T0133963

Software Specification and Design

Software Specification and Design

An Engineering Approach

John C. Munson

Auerbach Publications
Taylor & Francis Group
Boca Raton   New York

Published in 2006 by
Auerbach Publications
Taylor & Francis Group
6000 Broken Sound Parkway NW, Suite 300
Boca Raton, FL 33487-2742

Library of Congress Cataloging-in-Publication Data

Munson, John C.
    Software specification and design : an engineering approach / John C. Munson.
        p. cm.
    Includes bibliographical references and index.
    ISBN 0-8493-1992-7
    1. Computer software--Development. 2. Software architecture. I. Title.

QA76.76.D47M853 2005
005.1--dc22   2005045313

Taylor & Francis Group
is the Academic Division of T&F Informa plc.

**Visit the Taylor & Francis Web site at
http://www.taylorandfrancis.com**

**and the Auerbach Publications Web site at
http://www.auerbach-publications.com**

Dedication

To Mary

Contents

Preface

The goal of this book is to provide a foundation for engineered software. In order that we develop some engineering rigor in the software development process, we must first have a real clear idea as to what is happening in the various stages of software development. It is quite clear that we really do not know what software design is all about. When discussing the subject of design, it is generally intertwined with a particular programming language metaphor. Thus, there is a real confounding between the language metaphor and the design activity itself. It is my object in this book to parse the various stages of software specification, design, and coding into compartments that can also used to deal with each of these topics as a separate entity.

In the near term, there are going to be some major changes in the software development community. Some of today's biggest players in this market will begin to falter. The principal reason for this is that there is a functional limit to what hand-crafted systems can deliver. Unless the rigors of engineering discipline are brought into play in the software development process, the size of new systems alone will initiate the collapse of the companies trying to build them.

To ward off the inevitable collapse, a number of new software development strategies such as Extreme Programming have gained some popularity. Unfortunately, the problem is far too complex for such a simple solution. There are no miracles in the software development process. There are no magic amulets or gurus that can assist in this process. There is only real hard work. That is the rub. Managers in the software development arena are more than willing to invest in the latest magic nostrum — however, no solutions will be found there. To solve the problems created by the new and enormously complex software systems, they must be engineered. This is going to involve a lot of work and a lot of training. The good news is that this is not new ground that we are plowing.

The approach that I develop in this book was strongly influenced by my measurement experiences with the Space Shuttle Primary Avionics Software System (PASS). I would like to claim that I contrived the whole approach quite on my own. I did not. The PASS software development environment was the model for the CMM Level 5 software development organization. Many researchers have, however, looked at this system and have come away with exactly the wrong impression of what was going on within this environment and why it worked as well as it did. There was a great deal of interest in the software process within the PASS development group at IBM FSD. The software process, however, was only a small part of the operating environment. This process was built on top of a very well-defined requirements specification and design system. This infrastructure was a vital part of the development environment. In fact, it was the key to the success of the development of PASS and the entire software development process. Until you have the necessary infrastructure in place to manage the requirements, the design, the code, and the testing processes, there cannot be an effective software development process.

I am distressed by the fact that the lessons learned from PASS have become the basis for the CMM religion. They have learned, unfortunately, that if you spin the software process prayer wheel often enough and say the appropriate mantras that miracles will happen. No such miracles have been forthcoming, but this does not deter the true believers in the least. The truth of the matter is that if you wish to attain the Nirvana of software development, then you are going to learn how to engineer the software. This is going to be a lot of work. Most folks would rather recite the mantras than to do the necessary work. It is my belief, however, that there are people out there who really want to learn how to engineer software. They are ready and willing to cast away their software process prayer books and their computer science dogma. It is that audience to whom I address this book.

There are no mantras in this book. I have also tried to develop it relatively free from dogma. If we are going to make real progress in the area of system analysis and design, we had better start from the premise that little is known about this discipline. There is precious little science or engineering that has been done in the area. We are going to have to learn to discover much of what we will need to know. Fortunately, the path to knowledge has been well established in other sciences. We have only to learn how they did it and follow in their footsteps. In my previous book, *Software Engineering Measurement*, I attempted to lay the framework for both the conduct of scientific inquiry and the foundations for software measurement. I will refer to this material from time to time in this book.

Over the years, I have worked the general idea of requirements traceability that I first saw in operation in the Shuttle software organizations at Rockwell, IBM FSD, and NASA. I have learned to formalize what I saw in operation. In this book, I construct a model for this software development process. At the core of this approach is the overriding consideration of measurement. We would like to be able to measure every aspect of the software environment — from the initial requirements through the test activity to the operation of the developed software when it is placed into service.

There have been some rather unpleasant trends in the software design arena recently. At the top of this list is the UML debacle. In this case, the design process is almost completely obscured in a very complicated and unwieldy language model. We need to divorce the act of design from the language metaphor. The design focuses on the needed algorithms and the transformations that these algorithms will do on data. We worry about the language context only when we know what the problem is that we wish to solve.

There are really three distinct models that we must wrestle with to create software systems. First, there is the user's view of the system. This view of the system addresses the single consideration of *what* the software will do for the user. The user will interact with an operational model that we create for him through a precise set of operations. The software designer is obliged to convert the operational model into a functional description of the system. This functional model will create an abstract machine that will determine *how* each of the operations is to be converted to functionalities that will drive this abstract machine. Finally, once we have a good and clear understanding of what is to be done and how we wish to achieve this goal, the final task is to identify the appropriate language metaphor that provides the best capabilities for mapping the functional model into set of machine instructions.

The engineering problem that we now confront is exactly the same one confronted by the civil engineers in ancient Egypt. These engineers wanted to construct big buildings to shelter the eternal remains of their great leaders. Initially, the materials at hand were simple mud bricks. You can stack mud bricks only just so high before they collapse under their own weight. The use of mud bricks for building pyramids soon fell by the wayside. Stone was a much better building material, although much more difficult to shape into building blocks. The use of stones allowed the civil engineers to build much higher buildings. The Great Pyramid of Giza, for example, is a grand 246 meters high. It weighs some 55,000,000 tons. This proved to be an extremely expensive way to get to the rarified air of the Gods.

A very different building technique was used several millennia later to build the Eiffel Tower in Paris. It is 300 meters tall and weighs in at 7000 tons. The Eiffel Tower was "engineered." It was a very much cheaper way to visit the Gods in terms of total human effort expended on the project and also in terms of the simple materials cost of the structure.

Ancient pyramid designers simply stacked the building blocks on top of one another until they reached the maximum height permitted by the structural building blocks. If they exceeded this structural limit, the structures cracked and began to disintegrate. That is because the structure grew progressively heavier as it got bigger. Ultimately, the load that each of the individual building blocks was forced to carry became too great and they lost their structural integrity.

We are exactly at this same pass in the design of software systems. We are rapidly approaching the physical limits of software systems. They are rapidly beginning to crack and break under their own mass. We have built these systems in exactly the same manner that was used to build ancient pyramids. We simply stack code modules on top of one another until we reach the functional limits of the language metaphor. We build by brute force. When these structures reach the limits of human comprehension and maintainability, they crack and break.

There is a fantastic difference between the great pyramids and the Eiffel Tower. The pyramids are very impressive because of their size and the astonishing amount of effort employed in their manufacture. The Eiffel Tower is impressive because of its size and its engineering elegance. And, the Eiffel Tower was built in 1889. Modern computer operating systems are very impressive for their size and the amount of human effort employed in their manufacture. However, we simply have not yet learned to engineer software structures. No operating system software is an engineering equivalent for the Eiffel Tower. They are structurally similar to the pyramid of Giza.

There are, however, many software equivalents of the Winchester House in San Jose, California. This house was continually constructed by the widow and heiress to the Winchester rifle fortune. There were no plans for any of the construction additions made to the house by Mrs. Winchester. Three construction crews were employed so the construction of the house could occur unabated 24 hours a day. Mrs. Winchester reckoned that all the construction activity would keep the spirits of those who had been killed by Winchester rifles at bay. This construction methodology set a standard for most modern software development organizations. There are stairways in the Winchester house that lead nowhere (dead code). There are closet doors that open to expose walls (function stubs). But first and foremost, there are no blueprints (specifications) for the Winchester house. The house was simply hacked for a group of carpenters (developers) who worked around the clock on the project. Because there are no blueprints for this structure, it is also a maintenance nightmare.

Perhaps the most distressing fact to me is that we have been conditioned to accept such bad software. The incredible operating overhead bloat that is created by the object-oriented (O-O) programming religion is a very good example of this. The rationale for the O-O methodology is a simple one (although not one supported by fact or science). It supposedly cuts software development costs. What is happening, however, is that systems developed using this metaphor literally suck out all the juice from the user's computer. This disparity between the computer power of these computer systems and the power actually delivered to the customer represents an absolutely incredible business opportunity for new software organizations. Pretty soon, it will occur to someone that we can deliver a simple, reliable, and economical software product to the market complete with a real warranty. These new companies will rapidly own the market. It happened to the automobile industry in the 1960s — It will soon happen in the software industry as well.

The task at hand for modern software engineers is a simple one: we must stop building pyramids and learn how to build very lean, well-engineered systems. That is the major objective of this book: to establish the foundation for the engineering discipline in the software development process.

I would like to believe that this book will not be used to build systems based on the *Munson design model*, whatever that is. Nothing would disturb me more. I am not a prophet. This book was not written with divine inspiration. I do not wish to found a new religion with an appropriate accoutrement of disciples. I have, however, had the splendid opportunity of witnessing the evolution of some significant software projects. This book was designed to show the path to enlightenment in software specification and design. Each problem that we encounter will be different. Each project will be brand new. There are no universal solutions. Each systems analyst and each designer is going to have to learn how to do his own thinking. What I do wish to achieve is to establish a foundation for the *discipline* of software engineering.

I will spend very little time with software specification formalisms such as Z. It is not that I do not think that there is merit in formal specification … there is. Formalisms, however, have had a way of becoming ends in themselves. That is the danger. I have seen students come out of software specification classes using formal approaches. These students do not really have a clue about what software specification really is. If I were designing a safety-critical system, there are certain components that I would certainly wish to understand and describe completely and unambiguously. This is a natural for Z. I will employ a rather more informal natural language for the specification and design of software modules. I do this merely for reasons of economy of space. There is only just so much that one can hope to cover in a single book.

This book is about engineering discipline. Let us never confuse mathematical rigor with engineering discipline. They are simply not the same thing. A true mathematician really does not care whether a theorem that he is busily proving is in any way tied to reality. That is not the point. The proof exists for its own sake. An engineer, however, must be very concerned with the applicability of his work. It will have real-world consequences. We must certainly be assured that our engineering constructs are theoretically rigorous. They must also have relevance to the engineering environment.

The material presented in this book was developed in a graduate level class in software specification. Since that point, I have used much of this material in an introductory software engineering course. A background in both probability and statistics would certainly facilitate the reading and understanding of the material presented herein.

Chapter 1
An Overview of the Software Development Process

1.1 Introduction

Long gone are the days when folks worried about software performance. When machines were terribly slow and memory was horribly expensive, there was great need to ensure that programs were streamlined and efficient. In that these concerns have taken a back seat in the software development process, the new programming language environments have grown in size and waste in an essentially unbounded fashion. Feature bloat abounds. Runtime inefficiencies abound. Software systems have gotten huge, unreliable, and completely insecure.

We are, however, very rapidly approaching the point where Moore's Law of hardware speed and capability is about to break down if for no other reason than it is becoming more and more difficult to dissipate the heat that is generated by the ever-denser integrated circuit assemblies. Perhaps this crisis is a blessing in disguise. The attention must now turn to engineering software systems in a disciplined manner. The heady days of "cowboying" code are over.

If there are to be new gains in our future processing capabilities on our computer systems, it is clear that these new gains will probably not be so readily forthcoming from the hardware developers as they have been in the past. These gains will certainly have to come from the software developers. The huge bloated software systems that are created by today's software craftsmen represent a business opportunity of colossal proportions. This business opportunity is literally unmatched in the history of mankind.

Imagine, if you will, a fully functional word processor that would run in less than 500 KB. Now further imagine that it would start instantly, save your work transparently, and never break. Imagine that the vendor of this system would warrantee the product against any losses that you might incur as a result of the failure of the program because of reliability or security problems. The vendor of this product would own the market.

If similar strides were made across the board for all software products, the old Intel 286 and 386 boxes that now are gathering dust while waiting to become landfill would suddenly have real value. They would work surprisingly well with our new software. The major problem confronting the computing industry today is not the speed of the hardware; it is the colossal inefficiencies in the software systems.

The etiology of the current software crisis is a lack of engineering discipline in the software development business. This, of course, is not surprising. None of the **software engineers** now hacking code has probably ever had any exposure to basic engineering principles. Regrettably, those individuals who have come from engineering disciplines to software development have reverted to the lowest common denominator of software development and have forgotten whatever they once knew of best engineering practice.

In this book, we learn to identify the essential elements of engineering practice that we can put to work to create a disciplined software engineering development environment. There is real incentive for us to do this. The financial rewards that we will reap for doing so will be unprecedented in the history of mankind.

The path is a difficult one. We are going to have to learn to do some serious work. We have been lulled into incredible sloth by bloated object-oriented design and coding systems. To do real engineering we are going to have to take direct control of our future, learn to do measurement, learn to do real design, and learn to learn how to discover answers for problems that we uncover as we progress.

It is our objective, in this book, to define, very precisely, the salient features of the software design process. We will cut to the heart of the matter. More importantly, we will learn to question everything we do. We will begin very simply and then add to our disciplined software development environment only those features that will contribute to our making more maintainable, more reliable, and more secure software systems. More important than anything else, we will learn what these terms really mean.

1.2 An Overview of the Software Engineering Environment

Each software system begins with a set of requirements. The system requirements are really an attribute of a user or customer. Customers need a system that will perform certain functions for which they are willing to pay. These requirements can be both explicit and well defined, or they can be implicit and not so well defined. It is not always easy to ascertain what customers really want in a new software system. Sometimes they do not really have a good, clear idea of what their requirements are. From the software perspective, we are going to have to work with the customers to build a suitable abstract machine that embodies their specific needs.

In reality, there is more than one abstract machine with which the development staff must contend. First, they are going to design a software machine that will behave in accordance with the user's requirements. That is, they will work with the customer to design an operational model of a software machine that will satisfy the customer's needs. The operating characteristics of this machine will be defined by a set of operational specifications. This set of operational specifications will specify *what* the software system will do. These specifications will delineate two things. First, an operational model or metaphor will be defined to represent the abstract operational machine; and second, a set of *operations* will be established that will define how a user will interact with the system.

Once we have defined what the system will do, we next will turn our attention to *how* the operations will be accomplished on our computer system. This means that we are going to have to design a new abstract functional machine that will actually drive the operational abstract machine. The design of this functional machine will articulate a set of *functionalities* that describe how each operation will be implemented in the new software system. The goal, then, of the functional machine is to implement the functionality of the machine specified by the operational model. The characteristics of this functional machine are specified by a functional model and a set of functionalities that will animate this model.

The third abstract machine that the developers must determine is the machine that has been created by the developers of a programming language. There is, for example, an Ada machine, a C++ machine, a Java machine, etc. The functional machine must be mapped onto one of these programming language machines. The primary objective of a system designer should be to choose the programming language model that was the very best match for the functional model.

In more primitive applications there is great connectivity between what the user will do with the system and how the system works. Take, for example, the early automobiles, the Ford Model T in particular. Directional control of the vehicle was achieved by gearing a steering mechanism to give typical users sufficient mechanical advantage to control the vehicle with the large muscles of their arms. Braking was achieved through the use of a pedal on the floorboard of the vehicle that would enable a user to employ his strongest muscles, those of his upper thighs, to the braking function. In a modern vehicle, directional control can be achieved in a host of different ways, none of which rely on muscle power. The braking function can also be achieved in a variety of different schemes. Again, none of these schemes need to consider the muscular strength of the user. This means that the designers of modern automobiles have considerable freedom in their choice of both operational and functional models. Unfortunately, there are considerably more degrees of freedom in the design of new automobiles as a result of this lack of dependence on specific factors of human ergonomics. This makes the automotive design process much more complicated.

In the software development environment, the number of design alternatives for the operational models is very large, almost unconstrained. The set of design alternatives for the functional models for these operational models is also very large. As a result, we must learn to invest our development resources very wisely. In today's software development environment, the vast majority of expenditures occur at the back end of the software life cycle. These resources could be more wisely spent on the earlier stages of the software life cycle in the specification and design of the operational and functional systems.

With modern computer software systems, we build abstract machines. This means that there can be almost complete separation between the operations that the user will perform and the functionalities that the software will perform to execute these operations. A user could, for example, control a cursor on a computer screen with simple eye movement or voice commands. Neither of these two operations has anything remotely to do with how the little image of an arrow gets translated from one x,y coordinate pair on the computer screen to another x,y coordinate pair. Obviously, we need to establish a foundation of criterion measures so that we can quantify the attributes of each of the possible design alternatives and select from this very large set only those solutions that will produce a maximally useful and cost-effective solution. The specification and design methodology that we explore in this book is motivated by our need to quantify and measure design alternatives. We would like to learn how to engineer software. The discipline of engineering is based on sound scientific principles. Science has at its heart empirical validation processes that are based on measurement. The framework for the specification and design process, then, will be built around this need for measurement and empirical evaluation.

To assist in the subsequent discussion of program specification, it will be useful to make this description somewhat more precise by introducing some notation conveniences. From a user's perspective, a software system will implement a specific set of operations, O, on a suitable operational model. A system designer will implement the operational module through an appropriate functional model that will be driven by a set of mutually exclusive functionalities, F. Thus, if the system is executing a function $f \in F$, then it cannot be expressing elements of any other functionality in F. Each of these functions in F was designed to implement a set of software specifications based on a user's requirements. This mapping from the set of user-perceived operations, O, to a set of specific program functionalities, F, is one of the major tasks in the software specification process.

A pilot astronaut on the Space Shuttle need not be aware of the functionality of the Primary Avionics Software System (PASS) that governs the complete operation of the shuttle. Systems designers have carefully constructed a model that permits the pilot to control the shuttle as if it were a standard airplane. The pilot, for example, has a control stick that controls two user-perceived operations: roll and pitch. These operations are implemented in software functions that monitor, for example, the change in resistance in x and y coordinate rheostats in the base of the control stick. The pilot *operates* the spacecraft. The software *functions* monitor the change in resistance in the rheostats.

Ultimately, the structure of the system will be resolved in a low-level design process into a set of program modules. Each of the modules will implement one or more of the functionalities. At the design stage, these modules can be specified with some level of precision in the low-level design. More typically, the modular structure will simply emerge in source code as developers struggle to implement their ad hoc design. For measurement purposes, we need much more definition on the software development process. To that end, we need to specify each of the activities in the software specification process a little more precisely.

1.3 Historical Perspective on Software Development

So that we might better understand where we are today in terms of software development, we must understand our past. In a sense, we are victims of our past. The way we think about software is conditioned by our thinking that it is just software. When we need some of this software, we will just sit down and have a go at creating it. Computer hardware was never built this way because it was just too expensive. Essentially all of the design issues had to have been resolved before the first wires were soldered. Software is ethereal and easy to modify. It did not warrant such close scrutiny during the design process of the initial software systems.

The first code that was written for early machines was, of course, written in binary. Binary strings representing data and instructions were placed in a map of memory. The number of available memory locations was very small. This meant that the number of program modules had to be very small, which meant that the set of functionalities that could be implemented in that small memory space was also very small. This, in turn, meant that the number of operations that could be performed by a simple program was quite small.

5

The net result of the constraints imposed on the operational space by the memory constraints meant that early computers were used primarily to handle very simple repetitious tasks such as printing payroll checks, tallying results of punch card inputs, and other such simple tasks.

One of the early lessons of programming was that human beings do not deal well with binary numbers. It is very difficult for a human being to look at a string of 36, or so, binary digits and make sense out of it. As a result, early programming was a fault-prone and arduous process simply from a human factors standpoint. The first step along the road of humanizing the program development process came with the advent of the octal programming. Through the use of the octal number system, groups of three binary digits could be represented as a single octal digit. Thus, a 36-digit binary number could be represented as 12 octal digits. This meant that the complexity of the programming task, visually, diminished by nearly a factor of three for a programmer. The downside of the use of the octal number system is that computers only use binary numbers, which meant that there had to be an octal-to-binary translator system interposed between the programmer and the computer.

The next logical development in the humanization of the software development process was the appearance of the symbolic assembler. This meant that the programmer or developer was no longer responsible for maintaining the memory map of the program. Further, the developer could talk about places on the machine in terms of symbols that he or she could understand. The assembler also provided the programmer with the ability to describe the operations to be performed on the machine in terms of symbolic machine codes instead of numeric values.

The ultimate payoff in the use of an assembler program to handle the symbolic translation process for the programmer was increased productivity from the programmer in two ways. First, a programmer was using symbols that represented places and operations in a manner convenient to the programmer. Second, programmers made fewer errors, in that they were manipulating symbols and not numbers. The downside in the use of the symbolic assembly process was that the developer was yet another step removed from the actual machine. He or she was programming on a symbolic computer and not a binary one.

The next evolution in software development systems were transitional procedural languages such as DIBOL or FORTRANSIT. These languages were essentially extensions to the growing macro capabilities of the symbolic assemblers. They moved the programming activity much closer to the language of the programmer. Each of these languages created a hypothetical machine that the user could manipulate with much more ease than the simple binary machine. Again, as a consequence, there was a large gain in programmer productivity, as measured at the machine instruction level. One statement in DIBOL or FORTRANSIT would result in quite a few machine instructions. Because the programmer was working with a machine that was more suited to the problem that was being encoded, he or she was much less apt to make mistakes in the program.

With the advent of these new higher-level abstract machines, the programmer was now well removed from the actual machine. This meant that there was substantial mapping that had to be made by the language translators from the language of the abstract DIBOL/FORTRANSIT machines to the actual machines. In addition, the DIBOL machine and the FORTRANSIT machine were very different machines. The DIBOL machine was designed for business types of applications. The FORTRANSIT machine, on the other hand, was designed for mathematical computation. These two machines presented a very different outward face to the programmer. This meant that the programmer had to match the application to the appropriate machine. A payroll system could best be written in DIBOL. A program for computing the trajectory of a cannon shell could best be written in FORTRANSIT. There had to be a match between the nature of the problem space and the abstract machine that would be used in the development of a program in that problem space.

Then the world of software development began to change very rapidly. The number of programming languages began to proliferate. So too did the number of abstract machines represented by each of these languages. The complexity of the abstract machines began to grow seemingly without limits. Not all of these abstract machines are well specified. In fact, their operation is ambiguous. It is really a challenge for a software developer to construct a program that will work according to its operational specification within a language whose semantic rules are ambiguous.

Up to this point, the whole focus has been on the code development process, on creating the program and getting it to execute on the target machine. That, unfortunately, is pretty close to the state-of-the-art of software development. Design was never a strong component of the initial software development methodology. And it is certainly not a strong component of current software development methodology. If we were to look at the distribution of development resources in the current software development life cycle for most organizations today, it would look very much like the distribution shown in Figure 1.1. This means that the vast majority of the design problems are solved during the coding process. Further, there is a conspicuous effort to test quality into software.

A much more meaningful distribution of software resources is shown in Figure 1.2. In this case, there is great effort to determine the needs of the customer and build an operational model that will meet the customer's needs. Only when the product has been well defined is an effort made to transfer the operational model to a functional model. Coding is a relatively

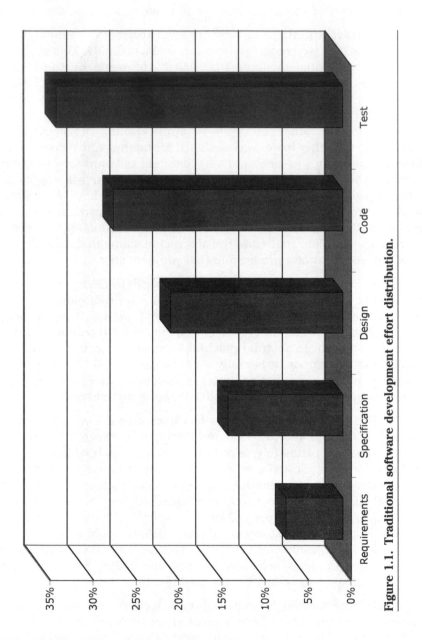

Figure 1.1. Traditional software development effort distribution.

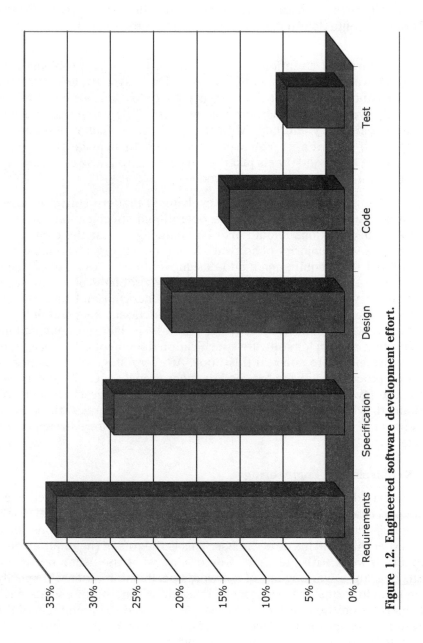

Figure 1.2. Engineered software development effort.

simple process. It is merely a question of implementing the design. Testing consumes very little of the resources because the design and development activities leading to the testing process are well defined. The purpose of the test activity is to ensure that the software will work correctly for the operational profile determined during the requirements and specification phases.

Now we turn our attention briefly to one of the major problems confronting software development efforts today. These systems are very large (>1 MLOC) and are designed for very complex abstract machines (C++). In a rapidly evolving system, there may well be a 5 percent code churn in any one week. To try and cope with this problem, configuration control systems such as sccs or rcs were developed to manage the rapidly evolving code base. And that is just the very problem. These configuration control systems manage the source code.

Just as the source code is rapidly evolving in modern software development scenarios, it is clear that the operational specifications and the functional specifications should also be changing at just the same rate. However, the vast majority of software development organizations never figured it out that requirements and design would have to be under configuration control as well. This is the crux of the problems of the software development world today. The code base is changing and that change process is managed. The operational and functional specs should be changing as well — and they are not. There is, in fact, no concomitant configuration control for software specification documents. This is a problem that we intend to solve in this book. At every stage of the software evolution process, a linkage between the operational specs, the functional specs, the low-level design documents, and the source code must be maintained. Whenever any one of these documents changes, there must be a concomitant change to documents upstream and downstream of the change.

1.4 Requirements Engineering

The software development process is driven by a real or perceived need on the part of a user for a software capability. In the vast majority of cases, the user cannot be relied upon to develop a set of specifications for a system that will fulfill his or her needs. This is the role of the requirements engineer: to work with the user to determine what the user's needs are and to develop a working set of software specifications that will specify this system in terms of a basic set of operations. The requirements engineer operates on the interface between the user and the architects of the operational design for the software. The objective of the requirements phase will be to design and develop an abstract machine, the operational model that best meets the needs of the user.

Software systems are abstract objects. The real challenge of the requirements process is to build a new virtual reality that will fulfill the user's needs and expectations. The number of degrees of freedom available to the requirements engineer in this process is really astonishing. We can build new worlds of abstract objects with very few constraints. Our imagination is the only real limiting factor in this process. For some, it is better to reinvent the wheel than it is to let the mind soar. It is nice to know that we are constrained only by our creativity in the creation of new abstractions. If we can imagine it, we can build it.

There are really two distinct objectives of the requirements engineering process. First, we must work with the user to elicit his or her requirements and then develop an operational model for a system that will best meet the user's needs or requirements. This operational model is the design of the abstract machine or environment that we are going to work with the user to create. If we are going to create a computer game, we must build a storybook for the game, an imaginary world for the game to take place, and objects that we will manipulate to fulfill the story. This is the operational model.

Once we have built the operational model, we can then develop a set of interactions for the imaginary world that we have created. This set of interactions will constitute the set of operations that will be employed by the user to manipulate and interact with the operational model that we have created.

Unfortunately, the requirements engineering process is not a single-cycle process. That is, we simply cannot sit down with the user and develop an operational model and a set of operations on that operational model in one single interaction with the user. As we build the operational model with the user, his own view of his needs will, in all likelihood, begin to change. It might well be that our initial impression of a user's needs was not completely accurate. This will become obvious when the user has the opportunity to interact with the evolving operational model.

To put this process in its proper perspective, let us imagine that we have returned to the past and brought Benjamin Franklin forward in time with us. For his time, Ben was a real progressive thinker. He will be a good subject for us to work with. We are going to bring Ben into a darkened room that contains only a television set, a remote control for the television, and two comfortable chairs. We are going to explain to him what the box in front of us does. Technologically, there will be a really large disconnect between the world that Ben has come from and the world into which we have introduced him. This is a good example for us to ponder in that, in many cases, the disconnect between the user of a modern software system and current technology will be almost as great.

We begin this process by explaining the operational model. Before turning the television set on and scaring the wits out of Ben, we must first lay a little foundation for what is about to happen to him. There will be a number of abstractions that he will have to wrestle with to grasp the concept of the television. First, images of people and places will appear on the glass screen in front of us at our command. These images are sometimes meant to inform us or to tell stories to entertain us. The people who will appear on the glass will be dressed strangely and will talk about things from a new magical world. The events that are taking place on the glass screen have happened in the past or are currently happening. Above all, these images are like pictures; they are painted on the screen by some device behind it. The scenes that they represent are not really in the television.

We now attempt to discuss some of the basic principles of radio and television so that Ben will have a foundation for what we tell him next. Fundamentally, the images are transmitted by a number of different transmitters and then grabbed from the ether by the television. We can, at our option, select from which transmitter we wish to receive information. There will be different content from each of the stations. By switching from one station to another, we will, *de facto,* be switching content.

Once Ben has a good foundation of the operational model for the television, we will then give him the remote control for the set. On this remote control, there is a series of buttons. Each of the buttons represents an operation that we can perform on the television model. Imagine the wonder of it all when he first pushes the button labeled POWER. Ben can now manipulate the television operational model through the use of the remote control device that is, in turn, an extension of the operational model.

Our operational model contains a special user interface. We will have incorporated all the operations for our television model into this device. We will probably first show Ben how to turn the set on and off. In this manner, he will know that if anything too extreme happens in the picture, he can immediately retreat from the new reality by turning off the power. We will then show Ben how to turn up and down the sound. Next we will introduce him to the concept of program selection through the various channels of the set.

It would be reasonable to expect that once Ben got through the period of culture shock, he would be able to manipulate this new magic lantern box and its remote control with some degree of facility. He would be quite capable of interacting with the operational model that has evolved over the years for the television medium. We can imagine that within a very short period of hours, Ben would be up to speed with the manipulation of the operational model that we have created for him. Admittedly, it would take him quite a bit longer to make sense of the content of some of the channels.

The one thing that we probably could not realistically expect to achieve with Ben is an understanding of just *how* the television set works. Of the many users of television sets worldwide today, not very many viewers have a clue about what is going on inside their television sets. There is a complete disconnect between the operational model that we have created for the user that describes what the device will do and the functional model that the television set designer used to develop the operational model. It is a characteristic of a good system design that the user needs to know only the operational model and nothing about the functional model to make the system work.

To return to Ben for a moment, it is reasonable to suspect that within a number of days he could begin to identify new operations that he would like to have incorporated on his remote. He might well be capable of suggesting improvements in the usability of the system for him. Our requirements engineer could work with Ben to modify both the operational model and the set of operations on that model. Neither individual will be concerned about how the operational model will be implemented. (They will rapidly learn, however, from the system designers that whatever modifications need to be implemented on the current system simply cannot be done.)

In summary then, the objective of the requirements engineering process is to work with a customer (user) to build an operational model for the user and a set of operations that will manipulate this operational model.

1.5 Software Specification

For our purposes, the software specification process occurs in four distinct phases. First we develop the operational specification driven by a set of user requirements. This consists of the operational model and a set of operations that the user will employ to manipulate the operational model. Again, the sole purpose of this set of specifications is to define a virtual system that can be manipulated by the user by a set of very well-defined operations. The operational mode, together with the set of operations, defines what the new system is to do.

The next step in the software specification process is intimately bound to the software design process. During this phase we map the operational model onto a specific functional model. We solve the problem of how the operational model works within the confines of a new virtual architecture. This functional model is manipulated by a set of functionalities. The functional model, together with its set of functionalities, constitutes our high-level design specification.

The third step in the software specification process is the decomposition of functionalities into specific program modules. This is the low-level design process. Each module receives data from a set of modules from which it can potentially receive execution control. Through an algorithm specified in the module design, this data is transformed according to the dictates of the algorithm and made available to the module that transferred control to the current module. At this stage, we are concerned with the specifics of each datum and the transformations made on that datum.

The final step in the specification process is to select a programming language model that we can use to implement the low-level design. We will not be able to modify these models; we must simply choose the least bad model from a repertoire of simply awful and inefficient language models to use in our application.

1.5.1 Operational Specification

The operational specification and its constituent elements are the product of the requirements analysis phase of the software development life cycle. For the moment, the operational specification consists of the operational model and a set of mutually exclusive operations to manipulate that operational model. That is the easy part. The next problem and perhaps the most difficult part of the requirements analysis phase is to determine exactly how the software will be used when it is deployed. We need to know this for two reasons. First, we cannot test everything that the software can possibly do. We need to ensure that it is tested in the same manner in which it will be used. Second, if we are to meet predetermined performance goals in the operation of the system, then we must also know how it will be used.

Nature assigns to each user of our software system a specific likelihood or probability distribution across the set of operations. This probability distribution is the user operational profile. We simply cannot know this operational profile or make an educated guess as to what it might be. We have to design an experiment, conduct the experiment, and make observations as to the user's behavior. This behavior will be embodied in the user operational profile.

The operational specification is a living document. It changes very rapidly during the initial stages of the project and continues to change during the entire life of the project. It is vital that we understand the nature of this change and create a mechanism to manage this change process.

There are three parts to the operational specification. First there is the operational system overview. This is, in essence, an executive summary of the user's operational system. Next is the operational model. This is a very precise description of the abstract machine that best meets the user's requirements. Finally, there is a set of operations that will animate the abstract machine.

1.5.2 Functional Specification

The functional specification documents the abstract machine that will be used to implement the operational machine. Just as was the case in the operational specification, there are three parts to the functional specification. First, there is the functional system overview. This is also an executive summary of the functional machine. Second, there is the functional model, a very detailed description of the functional machine. Third is the set of functionalities that will animate this abstract functional machine.

The functional specification is also a living document. It can be expected to change very rapidly during the initial stages of the development of the functional design process. It is most important that we recognize this fact. It is clear that we must have the infrastructure in place to manage this change process. The functional specification should be placed under a configuration control system in precisely the same manner as the source code.

Each of the functionalities is used to implement one or more of the operations in the operational specifications. A linkage must be established between each of the functionalities and the operations they implement. Similarly, there must also be a linkage between each of the operations and the set of functionalities used to implement these operations. If the operations change, this implies that they will be implemented differently at the functional level. Therefore, we must have a concomitant change in each of the functionalities involved with every change at the operational level. Similarly, change activity in the functional machine may have a dramatic impact on the operational machine. The linkage between the operations and functionalities will minimize the maintenance effort of synchronizing these two systems.

1.5.3 Module Specification

Once the basic operating characteristics of the functional machine have been established, the process of low-level design can begin. At this level, each of the functionalities is implemented in one or more low-level design modules. These modules actually transfer control from one to another. They pass data across an interface that will be transformed by an algorithm in the module.

Each design module is ultimately implemented by exactly one programming language module. The exact activity of the source code is dictated by the design module. The source code module associated with each design module is locked to the design module. The source code module never changes without a concomitant change in the design module. The only exception to this rule is the circumstance in which the source code module does not precisely implement the design module. Then, and only then, can the source code module change without a change in the design module.

Obviously, the design module specifications are subject to the same change activity during the software evolution process as the functional specifications and the operational specifications. Therefore, it is appropriate to place the module specifications under configuration control in exactly the same way that will be used to manage the source code, the operational specifications, and the functional specifications. All of these documents are living documents.

Now that the word "document" has been used, it is appropriate to talk a little about the documentation process. A system is documented precisely by its operational, functional, and module specifications, not by its source code. We never read source code to figure out what a software system is doing. The source code is there merely to animate the language model to perform the system functionality for us. Well-designed systems never have comments in the source code; there is absolutely no reason for these comments. From an infrastructure point of view, we might elect to use a comment statement as a mechanism of linking each source code module to its design module, but there is no reason that comments should be placed in the code beyond this consideration.

Each design module is to implement at least one functionality. This means that in the event there is a change in the functionality of the functional machine, the modules associated with the functionality must also change. Each of the functionalities must then be linked to their associated design modules. Similarly, each design module must be linked to the functionalities in which it is used. Changes in the design module will certainly impact these functionalities. Furthermore, each design module is implemented in exactly one code module. It must be linked to this source code module.

With the linkage in place between the design module, the associated source code module, and the appropriate functionalities, it is now possible to determine exactly which source code modules are used to implement an operation or a functionality. Further, it is also possible to determine exactly which functionalities and which operations use a particular source code module. Under configuration control, all of the most current versions of all specification elements and source code elements are linked together. This solves one the biggest and most costly software maintenance issues. The overwhelming amount of human effort spent in the software maintenance process is spent simply trying to determine what the system is today and how the system works.

With the low-level design will come the ability to measure the design with some degree of precision. This is the whole goal of this software specification methodology: to learn to measure the design artifacts, model their behavior, and build the right system the first time without massively rewriting the system to deal with specific design problems. In essence, the software specification methodology developed in this book will permit software to be "engineered" and not "crafted."

1.5.4 An Example

It would useful, at this point, to consider an example. Consider the gentleman in Figure 1.3. He would like a three-dimensional mouse to manipulate the object on the screen of his display unit. That is, the object on the screen would move in precisely the same fashion as his mouse in three dimensions. That is his requirement. That is his felt need. Now consider the fulfillment of his requirement.

The first thing to do is to construct an operational model for a system that will meet this user's needs. This operational model consists of a machine, some parts of which may be tangible and others may be abstract. We then construct a set of operations that will animate this model. The one thing that we do not worry about at this stage is how we are going to make this machine work. We are just concerned with what the user will do to interact with it.

To build this three-dimensional mouse, we take an ordinary tennis ball and suspend it within a frame with rubber bands. To operate his mouse, the user will simply grab the mouse and move it precisely as if he were grasping the object on the screen. We have now completed the operational model. We now define a set of operations for the user. There are three operations that relate to the translation of the object in each of the three coordinate axes. There are also three operations that relate to the rotation

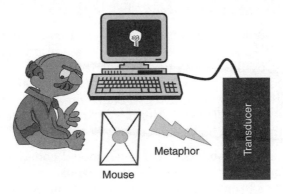

Figure 1.3. An example.

of the object on each of the three coordinate axes. We can summarize these operations as follows:

- o_1: Translate the ball on the x-axis.
- o_2: Translate the ball on the y-axis.
- o_3: Translate the ball on the z-axis.
- o_4: Rotate the ball on the x-axis.
- o_5: Rotate the ball on the y-axis.
- o_6: Rotate the ball on the z-axis.

That is all there is to the operational specifications. We have defined the operational model, the tennis ball. We have animated this model with the operations. We have now defined what the user will do with the new three-dimensional mouse.

Now the interesting work begins. We need to solve the problem of how we are going to figure out what the user is doing with the tennis ball mouse. There are a number of ways that we can do this. In the initial stages of the design process, we attempt to identify as many ways as we can think of to solve this problem. For each of these strategies, we do some initial pencil sketches to aid in our thinking. As we begin to understand each of the design alternatives, certain elements of reality will kick in. One of the biggest drivers in this initial exploratory process is cost. Some approaches will be much more expensive in either or both of physical and human resources. We examine two alternative approaches to the functional aspect of the design.

In the first design alternative, the motion of the ball is sensed by a video camera. To do this, a video camera is placed in front of the tennis ball. So that the precise position of the ball can be sensed, two black circular dots are placed on the side of the tennis ball that faces the video camera. When the tennis ball is moved by the user, the relative position of the two dots imposed on the two-dimensional plane of the video raster scan will indicate how the ball has been moved.

Now take a look at the software problem presented by this design solution. What the software must cope with is a grid of points or pixels strung together by the raster scan of the video camera. In essence, every 300 milliseconds or so, a new plane of, say, 1000×1000 bits is delivered to the software. Somewhere in these bits there are two black patterns representing the dots. These patterns shift over time, representing the relocation of the tennis ball by the user.

In this context, the software functional model consists of an abstract machine containing a 1000×1000 bit plane whose coordinate values are the binary values from zero to one. Every 300 milliseconds, the contents of this bit plane change. The functional model must contain registers that contain pertinent information about the past frame and the current frame.

We can begin to identify some of the basic functionalities that we will need to implement this design solution. The problem that we are trying to solve is basically one of pattern recognition. First we need to find the black dots by identifying the edges of the dots. Next we must determine the relative size of each of the dots, the position of these two dots in relation to each other, the length of each dot along the x- and y-axes, and the relative position of the bottom of each of the dots. These calculations must be performed for each frame as it is received. Changes in these four features of the dots from one frame to the next will contain the necessary information to deduce the movement of the tennis ball. For example, if the ball is moved toward the camera, the distance between the dots increases, their size increases, their shape does not change, and the bottoms of the dots maintain their relative distance from the lowest dot. We can now identify some of the basic functionalities needed to implement to solve this problem to wit:

- f_1: Find the outline of the two dots.
- f_2: Find the distance between the two dots.
- f_3: Find the length of the two dots on the x- and y-axes.
- f_4: Compute the relative change in the bottom of the two dots.
- f_5: Evaluate the changes between the current frame and the previous frame.
- f_6: Set the current frame to the previous frame.
- f_7: Send the new rotation and translation information to the graphics imaging system.

Admittedly, these represent some relatively high-level functionalities. It may be possible to decompose these into much more detailed functionalities. What is at issue here is the notion that the functional statement of the solution and the operational statement are very different. The user of this three-dimensional mouse would never be aware of the functional model. In fact, no part of it would ever be in his cognitive model. The model that the user interacts with is very different from the functional model that will actually implement the user's operational model.

This particular functional model was implemented using a video camera. This solution might be criticized from a number of different perspectives. If, for example, the user were to grip the tennis ball so that his fingers covered the black dots, then it would be difficult or impossible to deduce the movement of the ball.

Another approach to the functional design of the system might work along the following lines. We could bisect the tennis ball and place three accelerometers at three different positions inside the ball. Each of these accelerometers would sense the movement of the ball along each of the three coordinate axes. Attached to each of the accelerometers would be fitted a little transmitter that would transmit encoded signals corresponding to inputs obtained from the accelerometer. This scheme would permit us to sense the motion of the ball on all three axes.

After completing surgery on the tennis ball to insert each of the three accelerometers and their transmitters, we would then glue the halves of the ball back together and restore it to its position in the rack suspended by rubber bands. Presumably, each of the transmitters would encode the output of its accelerometer and transmit a signal representing the movement of the ball on the axis corresponding to that accelerometer. Now we must build a receiver to monitor the output of each of the transmitters inside the ball. This receiver will decode each of the signals and present the sense of the motion of each of the accelerometers to an associated analog-to-digital (A/D) interface on a computer. There will be three such A/D interfaces, one corresponding to each of the accelerometers inside three-dimensional mouse.

The software task under this new functional model is profoundly different from the video-based functional model. In this new scheme, the functional model consists of three registers within each of the three A/D interfaces, a set of three registers representing the previous contents of these three registers, a computational engine to difference the contents of these registers, and an interface to a graphics software package for image rotation and translation.

The software created under this functional model monitors the contents of three registers, one in each of the A/D interfaces. We assume that the register contents will be a number corresponding to the changes in a voltage level that varies directly in accordance with the values transmitted by each of the accelerometer or transmitters. The software system will interrogate each of these three registers at fixed intervals, determine the new values of these registers, compare these new values with values from the previous interrogation cycle, and then determine the relative motion of the tennis ball. We might partition these functionalities as follows:

- f_1: Initialize all program registers.
- f_2: Initiate data capture cycle.
- f_3: Capture the contents of register x.
- f_4: Capture the contents of register y.
- f_5: Capture the contents of register z.
- f_6: Compare new x, y, and z values to previous values.
- f_7: Move the contents of the x, y, and z register set to the holding register set.
- f_8: Send the new rotation and translation information to the graphics imaging system.

This new design solution is completely different from the previous video design solution. Our objective in the early stage of the design process is to identify a host of such possible feasible design solutions. In the last analysis, resource issues outside the solution domain will probably determine the particular choice of the operational model. We might have a very good staff of designers and developers who are quite experienced and good at pattern recognition problems. They might know little or nothing about A/D interfaces, or how to capture and interpret data from these interfaces. The staffing considerations would probably weigh heavily in our particular choice of which of the two functional models we might actually choose to implement.

1.6 Software Development: Past and Present

Much of our standard software development practice today is simply a carryover from the days when developers came to their jobs equipped with stone axes and wooden spears. In the good old days, the scope of the problems to solve on the computer was not very large. There really was not much that you could do with 5K words of memory. Each program essentially solved one problem. The program could easily be written on the back of a long piece of butcher paper that contained the octal memory map of the program.

As the size of memory space has increased over the years, the complexity of the programs that could run in this space has increased accordingly. The fundamental software development methodology has changed very little. This is largely due to the fact that folks in the software development world have really been isolated from basic engineering methodology. Software development folks were called in to craft new operating systems for hardware systems that were designed according to best engineering practice. Software was always an afterthought, an add-on. Everyone knew that the real value was in the engineering of the hardware systems. This notion was fostered by most of the great computer firms of yesteryear. Unfortunately, what never really happened was the introduction of engineering practice into software development. As a result, this field has been left to reinvent the basic notions of engineering.

1.7 Testing

From an engineering standpoint, there are really two distinct objectives of the software testing process. First, we must ensure that the software does what the user needs it to do. This type of testing will, of course, not be easy to do if we do not have a good, clear idea of what the software is supposed to do. During the requirements determination phase, we will develop a good, clear, and unambiguous statement of the operation of the system that we are going to develop. In subsequent phases of the software development process, this operation specification is mapped to specific code elements. Thus, each code element implements some element of an operational specification.

The set of code modules developed to implement a low-level design will be capable of demonstrating a very wide range of behaviors. Within this set of all possible behaviors is a very small subset of feasible behaviors. These are the behaviors derived directly from stimuli presented to the system by the user of the system as he or she exercises a set of operations. It is our objective in testing, therefore, to identify *a priori* the set of feasible behaviors of a system and test only those behaviors.

The second objective of the test process is to ensure that the software system must be reliable when placed in the user's hands. Not all operations of the software system being built can be used when the software is placed in service. It would be folly for us to devote scarce test resources to operations that would never be expressed by the population of users that the software will serve. Before beginning to test the software system for its operational reliability, we must first have a clear idea of how the software will be used when it is placed in service. It may well be, for example, that when a system is deployed, a number of operations it is capable of performing will never be expressed by a user. Again, given a model where test resources are limited, it would be folly to expend test resources to a set of operations that will never be expressed in the field. Far better would it be to ensure that the operations that the user will commonly exploit be those that will receive adequate testing.

Not all operations, then, are equal from a test perspective. The way that a typical user will use a system is reflected in the user operational profile. Informally, the operational profile is a statement of the probability that a given user will exercise a particular operation. We could assume that we have no information as to this distribution. We would then be obliged to test every operation to the same degree. In the extreme case, however, a user might well use one and only one operation from a large set of operations. Any test resources that we were to devote to other operations in the operational set would then be wasted. Realistically, we would like to test the software in the manner that it will be used. We must learn to allocate our test resources, which are very limited resources, in such a manner as to maximize the apparently reliability of the system for the way that the software will be used when it is deployed.

Unfortunately, the software engineering discipline has recently fallen victim to some very unproductive thinking. The notion of defect-free software has very recently been bandied about. This is a most unrealistic goal. Modern software systems typically contain a very large number of modules. These systems are growing almost geometrically with respect to time. They are also evolving very rapidly. There may be multiple builds of a system on a daily basis. With the size of these systems and the rate of code churn that they experience, the notion of defect-free systems is a most unattainable goal. No structural engineer ever thought to design a perfect, defect-free bridge. No architect ever thought to design and build a perfect skyscraper. It might be possible to do these things but it certainly would not be practical to do them. A bridge need not be perfect. It must simply stand, despite structural flaws that will be an inherent artifact of the materials used and the building process.

We simply cannot build perfect software systems — nor should we try. Because we are human, there will always be flaws in any of our elaborate constructions. The problem is not the flaws; the problem is that flaws destroy the operability of the system. We need to focus on the idea that we are building software systems that will be ***good enough*** — not perfect, just good enough to meet suitable reliability and availability considerations.

The computer security community is beset with the same impossible dream as the reliability community. They seek to build systems that are vulnerability-free. This is just as improbable a goal as building defect-free software. Any system that we have ever built has a way of being compromised. As we build new systems with brand-new capabilities and features, these systems will create new possibilities for exploitation. The problem is not the vulnerabilities. We can never test for them because we can never know what they are in advance of their being exploited. We can, however, instrument the systems that we build and monitor their execution when they are deployed. With the appropriate control mechanisms in place, we can know when the security of our systems has been compromised. We can test these control systems to ensure that they will perform their detection role when the software systems they are monitoring are placed into service. In so doing, we have incorporated in our design the notion that we will be able to detect aberrant behavior should it occur as a result of potential vulnerabilities.

One of the major difficulties in the software testing process is attributable to the process of software evolution. Software systems change very rapidly during their evolution. Thus, the object of the test process may change very rapidly during the software testing process. No software testing process can begin to be adequate unless the infrastructure is present to ensure that the tests being executed today, in fact, reflect the status of the system as it is right now. The source code base may change substantially in a very short period. As it does, the operational specifications and functional specifications must also change to maintain complete specification traceability. All operation and functional test cases must be linked to this change process. That is, if changes are made to the design during the evolution, then test cases associated with the previous functionality must be changed to reflect the new functionality. If changes are made to the operational specifications during the evolution process, then changes must be made to the test cases that deal specifically with the operations that change.

1.8 Software Availability Considerations

Software can fail to work for a number of reasons. The software may be broken. When we attempt to execute a particular functionality, the system might invariably fail. The software system may be under attack from either inside or outside the organization. Some will be performing unauthorized activity to either compromise the software itself or gain access to corporate intellectual property. In either event, once the software system has failed for whatever reason, it will continue to have the same liability that brought about the failure event until the system can be fixed.

1.8.1 Software Reliability

Software reliability has always been a real problem for large software systems. This is largely attributable to the fact that the notion of reliability in a software context has been greatly misunderstood. Researchers have tried to model software reliability as if a software system is a monolithic system. It is not. Software is really a loose collection of software modules. Only one of these modules is executing at any moment. If the module being executed is fatally flawed, then the execution of the module will fail. The system will crash. It should now be obvious that a software system is a different thing to different people. Each person who runs a software system will select from the repertoire of all operations a small subset that he or she will execute. In this subset, some operations will receive more attention than others.

It is clear, under the new scheme of specification traceability, that there are distinct subsets of program modules associated with each operation. If there is a flawed module in a subset that is used to implement a particular operation, then the system is likely to fail when that operation is made manifest by a user. Some users will execute this operation quite frequently. The system will fail regularly for them. Other users may not execute this same operation at all. They will think that the software system is very reliable.

Quite simply, the reliability of a software system depends entirely on its use. Tell me how you intend to use the system and I will tell you how reliable the software will be for you.

1.8.2 Software Security

Software security is also a badly misunderstood problem. There really is no security issue with software. There is, however, a very serious control problem with software. Massive software systems are crafted that have no built-in monitoring function designed into them. In essence, there is no one minding the store for these systems. It is relatively easy to break into these systems because they are very poorly designed and to compromise the system when the break-in is successful. If the necessary controls were designed into the system, its activity could be continuously monitored. The moment that an abnormal event occurs, it could be detected and arrested.

Thus, software security problems occur because of very poor design practice. It is more likely that insecure systems have been designed at all. More than likely, they have been cobbled together by software craftsmen. It is possible to exploit this bad design because nobody is minding the store. There are no processes in place to ascertain when a system is operating off nominal.

1.8.3 Software Maintainability

Finding and fixing a software fault has historically been regarded as a very difficult problem. It is a very labor-intensive and, consequently, very expensive task. This is the case because it is very difficult to deduce what the system is doing by simply reading the system source code. This is, in fact, the way most software maintenance is done. This maintenance activity would be absolutely unacceptable in most hardware contexts. If changes are made to an office building, the blueprints for the building are updated to reflect those changes. If new elements are added to an electronic system, the schematics for this system are updated. Problems on these systems are solved through an understanding of the design elements of the system. They are designed and built by engineers and not by craftsmen in the trades.

To make massive inroads on both the time and the expense of the maintenance problem, it is merely necessary to provide the necessary engineering documentation (i.e., design documents) for the system. Unfortunately, much of the current work in software maintenance focuses strictly on the notion of maintaining the source code for a system. This is an impossible task. There have been significant trends in recent years toward the creation of almost unreadable programming languages. Consider the C program shown in Table 1.1.

This is a very good example of source code that is not meant to be read. It would take a very good C programmer many hours to figure out what this program is supposed to do. And, it is only 18 lines long. If a program that is only 18 lines long presents a stygian task of program understanding, then a similar program several orders of magnitude larger would be an impossible one.

It would help to know what the program in Table 1.1 is supposed to do. Let us compile and execute it and see what happens. The result of this execution can be seen in Table 1.2.

My, my...what an interesting result. There was nothing in the C code to remotely suggest this outcome.

Table 1.1. A Sample C Program

```
#include <stdio.h>

main(t,_,a)

char*a;

{

return!0<t?t<3?main(-79,-13,a+main(-87,1-_,main(-
86,0,a+1)+a)):

1,t<_?main(t+1,_,a):3,main(-94,-27+t,a)&&t==2?_<13?

main(2,_+1,"%s %d %d\n"):9:16:t<0?t<-72?main(_,t,

"@n'+,#'/*{}w+/w#cdnr/+,{}r/*de}+,/*{*+,/w{%+,/w#q#n
+,/#{1+,/n{n+,/+#n+,/#\

;#q#n+,/+k#;*+,/'r :'d*'3,}{w+K w'K:'+}e#';dq#'1 \

q#'+d'K#!/+k#;q#'r}eKK#}w'r}eKK{nl]'/#;#q#n'){)#}w')
{){nl]'/+#n';d}rw' i;# \

){nl]!/n{n#'; r{#w'r nc{nl]'/#{1,+'K {rw'
iK{;[{nl]'/w#q#n'wk nw' \

iwk{KK{nl]!/w{%'1##w#' i;
:{nl]'/*{q#'ld;r'}{nlwb!/*de}'c \

;;{nl'-{}rw]'/+,}##'*}#nc,',#nw]'/+kd'+e}+;#'rdq#w!
nr'/ ') }+}{rl#'{n' ')# \

}'+}##(!!/")

:t<-50?_==*a?putchar(31[a]):main(-
65,_,a+1):main((*a=='/')+t,_,a+1)

:0<t?main(2,2,"%s"):*a=='/'||main(0,main(-61,*a,

"!ek;dc i@bK'(q)-[w]*%n+r3#1,{}:\nuwloca-O;m
.vpbks,fxntdCeghiry"),a+1);

}
```

At its core, the example C code in Table 1.2 represents one of the major software development problems confronted by today's major corporations. As developers become more sophisticated in their programming skills, these skills are then put to work creating more and more creative solutions to problems that have been solved many times in the past. The result of this creativity is that incredibly complex and labyrinthine source code modules are built that will result in maintenance headaches for the not-so-skilled folks who will have to maintain the code in the future. The

Table 1.2. The Result of Executing the Sample C Program

On the first day of Christmas my true love gave to me
a partridge in a pear tree.

On the second day of Christmas my true love gave to me
two turtle doves
and a partridge in a pear tree.

On the third day of Christmas my true love gave to me
three french hens, two turtle doves
and a partridge in a pear tree.

On the fourth day of Christmas my true love gave to me
four calling birds, three french hens, two turtle doves
and a partridge in a pear tree.

On the fifth day of Christmas my true love gave to me
five gold rings;
four calling birds, three french hens, two turtle doves
and a partridge in a pear tree.

On the sixth day of Christmas my true love gave to me
six geese a-laying, five gold rings;
four calling birds, three french hens, two turtle doves
and a partridge in a pear tree.

On the seventh day of Christmas my true love gave to me
seven swans a-swimming,
six geese a-laying, five gold rings;
four calling birds, three french hens, two turtle doves
and a partridge in a pear tree.

On the eighth day of Christmas my true love gave to me
eight maids a-milking, seven swans a-swimming,
six geese a-laying, five gold rings;
four calling birds, three french hens, two turtle doves
and a partridge in a pear tree.

On the ninth day of Christmas my true love gave to me
nine ladies dancing, eight maids a-milking, seven swans a-swimming,
six geese a-laying, five gold rings;
four calling birds, three french hens, two turtle doves
and a partridge in a pear tree.

On the tenth day of Christmas my true love gave to me
ten lords a-leaping,
nine ladies dancing, eight maids a-milking, seven swans a-swimming,
six geese a-laying, five gold rings;
four calling birds, three french hens, two turtle doves
and a partridge in a pear tree.

Table 1.2. (Continued)   The Result of Executing the Sample C Program

On the eleventh day of Christmas my true love gave to me
eleven pipers piping, ten lords a-leaping,
nine ladies dancing, eight maids a-milking, seven swans a-swimming,
six geese a-laying, five gold rings;
four calling birds, three french hens, two turtle doves
and a partridge in a pear tree.

On the twelfth day of Christmas my true love gave to me
twelve drummers drumming, eleven pipers piping, ten lords a-leaping,
nine ladies dancing, eight maids a-milking, seven swans a-swimming,
six geese a-laying, five gold rings;
four calling birds, three french hens, two turtle doves
and a partridge in a pear tree.

opportunities for software faults and security-related vulnerabilities in the coding milieu are literally unbounded.

For a small taste of the maintenance nightmare represented by the source code in Figure 1.2, let us imagine that we have observed a problem with the code. In Figure 1.3 we see that the program outputs the phrase "three french hens." It should read "three French hens." As an exercise left to the savvy reader, modify the program to correct this problem.

The bottom line of this exercise is that, realistically, there is no such thing as code comprehension. We will, therefore, assume hereafter that source code is essentially incomprehensible. The source code merely implements a low-level design specification that, in turn, implements a high-level functional design specification. If we wish to understand the program, we will refer to the design specifications for that program. To ensure that the source code faithfully implements these specifications, we retain a very small group of inspectors whose job it is to ensure that the source code does, in fact, represent exactly the intent of the design.

1.9   Software Performance Considerations

As we begin to work with the user in the formulation of an abstract machine for the operational system, it will soon become clear that the operations of this machine have attributes outside those of a software computational model. In the world of software machines, there is no real concept of time in the sense of the physical world. Time is not a relevant attribute to a software system. Software, then, cannot be described in terms of the physics of our universe.[2] On the other hand, time is a very relevant property of the universe in which the user exists. Therein lies a significant problem for the software developer. The consumer of the software is sensitive to the latencies present in the expression of the operations — the software is not.

The operational model, then, of a system that we are designing must exist in the physical world of the user. The functional model that we use to implement this operational model is not in this same space. That is a real challenge to us. The latencies between the start of an operation and its completion must be part of the functional design process. We can determine what satisfactory values for these latencies may be directly from the user or through a series of empirical investigations. We must then invent a way in the functional system to ensure that the upper bound on the latencies is never violated.

Imagine, for example, that the software system we wish to implement will intercept a signal from each of the user's keystrokes on a keyboard. We then map the keystroke to an appropriate bitmap to represent the key that the user depressed and then display this on a display in front of the user. There will be a slight delay between the time the user perceives that the key has been struck and when it appears on the screen. This is the latency induced by our software system. This latency is irrelevant to our software — but it is very relevant to the user. Unfortunately, we will not be able to ask our customer for this software what an acceptable latency value might be. We are going to have to conduct an experiment to determine exactly what the upper bound on this keystroke latency might be.

To make our proposed experiment more interesting, suppose that our cost to develop our software will be inversely related to latency. That is, the faster our program must be, the more it will cost to develop it. In this case, it is in our interest to make a very high latency application. Before we perform the experiment, we must first establish a reasonable criterion measure for evaluating the experimental outcome. For our criterion measure, we have our experimental subjects type from a standard text. We then count the effective number of correct words that were typed during each test interval. At each test interval we increase the induced latency in the keystrokes from 0.0 to 0.55 seconds in steps of 0.05 seconds.

Now suppose that we have conducted said experiment and have plotted the criterion measure for all subjects. The results of this hypothetical experiment are shown in Figure 1.4. We can see from this figure that there is a fairly significant deterioration in the quality of typing of the subjects when the keystroke latency exceeds 0.15 seconds. We must then design our functional system in such a manner as to ensure that the keystroke latency will not exceed 0.15 seconds.

In that our customers live in a universe governed by a different physics than that of the software universe, it is clear that there will be a temporal element to every operation in our operational model. Every operation will

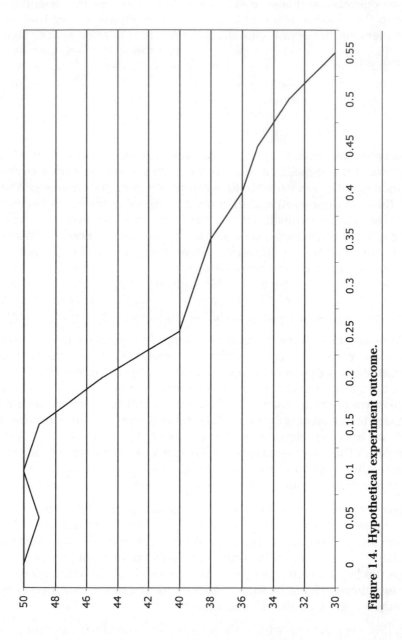

Figure 1.4. Hypothetical experiment outcome.

have this property, but none of the functionalities that will implement these operations will have this property. That will be a major problem in the specification and design of the functional systems that we create.

1.10   Hardware Software Decomposition

Computer software is an abstract object. As such, it simply cannot have a life of its own. It lives in a hardware system. It contributes to the functionality of a complete system. Modern aircraft such as the B-2 or the F-117 simply cannot be flown by a human being because of their aerodynamic instability. They are systems of hardware components and software components. The B-2 is a notable project in its own right. The cost of software development for this project exceeded the hardware development costs. In all fairness, this aircraft is really a flying software system. We only see the airframe so we think of it as a piece of hardware. Without its avionics systems, it is merely an empty shell. Our automobiles have also lost their autonomy as driving machines under the control of a human operator. They are under the control of multiple computer systems. In short, much of the functionality of the vast majority of modern hardware systems is now under software control.

Following best engineering practices, we set about to develop our new systems; we first engage the potential consumer of our new system, whether it is a telephone switch or a microwave oven. We derive from the potential customer base a list of requirements that these customers have and that our new system must fulfill. We then set about to build the operational model. This is best regarded as an iterative process. Customer requirements are embedded within the customer and are perhaps not even well known to the customer. We begin to architect an operational model that we think best meets the customer's requirements. In many cases we can construct prototypes that are animated with vaporware on the software side. These semi-animated prototypes will assist us in building the right operational model. Again, this operational model is animated by a set of operations.

The user will interact only with the operational model. This, of course, must be a tangible system, just as was the case for our example in Section 1.5.4. The user interacted with the tennis ball. His operations were made explicit on this interface. We then identified two different design solutions that would implement this operational model. In either case, much of the functionality, such as the system that employed the video camera, was a hardware system. Only certain aspects of the functionality were implemented in the software. Clearly, the system that we build will be a hybrid of software and hardware functionality.

After the formation of a viable operational model, we have to parse the hardware and software functionalities. This is a very complex process and involves considerable interaction between a staff of hardware engineers and software engineers. This interaction is the subject of a book in its own right. Therefore, we choose to focus strictly on the software side of the house for the remainder of this book.

1.11   The Bottom Line

The software specification and design methodology developed in this book is definitely a front-end loaded model. Most of our development resources will be committed to the early stages of the software life cycle. That is where they belong.

We have very frequently been told by many different software development organizations that they simply cannot afford to develop software in this manner. They incorrectly observe that they are currently not spending any money on the early stages of software development. The truth is that they are heavily invested in specification of the software they write. Unfortunately, most of this investment in the front-end process is really made at the back end where it is painfully expensive. What is worse is that much of the specification documentation is intimately woven into the source code of the document where it is difficult to find and to read. In the worst case, the specifications are, in fact, the code. Any attempt to understand the functional characteristics of such a system means that a process of retrofitting, at least temporarily, a set of functional specifications from the source code must be initiated. This is indeed a very expensive way to develop software.

At the back end of the software life cycle is the test process. As seen from Figure 1.1, a great deal of the software budget for a software development project is allocated to this stage. This is so because it is difficult to impossible to test a system whose operational characteristics are not known. Again, from an engineering perspective, we do not really worry that much about the fact that an engineered system has faults or flaws. What it important is that these flaws do not impact the operational characteristics of the system under construction. If we are manufacturing a mirror for a new reflecting telescope, we understand at the outset that it will not be possible to build a perfect mirror. The whole objective is to build a mirror that is "good enough." If we are designing and building a new highway bridge, we do not attempt to build a perfect bridge that will carry any load for eternity. The bridge will be designed to carry a given load for a finite life cycle. It will be built with structurally flawed materials. It will be engineered with this fact in mind. It is part of the specification of the bridge. We will all agree, in advance, as to what these limitations will be. They will be part of the specifications.

The driving force for the development of new products in today's marketplace is time to market for the products. The biggest sources of delay in the time to deliver a new software product to today's software market happen to be at the back end of the software development process. It takes weeks to test a software product that should be testable within a matter of very few hours. It takes months to code a new subsystem that should be coded in a matter of hours.

It is difficult to impossible to test an ill-defined system. It is really difficult to design a functional machine and write code for this machine at the same time. If, for example, we had a complete module specification written down for a source code module, it would take very little time to write the module and verify that the source code module did, in fact, implement the design correctly. We could even outsource this process with complete confidence that the supplier would deliver correct source code back to us.

It is really easy to test a software product whose operation characteristics are completely specified and to code projects that are completely designed. It is really straightforward to design the functional machine for an operational machine that is well specified. Because it is relatively simple to perform these tasks under a well-specified system, it is also very fast to perform them. This means that new products and new releases to these products can get to market much more rapidly. This is not new ground that we are plowing here. This is a lesson that the car manufacturers in Detroit have had to learn the hard way in their competition with their Japanese counterparts. Time to market is a major consideration for survival in the automobile industry.

Software maintenance costs have now risen to the point that they dominate the cost of a software product across its useful life. In some cases, the software maintenance function will account for more than 80 percent of the total software life-cycle costs. Much of this maintenance cost is simply wasted money. The overwhelming majority of this money is now spent on the momentary reconstruction of design specs for the source code base.

Sometimes it is not easy to see this problem from a software perspective. Let us turn, instead, to the problems of updating the electrical circuits in a house. In the Boston area, there are a quite a few very old houses that have been wired for electricity and then rewired again and again to try and accommodate the demands of a rising need for increased electrical capacity. Suppose that we want to change one of the bedrooms in such a house to a multimedia room. To do this, we hire an electrician who will add additional circuits to the room to meet the needs of the new equipment we wish to run. Our electrician will spend the better part of a day in the house just trying to figure out where the existing wires go. In essence, he must first retrofit a blueprint for the house with an electrical diagram. This is the design spec for the house as it now exists. Once he has a clear understanding of how the house is now wired, he can then proceed to introduce the changes that will be necessary to add the new circuitry to the house. If, on the other hand, we had given our electrician an accurate and up-to-date set of blueprints for the house, we would have had to pay only for his services to implement the change. The ratio of the time it takes to retrofit a set of temporary specifications to the time it takes to make the necessary modifications is astonishingly large. We are paying the electrician to learn about our house, and the majority of the electrician's bill will reflect this learning experience. The distressing thing is that unless we preserve the specification for the changes that we have just made to our electrical system on a new set of blueprints, we are going to have to pay the next electrician that comes to work for us to learn about our house all over.

This is a very expensive way to modify a house. It is also a very expensive way to modify a computer program. In fact, the practice is so prevalent in the software industry that it is the *de facto* standard. In software development shops throughout the industry, there are never accurate software design documents. Any software maintainer who modifies the code in any way must first be paid to develop a set of temporary design specs for the code he or she is modifying only to throw away those specs when the task is finished. It is a very costly and inefficient way to do business. If for no other reason, the cost of software maintenance should clearly mandate the need for developing and maintaining accurate specification and design documents for a software project.

References

1. http://research.microsoft.com/ntball/papers/xmasgift
2. Munson, J.C., *Software Engineering Measurement*, Auerbach Publications, Boca Raton, FL, 2003.

Chapter 2
Requirements Analysis

2.1 The Requirements Process

To simplify and disambiguate our subsequent discussion, let us accept the fact that a requirement is an intrinsic property of an entity, either in the form of a business or a person. Requirements are not attributes of software documents. People and corporate entities have requirements or needs. In the development of a new software system, we seek to meet the needs of a person with this felt need or requirement. In the context of this book, the notion of a requirement is different from the standard use of the term in the literature. It is our thesis that a requirement is a property of an entity, corporate or corporeal. We interact with the entity to develop an abstract machine, the operational model that will best fulfill the user's requirements. The documentation surrounding the operational machine that we develop in response to the user's requirements is known as the operational specification. The customer's requirements are fulfilled in the operational specification.

A significant part of the software development process involves working with customers to ascertain what their needs are. This process is not as simple as it might at first seem. In some cases, perhaps the majority of them, customers have only a vague idea of what their needs (i.e., requirements) really are. They must be educated so that they can assist in the process of fulfilling their needs. The process of squeezing out the requirements from customers is called *requirements elicitation*. In general, the services of a specially trained person called a requirements analyst are needed to work with customers to match up a set of operational specifications for a system that can be built with the requirements or felt needs of these customers.

2.2 The Concept of a Customer

Software is written for a reason. This might seem an obvious conclusion but there is always someone with a felt need to use the speed and accuracy of a computer to help them solve a problem in their intellectual world. Sometimes, the author of the software will be the consumer of this software.

Software can also be written under contract to fill a particular need of a third party. The most lucrative aspect of software creation is to fulfill a perceived need in a much larger class of potential customers. In this case, the customer is an abstraction created by observations on a potential market.

A customer for a software project need not always be flesh and blood. In the case of embedded systems, it is best to think of the customer as the hardware system that the software is driving. Perhaps a much better term than "customer" would be the term "client." Unfortunately, the notion of a client has recently acquired many different meanings, particularly in the area of computer networks. So, *customer* it is.

2.2.1 The Customer as a Real Person

When software systems are developed for a real customer under a contract, it is possible to interact directly with the customer to determine what capabilities he or she must have for the proposed software system. Again, the customer requirements represent a need that the customer has to gain some new or extended functionality.

Having a real customer to interact with is a fortuitous event for a requirements analyst. Questions about the operational specifications for the system that will satisfy the customer's requirements can be resolved with direct interaction with the customer.

Customers will really vary in their ability to articulate their requirements. At the one extreme there is a person who "recognizes the right system when he sees it." At the other extreme is the very well-informed person whose requirements leave no room for discussion. Each customer falls somewhere on this continuum. One of our first tasks in the development of a new system is to determine exactly where the customer is on this continuum.

2.2.2 The Customer as a System

Most modern hardware products are really hybrids. Much of the functionality of the system is now being embodied in software. These embedded systems are ubiquitous. The microwaves in our kitchens run under software control. Modern automobiles have multiple computer systems that handle everything from braking to climate control. In fact, it would probably be easier to identify things that do not have computer controls in them than it would be to try to identify systems running under computer control.

In the case of these embedded systems, the customer is really the hardware system. The software is sharing the functionality of the system with the hardware. The software is really interacting with the hardware to operate the system. The customer requirements are those of the hardware.

One of the most difficult areas of design in embedded systems is the determination of exactly which functions will be handled by software and which by hardware. As microprocessors began to be incorporated into radios, for example, these systems typically ran the user interface. The electronics were used exclusively to decode the radio signal and amplify it. These activities were regarded as intrinsically analog in nature. New radios, however, have a software component that performs this functionality. Most of the functionalities of these new radios are now software. In Chapter 10, we explore the design process of embedded systems in more detail. This design process involves parsing the functionality of the system into hardware and software.

In any event, the requirements for the software component of embedded systems are derived from this parsing of functionality into hardware and software. In general, the operation specifications for the system are developed initially without regard to implementation in hardware or software. The operational model, in this case, is a hardware system with a set of operations that will be used by the customer of the system to manipulate this real machine.

2.2.3 The Customer as a Marketing Abstraction

In the case of general application software systems such as word processors, spreadsheets, and accounting packages, there is no single customer. These systems are written to perceived requirements of a market. The operational specifications for these systems will be derived from requirements developed by a staff of professionals in the marketing division. If there is a good match between the actual requirements of the potential users of the software and the system that is articulated in the operational specification, then the software will likely be a success.

The important distinction for these software applications is that the customer is not a single individual. Rather, the customer consists of a class of software consumers whose needs (requirements) are fulfilled by the software underlying the operational specification. If the marketing staff has done a good job of assessing the requirements of the projected customer base, then the software product will be a success.

2.2.4 Stakeholders

There are really two levels of individuals who will be impacted by a new system. There are those who will be direct consumers of the services provided by the new system and there are those individuals who will be impacted by second- or third-order effects of the system. We might be designing a new decision support system for the top-level managers within an organization. They are the direct users of the system. The effect of the new decision support system will, however, ripple through the management hierarchy in a multiplicity of ways. Managerial decisions made by the top-level managers are passed down the hierarchy to subordinates for implementation. The information that the decision support consumes in its analysis process is obtained from employees throughout the organization. A thorough requirements analysis process strives to identify all potential stakeholders in the organization and incorporates their requirements into the complete requirements picture.

2.3 Requirements Capture

Again, the stated purpose of the requirements capture phase of the software development process is to map the set of user requirements onto a set of operational specifications that most closely matches the customer's needs. Unfortunately, the user requirements will prove a most illusive target. The further that this customer gets into the project, the more aware he or she is of all the possible alternative solutions. Also, the more educated the customer becomes, the more his or her needs will change. The bottom line is that the interaction with the customer during the requirements capture process is an iterative process. At any stage in the process, the operational model is the most current manifestation of these requirements. The user interacts with the requirements analyst to build an operational model that best fulfills his or her needs. The user also works with the requirements analyst to develop a set of operations that will animate the operational model. In that manner, the operational specifications constitute the best and most cogent statement of our current understanding of the customer's requirements.

2.3.1 Requirements Elicitation

We cannot begin to construct a software system without some notion of what a user's needs are. It is clear that these needs might even not be well formulated in the user's mind. We must extract these needs with the user's cooperation. This is the process of requirements elicitation. The problem is quite similar to that faced on a daily basis by a car salesman. A typical customer enters a showroom with a vague notion that he needs a new car. The first step in the elicitation process that a good salesman always performs is to qualify the customer. Many folks would like to buy a new car but not every potential customer has the financial ability to buy one. It would be a waste of the salesman's time to attempt to show cars to these people. They would like to buy a car but they cannot afford to do so. They may like to see models at the top of the model line but their budget will only permit them to purchase an entry-level vehicle. In qualifying this customer, the salesman is, in essence, placing constraints on the interaction with the customer. He is helping the customer understand the range of vehicles that the customer might purchase.

After the salesman has constrained the problem space by determining exactly what the customer is capable of spending on a new car, there are many hoops yet to jump through. Within a given price range, there are many possible vehicles to show the customer. Cars come in a variety of colors, have many different options packages in them, come in a variety of body styles, and with a variety of different engines in them. The very worst scenario from the salesman's standpoint is that the customer really does not have a good idea what color, body style, engine, or options he would like. In this case, the salesman must elicit information from the customer to constrain the problem so that it has a near-term solution. He might choose, for example, to show a customer a color chart for the models that are in the customer's price range. A happy outcome for this process would be to discover that the customer only likes white cars. This would really limit the sales effort. On the other hand, the customer might be color-blind and thus have no particular preference for color.

The main problem confronted by the car salesman, then, is the elicitation problem. He must work with the customer to define a solution to the purchase decision that also lies in the domain of the inventory of the car dealership. This elicitation process may be very short. The customer knows that he wants a green, four-door sedan with a six-cylinder engine. Satisfying this need is just a matter of finding the appropriate vehicle on the car lot. On the other hand, the elicitation process may be very long. The only clear requirement that a customer may exhibit is the need for a new car.

The requirements elicitation process for a software project is very similar to the problem confronted by our car salesman. The customer has a felt need for a software system. The customer's notion of just what that system is may be very clear but it may also be very cloudy. The main objective of the requirements elicitation process is to make the customer's requirements manifest in an operational specification that best describes this need.

It is very useful for both the customer and the requirements analyst to know the objective of the elicitation process. We have seen quite a number of requirements documents that are the result of this elicitation process. They share a common characteristic: they are fraught with ambiguity. Indeed, it is very difficult to disambiguate such a document. In most cases, it is difficult for the customer to relate to the content of this document. If, on the other hand, we look at the requirements elicitation process as building a model of the system that will be built for the customer, this is a process that is much easier to engage the customer in.

Let us examine this requirements elicitation process as it might occur between an architect and a customer who wants to have the architect design a new house. There are two possible scenarios for this interaction between the architect and the customer. In the first scenario, the architect might perceive his role of soliciting from the customer a list of requirements that the customer might have for a house. This list might include such things as cost constraints, site construction constraints, the number of bedrooms that a customer might need, etc. What the architect does not know, however, is that the customer has in his mind's eye a two-story antique colonial reproduction house with knotty pine floors, an old-fashioned kitchen with a fireplace in it, and a rustic look throughout the house. The architect is operating from a very different perspective. His notion of the requirements process is to obtain from the customer the list of cost factors and other details that will affect the construction process. Unfortunately, there is probably not an item on this list for antique colonial reproductions. At a later stage, when the architect begins to design a modern ranch-style house, then and only then will both the client and the architect realize that the customer's needs are not going to be met. There was just no formal mechanism during the requirements elicitation process for the user to express the notion that he had of the house that he wanted the architect design.

An alternative approach to this requirements elicitation process is for the architect to realize that a customer may not have a real grasp of the design and construction of a house. The customer has an image of a house in his mind. The best way to see that a customer's needs are met is to develop an operational model of a house that meets those needs. With the advent of computer-aided design (CAD) software, this is a particularly easy process. The architect and customer would first engage in a short dialog to determine the financial and physical constraints imposed by the building site. From that point, the architect would have a reasonably good idea as to the size of the structure that the customer can afford and that can be built on the customer's chosen building site. The architect would then turn to his computer and lead the customer through a tour of house styles. From this very brief tour, it would soon be apparent that the customer wanted an antique colonial reproduction. Most houses of this genre tend to be three-story houses. The architect would then display a three-story antique colonial reproduction house as a model for the customer. Once the overall nature of the structure has been determined, attention can then be turned to the three different levels of the house and how bedrooms, bathrooms, the kitchen, etc. might be assigned in rough proportion to each of these levels. Using the CAD modeling approach, the architect can build a very reasonable first approximation of the operational model of the house during this interaction with the customer.

The important thing to remember is that during the requirements elicitation process in this hypothetical interaction with an architect and his customer we are strictly talking about what the house will be from the customer's perspective; we do not discuss how it will be built. The typical customer has no knowledge of building codes, electrical code, or plumbing codes.

2.3.1.1 Obtrusive Observation. Requirements can be obtained directly from the stakeholders of a new software system. In this process, direct contact is made between the requirements analysts and the stakeholders of the system. The stakeholders can be queried directly through the use of questionnaires and interviews. They can also be monitored directly in their daily routine by an observer. All of these observation processes are obtrusive. We actually enter the stakeholder's space to obtain the requirements information we seek.

The main problem, then, with obtrusive or direct observation is that it will alter the environment we are attempting to understand. If we were to place an observer in a cubicle to monitor an employee's use of the PC on the employee's desk, it is reasonable to assume that we would learn very little from this observation. The presence of the observer will cause the employee to alter his or her behavior to meet the expectations of his or her job definition. Just as soon as the observer leaves the cubicle, it is reasonable to expect that the employee will resume his or her normal activity of Web surfing, gossiping in one or more chat rooms, and sending instant messages.

The use of questionnaires is also suspect as a viable means of requirements elicitation. There are really two different types of requirements information we might want to collect on a questionnaire. First, we might choose to use the questionnaire to determine how an employee is currently using a system. Second, we might wish to learn how they might use a new system.

2.3.1.2 Unobtrusive Observation. One of the first lessons that every requirements analyst learns is that there is a great disparity between what a customer says he will do with a software system and what he will really do. If, for example, you were to ask one of the employees buried deep in the catacombs of cubicles of a typical modern office what kinds of things he does on a typical day, you might discover that he spends the majority of his time in report generation, principally using word processing and spreadsheet applications. If you were to place a software monitor on his workstation and actually record his activity during a typical workday, a vastly different picture would emerge. You would find, typically, that this employee spends the majority of the day either surfing the Web or chatting with friends, relatives, and an occasional colleague in one or more chat rooms or instant messaging systems.

The actual observation of the employee is taken without the employee's knowledge. It is unobtrusive. When this same employee feels that he is being observed, he will change his behavior to meet company expectations. This change in behavior will greatly bias our understanding of the system user requirements.

In a similar fashion, we could interrogate each user of a company local area network to find out what network services they might use. Alternatively, we could monitor packet traffic on the network to get a much more precise estimate as to the services being provided by the network. In the latter case, the user network requirements are derived from unobtrusive observation of network activity.

2.3.2 Requirements Formulation

In the commercial sector there are really two separate entities that must be considered in the requirements elicitation phase. On the one hand there is the business itself, the corporate entity. On the other hand there is the individual who will interact with the system, in which case we must consider both the requirements imposed by the business entity and the individual user requirements.

2.3.2.1 Business Requirements. Business requirements are the needs of an organization to achieve its goals and objectives. The specific nature of the business requirements will vary, of course, with the nature of the system that is needed. If the specific requirements relate to a new IT infrastructure, then we must determine what information is required to support the business enterprise in terms of connectivity, security, and functionality. The process of requirements formulation in this case is a matter of determining the specific needs and capabilities of each of the departments in the business entity that will be impacted by the new system.

On the other hand, we might speak to the business requirements for a new product that the company is proposing to develop for commercial release. This set of business requirements is developed from a detailed analysis of the needs of the market and the business model of the company. The process of requirements formulation for a product will be very different. This process involves a substantial dialog between the corporate marketing organization and its research and development organization.

In both cases, the end result of the requirements formation effort should not be an unstructured list of needs. Rather, the end product of the requirements formulation process should be a viable set of operational specifications for the proposed system.

2.3.2.2 User Requirements. Each user of a new or evolving software system has a specific set of needs that must be fulfilled by this system. These are the user requirements. In most cases, these needs are not completely understood or formulated in the user's mind. It is a very rare individual who can specify precisely what a new software system must do for them. They must be guided by a structured process and by a trained person to enable them to articulate these needs.

Unfortunately, a list of user-felt needs listed in a "requirements docu-ment" will not serve the user well. We can see this process at work in our daily lives and note immediately the disparity between our statements of need and our subsequent actions. Let us consider, for example, the purchase decision for a new automobile. The rational approach to this purchasing process would have us very carefully list our needs for the new automobile in terms of the number of passengers that we need to transport, the amount of baggage or stuff that we need to carry with us, the fuel economy that we would like to have, etc. When we arrive at the dealership, however, a very different set of implicit needs takes over. Our intentions at the outset may have been to buy a cheap and economical van to transport the kids to soccer matches. The sight of the red, high-powered convertible just overwhelms our rational side. We leave the showroom in our new red convertible with the wind in our hair. It is clear, then, that there is a set of implicit requirements that is really governing our lives. The operational model of the conservative, economical van simply did not match the actual operational model we had in our head. While this example represents an extreme case, it clearly indicates the efficacy of our preparing lists of what it is that we think that we want — our requirements. Far better it would be for us to develop an operational model very early in the game against which we can test our actual requirements.

2.4 The Requirements Analyst

The requirements process is clearly one that involves direct interaction with a customer or an abstraction of that customer. The skill set of a person who can work with a customer to convert requirements into a viable operational model is very clearly different from that of a software devel-oper. The operational model is an abstract machine whose functionality is hidden from the customer. It takes a person with special training to perform the mapping from requirement to model. This function is per-formed by a person called a requirements analyst.

There have been many different definitions of this person and what his or her role might be. Ostensibly, a requirements analyst works closely with the customer to determine the nature of the system that the customer would like to have built. For our purposes, we are going to stereotype this person's role in terms of the operational system specifications. Our require-ments analyst is trained, first and foremost, in the development of system operational specifications. He knows, for example, that his role is to work with the customer to create an operational model of the proposed system. Further, this operational model is animated by a specific set of operations.

Let us imagine that we are employed by a bank that is just beginning to consider implementing its own automated teller machine (ATM) system. The bank officers have a clear idea of what this ATM system means and how they want it to work. That is, they have a set of requirements for the operation of this system. We presume that they share a common vision of what this system should be. A more realistic scenario would have each bank officer holding a slightly different set of requirements. In any event, our first task is to work with the bank officials to build a working operational model of the system that they envision.

Again, the requirements of the bank officers for their new ATM system is not well articulated. These requirements are abstractions in the minds of the bank staff. Our task is not to play a guessing game with these folks to try and tease out the requirements. Some of these requirements may not be really well defined in the minds of the staff. It will be an exercise in frustration to tease these requirements from the staff. Our objective is very different. We are going to build an operational model of the ATM system. As the model emerges, the bank staff will either agree with the nature of the emerging system or offer suggestions to change it so that it does match their requirements. We must view the operational model as a communication mechanism in the requirements elicitation process. What we do want to cultivate in the minds of the bank officers is the notion that we are working together to build the operational model. Altogether too often, what emerges from the requirements elicitation process is a very abstract "requirements document" that consists of endless pages of lists of things each user feels is important to the new system. From our perspective, the most successful outcome of the requirements analysis phase is an operational model of the proposed system that clearly represents a consensus among the customers of the system.

As the operational model of the system begins to coalesce, we can then begin to define a very precise set of operations that will be performed on the ATM device, both from the standpoint of the bank's customers on the front end of the machine and the bank staff on the back end of the machine. These operations will animate the machine. They will also serve as a framework for determining exactly what kinds of data the system will accept and how this data will drive the system. They will also serve as a framework for identifying nonoperational considerations such as response latency or performance, security, and reliability needs.

2.5 Specification Traceability

The ultimate goal in any software development exercise is to build a product that meets a customer's needs. To make this happen, there must be a fairly rigorous statement of the operational model that we have agreed to build for the customer. As the design phase progresses, this operational model is mapped into a design framework consisting of the functional model and a set of functionalities that will animate this functional model. In the best of all worlds, this mapping process is performed by the requirements analysts and the software designers. Finally, the design is mapped onto source code by software developers.

It very frequently happens that the operational specification does not map well into the set of functional specifications. Unless the customer is brought back into the loop and an updated set of operational specifications is created to ensure the correct mapping from the operational specifications to the functional specifications, there will be a significant mismatch between the system that was designed and the system that the customer really wanted.

At the next stage of the software development process, the functional specification is mapped onto source code by the software development team. As they read and interpret the functional specification, there will be plenty of opportunities for misinterpretation; that is, the system that actually gets built will differ from the design. In some cases, new features will be added to the system at the whim of a development team. Ultimately, the system that gets developed may have significant departures from the system that the customer actually wanted — hence the cover of this book.

The objective of the software specification process is to provide a complete and unambiguous path from an operational model that meets the user's precise needs to the source code that will actually implement that operational model. It is pointless, however, to define this specification traceability at the inception of a software development process without implementing processes to maintain the traceability paths.

2.5.1 The Motivation

It is a very complicated and time-consuming process to engage in the generation of a viable operational and functional specification. Most software development organizations are driven by the need to get some code on the system to feel a sense of accomplishment. Code created in this manner, however, is practically guaranteed to satisfy the needs of the developers and not the needs of the customer. It is well worth the time taken to work with the customer to build a very precise set of operational specifications, then to build a set of functional specifications that meet those operational specifications, and, finally, to build source code that matches the functional specifications.

The drive to begin to build a system as soon as possible must be resisted. It would be complete folly to think about building a new office building without a complete set of blueprints covering every conceivable detail of building construction. It would never occur to the staff of Boeing to hire some mechanics to build a new airplane. That may have been possible in the early days of aviation, but it is simply not realistic in light of the complexity of modern aircraft. It is astonishing, then, to watch new software systems being developed in this manner.

An engineered software system has the same attributes as a new airplane development project. The majority of the development costs are spent in the early stages of the development effort. All aspects of design and operation have been resolved before the first line of source code is written. There should be practically zero degrees of freedom in the programming of a software system. The act of programming should be simply a matter of translating the design of the software system to a specific language format.

There is tremendous inertia in the current software development methodology. This was established in the early days of computer programming when machines were simple and programs could be written and understood by a small team of programmers. Software development organizations are quite accustomed to spending enormous amounts of resources in the testing and "debugging" of ill-defined systems. They are not at all accustomed to spending far less money to engineer the system correctly from the start.

2.5.2 The Payoff: Maintainability

The sample C program shown in Table 1.1 is a textbook example of unreadable and unmaintainable code. There is little about this program that suggests what it will do. Given that it has been faithfully reproduced and will compile and execute correctly, the program is still very much a mystery. When it executes, the results are even more mysterious. This program, as shown in Table 1.2, will print the verses to the song, "Twelve Days of Christmas." Now that we know what it will do, the program is still a mystery. This is a very good illustration of the write-only feature of the C programming language.

Clearly, the set of operational specifications for this little program is quite simple. The user simply wants a program that will print out the verses for the "Twelve Days of Christmas" whenever it is invoked. The set of operations is very small as well. There is one operation; that is, print out the verses.

The functional specification that dictates the design is where the complexity of the program really begins to grow. A simple functional model for this program might suggest that the text for the verses of "Twelve Days of Christmas" might reside in a disk file, in which case the program would have a small repertoire of functionalities. An even less complex functional specification might suggest that the entire set of verses resides in one string that would print out when the program executes. This sample specification would result in the C code shown in Table 2.1. The precise characteristics of this program can be deduced immediately.

Table 2.1. Another Sample C Program

```c
#include <stdio.h>
main()

{
printf ("On the first day of Christmas my true love gave
to me\na partridge in a pear tree.\n\nOn the second day
of Christmas my true love gave to me\ntwo turtle doves\nand
a partridge in a pear tree.\n\nOn the third day of Christmas
my true love gave to me\nthree french hens, two turtle
doves\nand a partridge in a pear tree.\n\nOn the fourth
day of Christmas my true love gave to me\nfour calling
birds, three french hens, two turtle doves\nand a partridge
in a pear tree.\n\nOn the fifth day of Christmas my true
love gave to me\nfive gold rings;\nfour calling birds,
three french hens, two turtle doves\nand a partridge in a
pear tree.\n\nOn the sixth day of Christmas my true love
gave to me\nsix geese a-laying, five gold rings;\nfour
calling birds, three french hens, two turtle doves\nand a
partridge in a pear tree.\n\nOn the seventh day of Christmas
my true love gave to me\nseven swans a-swimming,\nsix geese
a-laying, five gold rings;\nfour calling birds, three
french hens, two turtle doves\nand a partridge in a pear
tree.\n\nOn the eigth day of Christmas my true love gave
to me\neight maids a-milking, seven swans a-swimming,\nsix
geese a-laying, five gold rings;\nfour calling birds, three
french hens, two turtle doves\nand a partridge in a pear
tree.\n\nOn the ninth day of Christmas my true love gave
to me\nnine ladies dancing, eight maids a-milking, seven
swans a-swimming,\nsix geese a-laying, five gold
rings;\nfour calling birds, three french hens, two turtle
doves\nand a partridge in a pear tree.\n\nOn the tenth day
of Christmas my true love gave to me\nten lords a-
leaping,\nnine ladies dancing, eight maids a-milking, seven
swans a-swimming,\nsix geese a-laying, five gold
rings;\nfour calling birds, three french hens, two turtle
doves\nand a partridge in a pear tree.\n\nOn the eleventh
day of Christmas my true love gave to me\neleven pipers
piping, ten lords a-leaping,\nnine ladies dancing, eight
maids a-milking, seven swans a-swimming,\nsix geese a-
laying, five gold rings;\nfour calling birds, three french
hens, two turtle doves\nand a partridge in a pear
tree.\n\nOn the twelfth day of Christmas my true love gave
to me\ntwelve drummers drumming, eleven pipers piping, ten
lords a-leaping,\nnine ladies dancing, eight maids a-
milking, seven swans a-swimming,\nsix geese a-laying, five
gold rings;\nfour calling birds, three french hens, two
turtle doves\nand a partridge in a pear tree.");

}
```

47

The moral to this story is that if the functional specification for a program is very simple, then the resulting code will be very simple.

Functional specifications, however, are written for people and not for C compilers. Therefore, the set of functional specifications for the program represented in Table 1.1 would specify precisely how the single string in the program,

```
"@n'+,#'/*{}w+/w#cdnr/+,{}r/*de}+,/*{*+,/w{%+,/w#q#n+,
/#{l+,/n{n+,/+#n+,/#\;#q#n+,/+k#;*+,/'r  :'d*'3,}{w+K
w'K:'+}e#';dq#'l
\q#'+d'K#!/+k#;q#'r}eKK#}w'r}eKK{nl]'/#;#q#n'){)#}w')
{){nl]'/+#n';d}rw'  i;#  \){nl]!/n{n#';  r{#w'r
nc{nl]'/#{l,+'K  {rw'  iK{;[{nl]'/w#q#n'wk  nw'
\iwk{KK{nl]!/w{%'l##w#'  i;
:{nl]'/*{q#'ld;r'}{nlwb!/*de}'c  \;;{nl'-
{}rw]'/+,}##'*}#nc,',#nw]'/+kd'+e}+;#'rdq#w!  nr'/  ')  }
+}{rl#'{n'  ')#  \}'+}##(!!/"
```

could be parsed in nested loops to produce the strings of text representing the stanzas of the song.

The very worst thing that could happen to a developer trying to execute the original C program shown in Table 1.1 is that there is a fault in the code. One or more characters have been altered. It would be a stygian task to find the problem and fix it. For a novice developer, it would be an almost impossible task.

If, on the other hand, there were a very precise set of low-level design documents that identified the contents of the string and the algorithms used to parse it, the task would immediately become a relatively simple one. We would only have to identify where the program differed from the design specification and then change the program to reflect the design specification. The effort to do so would be minimal.

Maintainability, then, is not a property of the source code; it is a property of the complete specification process. Code that is well specified can be easily maintained. Code that is not well specified can be a nightmare from which a maintainer will be unable to awake. We do not build bridges or office buildings without blueprints. It is astonishing that we would think to build software without them.

It is very, very rare to find a customer who can precisely articulate his or her needs for new software at the outset of a project. In the vast majority of software development exercises, there will be an astonishing amount of churn in the operational specification. The advantage of requirements traceability (or as we would prefer to call it, specification traceability) is that each element of the operational specification is very precisely bound to a set of functional specifications that are, in turn, bound to a specific set of code.

2.5.3 The Payoff: Time to Market

Perhaps the greatest payoff for the investment in specification traceability is the problem that is killing most software developers today. That is, the time it now takes to bring a new product or revisions to an existing product to market. As a new product matures in a typical software development organization, there is less and less certainty about what the product actually does. There is even less certainty as to how the product really works. New features have been added to the system by essentially anyone who could sneak them in. As a result, the test process now becomes a major factor in delaying the introduction of the new (or updated) product.

A software product whose operational specification maps directly to it functional specification, which, in turn, maps directly to source code elements, is a product that can be readily understood by managers, marketing, developers, and software quality assurance. It is very easy for each of these software teams to understand and it is easy to test and to certify. All of this translates directly to reducing the time it takes to get a new product on the market. This, in turn, translates directly into reduced development and testing costs and also to the business opportunity of being a market leader.

Very frequently we have heard software development organizations say that "requirements traceability is a very nice objective, but we simply cannot afford to implement it." Quite the opposite is true. They simply cannot afford not to implement it. From a business perspective, the result is quite astonishing. The lack of engineering discipline in the software development process has created the greatest business opportunity that the world has ever seen. The first company to understand this fully has the potential to completely dominate the software marketplace.

Chapter 3
Operational Specification

3.1 Software Operational Specification

The first step in the software specification process is the definition of our system at the operational level. This is the user's view of the system. With our software skills, we can create virtually any reality that we wish. However, we must first specify the reality that we want. The real interesting prospect of software development is that we can operate essentially without constraint in the reality that we can fabricate for a user. Before we can begin the operational specification process, we must first define this reality. This virtual system that we create for the user is called the operational model.

There are three components to the complete operational specification. The first component is the operational system overview, a high-level description of the system and its operational characteristics. The overview is the grist for the mill of the people in sales and marketing. The operational model is a very precise description of the abstract machine with which the user will interact. It will consist of three parts: (1) a diagram or pictorial representation of the abstract machine; (2) a general description of what the user must do to interact or animate the operational machine; and (3) the embodiment of the constraints on the operational requirements that must be formalized to ensure that the software meets the user's needs. The final component of the operational specification is a set of operations that define the interactions that a user will have with the operational machine. From a high-level perspective, this set of operations will constitute the users manual for the operational machine.

There are two major objectives in the development of the operational specification: (1) to construct an abstract machine that we can validate against a set of business requirements, and (2) ensure that the operational specification will be an unambiguous statement that performs in developing the system. With regard to the first objective, the documents that describe this abstract machine, the operational specification, constitute a legal and binding contract either with a user or a business unit.

Second, the operational specification will be an unambiguous statement of work that is to be performed in developing a system. When a software system reaches operational status, it must behave exactly in the manner of the abstract machine outlined in the operational model. It will do no more than that and it will do no less.

3.2 Operational System Overview

We begin the operational specification with the operational system overview. This is a simple précis of the system. It is a concise statement of the basic operation of the system from the user's perspective. It gives the customer, the designer, and the developer an overview of the operation of the system. This is the kind of thing that would be printed on the cover of a CD-ROM containing the software. We will be able to read this description and know what the system will do for us.

The term "user" or "client" does not always imply the existence of a human being in this process. For embedded systems, the client is the hardware being driven by the software. In yet other circumstances, the user or client might be one or more independent software systems.

The most important aspect of the operational system overview is that it constitutes an executive summary of the purpose and intent of the system. It should serve to clarify the thinking of everyone associated with the project. With very large systems, it is increasingly difficult to form a concept or perceive the gestalt of these systems from a detailed description of these systems. Thus, the role of the operational system overview is vital to our understanding of the nature of the system.

3.3 Operational System Model

The next step in the specification process is to construct the operational system model. Again, we can create virtually any reality that we want with our modern software technology. We are going to build an imaginary castle in the sky for our user. The precise description of this castle is the operational system model. It defines very precisely the user's overview of the system operation. It answers the question of *what* the system does. It should provide the system user with a complete description of the abstract model that will interact with the user.

If, for example, our task is to construct a calculator for a user to deploy on his or her desktop, we must work to define the precise model for the calculator. One calculator that we could build would work in the command mode and would behave in a similar fashion to the traditional UNIX dc calculator. We would then define for the user how many decimal places the calculator would maintain for calculations, what operations were permissible, how the data would be entered, and how the data would be displayed. In essence, we would write a simple user's manual that would describe our calculator model so that the user could operate it correctly within the framework of the command-line calculator.

3.3.1   Constraints on the Operational Model

With every software system there are some very reasonable and abiding considerations that every user has about the software that she or he is about to acquire. Users would like the system to run well, have minimal impact on their system resources, and above all, not break frequently when placed into service. These are not operational issues insofar as they describe considerations ancillary to the operational characteristics of the system.

3.3.1.1   Reliability. A *reliable* software system is one that does not break when placed into service at the customer's site. Reliability, however, is not a static attribute of a software system. Reliability is a function of how the software will be used by that customer. Some operations of the software will perform flawlessly and forever. Other operations of the same software system will be flawed and subject to repeated failure events. Software reliability, then, is determined by the interaction between the structure of the code and the user's operation of the system as reflected in his or her operational profile.

The failure of a software system depends only on what the software is currently doing: the operations that a user is performing. If a program is currently executing an operation that is expressed in terms of a set of fault-free modules, this operation will certainly execute indefinitely without any likelihood of failure. Each operation causes a program to execute certain program modules. Some of these modules might contain faults. A program might execute a sequence of fault-prone modules and still not fail. In this particular case, the faults might lie in a region of the code that is not likely to be expressed during the execution of a function. A failure event can only occur when the software system executes a module that contains faults. If an operation is never selected that drives the program into a module that contains faults, then the program will never fail. Alternatively, a program may well execute successfully in a module that contains faults just as long as the faults are in code subsets that are not executed.

Computer programs do not break. They do not fail monolithically. Programs are designed to perform a set of mutually exclusive tasks or functions. Some of these functions work quite well, while others may not work well at all. When a program is executing a particular function, it executes a well-defined subset of its code. Some of these subsets are flawed and some are not. Users execute varying subsets of the total program functionality. Two users of the same software may have totally different perceptions as to the reliability of the same system. One user might use the system on a

53

daily basis and never experience a problem. Another user might have continual problems trying to execute exactly the same program. The reliability of a system is clearly related to the operations that a user performs on the system.

3.3.1.2 Security. A *secure* system is one that can repulse all attempts for misuse. A software system can be assailed from outside the designated and authorized user community by agents who wish to stop the normal use of the software. A software system can also be invaded by an outside agent who exploits the weakness of our defenses for his or her own purposes. Such misuse might divert financial resources or goods to the agent. The agent might also misuse the software to steal intellectual property. At the heart of a secure software system is a real-time control infrastructure that can monitor the system activity and recognize insidious behavior and control it before damage is done to the system. From the availability standpoint, the essence of the security problem is that outside agents are actively trying to subvert the system. They will cause the system to fail to perform its normal activities. In the worst case, they can cause the system to fail, destroy system resources, or consume system resources through a denial-of-service attack.

3.3.1.3 Availability. A system that has been developed for *high-availability* applications can identify potential problems as they occur and seek remediation for these problems before the system can fail. Typically, a system that has been tested and certified for certain operational behaviors will run without problems when it is placed into service. When the software is driven into new and uncertified domains by new and uncertified user activity, it is likely to fail. A system based on principles of survivability will be able to identify new usage patterns by the customer and communicate these new uses to the software developer. The developer then has the ability to recertify the system for its new usage patterns and ship a new release of the software to the customer before the system has the opportunity to fail in the user's hands.

3.3.1.4 Maintainability. From a user's perspective, the concept of software maintenance is very different from that of a developer. A user is not trying to fix a code problem or solve a design problem. A user is first confronted with the task of installing the software on his computer. This process must be easy and straightforward. A reasonable expectation is that any software system should be installable by a typical user without consultation with the software development organization. Further, a system must be easy to remove or uninstall. Absolutely nothing in the world is worse than a system that builds program modules unseen to the user and keeps them in undisclosed locations. Any system should be completely encapsulated so that it is easy to install and easy to remove.

Great consideration should be given to the software update process. Ideally, this process should be completely transparent to the user. With the Internet connectivity available today, this process should be an accounting exercise and not a matter for system administration staff. That is, the transfer of money for the new software update should consume more resources than the update activity itself.

3.3.1.5 Survivability. It is a characteristic of most modern software systems that they are very fragile. If any faults are encountered during their operation, the entire system is likely to fail. This would be analogous to having an automobile stop dead in the road due to the failure of a headlight or a taillight. This level of survivability for an automobile would be completely unacceptable.

So that we might have a point of definition for the concept of survivability, a system will have the attribute of survivability if it can continue to operate minus the services of one or more of its operations. We will discover that basic notions of operational survivability depend directly on the design of the software. If the functional components of a system are tightly woven together, then a system will be very fragile. If, on the other hand, the functional components are tightly compartmentalized and of limited scope, then a system can be gracefully degraded in its operation.

Context is very important to the notion of survivability. It is one thing for a car to lose its headlights in the middle of the day; it is quite another for them to fail in the middle of the night. The service provided by the headlights, illumination of the road, is not vital during the day but it is at night. Precisely the same notion of context dependency is true in the software arena as well.

3.3.1.6 Performance. There are two parts to every operation: (1) the stimulus and (2) the system response to that stimulus. The elapsed time between these two events is the *latency* of the operation. Latency is an attribute of every operation. Some operations will have relatively high latencies while other will have a relatively short latency. The actual performance of the system will depend on the proportion of time spent in each of the operations. This, of course, we can learn from the operational profile. If a user spends a great deal of time executing high-latency operations, then his perception of the system is that it is very slow. If, on the other hand, a user tends to use a suite of very low-latency operations, then the same system will appear to be very fast to this user.

3.3.1.7 Compatibility Considerations. Very often, the hardware context for a software system exists before the development of the software. In such a case, it is evident that the software system to be developed must function correctly in the hardware system in which it must operate. The hardware needs will impose real constraints on the design process. These constraints must be clearly articulated early in the software specification process, particularly at the operational specification level.

The next compatibility consideration relates directly to the potential need to function with other existing software systems. A large part of the process of ensuring the interoperability of the new system with other software systems will be the complete and unambiguous specification of the interface between the software systems.

On many occasions, the interface with other software systems occurs across a computer network. In these cases, the vehicle for information exchange between software systems is via a well-defined network protocol. Hence, the software system is constrained by the standards that define the communication protocol.

3.3.1.8 Size Considerations. Memory real estate is a very expensive commodity. We would like to be parsimonious in our use of it. For embedded software systems, this memory translates directly into power consumption. For object-oriented systems, there is a tremendous price extracted for the runtime environment. Regardless of the context for the system, there are always cost considerations for memory. Memory utilization should be a part of all operational specifications, just as any other cost consideration would be considered at this stage.

There is also a direct relationship between the size of a program and its operational overhead. As memory costs have dropped and processing speed has increased over the past two decades, very little consideration is given, anymore, to the size of a program. This trend is about to experience a dramatic reversal — the size of a program does matter.

There is also a strong reliability component in the size issue. Modern programming language environments rely heavily on the runtime support of an extensive library of services. A very simple program, thus, can become very complex when all the necessary runtime support baggage is added on by the language system. We have watched with amazement as the size of the load module for the simple C "hello world" program has grown over the years. We have not written any of these runtime support modules. We do not know what they do. We do not know what quality standards, if any, were imposed on their development. In other words, the vast majority of the runtime object module of our software is code written by others. In some cases, this may be the majority of the actual object code. We can impose strict software quality standards on our own development work. The majority of the code that we ship, however, will have been written by unknown developers working to unknown standards. It will be difficult to certify a software system that we did not write. Thus, if we are attentive to the size of the program that emerges, we can work to minimize our exposure to code that we did not create.

3.3.2   Graphical Representation of the Operational Model

It is a common saw that a picture is worth a thousand words. This is particularly true in the case of the operational model. The graphical representation of the operational model shows the constituent elements of the abstract machine that the user will operate. It also shows how the components of the machine are related to one another.

The real value of a picture, however, is that it is very easy for a customer to understand. Again, the role of the operational model is to disambiguate the system for the customer. We are trying to design a system that will best meet the user's needs. Technical jargon tends to baffle the uninitiated. Pictures, hence, are vital in this process. Architects are very cognizant of this fact; they regularly work with customers who cannot deal well with the operational specification for a house that is being designed for that customer. The very best strategy for the architect to pursue is to build a simple three-dimensional model of the house that the customer can see and touch. The customer can then examine the house for its aesthetics and also for how it will work as he or she moves from one room to another.

3.4   Operations

An **operation** is an external event to which the operational model must respond. These events occur in the external environment and then impinge on the operational model. The operational model attends to each of these events one at a time. In this sense, the operations are mutually exclusive. Associated with each operation there is a **stimulus** to the operational model that announces the presence of the operation. Some of these stimuli can be considered to occur at random. They do not depend on other stimuli or the state of the operational model when they occur. Other stimuli can only occur in a sequence of other stimuli; they depend on other stimuli.

An operation is an attribute of the user and not the system. The external environment initiates an operation. A software system is conditioned to respond to the initiation event. It is also an attribute of each user that he or she will distribute his or her activity across the set of operations in a different manner. The frequency at which each user selects each operation from the set of all operations constitutes the **behavior** of that user.

The repertoire of operations can vary substantially, depending on the nature of the system being specified. A program that emulates a clock will have a very limited set of operations. We could conceive of operations to start the clock, set the hour, and set the minutes. Beyond that there would be little further interaction with the clock. Other operational models may be much more complex, with very complex temporal relationships.

In essence, the operations animate the operational model. Getting the set of operations right is a very difficult task. For a large complex system, there may be several thousand such operations. Perhaps the best way to proceed in developing the operations is in a top-down fashion. This exercise is very similar to that of preparing an outline. We first begin with the major headings. An operating system, for example, might be partitioned into operations on the file system, on memory management, on networking services, and on scheduling. The file system might be further subdivided into operations on directories and operations on files, etc.

The inevitable granularity question always arises. How do you know when operations have been partitioned to the lowest possible level? Consider the case where we have an operation for which the user provides our software system with a decimal number. We can define an operation to read that number. We also realize that the number is composed of multiple digits. As far as the user is concerned, a number is atomic. We do not think about numbers as digits. Therefore, we should not have an operation that reads digits.

As we progress in our definition of system operations, we are, in fact, developing a set O of operations. These operations must be mutually exclusive. If, for example, the user is currently expressing operation $o_i \in O$, then he must cease this operation before commencing another.

3.4.1 The Stimulus

For each of the operation stimuli, there is a suite of responses from the system. The precise nature of the stimulus depends heavily on the nature of the software system being developed. In the case of a simple command-line calculator, for example, there are two basic classes of stimuli with which the system must cope. First, the calculator will be brought into existence by the operating system in response to a command from the user. In response to its initial animation, the typical machine initiates some activity to initialize its internal state and then sets the stage for interaction with the user by initiating some type of prompt to the user indicating that the system is now open for business. The bottom line is that there can be many different sources of stimuli to which a program must respond. Stated another way, there can be multiple classes of users, each of which has a different set of operations they can invoke.

3.4.2 The Operational Response

Each of the operations that will be defined only manipulates the abstract operation model. That is all they do. The operational response is simply the change that occurs in the operational model in the presence of a stimulus for that operation. The operational stimulus is received by the operation model and it then acts to perform some work for the user. The precise specification of this piece of work is, in fact, the operational response.

Under no circumstances do any of the operations specify *how* it is to be implemented. Operations specify only *what* is to be done. In the specific case of a simple clock system, we could specify an operation to set the hour on the clock. In describing this operation, we might say, for example, that we would enter a command to the clock system on a command line with the following syntax "hour = 0700". If, on the other hand, we were to specify that we wanted the value "7" to be placed into an hour display register, we are now dealing specifically with how the operation will proceed. This is clearly not an operation; it is a functionality. It is manipulating an abstract machine other than the one specified in the operational model.

3.4.3 Temporal Constraints

Each operation animates the operational model. In some cases, other operations must first be performed for an operation to have a successful outcome. Thus, an operation might depend on the sequence in which the operations are performed. Further, an operation might well be constrained to be performed within a certain real-time interval. These two attributes constitute the temporal operation bindings.

3.4.3.1 Sequential Binding. It is clear that some operations must occur in sequences. A brake pedal must first be depressed before the transmission level can be moved to select a gear. The radio must first be turned on before a station can be selected. These are examples of the sequential binding of operations. That is, we must first perform operation o_i before we can perform operation o_{i+1}. Thus, as we define each operation, we must then list the direct antecedent operations for that operation. It is clear that a radio must first be turned on before selecting a station. In that sense, the station selection operation depends on the power-on operation. It might well be that we first set the volume of the radio before selecting the new station. The station selection operation does not depend on the volume adjustment operation, only on the power-on operation.

As we begin to develop the suite of operations that will animate our operational model, we discover that there are two sets of operations. One set consists of those operations that do not have sequential dependencies on any other operations. The second set consists of those operations that do have sequential dependencies on other operations. Within this latter set, the operations are organized into a forest of trees. Some of the operations in this set are the root nodes of these trees; that is, they have no direct sequential dependencies on other operations but they do have one or more modules that depend on them. Other operations are root nodes of sub-trees of one of the trees in the set. Other operations are leaf nodes in the dependency trees; that is, they will have no operations that depend on them.

A significant part of the design of the operational specification of an emerging software system is to create and maintain the forest of these operational dependencies. It would be very useful to build and maintain a flow graph representation of these dependencies as a visual display as part of the operational specifications.

3.4.3.2 Real-Time Constraints. Computer software does not really operate in our four-dimensional world. The physics we use to describe our universe simply do not apply to computer software. Of greatest concern to us at this point is the notion of time. The performance of an operation by our operational model could take years or microseconds. The success or failure of this operation has nothing to do with the elapsed time in our universe. Time, however, is very important to the human organism that will ultimately interact with the software. If, for example, the pilot of an F-16 jet aircraft pulls back on the control stick, it is very important that this stimulus be sensed in a millisecond framework and responded to with similar alacrity. The fact that the elevator surfaces of the aircraft are moved upwards by the avionics software would constitute a successful response to the control stick stimulus. For this action to be useful to the pilot, it must happen in a temporally meaningful context for the pilot.

Therefore, we are going to insist that some operations must happen within a certain time interval, or latency. Thus, we can assign a latency value to each operation. Let $l(o_i)$ represent the latency of operation o_i. For some operations we can be indifferent to the value of $l(o.)$. For other operations, we might insist that $l(o.) < a$; that is, the operation must occur with a latency less than some value a measured in human timeframe. Other operations may constrain latency to an interval such as $b \leq l(o.) \leq a$. As the operational model develops, it is vitally important that we ascertain what these latencies should be. We, of course, derive these values either directly from the user or empirically during the simulation of the operational system.

3.4.4 The Attributes of an Operation

The notion of an operation can now be defined with some degree of precision in that we now have a good understanding of what the attributes of an operation really are. To specify an operation, all of its attributes must be specified. These attributes are shown in Table 3.1.

Table 3.1. Operational Attributes

Attribute	Description
Operation Name	A unique identifier for this operation
Stimulus	Text describing the precise event that occurs in the external environment that will announce the initiation of the operation
Operation	Text describing the actions taken by the operational model in response to the stimulus
Sequential Dependencies	A list of operations that must occur prior to the initiation of the current operation
Latency	Possible upper and lower bounds on the real-time performance of the operation by the operational model

Each operation has a unique operation name. We can see the value of this identification when we attempt to map between the operations and the functionalities. There is a distinct stimulus from the external environment that will initiate this operation. This stimulus might be a direct input from the user or it might even be a hardware signal in the form of an interrupt. In response to the stimulus, the abstract machine specified in the operational model takes some action based on the nature of the stimulus. This is the distinct characteristic of each operation. Further, each operation can be bound to other operations in a temporal structure.

It is clear that our abstract software machine represented by the operational model will not exist in the same universe in which the external user exists. Other than a sequential dependency, there is no sense of time in the abstract machine. However, for our abstract machine to be useful in the physical universe, we must impose some temporal constraints in terms of latency to each operation.

Thus, each operation in the operational specification must have these five attribute dimensions specified for it. If there are no sequential dependencies, then this fact should be noted. If there are no sequential dependencies, then this also must be noted.

3.5 The Operational Profile

The sense of real-time or clock time does not really exist for computer software. Time is relevant only to the hardware on which the software will execute. A given piece of software can run in many different environments on many difference machines. Some of the machines may be fast, while others are very slow. The consequences of execution of the software are the same in each of these environments. The notion of clock time in this highly variable environment is neither pertinent nor relevant. The simple fact is that computer software does not exist in our four-dimensional world.

However, we do need to have some sense of the order in which activities occur. We can use the term "epoch" to provide this order. The transition in the user's environment from one operation to another is an operational epoch. The transition from one functionality to another is a functional epoch. Finally, the transition from one module to another is a module epoch. We measure the duration of a user's interaction with the system in terms of operational epochs, and we measure the duration of system activity in terms of module epochs.

The transition from one mutually exclusive element of the system to another can be described as *a stochastic process*. The system elements, of course, can be user operations, system functionalities, or module executions. As such, we can define an indexed collection of random variables $\{X_t\}$, where the index t runs through a set of non-negative integers, $t = 0$, 1, 2, ... representing the epochs of the process. At any particular epoch, the software is found to be executing exactly one of its M possible elements. The fact of the execution occurring in a particular element of a set of operations, functionalities, or modules is a *state* of the system. For this software system, the system is found in exactly one of a finite number of mutually exclusive and exhaustive states that can be labeled 0, 1, 2, ..., M. In this representation of the system, there is a stochastic process $\{X_t\}$, where the random variables are observed at epochs $t = 0, 1, 2, ...$ and where each random variable can take on any one of the $(M + 1)$ integers, from the state space $A = \{0, 1, 2, ..., M\}$, the set of program modules. The elements of $\mathbf{P}$ are then $p_{ij} = \Pr[X_n = j \,|\, X_{n-1} = i]$.

Interestingly enough, for all software systems there is a distinguished event that represents the start of the stochastic process. In the case of the set of program modules, for example, the main program module will always receive execution control from the operating system. If we denote this main program as module 0, then $\Pr[X_0 = 0] = 1$ and $\Pr[X_0 = i] = 0$ for $i = 1, 2, ..., M$. Further, for module epoch 1, $\Pr[X_1 = 0] = 0$, in that control will have been transferred from the main program module to another function module.

When a particular user exercises a system, that user exhibits a characteristic distribution of activity across the set of operations O. Some operations occur with a greater likelihood than others. The distribution of user activity across the set of operations constitutes the **operational profile** of that user. The operational profile is a characteristic of the user.

When the software developer constructs a software system, it is designed to fulfill a set of specific business requirements. The user runs the software to perform a set of perceived operations. In this process, the user does not typically use all of the operations with the same probability. The *design operational profile* of the software system is the set of unconditional probabilities of each of the operations O being executed by the user. Let Z be a random variable defined on the indices of the set of elements of O. Then, $o_l = \Pr[Z = l]$, $l = 1, 2, ..., |O|$ is the probability that the user is executing an operation l as specified in the operational specification of the program and $|O|$ is the cardinality of the set of operations. A user can only execute one operation at a time. The distribution of o, then, is multinomial for programs designed to fulfill more than two distinct operations.

As we will discover, considerable effort should be directed toward understanding just what the software should do for the user (the set of operations) and how the user will select among the operations. The prior knowledge of this distribution of the operational profile should be a principal guide to the software design process. It seems improbable that we would not want to know how a system will be used before we build it. Imagine, if you will, if the designers of the Golden Gate Bridge had lacked this foresight when they built that bridge. They clearly had to anticipate both the projected traffic for the bridge and the weight of that traffic on the bridge to build the right bridge.

The design operational profile is a single point in an $n-1$ dimensional space. It is, in fact, the centroid in a range of possible departures from the design operational profile. That is, each user uses the system in a slightly different manner. This creates a slightly different operational profile represented by a different point. Let O^p represent the design operational profile. Each user has a slightly different behavior, represented by an operational profile, say O^u. Each of the operational profiles is, in fact, a point in an $n-1$ dimensional space. Note that we lose a degree of freedom due to the fact that $\sum o_i^p = 1$. It is possible to compute the distance in this $n-1$ dimensional space, the two points representing a user's operational and the design operation profile, as $d = \sum(o_i^p - o_i^u)^2$, where n represents the number of operations and $0 \le d \le 2$.

In that no two users will use the system in exactly the same way, it is necessary to understand the distribution of the distances, d. Let d_i represent the distance between a particular operational profile for user, i, and the design operational profile. We can then talk about the average distance

$$\bar{d} = \frac{1}{m} \sum_i d_i$$

for a group of m users and the variance of this distance across all users,

$$Var(d) = \frac{1}{m} \sum_i (d_i - \bar{d})^2 .$$

The real problem, from a design perspective, is that we really do not know what the mean and variance of these distances will be when the system is developed. There are two distinct solutions to this dilemma. First, we can conduct a controlled experiment to develop reasonable estimates of what these statistics will be. Second, we can design a **robust** system. A robust system is one that works reliably in the face of large values of *Var(d)* when the system is deployed.

As we begin to gain some detailed knowledge of the operational profile, we can now begin to examine the system more closely from the performance standpoint. We recall that the latency of each operation is $\lambda_i = l(o_i)$. The first statistic that we can develop is the expected value for the operational latency of the system under an operational profile O; this is $E(\lambda) = \sum_i o_i \lambda_i$. The variance of the operational latency is then under the same operational profile:

$$Var(\lambda) = \sum_i o_i \lambda_i^2 - E(\lambda)^2 = \sum_i o_i \lambda_i^2 - \left(\sum_i o_i \lambda_i \right)^2$$

It should be eminently clear, then, that if a system is experiencing performance problems, a very good place to look for improvement would be on those operations where $\lambda_i o_i$ is very large. In fact, if we were to sort the $\lambda_i o_i$ from largest values to the smallest, we would have a pretty good idea where the real performance issues lie.

It is important to note that performance, just as for reliability and availability, depends on the operational profile. It does little or no good to attempt to deal with latency issues with an operation that is seldom, if ever, expressed by a user. The real operational latency problems occur on those operations that are frequently expressed by the users.

3.6 The Evolution of the Operational Specifications

The operational specifications are living documents. They are subject to almost constant change during the course of the natural life of a software system. These documents change over time to reflect changes in the operational machine. There are essentially four different types of documents that must be managed under some type of configuration control. These are as follows:

1. Operational overview
2. Operational model (as text)
3. Operational model (as figures)
4. Set of operations

As the system evolves, there will be new versions of each of these documents. In essence, the system defined by the operational specification is a moving target. The management of the operational overview and operational model in this context is relatively straightforward in that there will always be one each of these documents. All we need to do for future systems is track the version numbers of these documents. The set of operations is very much more dynamic. At its inception, a system might consist of, say, n operations. As the system evolves, some of elements of the original set of operations may vanish and new operations will be introduced.

It is absolutely vital that we be able to identify the structure of the system in terms of the set of operations at any particular point in time. Without this structure, it would be practically impossible to conduct meaningful conversations about the system if every participant in the conversation is, in fact, talking about a different system. To aid in this discussion, let us define an index vector, ι, that will maintain the versioning data on each of the operations. Let ι_i represent the version number of the ith operation of the system. For the initial system, then, consisting of n operations, the index vector would be $\iota = \langle 1.0,\ 1.0,\ 1.0,\ 1.0,\ 1.0 \rangle$ for a system with five operations. Let us now assume that operation 2 has been modified. The new index vector would be $\iota = \langle 1.0,\ 1.1,\ 1.0,\ 1.0,\ 1.0 \rangle$.

At some future time, a new operation can be added to the system. The index vector might then look something like this: $\iota = \langle 1.1,\ 1.3,\ 1.0,\ 2.1,\ 1.3,\ 1.0 \rangle$, where $\iota_6 = 1.0$ represents the version of the new operation. Not only do new operations enter the system, but others can be removed. When that happens, we preserve the initial structure of the index vector. Let us assume, for example, that the third operation in the original set of operations has been deleted from the system. The new index vector will have a zero placed in the third position to represent this event to wit: $\iota = \langle 1.1,\ 1.3,\ 0,\ 2.1,\ 1.3,\ 1.0 \rangle$.

In systems that employ source code control for managing the evolution of the source code, there are distinct points in time where all of the most current versions of all modules are compiled and linked into a **build** of the system. The build represents a distinct point in the evolution of the system. A build is characterized by a list of source code elements that went to the compilation. This list of modules, together with their version numbers, is called the build list. A very similar concept can be developed for the operational specifications.

The elements of an operational specification are assumed to be under a constant state of flux. At periodic intervals, these elements are bound together to define a build of the operational specifications. As we will see in subsequent chapters, this build event is defined by the build of the source code system. Each source code element is bound to one or more operations. The system that is built from source code reflects exactly one state of the vector ι. This permits the unambiguous interpretation of the operational system that is reflected in the current build of the source code.

We can identify the build points of the operational specifications with the nomenclature $\iota^{(k)}$ for the kth build of the operational specifications. In general, the builds of the operational specifications correspond directly to builds of the system source code.

As it turns out, then, the set of operations O is not really a static set of fixed operations. We need the ability to distinguish these sets from one another to eliminate ambiguity in the discussion of set characteristics. Based on the notion that a build is a defining moment in the operational specifications, we can identify the evolving sets of operations in concert with the build nomenclature. Thus, $O^{(k)}$ identifies the set of operations at the kth build of the operational specifications

Each build of the system may well represent a new build in the operational specifications. This, of course, has some real consequences in the operational profile. This is a problem that we will return to and study at greater depth at a later point in the book. For the time being, we should note that the operational profiles of two sequential builds, $O^{(k)}$ and $O^{(k+1)}$, are not necessarily comparable, particularly in the case where the cardinalities of these two sets are different. The operational profiles, then, are an artifact of the set $O^{(k)}$ on which they are defined.

3.7   An Example

At this point, it would be useful to introduce a sample system that we can track through all the stages of specification, design, development, and test. For this simple example, a software calculator is implemented for use on a UNIX platform. This is a simple RPN calculator similar to the dc calculator supplied with many UNIX systems.

3.7.1   The Operational Overview

The calc software system is a simple desk calculator. It is designed to run in command mode. This means that it will be invoked from a UNIX command line by typing the name calc with no arguments. The calc machine is capable of the basic arithmetic operations of add, subtract, multiply, and divide. The arithmetic it performs is integer arithmetic. No decimal points can appear in the numbers entered in the machine. All integers will be limited to ten digits. The integers can be signed or unsigned.

The calc machine is an RPN calculator. This means that all numbers entered by the user are placed on top of a stack. This stack can hold four numbers. Whenever an operation is entered by the user, such as +, −, *, or % (for divide), this operation is applied to the top two numbers on the stack. The user can display just the top entry on the stack or can elect to display the entire stack, in which case the numbers will be printed from the top of the stack to the bottom. The result of an addition or subtraction operation replaces the topmost number on the stack. The third and fourth numbers on the stack replace the second and third numbers on the stack at the conclusion of either a addition or subtraction operation. The fourth register contents are replaced with a zero. The result of a multiplication operation replaces the top two numbers on the stack. Each of the numbers is a signed decimal number. The topmost entry will be the ten most significant digits of the calculation, and the next register will contain the ten least significant digits of the calculation. The division operation (%) produces two numbers (1) the quotient of the divide appears in the top-most register, and (2) the remainder of the division operation appears in the next register in the stack. For all calculations, the top register is the left operand of the infixed operator.

The `calc` system prompts the user with a ">" symbol when it is ready for either an operator or operand input. At the prompt, the user can type any one of the operations listed in Table 3.2, followed by a carriage return keystroke. The description of each of the permitted operations is shown in the second column of Table 3.2.

3.7.2 The Operational Model

In the context of the `calc` operational model, it is necessary to explain completely and unambiguously how the decimal calculator works for the user. This is in contrast to the operational overview that is a more glib and general statement about the nature of the calculator. There are two components to the operation model: (1) a graphical representation or picture of the components of the operational system that will show both the structure of the components and how they interact with one another; and (2) a written description of the constituent element of the system, again specifying how these components interact with one another.

3.7.2.1 A Graphical Representation of the `calc` Machine. The essential user operational model is shown in Figure 3.1. In this case there is very little to represent. The user can interact with the `calc` machine through the keyboard. The commands that the user gives to the `calc` engine are applied to the register set.

3.7.2.2 The `calc` Operational Model. The `calc` machine performs basic arithmetic operations on signed decimal numbers. A signed decimal number is composed of a non-empty string of decimal numbers, a sign, and a decimal point. The first character in the string must be a sign (+ or −). The remaining characters can be decimal numbers and a single decimal point. The user may or may not enter a sign. The user may or may not enter a decimal point.

Basically, a user can submit either operators or operands (decimal numbers) to the `calc` machine. If a decimal number is entered, the contents

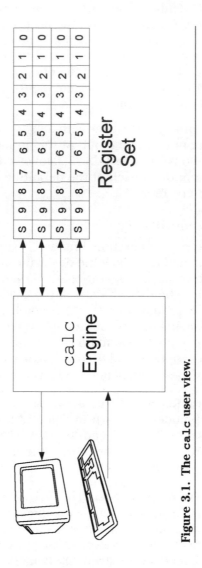

Figure 3.1. The calc user view.

of the stack are pushed down one level by the calc engine. The new decimal number is now placed on top of the stack. The contents of the last register on the stack are lost during the push-down process. If a user does not enter a decimal point, one will be concatenated to the end of the nine-digit decimal string.

There are two distinct types of operators. There are arithmetic operators that control the arithmetic that calc performs on the stack, and there are calc control commands that permit calc operations on the stack, such as displaying its contents.

The calc machine can be initiated as a UNIX process. There will be no arguments on the command line. When it is initiated, calc will prompt the user with the ">" prompt. The user can enter either an operator or an operand. The system will terminate when the user types in the "q" operator.

3.7.2.3 Reliability. Software reliability is a function of how the software will be used. We cannot begin to make an assessment as to the reliability of our system until we know how it will be used. Stated much more precisely, one of the first things that we must know about our system is how the user will distribute his or her activities on this system. This distribution will be the prior distribution for the operational profile.

A good case can be made that the prior distribution of the operational profile cannot be readily obtained. That response is always a cheap shot. We can obtain a reasonable distribution of the operation profile calculator by watching what a group of experimental subjects does with a Hewlett-Packard RPN calculator. That is, we can design and conduct an experiment with a group of typical RPN calculator users to see just how they would use the calculator on a series of problems that we would ask them to solve.

Another very good tool for obtaining experimental data on operational profiles is the prototype. That is, we can construct an emulator for our calculator and then see how our experimental subjects will interact with it. In the case of the calc software, of course, the exercise of constructing the emulator will be the same as the construction of the machine itself. This is not really a viable alternative for this trivial problem.

3.7.2.4 Security. Common sense prevails here. There are no activities of calc that will demand that it operate with root privileges. We do not go out of our way to introduce features to our calculator that will introduce both features that are extraneous to the operation of the calculator and unwanted by the user.

3.7.2.5 Availability. Again, a system that has been developed for *availability* can identify potential problems as they occur and seek remediation for these problems before the system can fail. We will have built our `calc` system around a prior distribution of the operational profile. When our software is placed into service, it is reasonable to believe that it will work reliably when used as we have tested and certified it under the prior operational profile. To ensure that we continue to operate within the certified reliability of our `calc` software, we must monitor the users to ensure that they are using it in a manner consistent with our certification procedure. At the point that we observe significant departures on the part of users from the certified operational profile, the reliability of the `calc` software becomes suspect. The only way we can continue to ensure the reliability, and availability, of `calc` is to capture the operational profile of this new use of the system and then certify the system under that operational profile.

3.7.2.6 Maintainability. The software for `calc` is delivered to the user in source code form. The user is provided with a complete and unambiguous description of how the system is to be built for his or her machine. We must also design mechanisms for the user to follow to merge updates for the source code.

3.7.2.7 Survivability. Our calculator is a very simple machine, yet even here there are some critical survivability issues. In that we are emulating a stack-oriented calculator, all of the intermediate results of calculations are held in the registers that constitute the stack. If our calculator begins to fail, it would be fine if it refused to do addition operations. It would be fine if it refused to multiply. But it would not be fine if it refused to display the stack contents. Thus, we insist that the stack display operations must function correctly regardless of the status of the arithmetic operations that the calculator may perform.

3.7.2.8 Performance. The complexity of our calculator will be sufficiently low that we would not begin to encounter performance problems with it. Because, in this case, the user is a human, all operations are performed at human speeds measured in seconds and not machine speeds measured in nanoseconds.

3.7.2.9 Compatibility Considerations. Our calculator must run on any platform on which UNIX (or Linux) currently runs. Thus, we must avoid designing in features that are Intel specific, for example. The calculator is to run in command-line mode. This means that it will not use any of the capabilities of the X-Windows environment.

3.7.2.10 Size Considerations. Given the acceptable level of feature bloat and system overhead in today's standard software development practice, there is very little that we can do to our system to cause it to be competitive with even the simplest calculator program currently on the market. It would be a valuable exercise, for this example, to measure the size of the resulting object system and determine precisely how much of the functionality of this system is contributed by the programming language system.

3.7.3 The Set of Operations

The `calc` system operations are a set a mutually exclusive activities or operations that the user can execute. A list of operations for our hypothetical `calc` software is shown in Table 3.2.

Each operation is distinct. We cannot combine them. The user is constrained to doing one of them at a time in serial order. Essentially, we must insist that each operation be entered, followed by a carriage return. It should be obvious that there are no implementation details considered in the set of operations. These operations are strictly what the user will do to interact with our `calc` software.

3.7.4 The Operational Profile

It is vital to the design process that we understand the prior distribution of the operational profile. It is also very important to understand just how much variability there will be in this operational profile across multiple users. To obtain such data, we must conduct at least two experiments. The first experiment focuses entirely on the variation in users for a given operational profile. If we find a great deal of variation in the manner that different people use a calculator, this will have great implications for the nature of the second experiment. We need to have lots of subjects in our second experiment to ensure that we have observed the full range of behavior typical of the larger user community. If, on the other hand, we find in our first experiment that there is very little variation in the way that a calculator is used, then we can learn a great deal about the operational profile for our calculator from an experiment with very few subjects.

Now imagine that we have conducted an experiment. We have selected six people at random from a group of UNIX users on our computer system and asked them to participate in a study we are conducting. We have written a version of our calculator in PERL. This experimental version of the calculator has been instrumented so that we can capture the frequency of use of each operation. All subjects have been instructed to use our calculator when next they have some integer arithmetic they would like to perform. We have designed the prototype system so that we can capture the frequency data for the operations directly from the PERL script.

After we have performed our experiment, we now have usage data for the six subjects on their use of the `calc` machine. This hypothetical data is shown in Table 3.3. In the rightmost column are the totals for the distribution of activity on each operation across all subjects. In the last

Table 3.2. Operations for Hypothetical Software

Operation	Stimulus	Response
O_1	\<enter operand>	The value of the number is pushed on the stack. A number is a string of the digits "0" to −"9." It can be preceded by an optional sign ("+" or "−"). If the integer does not follow the form of a decimal number, the system will display the response "error," followed by a carriage return and a new prompt.
O_2	+	The top two values on the stack are popped, added, and their sum pushed back on the stack. The contents of the last register are replaced by a zero.
O_3	−	The top two values on the stack are popped, the second number is subtracted from the first, and the difference is pushed back on the stack. The contents of the last register are replaced by a zero.
O_4	*	The top two values on the stack are popped, multiplied, and the least significant ten digits of the product are pushed back on the stack and then the most significant ten digits of the product are pushed into the stack. Both registers carry the sign of the result.
O_5	%	The top two values on the stack are popped; the first number is the dividend and the second number is the divisor. The signed remainder is pushed onto the stack, followed by the signed quotient. If the divisor is zero, the system will display the response "error," followed by a carriage return and a new prompt. The contents of the register set remain unchanged.
O_6	d	The top value on the stack is duplicated. That is, it is copied out by the calc engine and pushed back onto the stack.
O_7	p	The top value on the stack is printed. The top value remains unchanged.
O_8	f	All values on the stack are printed with a carriage return separating them.
O_9	q	Exits the program.
O_{10}	c	The top stack entry is popped. The contents of the last register are replaced by a zero.

row is a count of the total number of operations performed by each of the subjects as he or she interacted with the calc machine. From these hypothetical frequency data, we can now derive the operation profile for each of the subjects. We will compute an estimate for the individual operational profiles by dividing the column marginals (last row entry) into

Table 3.3. Frequency Data for Operations in Prototype calc Machine

Operation	Subjects						Total
	1	2	3	4	5	6	
1	10	30	52	12	48	11	163
2	5	12	24	3	24	5	73
3	2	8	10	4	8	5	37
4	1	4	0	4	12	0	21
5	1	1	0	1	0	0	3
6	0	1	0	0	0	0	1
7	2	10	5	2	4	1	24
8	0	8	0	1	1	0	10
9	1	1	1	1	1	1	6
10	1	4	1	3	2	0	11
Total	23	79	93	31	100	23	349

the frequency count for each operation. These operational profile data is shown in Table 3.4. We can also compute an operational profile across all subjects using the frequency data from the last column of Table 3.3. This global operational profile is shown in the last column of Table 3.4.

As mentioned previously, each user operational profile represents a point in a nine-dimensional space. We can compute the distance between each of the user profiles and the total profile by

$$d = \sum_{i=1}^{10} \left(o_i^s - o_i^t \right)^2,$$

where o_i^s is a subject profile value and o_i^t is a total profile value. These distances are shown in the last row of Table 3.4. The distances, of course, are distributed on the interval [0,2]. Among the hypothetical subjects, we see the greatest departure from the total profile on subjects 2, 4, and 6. Subjects 1 and 5, on the other hand, were relatively close to the total profile.

Let us now take these same hypothetical operational profiles and explore the performance implications. Let us assume that we have collected performance data on each of the operations. This data is shown in the last column of Table 3.5. Each operation can be characterized in terms of the length of time it takes to execute that operation (in milliseconds).

Table 3.4. Operational Profiles in Prototype `calc` Machine

Operation	Subjects						Total
	1	2	3	4	5	6	
1	0.43	0.38	0.56	0.39	0.48	0.48	0.47
2	0.22	0.15	0.26	0.10	0.24	0.22	0.21
3	0.09	0.10	0.11	0.13	0.08	0.22	0.11
4	0.04	0.05	0.00	0.13	0.12	0.00	0.06
5	0.04	0.01	0.00	0.03	0.00	0.00	0.01
6	0.00	0.01	0.00	0.00	0.00	0.00	0.00
7	0.09	0.13	0.05	0.06	0.04	0.04	0.07
8	0.00	0.10	0.00	0.03	0.01	0.00	0.03
9	0.04	0.01	0.01	0.03	0.01	0.04	0.02
10	0.04	0.05	0.01	0.10	0.02	0.00	0.03
Distance	0.005	0.020	0.016	0.029	0.007	0.019	

Table 3.5. Operational Latencies in the `calc` Machine

Operation	Subjects						Latency
	1	2	3	4	5	6	
1	34.27	29.93	44.07	30.51	37.83	37.69	79
2	29.92	20.91	35.52	13.32	33.04	29.92	138
3	12.00	13.97	14.84	17.81	11.04	30.00	138
4	5.47	6.37	0.00	16.23	15.09	0.00	126
5	5.24	1.53	0.00	3.89	0.00	0.00	121
6	0.00	1.01	0.00	0.00	0.00	0.00	80
7	8.00	11.65	4.95	5.94	3.68	4.00	92
8	0.00	9.32	0.00	2.97	0.92	0.00	92
9	4.57	1.33	1.13	3.39	1.05	4.57	105
10	1.45	1.69	0.36	3.23	0.67	0.00	33
Average Latency	66.65	67.77	56.80	66.76	65.48	68.49	

The operational profile for each subject represents the relative likelihood that he will execute a particular operation at any point in time. The product of each subject's operational profile and the latency vector represented by the last column in Table 3.5 are listed in columns 2 through 7 of this table. We can obtain an expected value for the latency for each subject by adding the individual columns 2 through 7. The results of this are shown in the last row of this table. We can see that there is substantial variation in the average latency for each user. For subject 4, the average response time of the system for the work that he will do on it is about 67 milliseconds. Our hypothetical subject 3 will have a slightly different view of the same software; each of his operations can be expected to take about 57 milliseconds. The net result of this is that subject 3's machine appears to run faster than subject 4's machine.

Chapter 4
Functional Specification: High-Level Design

4.1 Introduction

The system functional requirements specify the high-level design of the system that we develop to implement the operational model. In the functional requirements, we design a new abstract machine onto which we map the behavior of the abstract machine we created for the user in the operational specification. This new abstract machine ultimately maps onto a particular programming language model that, in turn, will map onto a real computer system. At the functional level, we tackle the problem of *how* each of the operations is performed. The end user neither sees this machine nor does he have any need to know about its operation.

In architectural terms, the operational specifications would represent the floor plan and the elevations of a house. The architect uses these two-dimensional representations of a house to describe what the structure will look like and how the space in it will be organized. This is the reality that the homeowner will perceive. It would be difficult to impossible to build a house from this level of specification. There are really quite a variety of different ways to frame out a house. There are quite a number of different roofing systems that we can use to create the same visual effect. The floor plans and the elevations do not speak to these issues; they merely show what the house will look like. The actual structural details of the house are developed on another set of detailed plans. This is where the real design work occurs. The plumbing runs are drawn, as are the electrical systems. The precise construction technique to be used for the foundation is drawn with complete specificity.

The functional specifications are an exact analog for the detailed blueprints that an architect draws for the construction firm that will build the house that the architect has just designed. The functional specifications are the architectural blueprints for the software system. The primary objective of this specification process is to eliminate any ambiguity in the

nature of the system that is to be built. As we get further into the specification of the system, we are systematically constraining the problem and
eliminating degrees of design freedom at every step. Ultimately, when the
time comes to code the system, a developer will literally have zero degrees
of design freedom. Developers should be automatons: slaves to the design
documents. The system architecture is completely specified in the functional specifications and the module specifications. The sole role of the
software developer is to map the functional and module specifications
onto a particular programming language model.

As was the case for the operational system specification, there are three
parts to the functional specification. First, there is the functional overview,
a glib statement about the fundamental nature of the abstraction machine
and how we wish to animate it. The actual abstract machine that we are
going to design to solve the implementation of the operational specification is described under the heading of the functional model. The functional
model makes our software system appear to operate in the manner articulated in the operational specification. It represents the high-level design
of an intermediate system to implement the operational specifications.

Finally, we animate this new abstract machine, the functional model,
with a set of functionalities. The use of the term "functionality" is somewhat unfortunate. It would have been so much better to call the activities
that are to be performed on the functional model by the name "function."
Unfortunately, the term "function" is tightly bound to a number of different
programming languages. In these contexts, a function is a program module.
That is certainly not what we are talking about in this chapter.

4.2 Functional System Overview

Just as was the case with the operational system overview, we need to
create a statement of purpose for the system designers. That is the role
of the functional system overview. The functional system overview sets
certain design parameters and takes the first step in the restriction of the
degrees of freedom in the design process. It constitutes the intended
direction that the ultimate system will take. This overview is an executive
summary of the systems that is to be designed. It is written first. It is a
consensus-building document. All interested parties in the design process
use this document to guide the subsequent detailed exposition of the final
product.

To return to the `calc` system whose operational specifications were
laid down in the previous chapter, the arithmetic that will be performed
on this calculator is decimal. The user will enter decimal numbers and get
decimal results. Discounting the notion, for the moment, of using LGM
inside our calculator, we must come to terms with the idea of decimal
arithmetic. When we look at the instruction repertoire of modern computers,

there are a host of different ways we can do the necessary arithmetic. We could, for example, choose to use the decimal instructions in a computer, in which case all the functional specifications for the `calc` functional model will use decimal registers and decimal arithmetic. Unfortunately, in the desert of today's programming language models, there is a dearth of decimal arithmetic capability. Another alternative that we might consider, then, is to accept ASCII decimal digits from the user, convert them to a decimal number, perform the necessary arithmetic, and then convert the decimal results back to decimal numbers for presentation to the user. There are a lot of programming languages that we can use to do this. Thus, in our functional system overview, we elect to map the decimal calculator problem onto a decimal machine. The functional system overview clearly defines this context.

4.3 Functional System Model

The functional system model provides a system-level description of ***how*** the system will be implemented. The basic architecture of the functional machine is established in the functional model. A modern car might have any number of propulsion systems under the hood. From an operational perspective, none of this is relevant. What the user is concerned with is that the vehicle will move forward when placed in gear and the accelerator depressed. The user is interested in what happens when the accelerator is depressed and not how the acceleration actually occurs. The only place where the specific nature of the functional mechanism that is actually propelling the car comes into play at the user level occurs when the time comes to replenish the energy supply for the vehicle. Then it matters as to whether the user will put diesel fuel, gasoline, or electricity into the vehicle to replenish its energy supply.

As we begin the decomposition of the functional model (that is, the high-level design) to the module level (that is, the low-level design), our atomic datum will be the scalar number. These are the bricks and mortar for our design process. In primitive societies, all building materials can be crafted directly from those resources provided by nature. In modern civilizations, building materials are assembled into subsystems. If we want a window, we merely identify the appropriate window and specify it as a unit in the plans. We do not suppose that a carpenter will build the window by cutting and fitting the glass panels and the wood frame. In a similar vein, we can imbue the abstract machine in the functional model with whatever data structures capabilities we need. We can specify an array capability on this machine that would organize scalars into dense lists for indexing purposes. We can specify a table or record capability in this machine that would allow different types of scalars or structure to be assembled as sequential units.

There are two fundamental laws of nature that are far too often applied in the design process. The first law is the "law of the hammer." Simply stated, if you give a child a hammer, then everything in his environment becomes a nail. The second law is that "the design must fit the solution." We have provided our developers with the very best C++ development environment; therefore, they must develop a C++ application. This is an extremely poor development practice. The very worst problem is that the focus is on the language and its capabilities, and not on the problem and the exigencies of the design.

First let us look at the application of the first law, the law of the hammer, in the practice of design. Very early in their career in academia, computer science students are taught about dynamic data structures, and pointers in particular. These seem like very fine ideas. They completely obviate the need for planning. All of the space for the buffer can be obtained from the operating system at runtime. It is merely necessary to declare a pointer and the rest will happen as if by magic. A careful analysis of fault data shows us that an astonishing number of faults that can be classified as memory leaks occur because of the failure to keep track of these memory quanta obtained dynamically from the operating system. There is yet another, more subtle problem with pointers. Very early in the history of computing we learned that programming at the assembly level was not a very productive way to use programmers' time. Basically, it would be reasonable to expect ten lines of clean code per day per programmer. Ten lines of FORTRAN did a lot more work than ten lines of assembly code. As a result, designers and developers were enjoined from developing new software at the assembly level.

Unfortunately, it was well known among developers that only really good developers could code assembler. It was a macho thing. "Real men code in assembly language." The C programming language (and its derivatives) and its use of pointers arose to fill the void created by forbidden assembler language programming. "Real men now use pointers in C." The result of this very bad programming practice is that most C code has now been rendered almost unreadable. What is worse is that the practice creates very fertile ground for the breeding or nurturing of software faults. The design process should be governed strictly by considerations of performance, security, reliability, maintainability, and availability. It should not be governed by the rules of a programming cult.

Unfortunately, programming language environments have become the focus of the novice designer. We see evidence of this on a very regular basis. They happen to dominate the software development industry. When index sequential file access methods, for example, were first introduced, it was astonishing just how many applications looked like indexed sequential file management systems. Without regard for how the files might be used in their creation and maintenance, the applications were wrapped into an indexed sequential access method.

4.3.1 Decomposition of the System Functionality

The first step in the design of a system is the decomposition of the system into its major subsystems. A house, for example, is composed of a structural system, an electrical system, a plumbing system, a control system, and an HVAC system. The design process addresses all of these components in parallel as the system develops. It would be very unwise to design the structural components of a house only to find out that there was exactly no provision made to run heating and air conditioning ducts through the structure to the various rooms. Similarly, we could design a two-story house only to find that we had made not provisions for venting the plumbing fixtures on the first floor through the second floor.

The design of a house always occurs in top-down fashion. At the first stage in the design process, the form of the house takes place. The floor plan is laid out, elevations are created for the various views of the house, and then sections are drawn through the structure at key points. Once there is a reasonable functioning model of the house, it is then partitioned into its various subsystems. There is a plumbing system that brings fresh water into the various rooms of the house and carries soil water away from them. Then there is the electrical system. Electrical services are designed from the main power panel out to the various rooms of the house. The structural systems are then developed. The loads of the roof and the floors of the house must be carried to the foundation of the house. The house might well have modern control systems, such as security and lighting controls, integrated into the design. These subsystems are integrated into the design at this stage. Finally, provisions must be made to heat and cool the structure. This means that HVAC subsystems must be integrated into the structure.

All of these subsystems must be integrated into the original design of the house. During this integration process, we may well discover that the original design does not permit air conditioning ductwork to travel from one floor to the next. Consequently, the design must be modified accordingly. Similar accommodations must be made for essentially every single subsystem. The design process, then, is really an iterative process. As we descend to increasing levels of design specificity, problems will arise that cause modification of the original system.

Thus, each functional subsystem, at the top level, must be decomposed into discrete subsystems as well. For very large projects, this decomposition process can continue through many different stages. When a subsystem has been decomposed as far as is reasonable, the final system components will constitute the basic system functionalities. Thus, at its core or lowest

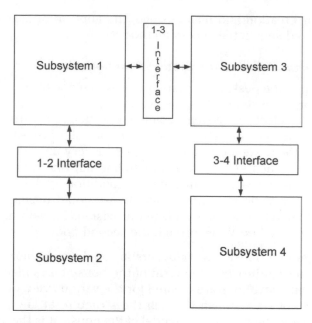

Figure 4.1. System elements.

level of design granularity, any system or any subsystem of that system is composed of a set of functionalities.

Let us look at a hypothetical system. Assume that we can partition this system into a total of four subsystems as is shown in Figure 4.1. Each of these subsystems interacts with a subset of the other subsystems. Each of the subsystems has its own architecture. Subsystem 1, for example, might be a graphical user interface. Subsystem 4 might well be a computational engine for finding solutions to very complex mathematical equations. Any interaction between any two systems will occur across an interface. Control occurs from one subsystem to another across this interface, as do data packets to be transferred between these two subsystems.

4.3.2 Interaction of the Functional Components

In a software system, the functional components interact in two distinct ways. First, each functional component obtains control of the computer that it is running on and maintains control completely until it passes this control to another subsystem. That simple fact is what makes computer systems unique. Other types of physical control systems have components that must function in parallel. Computer software systems do not work that way; they are very different animals. When a functional subsystem in a computer software system receives control, it effectively wakes up and begins to function. This functional subsystem continues to operate to the exclusion of every other system until it surrenders its control to another system.

The second mechanism of functional subsystem interaction in computer software systems is the data exchange. A functional subsystem may have data to share with another subsystem. This data is organized into a packet of data scalars that can be passed from one subsystem to another. The precise nature of the structure of this data packet is governed by a protocol. This protocol is an integral piece of the design of the functional model.

4.3.3 Definition of the Functional Model

A functional model is an abstract machine. It is functionally equivalent to the abstract machine of the operational model. It has exactly the same interaction with the outside environment as the abstract machine for the operational model. The inputs from the user space and the outputs from the system to its operating environment are identical to those of the operational model. The machine specified for the functional model, however, is composed of a set of functional subsystem components and their interfaces. In the specification of the characteristics of this machine, we must identify exactly how the abstract machine for the operational model works.

The user of the abstract machine at the operational level may well perceive that the machine he or she is working with is a decimal machine, as was the case for the BASIC programming language environment. All arithmetic on this machine was carried out to a specific level of decimal precision. Underneath the BASIC machine, however, there could well have been a functional machine that performed all arithmetic in binary.

Each of the subsystems of the abstract machine for the functional model is defined by sets of:

1. Functionalities that are the fundamental building blocks of the subsystem
2. Interfaces to other subsystems with which it can interact

An interface consists of the

1. Definition of the set of data packets that can be passed from one system to another
2. Protocol for the interpretation of those data packets

A data packet is a list of data items transmitted to a functional subsystem or received from it. There may be many different types of these data packets for any one functional subsystem, depending on the complexity of the interaction between two subsystems. A data packet need not be complex. It might, for example, consist of a simple integer scalar. Each data packet is an element of the interface.

A protocol is a set of rules that defines the structure of a data packet. It might be, for example, that one subsystem passes an array of integers to another. The first integer in this array is used to specify how many other integers are in the array. Notions of type and domain for scalar values are somewhat loose at this stage. At the module level we can specify very precisely what an integer and the domain that each integer is defined on mean.

The interface with the UNIX operating system is a very good example of the dialog that occurs from one software system to another. The fundamental communication mechanism between the UNIX system and an application program is through the `syscall` framework of system services. Each `syscall` is a request for specific services from the application program to the UNIX kernel. Each such call has a specific format and data structure that will be used as parameters for the information exchange.

4.3.4. *Graphical Representation of the Functional Model*

The functional model is best shown in graphical form. This graphical representation parallels the functional decomposition process. At the top level, the initial representation of the system is structured from components that interact with one another. In this diagram we show two distinct mechanisms for this interaction. First, there is the control path that shows how each subsystem transfers control to other subsystems that it can interact with directly. Second, there is a data path that shows the direction of dataflow and also references to a protocol for that dataflow.

4.3.5 *Constraints on the Functional Model*

Just as was the case in the operational model, there are constraints that must be imposed on the functional model. If reliability or performance is an issue at the operational level, then they are also issues at the functional level.

4.3.5.1 Reliability. Operations are implemented in specific functionalities. Thus, the reliability of each operational aspect of the system directly depends on the reliability of the functional subsystems. Quite unlike hardware systems, software systems are not simply the sum of their parts from the standpoint of reliability. Certain functional aspects of a software system can be mortally wounded yet the system functions quite normally for a given user. The manner in which a user distributes his or her activity determines how reliable the system will be for them.

At the functional level, then, the reliability constraints are driven by the direct relationship between the functional profile of the system and the user operational profile.

4.3.5.2 Security. Most computer security problems occur as a result of ambiguous program operation at the functional level. This means that there is functional program behavior a system is capable of performing that is not specified in its functional characteristics. The net effect of these implicit functionalities is to implement a set of implicit operations at the user level. That is, they permit the user to exploit at the operational level, functionality that has been inadvertently created at the functional program level.

There are three distinct aspects of computer security at the functional level. First, there is the notion of access control; that is, only specific classes of users can express certain classes of functionality. Unless the user has specific authorization, such as a key, to initiate a specific functionality, he will not be authorized to exercise that functionality. Second, there is the protection of program and data assets through the use of encryption techniques. The third aspect of security that can be implemented at the functional level is behavioral control. We provide for the design of real-time monitoring systems that will monitor the operational characteristics of the user; this enables us to identify departures from a system's normal behavior.

4.3.5.3 Availability. As a user exercises a system at the operational level, the distribution of his or her activity across the set of operations reflects itself on the set of functionalities. Each system is designed to operate under a given operational profile with high reliability. That is, the system can be certified to operate reliably within some reasonable limits around an operational profile. As we can see, the distribution of activity of a system at the functional level, the functional profile, directly depends on the operational profile.

A system can be tested and its operation certified at the operational level. It operates well within that operational profile. We can expect the system to become unreliable when there are departures from the certified program operation. These departures will be very visible within the framework of the functional profile. When the functional system is being used in a manner that is uncertified, then we must expect it to fail. Thus, to ensure a specified level of availability at the operation level, the system must be monitored at the functional level to ensure that it is operating within a nominal range.

The availability constraints at the functional level articulate the precise nature of monitoring of a system at the function level. That is, we must define very precisely how the use of the functionalities will be measured and monitored in real-time.

4.3.5.4 Maintainability. The primary criterion for establishing the maintainability of a system at this stage in the software development process relates directly to the mapping between the functionalities and the operations. Each operation is implemented by one or more functionalities.

Further, as the software system evolves, the mapping must remain current for every change in the operations specifications and the functional specifications as well.

4.3.5.5 Survivability. The key to the survivability attribute is to partition the functionality of the system into vital and nonvital functionalities. This classification can be achieved at the user level by a similar partition in the set of operations into a set of vital (necessary) operations and a set of nonvital operations. Each functionality will be used to implement one or more operations. Those functionalities that implement vital operations are vital functionalities.

4.3.5.6 Performance. The performance criteria are first established at the operational level. Again, each operation is implemented by one or more functionalities. Therefore, these functionalities operating in concert must meet the performance criteria established at the operational level.

4.3.5.7 Compatibility Considerations. As we move closer to the machine level in the specification process, a precise determination must be made as to the functional interface to hardware systems. As we see in Chapter 10, there is often a trade-off made at this stage as to whether a particular functionality will be implemented in hardware or in software.

On the software side of the house, if a system is to interface with another software system, then the functionalities handled by that software system must be completely articulated as a compatibility consideration.

4.4 Functionalities

The word "functionality" is used to convey the sense of the functional description of the things that the virtual machine described in the functional model will do. Functionalities should in no way be construed as software functions or subroutines. Functionalities are the operational properties of the functional system model.

A functionality is the lowest level of functional system decomposition. Each functionality temporarily commands the entire resources of a computer. This functionality possibly receives data passed to it, and this data is organized into a packet for transmission to the functionality. The functionality operates on the data, possibly restructuring the data into a new packet structure, and then it transmits the data to another functionality.

It is a characteristic of each functionality that it can receive control from one or more other functionalities. The complete specification of the incoming control structure for a functionality is an attribute of that functionality. Similarly, the functionality can transfer control to another functionality. The complete specification of outgoing control structure for a functionality is an attribute of that functionality.

Getting the granularity of definition of a functionality right is sometimes not easy. Perhaps the best way to do this is to start at the highest level and then decompose this functionality into the next level of specificity until all possible ambiguities have been removed. Consider, for example, the case of a functional system that performs decimal arithmetic. There are three types of arithmetic that must be performed by this subsystem. First, it must be capable of performing the adding operations of + and −. It must also be capable of performing multiplication. Finally, it must be able to carry out decimal divisions. It is clear that forming the sum of a decimal number is not an easy task. It is well beyond the scope of a high-level design discussion to partition this functionality further. The input to the decimal add functionality is a data packet that contains two signed decimal numbers and a command that tells the functionality whether an addition operation or a subtraction operation is to occur. The output from the decimal add functionality is a data packet that contains a signed decimal number. Somewhere in the description of the functional specification, we must come to grips with the fact that the domain of the sum of two decimal numbers will be an order of magnitude greater than that defined for the two operands.

Again, the purpose of the high-level design is to constrain the solution space for the functional model. We will have achieved the proper level of granularity of specification when all possible solution alternatives have been eliminated, save the one we wish to occur. We do not want programmers performing the design function. If we permit this to occur, they will simply tuck functional specifications into their code where they will reside implicitly. We want the entire functionality of our software to be articulated in the design specification and not in the code. This is a particularly vital consideration if the target language for our system is write-only code, such as C or C++.

Just as was the case for the operational model where the operations animated the abstract machine, so too will the functionalities animate the abstract machine defined in the functional model. There are really four elements in the definition of a functionality:

1. The *control bindings* between a particular functionality and all other functionalities from which or to which it can receive or give control must be specified.
2. The *temporal bindings* that constrain the functionality in relation to other functionalities must be specified.
3. The *data packets* that it transmits or receives from other functionalities must be specified, together with the protocol for the interpretation of that data.
4. The *functional transformations* that the functionality performs on each of the data packets must be specified.

Table 4.1. Specifications for a Functionality

Functionality Name	f_i
Control	Received from functionality: <List of functionalities> Transferred to functionality: <List of functionalities>
Temporal	List of functionalities that must be completed before performing this functionality List of functionalities that may directly follow this functionality
Data	Incoming packets: <Packet list> Outgoing packets: <Packet list>
Protocol	<Protocol list for data packets>
Functional Transformations	<List of data transformations>

Thus, in the process of defining a functionality, a table must be completed for each functionality. The contents of this table are shown in Table 4.1.

4.5 The Functional Profile

When a software developer constructs a software system, it is designed to fulfill a set of specific functional requirements. The user runs the software to perform a set of perceived operations. In this process, the user typically does not use all of the functionalities with the same probability. The functional profile of the software system is the set of unconditional probabilities of each of the functionalities F being executed by the user. Let Y be a random variable defined on the indices of the set of elements of F. Then,

$$q_k = \Pr[Y = k], \quad k = 1, 2, \dots, \|F\|$$

is the probability that the user is executing program functionality k as specified in the functional specifications of the program and $\|F\|$ is the cardinality of the set of functionalities. A program executing on a serial machine can only be executing one functionality at a time. The distribution of q, then, is multinomial for programs designed to fulfill more than two specific functionalities.

The q_k depend on how the user distributes his time across the suite of system operations. We can observe and understand the conditional probability distribution of the functionalities to wit:

$$w_{kl} = \Pr\left[Y_n = k \mid Z = l\right]$$

That is, if we know the particular operation being performed, then we can determine the distribution of activity among the various functionalities.

The joint probability that a given operation is being expressed and the system is exercising a particular functionality is given by:

$$\Pr[Y_n = j \cap Z = l] = \Pr[Z = l]\Pr[Y_n = i \mid Z = l] = o_l w_{jl}$$

where k is the index for the set of functionalities and l is the index for the set of operations. Thus, the unconditional probability, q_i, of executing functionality i under a particular operational profile is:

$$q_i = \Pr[Y_n = i]$$

$$= \sum_l \Pr[Y_n = i \cap Z = l]$$

$$= \sum_l o_l w_{il}$$

The distribution of q, the functional profile, is also multinomial for a system consisting of more than two modules.

Just as we did with the operational profile, we can characterize design *functional* profile as a single point in an $m-1$ dimensional space, where m is the cardinality of the set of functionalities. It is, in fact, the centroid in a range of possible departures from the design functional profile. That is, each user will use the system in a slightly different manner. Each user will have a slightly different operational profile represented by a different point. Because of the dependency of the functional profile on the operational profile, this, in turn, means that there will be some variation in the functional profile of a system across a number of users. Let F^p represent the design functional profile. Each user induces a slightly different behavior on the functional machine represented by a functional profile, say F^u. Each of the functional profiles is, again, a point in an $m-1$ dimensional space. It is possible to compute the distance in this $m-1$ dimensional space, the two points representing a user's actual functional profile, and the design functional profile as:

$$d = \sum_{i=1}^{m} \left(f_i^p - f_i^u\right)^2$$

where m represents the number of functionalities and $0 \le d \le 2$.

Because no two users will use the system in exactly the same way, it is necessary to understand the distribution of the distances d. Let d_i represent the distance between a particular functional profile for user i and the design functional profile. We can then talk about the average distance

$$\bar{d} = \frac{1}{m} \sum_i d_i$$

for a group of m users and the variance of this distance across all users:

$$Var(d) = \frac{1}{(m-1)} \sum_i (d_i - \bar{d})^2.$$

Just as was the case for the set of user operations, we can speak to the issue of the latency of functionalities. As we get closer to the actual machine that will run the user operations, we are in a better position to understand and model these latencies. We recall that the latency of each operation is $\lambda_i = l(o_i)$. Each operation is implemented through one or more functionalities. Thus, it is clear that there is a functional dependency between the latencies of the functionalities and those of the operations.

Let $\gamma_j = l(f_j)$ represent the latency of a functionality, j. It is clear that γ_i is an expected value for the functional latency to wit:

$$\lambda_i = \sum_{j=1}^{m} \gamma_j \Pr\left(f_j \mid o_i\right).$$

Just as was the case for the operational latency of a system, we can speak to the first two moments about the mean of the functional latency. The first statistic we can develop is the expected value for the functional latency of the system under a functional profile F. This is:

$$E(\gamma) = \sum_i f_i \gamma_i,$$

where $f_i = \Pr(Y = i)$. The variance of the functional latency, then under the functional profile F, is

$$Var(\gamma) = \sum_i f_i \gamma_i^2 - E(\gamma)^2 = \sum_i f_i \gamma_i^2 - \left(\sum_i f_i \gamma_i\right)^2$$

From a performance standpoint, if a system is experiencing performance problems, another very good place to look for improvement would be on those functionalities where $\gamma_i f_i$ is very large. In fact, if we were to sort the $\gamma_i f_i$ from largest values to the smallest, we would be able to identify potential performance problems in the software system based on its actual usage. It does not necessarily matter that a particular functionality is slow. What really matters is that it does not get used a lot.

4.6   The Evolution of the Functional Specifications

The functional specifications evolve in precisely the same manner as operational specifications. They also are subject to almost constant change during the course of the natural life of a software system. These functional specifications change in response to an evolving design concept. Again, there are essentially four different types of documents that must be managed under some type of configuration control. These are as follows:

1. Functional overview
2. Functional model (as text)
3. Functional model (as figures)
4. Set of functionalities

As the system evolves, there will be new versions of each of these documents. The design process is a particularly dynamic one. Very often, we really do not understand the true nature of the problem we are trying to solve until we are well into the design process. It is clear, then, that the documents describing the functional machine will be very fluid.

The management of the functional overview and model is very simple in that there will always be one each of these documents. All we need to do for future systems is to track the version numbers of these documents. The set of functionalities will change frequently. At its inception, a system might consist of, say, m functionalities. As the system evolves, some elements of the original set of functionalities may vanish and new functionalities will replace them.

We use precisely the same methodology to reference the set of functionalities that we developed for the set of operations. The same notion of the use of an index vector, η, that maintains the versioning data on each of the operations will work just as well with the set of functionalities. The elements, η_i, of the functionality index vector represent the version number of the ith functionaltiy of the system.

In systems that employ source code control for managing the evolution of the source code, there are distinct points in time where all the most current versions of all modules are compiled and linked into a ***build*** of the system. The build represents a distinct point in the evolution of the system. A build is characterized by a list of source code elements that went to the compilation. This list of modules, together with their version numbers, is called the build list. A very similar concept can be developed for the functional specifications.

The elements of a functional specification are assumed to be in a constant state of flux. At periodic intervals, these elements are bound together to define a build of the functional specifications. As we will see in subsequent chapters, this build event is defined by the build of the source code system. Each source code element is bound to one or more operations. The system that is built from source code reflects exactly one state of the functional index vector, η. This permits the unambiguous interpretation of the functional system reflected in the current build of the source code. The build points to the functional specifications with the nomenclature $\eta^{(k)}$ for the kth build of the functional specifications. In general, the builds of the functional specifications occur with the builds of the system source code. Thus, $F^{(k)}$ will identify the set of functionalities at the kth build of the system.

Just as was the case with the operations, each build of the system represents a new build in the functional specifications. This fact also has some real consequences in the functional profile. For the time being, we should note that the functional profiles of the sets of functionalities associated with two sequential builds, $F^{(k)}$ and $F^{(k+1)}$, are not necessarily comparable, particularly in the case where the cardinality of $F^{(k)} \cap F^{(k+1)}$ is less than the cardinality of either $F^{(k)}$ or $F^{(k+1)}$.

4.7 An Example (Continued)

We can now begin the process of designing the abstract machine that will run the `calc` machine whose operational specification was introduced in Chapter 3. In our first cut at this software system, only the operational characteristics of this machine were presented. For all the user knew or cared, we could well have implemented the calculator using LGM (Little Green Men) that live inside our computer, performed the arithmetic on abacuses, and kept the stack contents on little blackboards so they could report these values should the user ever request them. In this example, we reject the notion of LGM as a functional solution to our calculator, if for no other reason than they are in short supply. They are gainfully employed, currently creating problems in modern operating systems. We now set about to describe how we intend to solve the functional aspects of our `calc` machine in the context of the UNIX OS environment.

In our `calc` example, we could implement the operational model in any number of ways. We have several choices as to the nature of the arithmetic that we can use on the target machine. We can represent the contents of the stack as binary numbers, as character strings, as decimal strings, as packed decimals, or even as floating point numbers. The stack can be represented in a variety of different data structures, such as an array or as a linked list. Even for this simple `calc` machine there are an astonishing number of degrees of freedom in how we are going to really implement the operational model at the functional level.

One of the first design problems we face in the implementation of the `calc` machine is exactly how we are going to do the calculator arithmetic on the abstract machine that is the functional model. This is a top-level decision that will have a profound influence on the underlying machine. In that the arithmetic we propose to do is decimal arithmetic, we contrive a decimal machine that uses a nine-digit decimal floating-point representation. This will be a thirteen-digit number, with a digit for the sign of the number, nine decimal digits for the mantissa, a sign for the exponent, and a two-digit exponent. This underlying decimal machine works fairly well for the decimal arithmetic we have proposed. There is one slight problem, however, with this representation: the sum of two nine-digit decimal numbers can be a ten-digit number. This will be outside the range of valid numbers that can be represented in our decimal floating-point format. This, in turn, means that we must contrive some special provisions for handling this contingency when we do an addition operation. If addition is a trial to us, then multiplication will be a real problem. The product of two nine-digit decimal numbers can be a 17-digit number. Thus, multiplication requires some real additional computational burden on our decimal architecture.

The nature of the problem that we wish to solve is well within the capabilities of the decimal arithmetic instruction repertoire of most of today's personal computers. There is a real dearth of programming language environments available in the UNIX environment that will give us access to this decimal instruction repertoire. The two most obvious alternatives (BASIC and COBOL) are not really viable alternatives in the UNIX environment. Thus, if we wish to do decimal arithmetic, we are going to have to write all the code for the decimal operations in a language such as C. This may not be an unpleasant alternative to the use of binary arithmetic. There are now two design alternatives on the table. The time has come to evaluate each of these alternatives and then choose one over the other for the functional architecture of our `calc` machine. There are many factors that will mitigate in our choice for the ultimate architecture. The personal preferences of our developers will not be a factor in this decision. Quality considerations, availability considerations, and maintainability considerations will govern our choice of the underlying architecture.

The time has now arrived for us to make some pencil sketches of the competing alternatives for the architecture of our machine. We do not have to get too far into the sketch process to discover that doing our own decimal arithmetic will result in a very complicated and lengthy design process. In this case, it does not warrant the effort necessary to do the design work to get such a machine to work. If, on the other hand, we are going to permit the user of the `calc` machine to operate on integers of, say, 30 digits, then the design effort to implement this solution on a decimal machine would far exceed that of the proposed decimal arithmetic alternative.

The real essence of the high-level design process is that we can explore many alternative solutions and find the best one for our pre-established quality criterion. The very worst thing that we could do from the design aspect is to implement a solution that is an artifact of a programming language environment. These solutions are those that are the easiest to find and also those that will have tragic consequences for both the developers and the users of the system.

4.7.1 The Functional Overview

The `calc` program is a UNIX command-line program that performs decimal arithmetic. The program emulates a stack-oriented calculator. The inputs to this calculator are in reverse Polish notation. The calculator is invoked on a command line without arguments. At a ">" prompt, a user can enter either operands or operators. The operands will be a nine-digit or less decimal number with an optional sign. The operators will cause the system to perform arithmetic and display functions on the stack.

The `calc` program examines input strings received from the user's keyboard. These inputs are parsed into two categories, either operators or operands. If the input is neither a valid operator nor operand, the word "error" is displayed by the system. All operands are converted to signed nine-digit decimal floating-point numbers. These decimal numbers are placed into a register within the arithmetic-logic subsystem of `calc`. The arithmetic-logic subsystem emulates the stack concept through the use of an array of sequential registers maintained in this subsystem.

When an addition operation is indicated by the user, the arithmetic-logic system infixes the operator between the top two registers on the stack. The top stack element is the left operand of the addition operator. If the sum of the two registers produces a value that cannot be represented in nine decimal digits, the arithmetic-logic system will send an error indication to the user interface subsystem that will, in turn, display the word "error" on the user's display device. A multiply operation results in two signed nine-digit decimal numbers. The first number is on top of the stack and represents the nine most significant digits of the multiplication operation. The second number is the second entry on the stack and represents the nine least significant digits of the multiplication operation. A divide operation results in two signed nine-digit decimal numbers. The top of the stack after the divide operation contains the quotient and the remainder is the second entry on the stack.

In addition to the basic arithmetic operations, there is also a repertoire of stack manipulation operations provided in the calc machine. The stack manipulation commands **d** and **c** cause the arithmetic-logic unit to alter the contents of the local registers. The print commands **p** and **f** cause the arithmetic-logic unit to transfer the decimal number on the stack to the interface subsystem for conversion to ASCII strings.

Finally, when the finite state machine recognizes the **q** command, control is transferred from this subsystem to the operating system, indicating the normal completion of the calculator software.

4.7.2 *The Functional Model*

We now turn our attention to describing the virtual machine (the system model) that we will use to implement the operations. The most basic framework for this machine is shown in Figure 4.2. The user environment composed of the input mechanism and output mechanism is resourced and managed by the operating systems. That communication interface is not part of the calc machine. Rather, calc derives inputs from the user environment from the operating system and it sends responses to the user through the operating system/user interface.

If we expand the module labeled as calc Engine in Figure 4.2, an example partition of the calc functionalities is shown in Figure 4.3. From this figure we can see that there is an interface between all subsystems of the calc engine. There are also interfaces between the calc engine and the operating system (OS). The OS/Analysis interface represents the transfer of control only. When the system receives control from the OS, this control will be passed to the Analysis subsystem. At the conclusion of the execution of the calc program, control is passed back to the OS from the Analysis subsystem. The Analysis subsystem, then, is really in charge of the control function for the calc engine.

This simple calculator example is a trivial system. In a large software system, there may be hundreds or even thousands of subsystems, most of which will be much more complex than that of the simple calculator example. Realistically, the I/O subsystem and the Analysis subsystems could and should be combined into one subsystem. There is value, however, for pedagogical purposes in imagining them to be separate systems.

Each subsystem must be connected to at least one other subsystem across an interface. In the case of the calc subsystems, there are interfaces among all the subsystems. Data arrives from the user in an input string buffer. To begin our discussion of the functional model, we examine each subsystem in turn. The discussion of each subsystem contains three essential components. First, we elaborate on the precise nature of each

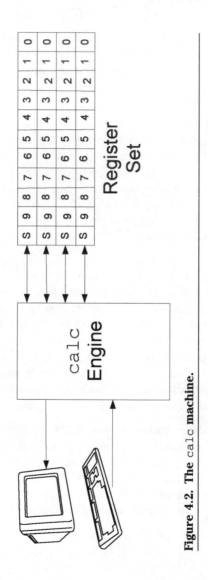

Figure 4.2. The `calc` machine.

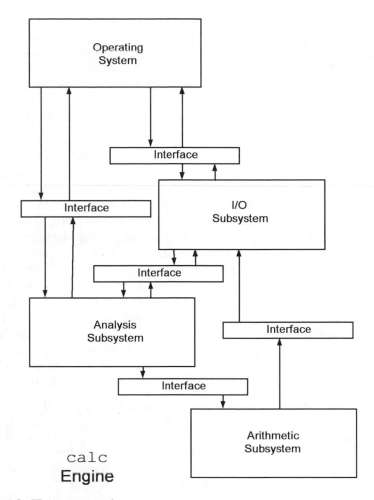

Figure 4.3. The `calc` **engine.**

of the interfaces. Second, there is a précis of functional aspects of the subsystem. Third, the functionalities of each subsystem are made explicit.

4.7.2.1 The Analysis Subsystem. There are three interfaces to the Analysis subsystem. There is an interface with the Operating System (OS), an interface to the Arithmetic subsystem, and an interface to the I/O subsystem. The interface with the Operating System is the easiest of the interfaces to describe. Control is passed to the Analysis subsystem across this interface and control is returned to the Operating System across this interface.

When the Analysis first receives control from the Operating System, the Analysis must first have some data from the user to process. It receives this data from the I/O subsystem. Thus, the first activity of the Analysis is to transfer control to the I/O subsystem to receive some input from the user. It is obvious, then, that control is passed between the I/O subsystem and the Analysis across the interface between them. The I/O subsystem returns a string of ASCII characters, the last character of which is a carriage return character. This ASCII string is received by the Analysis system across the I/O—Analysis interface. If the ASCII string received by the Analysis subsystem does not constitute a valid string, the Analysis will send the ASCII string "error" to the I/O subsystem.

The Analysis parses the ASCII string received from the I/O subsystem. The ASCII string can be an element of one of three sets: it can be a valid decimal number, a valid operator, or an invalid string. If the string received from the I/O system is not an invalid string, then it is either a decimal number or an operator. If it is an operator other than the **q** operator, the character representing the operator will be put on the interface between the Analysis and Arithmetic subsystems. Control is then passed across this interface to the Arithmetic subsystem. Control will return to the Analysis subsystem after the operation has been applied to the stack by the Arithmetic subsystem. If the string received from the I/O subsystem is a valid decimal number, then this number will be converted to a signed nine-digit decimal floating-point number and placed on the interface to the Arithmetic subsystem. Control is then transferred to the Arithmetic subsystem. If the operator received from the I/O subsystem is a "**q**," then the Analysis subsystem will transfer control back to the operating system.

There are really three different functionalities that we define for the Analysis subsystem. The first, f_1, initializes the system and accept/return control from/to the OS. The second functionality, f_2, gets an ASCII string from the I/O subsystem, parses this string, and sends the decoded user input to the Arithmetic unit. A third functionality, f_3, sends an error message to the I/O subsystem if the input is invalid.

4.7.2.2 The I/O Subsystem. The I/O subsystem is relatively simple. There are two simple functionalities here. The first functionality, f_4, simply gets an ASCII string from the OS. The second functionality, f_5, puts a string back to the OS for display. The outputs from the I/O subsystem are always on the interface between the I/O and the Analysis subsystems. The inputs to the I/O subsystem can appear on either the I/O—Analysis interface or the I/O—Arithmetic interface.

4.7.2.3 The Arithmetic Subsystem. The actions of the Arithmetic subsystem can be neatly compartmentalized into three sets of functionalities. First, there is an arithmetic functionality, f_6, that causes arithmetic to be performed on the contents of the stack. Next there is a stack functionality, f_7, that manipulates or interrogates the stack. Finally there is a translate functionality, f_8, that converts a decimal number to an ASCII string.

There are three arithmetic operations that the Arithmetic subsystem performs in its arithmetic functionality. In that addition and subtraction operations for signed numbers are essentially the same operation, they are combined into one activity. In this activity, the sign of the left operand can be changed (for subtraction) and then the sum of two decimal numbers is created. If the magnitude of the resulting sum cannot be represented in nine decimal digits (i.e., $\log_{10}(a+b) \geq 10$), then an error condition is generated and an ASCII string "error" is sent to the I/O section. To obtain the left and right operands for the addition, the stack functionality is invoked twice to pop the stack. The result of the arithmetic is pushed onto the stack by the stack functionality.

To perform the multiplication operation, the arithmetic functionality first invokes the stack functionality to obtain the left and right operands for the multiplication operation. The two operands are signed decimal floating-point numbers. Then the product is performed. The product is divided by 10^9 and the remainder for this divide (in decimal floating point) is pushed onto the stack. The quotient is pushed onto the stack next.

To perform the division operation, the arithmetic functionality again invokes the stack functionality twice to obtain the divisor and the dividend for the divide operation. The remainder from the divide operation is pushed onto the stack, followed by the quotient. Prior to the division operation, the divisor is checked for a zero condition. If the divisor has the value zero, then an error condition is generated and an ASCII string "error" is sent to the I/O section.

In addition to the arithmetic operations, there is the stack functionality. This functionality operates on the stack for rearranging the stack contents and for displaying one or more registers of the stack. To implement the stack on our machine, we organize the registers that hold the four operands into a dense list or an array. The first array element represents the top of the stack. Each of the registers holds a nine-digit decimal floating-point number. The push operator moves the contents of the penultimate register to the last register. It then moves the contents of the second register to the third register. Finally, it places the incoming number in the first register of the array. The pop operator causes the contents of the first register in the array or stack to be read into a temporary location. Then the contents of the second register are moved to the first register, the contents of the third register to the second register, and the contents of the fourth register to the third register. The contents of the fourth register are replaced with a decimal zero. The clear operator simply causes the contents of register 1 to be replaced with a decimal zero. The duplicate operator causes the contents of register 1 to be pushed onto the stack.

For the two print operations, the stack contents are sent to the translate functionality. In the case of the "**p**" operator, the contents of register 1 only are translated. In the case of the "**f**" operator, the register contents from registers 1 to 4 are retrieved and translated sequentially.

This decimal machine model is really a trivial example. Necessarily, it would be of limited utility in the real world. However, it does serve our purpose to convey the essence of the notion of what a functional model should embody. The important thing to note is that the functional model solves the problem of how we are going to implement the user operations. It has constrained the problem from the standpoint of design. There is no doubt as to how the numbers are represented in the virtual machine and how arithmetic is performed.

4.7.3   The Functionalities

The set of functionalities for the functional `calc` machine is summarized in Table 4.2. The functionalities listed represent the essence of the functional characteristics of the `calc` machine. The granularity of these functionalities is rather high level. As an example, the precise methodology used to implement the multiply operation is not specified. In fact, all the arithmetic operations fall under the umbrella of a single functionality, f_6.

There is a control relationship among the eight functionalities. Functionality 1, the initialization functionality, receives initial control from the operating system. It then performs its initialization duties and turns control over to Functionality 2. The control structure relationship among the functionalities is shown in Table 4.3. The control connections among the functionalities can be one-way or two-way connections. In the case of Functionality 1, for example, control is received from the operating system. When Functionality 1 has completed is initialization duties, it hands control to Functionality 2 and receives control again from Functionality 2 on receipt of the "**q**" character from the user.

Table 4.2. Functionalities from Hypothetical Software

Functionality	Description
f_1	System initialization
f_2	Accept string and convert
f_3	Send error message
f_4	Get string from OS
f_5	Put string to OS
f_6	Do arithmetic
f_7	Manipulate stack
f_8	Convert decimal floating-point number to ASCII string

Table 4.3. Control Relationship among the Functionalities

Functionality	2	3	4	5	6	7	8
1	2						
2		2	2		2	2	
3				2			
4							
5							
6							2
7				2			2
8				2			

Each functionality can be characterized by three distinct attributes. There is control binding among the functionalities; they receive control from other functionalities and they pass control to functionalities. This transfer of control is demonstrated in Figure 4.4. While it is not practical to represent the functionalities in this graphical form for large systems, it does serve our purposes in this simple example. A much more practical means of showing this transfer of control, of course, is the transition information shown in Table 4.3.

Functionalities also receive data packets from functionalities from which they receive control. They also pass data packets to functionalities to which they, in turn, pass control. Each functionality can also be characterized by the nature of the functional transformations that it makes to the data it receives. For each of the functionalities f_1 through f_8, the data is shown in Tables 4.4a through 4.4h.

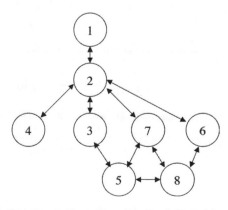

Figure 4.4. Graphical presentation of control relationship.

Table 4.4a. Functionality f_1

Functionality	f_1

Control	Received from functionality:
	  OS, f_2
	Transferred to functionality:
	  f_2, OS

Data	Incoming packets:
	  None
	Outgoing packets:
	  None

Functional Transformations	Stack initialization (registers set to zero)

Table 4.4b. Functionality f_2

Functionality	f_2

Control	Received from functionality:
	  f_1, f_3, f_4, f_6 , f_7
	Transferred to functionality:
	  f_3, f_4, f_6 , f_7

Data	Incoming packets:
	  ASCII string
	Outgoing packets:
	  Signed decimal number
	  Command code
	  Error message

Functional Transformations	Parse character input into:
	  Nine-digit decimal floating-point number
	  Operation code or
	  Error condition

Table 4.4c. Functionality f_3

Functionality	f_3

Control	Received from functionality:
	  f_2
	Transferred to functionality:
	  f_2

Data	Incoming packets:
	  None
	Outgoing packets:
	  Character string "error"

Functional Transformations	Generate error message for output

Table 4.4d. Functionality f_4

Functionality	f_4
Control	Received from functionality: f_2, OS Transferred to functionality: f_2, OS
Data	Incoming packets: Character string Outgoing packets: Signed nine-digit floating-point number Character code "d", "p", "f", or "c"
Functional Transformations	

Table 4.4e. Functionality f_5

Functionality	f_5
Control	Received from functionality: f_3, f_7, OS Transferred to functionality: f_3, f_7, OS
Data	Incoming packets: Character strings Outgoing packets: Character string
Functional Transformations	Data buffering

Table 4.4f. Functionality f_6

Functionality	f_6
Control	Received from functionality: f_2, f_8 Transferred to functionality: f_2, f_8
Data	Incoming packets: 2 nine-digit signed decimal numbers Outgoing packets: 1 or 2 nine-digit signed decimal numbers
Functional Transformations	Addition Multiplication Division

103

Table 4.4g. Functionality f_7

Functionality	f_7
Control	Received from functionality: f_2, f_8 Transferred to functionality: f_2, f_8

Data	Incoming packets:
	  Character code "d", "p", "f", or "c"
	Outgoing packets:
	  Signed nine-digit decimal numbers

Functional Transformations	Change stack locations Zero top of stack Data transfer from stack

Table 4.4h. Functionality f_8

Functionality	f_8
Control	Received from functionality: f_6, f_7 Transferred to functionality: f_8, f_7
Data	Incoming Packets Signed nine-digit decimal number Outgoing Packets Character string
Functional Transformations	Convert digned nine-digit floating-point decimal number to character string

Now that the functionalities have been specified, we can now fit them into the overall functional model. They have been associated with each of their functional subsystems in Figure 4.5. We can also see from this same figure that the functionalities are associated with particular subsystem interfaces. This association permits us to define exactly the nature of each of the interfaces between the subsystems.

We begin the discussion of the interfaces by examining the OS—Analysis subsystem interface. The functionality f_1 is connected to this interface. It receives control from the OS across this interface. No data, however, is exchanged across this particular interface. If we look at the Analysis subsystem—Arithmetic subsystem interface, we find a much richer structure. Functionality f_2 transfers control to functionalities f_6 and f_7 across this interface. In addition, f_2 will also send either a decimal number or a control

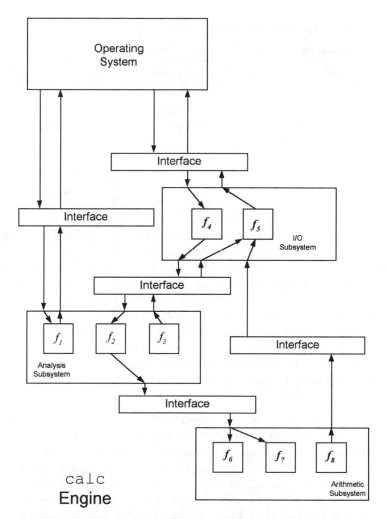

Figure 4.5. Connectivity between functionalities and interfaces.

code across this interface. The precise nature of each of these interfaces can now be constructed from the information collected in Tables 4.4a through 4.4h. The complete interface information is summarized in Table 4.5.

4.8 Configuration Control for the Functional Specifications

There are three distinct sets of documents that constitute the high-level design of a system. First there is the Functional Overview. This document is simple text. It can be managed under configuration control just like any other source code element. Then there is the Functional Model. There are really two elements to this model. First there is the text document that

Table 4.5. Interface Information

Subsystem Interface	Control	Data Packets
OS—Analysis	$OS \rightarrow f_1$	None
Analysis—Arithmetic	$f_2 \leftrightarrow f_6$	Nine-digit decimal number
	$f_2 \leftrightarrow f_7$	Control code
I/O—Arithmetic	$f_8 \leftrightarrow f_5$	Character string
I/O—Analysis	$f_3 \leftrightarrow f_5$	Character string
	$f_2 \leftrightarrow f_4$	Character string
OS—I/O	$f_5 \leftrightarrow OS$	Character string

describes the abstract functional machine. This is a source code file and should be managed under configuration control in precisely the same fashion as any other source code element. The second element of the Functional Model is the graphical representation of the model. For large systems, this may involve many different layers of system decomposition. Within each layer of functional decomposition there may be many different graphical elements, each representing a functional subsystem. Each of these graphical subsystems should also be under configuration control. Perhaps the best way to do this is to use a graphical system such as xfig, which represents the graphics in textual form. This can easily be managed by most configuration control systems.

The final set of documents managed in the functional specification of a system is the functionalities themselves. Each functionality can be thought of as a table. Examples of these tables are shown in Tables 4.4a through 4.4h. Each of these tables is a separate file in the configuration control system. What is most important is that the relationship among the various functionalities with regard to the control interface must be preserved. In our specific example, shown in Table 4.3, alterations to the content of, say, functionality f_5 will have a potential impact on functionalities f_3, f_6, and f_8. Thus, it is important that each of the functionalities be linked to one another in the configuration control system. Should functionality f_5 change, under configuration control it will have a new version number. Thus, the links kept in each of the files representing each of the functionalities would look something like the updated version of Table 4.4e, now shown as Table 4.6. In this new hypothetical table, we can see that the file represents the most recent version of functionality f_5 points to the most recent version of functionality f_3, which is Version 5.3, and the most recent version of functionality f_7, which is Version 4.1.

Table 4.6. Functionality f_5 under Configuration Control

Functionality	f_5
Control	Received from functionality: OS f_3 : linked to Version 5.3 f_7: linked to Version 4.1 Transferred to functionality: OS f_3 : linked to Version 5.3 f_7: linked to Version 4.1
Data	Incoming packets: Character strings Outgoing packet Character string
Functional Transformations	Data buffering

4.9 Summary

At the high-level design stage of development, much of the specificity of the system is missing. We do not, for example, define the domains for the operands. We do not specify exactly what a character string is. At the high-level design stage, we are merely trying to partition functionality into meaningful buckets or subsystems and understand how these subsystems relate to one another through their interfaces. At the low-level design stage, we will partition the functionalities into design modules. At this level, the granularity of definition of data and algorithms will be quite complete. Our fundamental design objective is to maintain some notion of the forest. At the point that we become over-specific too soon in the design process, we will see only trees and no forest.

High-level design is just that. It is our first cut at the description of how a system will work. The primary objective of the high-level design stage is to wrestle with how we are going to implement the operations specified in the operational specifications. The system is parsed at this stage into functional subsystems and then animated with specific functionalities.

Chapter 5
Mapping Operations to Functionalities

5.1 Introduction

It is now eminently clear that there are two levels of software specification that must occur in the early stages of a software development effort. First, we need to define a system around a user's requirements. This is the operational system that the user interacts with directly. Then we need to solve the problem of how to implement the user's abstract machine on another machine of our own design. This new machine will be defined by the functional model and animated by the functionalities that we design for it.

In the normal course of the current state-of-the-art software development, both the operational system and the functional system may or may not be specified adequately. In the unlikely event that both are carefully specified, they must be linked. In particular, each of the user operations will animate the operational abstract machine. This causes activity of the functional abstract machine. Thus, each user operation causes one or more functionalities to be expressed on the functional machine. There is clearly a linkage between the user operations and the set of functionalities. In fact, each of the operations maps directly to a particular set of functionalities. One of our primary considerations in the development of operational and functional specifications is that these two domains should be linked. We need to know exactly which functionalities are involved with each operation. If an operation is changed, this linkage permits us to identify the functionalities that implement it so that we can change them accordingly. Similarly, we would like to know which operations invoke a particular functionality. It is vital to know which operations might be impacted should a functionality change.

Linking the operation and functionalities is extremely important but it is also just as important that this linkage be *maintained* over the life of the software. Those organizations that do think to link functionalities with operations during the initial design stage uniformly fail to maintain these associations. As time progresses, there is a divergence between the functional machine and the operational machine. This is the stuff of maintenance nightmares. We will develop mechanisms for maintaining these linkages.

The various parts of the operational specifications and the functional specifications are, at the end of the day, simply a different kind of source code document. Everyone now seems to agree that maintaining source code under configuration control is a good thing. It turns out that the act of maintaining the functional and operational specifications under configuration control is an astonishingly good idea. In this chapter we explore the potential for using configuration control systems to maintain the linkage among all source code documents for us.

5.2 $O \times F$

We now turn our attention to the precise relationship between the operational abstract machine and the functional abstract machine. It is quite conceivable that we could construct a system wherein there is a one-to-one mapping between the user's operational model and the functional model. That is, for every user operation, there is exactly one functionality. In most cases, however, there may be several discrete functionalities that must be executed to express the user's concept of an operation.

Each operational system will have a set O of operations that animate it. Each functional system will have a set, F, of functionalities that animate it. For each operation $o_i \in O$ that the system may perform, there will be a subset, $F^{(o)} \subseteq F$, of functionalities that will implement it. It is possible, then, to define a relation IMPLEMENTS over $O \times F$ such that IMPLEMENTS (o, f) is true if functionality f is used in the implementation of an operation o. Within each operation, one or more of the system's functionalities will be expressed. For a given operation o, these expressed functionalities are those with the property

$$F^{(o)} = \{f : F \mid \forall \text{ IMPLEMENTS } (o, f)\}$$

An example of an IMPLEMENTS relation for a simple software system is shown in Table 5.1. From this table we can see that functionalities f_1 and f_2 are employed in the implementation of the operation o_1.

Table 5.1. Example of the IMPLEMENTS Relation

$O \times F$	f_1	f_2	f_3	f_4
o_1	T	T		
o_2		T	T	T

5.3   Distribution of Activity among the Functionalities

In Chapter 3 we established the fact that not all operations get the same amount of usage. The disparity in the distribution of activity was formalized in the notion of an operational profile. Each of the functionalities depends on the activity of the operations. The binding between operations and functionalities is formalized in the IMPLEMENTS relation. This binding is not strictly deterministic. If IMPLEMENTS(o_a, f_b) is true for operation o_a and functionality f_b, this does not imply that functionality f_b will always be expressed when operation o_a is invoked by the user. As a case in point, the functionality f_b might well be an error condition, in which case this functionality would be expressed only if an error condition occurred, such as a divide by zero in the case of our `calc` example. To capture the essence of these more tenuous relationships between functionalities and operations, we need to characterize the distribution of activity in two different ways. First, we would like to know the strength of the binding between operation and functionality. We can establish this relationship by measuring the proportion of activity each functionality receives under each operation. Second, we would like to establish prior probabilities for the conditional probability distribution, $\Pr(f_a \mid O)$.

For each operation $O \in O$, there is a relation p' over $O \times F$ such that $p'(o, f)$ is the proportion of activity that a functionality f will receive during the execution of an operation o. An example of the IMPLEMENTS relation for two operations implemented in four specified functions is shown in Table 5.1. What we cannot tell from Table 5.1 is the relative strength of the relationship between operations and functionalities. We observed, for example, that functions f_1 and f_2 were used to implement the operation o_1. We also saw that functionality f_2 is a functional part of both operations. In Table 5.2, there is an example of the relation p'. These numbers represent the proportion of time each of the functions will execute under each of the operations. In operation o_1, functionality f_1 may or may not execute. The functionality f_2, on the other hand, will always execute whenever operation o_1 is expressed.

The conditional probability distribution, $p(f \mid o)$, shows the relationship between each functionality and operation in a very different manner. A

Table 5.2. Example of the p' Relation

$p'(o, f)$	f_1	f_2	f_3	f_4
o_1	0.2	1.0	0	0
o_2	0	1.0	1.0	0.2

Table 5.3. Example of the Conditional Probability Distribution

p(f|o)	f_1	f_2	f_3	f_4
o_1	0.1	0.9	0	0
o_2	0	0.4	0.5	0.1

hypothetical distribution for these conditional probabilities is shown in Table 5.3. In this case, if we were to observe the operation o_1 during an arbitrary functional epoch, the relative likelihood of observing each of the functionalities f_1 and f_2 is 0.1 and 0.9, respectively. Let us suppose, for the moment, that the operational profile for the two operations shown in Table 5.3 is $p(o_1) = 0.3$ and $p(o_2) = 0.7$; then we can derive the functional profile for the functionalities as:

$$p(f_1) = \sum_{i=1}^{2} p(o_i)p\left(f_1 \mid o_i\right)$$

$$= 0.3 \times 0.1 + 0.7 \times 0$$

$$= .03$$

$$p(f_2) = \sum_{i=1}^{2} p(o_i)p\left(f_2 \mid o_i\right)$$

$$= 0.3 \times 0.9 + 0.7 \times 0.4$$

$$= .55$$

$$p(f_3) = \sum_{i=1}^{2} p(o_i)p\left(f_3 \mid o_i\right)$$

$$= 0.3 \times 0 + 0.7 \times 0.5$$

$$= .35$$

$$p(f_4) = \sum_{i=1}^{2} p(o_i)p\left(f_4 \mid o_i\right)$$

$$= 0.3 \times 0 + 0.7 \times 0.1$$

$$= .07$$

Again, the functional profile is the unconditional probability of executing a particular functionality during an arbitrary functional epoch. We can see from this trivial example that the functional profile directly depends on the operational profile. If the operational profile were to change, then the functional profile would also change.

One of the major problems in the determination of the reliability of a software system is that the past history of the operation of a software system is not very good predictor for its future reliability. The reason for this is squarely placed on the concept of the functional profile. Each functionality will exercise particular aspects of the functional machine. As long as the user operational profile remains stable, then the manner in which the functional machine actually executes is stable. However, when there is a major shift in the operational profile by the user, there will be a concomitant shift in the functional profile. This will redistribute the activity of the functional machine in a very different manner. It might well be that the shift causes an unreliable functionality that received little exposure under an initial operational profile to become a dominant player in the functional machine under a new operational profile. This will, of course, result in the diminution of the reliability of the system as a whole.

5.4 The Specification Build Process

As it turns out, the notion of the IMPLEMENTS relation is somewhat misleading. The set of operations is changing dynamically. New versions of each of the operations evolve. Some operations change fairly often, while other operations will seldom, if ever, be modified. What is even more important is that some operations will disappear as the system evolves, while other new operations will be introduced during this same evolutionary cycle. Exactly the same argument could be made for the functionalities. They are also subject to the evolutionary process. The IMPLEMENTS relation, then, can be expected to change repeatedly as the elements of the set of operations O and the set of functionalities F change as well.

The defining moment for the set of operations and the set of functionalities was established to be the build event. The specific set of operations for a build k is represented by the set $O^{(k)}$, and the set of functionalities by the set $F^{(k)}$. The set of operations is indexed by the vector $\iota^{(k)}$ and the functionalities are indexed by the vector $\eta^{(k)}$. A more realistic view of the IMPLEMENTS$^{(k)}$ relation for the kth build, then, is shown in Table 5.4. The

Table 5.4. Example of the IMPLEMENTS$^{(k)}$ Relation

$O \times F$	$f_{\eta_1^{(k)}}$	$f_{\eta_2^{(k)}}$	$f_{\eta_3^{(k)}}$	$f_{\eta_4^{(k)}}$
$o_{\iota_1^{(k)}}$	T	T		
$o_{\iota_2^{(k)}}$		T	T	T

**Table 5.5. Example of the
IMPLEMENTS$^{(j)}$ Relation**

$O \times F$	$f_{\eta_1^{(k)}}$	$f_{\eta_2^{(k)}}$	$f_{\eta_3^{(k)}}$	$f_{\eta_4^{(k)}}$	$f_{\eta_5^{(k)}}$
$o_{\iota_1^{(j)}}$	T	T			
$o_{\iota_2^{(j)}}$		T	T	T	
$o_{\iota_3^{(j)}}$		T		T	T

specific functionalities incorporated in the build k are those indexed by the vector $\eta^{(k)}$, which in this case has four elements. This means that there have only been four functionalities throughout the evolution of the functional specifications through build k.

At some later point in the evolution of the system — at, say, build j — the nature of the IMPLEMENTS relation will have changed. An example of the system at this new evolutionary point is shown in Table 5.5. In this case, a new operation, $o_{\iota_3^{(j)}}$, appears, as does a new functionality, $f_{\eta_5^{(j)}}$.

It is important to note that the operations $o_{\iota_1^{(k)}}$ and $o_{\iota_1^{(j)}}$ are not necessarily the same operations. The index vector $\iota_1^{(k)}$ records the version number of each of the operations on the kth build. Thus, the version number recorded in $\iota_1^{(k)}$ may be quite different from that recorded in $\iota_1^{(j)}$. The IMPLEMENTS relation then serves to provide an additional level of binding information. First, it binds functionalities to operations. Second, it binds versions of functionalities to version of operations.

It is clear, by this point, that there are multiple IMPLEMENTS relations, one for each build. Thus, a more appropriate nomenclature for this relation would be IMPLEMENTS$^{(k)}$ representing the IMPLEMENTS relation on the kth build.

The defining moment for the IMPLEMENTS relation is the document build. Each build will define a new IMPLEMENTS relation. This relation must be preserved at each build point in the form of a build list. The essence of a build list is that it associates a particular version of an operation to a particular version of a functionality that will implement it. Let us assume that at build k, the operation index vector is:

$$\iota^{(k)} = \langle 1.2, 1.3 \rangle$$

and that the functionality index is:

$$\eta^{(k)} = \langle 1.4, 1.1, 1.3, 1.6 \rangle$$

The build list for the IMPLEMENTS$^{(k)}$ relation is shown in Table 5.6.

Table 5.6. The Build List for Build k

Operation Version	Operation Index	Functionality Index	Functionality Version
$\iota_1^{(k)}$	1.2	$\eta_1^{(j)}$	1.4
$\iota_1^{(k)}$	1.2	$\eta_2^{(j)}$	1.1
$\iota_2^{(k)}$	1.3	$\eta_2^{(j)}$	1.1
$\iota_2^{(k)}$	1.3	$\eta_3^{(j)}$	1.3
$\iota_2^{(k)}$	1.3	$\eta_4^{(j)}$	1.6

Let us assume that the system has undergone substantial change between build k and build j. The operation index vector for build j would be:

$$\iota^{(j)} = \langle 2.3, 3.1, 1.1 \rangle$$

and that the functionality index might be:

$$\eta^{(j)} = \langle 1.5, 1.3, 1.4, 2.3, 1.0 \rangle$$

The build list for the IMPLEMENTS$^{(j)}$ relation is shown in Table 5.7.

The build lists, then, will identify which versions of each of the operations are associated with particular version of functionalities. There are several more layers of this binding process discussed in subsequent chapters. From a maintenance perspective, it is absolutely vital to ensure that the operational and design specifications are traceable directly to the

Table 5.7. The Build List for Build j

Operation Index	Operation Version	Functionality Index	Functionality Version
$\iota_1^{(k)}$	2.3	$\eta_1^{(j)}$	1.5
$\iota_1^{(k)}$	2.3	$\eta_2^{(j)}$	1.3
$\iota_2^{(k)}$	3.1	$\eta_2^{(j)}$	1.3
$\iota_2^{(k)}$	3.1	$\eta_3^{(j)}$	1.4
$\iota_2^{(k)}$	3.1	$\eta_4^{(j)}$	2.3
$\iota_3^{(k)}$	1.1	$\eta_2^{(j)}$	1.3
$\iota_3^{(k)}$	1.1	$\eta_4^{(j)}$	2.3
$\iota_3^{(k)}$	1.1	$\eta_5^{(j)}$	1.0

source code that goes to each build. Each build of the system represents a slightly different system. Each incremental system is described by its own operational, functional, and module specifications.

5.5 An Extended Definition of Operations and Functionalities

It is now possible to define the notion of an operation a little more precisely. An operation consists of two distinct parts. First there is a textual description of the operation that describes the user's activity in manipulating the abstract machine represented by the operational model. Second there is the linkage to the specific functionalities that will implement that operation. We can summarize this new definition of an operation by defining a new table to represent this idea. This information is presented in Table 5.8. In this table, each operation has a name, in this case o_i. Each operation also has a unique position in an index vector (*vis.* Section 3.6), in this case ι_j.

For each operation it is clear that there are one or more functionalities that will be employed to implement that operation. It is also quite clear that these functionalities may evolve quite rapidly during the development phase. It is also quite possible that the underlying functional model may completely change during the development of a system should it be discovered that the original design was unworkable. Thus, it is vital to provide a continuing linkage between each of the operations and the current functionalities that implement them. Each functionality, under our scheme of document management, exists as a file in a configuration control system. It can be retrieved from the configuration control system by its filename and version number. In essence, a pointer to a functionality will be the pair <filename><version #>, as is shown in Table 5.9. In the linkage section of the operator definition, then, we keep a list of all of the functionalities that implement each operation together with the links to the most current versions of those functionalities.

One of the major problems confronted by software development organizations today is that there is a rapid departure from the operational

Table 5.8. Updated Description of an Operation

Operation Name	o_i		
Operation Index	ι_i^j		
Description	<textual description of the user stimulus to the operational system>		
Linkage	Functionality Name	Functionality Filename	Version
	<functionality>	<filename>	<version #>

Table 5.9. Specifications for a Functionality

Functionality Name	f_i		
Functionality Index	η_i^j		

Control	Received from functionality:
	   <List of functionalities>
	 Transferred to functionality:
	   <List of functionalities>		

Data	Incoming packets:
	   <Packet list>
	 Outgoing packets:
	   <Packet list>		

Protocol	<Protocol list for data packets>		
Functional Transformations	<List of data transformations>		
Linkage	Operation Name	Operation Filename	Version
	<operation>	<filename>	<version#>

specifications (if they are, in fact, formalized) and the functional specifications. This means that it is very difficult to trace how a particular feature
or operations is currently implemented. This leads to maintenance nightmares. An astonishing amount of time is currently invested in most software
development organizations performing just this task. It is only appropriate
that this linkage between these two sets of specifications be preserved by
an automated system.

5.6 The `calc` System Example

We are now in a position to examine just how the functionalities for the
`calc` system are distributed to the operations. The mapping of operations
to functionalities for this system are shown in Table 5.10. Inspection of
this table reveals that some operations can be used in all operations. An
example of this would be functionality f_1. This functionality is the system
initialization function. It occurs with the first user activity. However, the
user may choose any of the many operations as the first one. Therefore,
the initialization functionality is potentially involved with all of the operations. It is, however, only invoked once and then never again. What we
do not learn from Table 5.10 is the specific nature of this relationship
between operations and functionalities; we only learn that a functionality
can be expressed when the user selects a particular operation. Functionality f_6, on the other hand, is associated with only operations o_2, o_3, o_4,
and o_5.

Table 5.10. The IMPLEMENTS Relation for the `calc` System

Operation	Functionality							
	1	2	3	4	5	6	7	8
1	T	T	T	T			T	
2	T	T	T	T	T	T	T	T
3	T	T	T	T	T	T	T	T
4	T	T	T	T	T	T	T	T
5	T	T	T	T	T	T	T	T
6	T	T	T	T			T	
7	T	T		T	T		T	T
8	T	T		T	T		T	T
9	T	T		T				
10	T		T	T			T	

5.6.1 Distribution of Activity in Functionalities

It is clear, then, that the IMPLEMENTS relation does not give us a feel for the relative strength of the binding between a functionality and an operation. To extract this binding information, we must instrument the system and measure it. Let us suppose that we have done this for our six test users of the system. The hypothetical results of this measurement exercise are shown in Table 5.11. From Table 3.2 we observed the frequency of each of the operations across all six users; this data is repeated in the penultimate column of Table 5.11. We are now going to observe the distribution of the functionalities for each operation. Operation 1, for example, employs functionalities 1, 2, 3, 4, and 7. As it turns out, operation 1 is to enter an operand. All the users chose this as their first activity. Thus, functionality 1 (the initialization functionality) was invoked six times in association with operation 1 and never with another operation. Although IMPLEMENTS (o_i, f_1) is true for all i, it is only actually invoked in operation 1 for these users.

The final column in Table 5.11 tallies all the instances of execution of all functionalities. Another way to say the same thing is that this column enumerates the total number of functional epochs for each user. The penultimate column enumerates the total number of operational epochs for each user.

If we divide each entry of the functional frequency count from Table 5.11 by the number of operational epochs, we can derive the p' relation shown

Table 5.11. Distribution of Activity across Functionalities

	Functionality									
Operations	1	2	3	4	5	6	7	8	Total Events	Total Instances
1	6	163	2	163			163		163	497
2		73	1	73		73	73	73	73	366
3		37		37		37	37	37	37	185
4		21	1	21	21	21	21	21	21	127
5		3	1	3	3	3	3	3	3	19
6		1		1			1		1	3
7		24		24	24		24	24	24	120
8		10		10	10		10	10	10	50
9		6		6					6	12
10			11	11			11		11	33

Table 5.12. Example of the p' Relation for the `calc` System

	Functionality							
Operation	1	2	3	4	5	6	7	8
1	0.04	1.00	0.01	1.00	0	0	1.00	0
2	0	1.00	0.01	1.00	0	1.00	1.00	1.00
3	0	1.00	0	1.00	0	1.00	1.00	1.00
4	0	1.00	0.05	1.00	1.00	1.00	1.00	1.00
5	0	1.00	0.33	1.00	1.00	1.00	1.00	1.00
6	0	1.00	0	1.00	0	0	1.00	0
7	0	1.00	0	1.00	1.00	0	1.00	1.00
8	0	1.00	0	1.00	1.00	0	1.00	1.00
9	0	1.00	0	1.00	0	0	0	0
10	0	0	1.00	1.00	0	0	1.00	0

in Table 5.12. This gives us some measure of the strength of the binding between each of the functionalities and operations *for this particular group of users*. We do know, for example, that whenever operation 1 was invoked by this group, that functionalities 2, 4, and 7 always occurred.

Table 5.13. The Conditional Probability Distribution for the Functionalities

Operation	Functionality							
	1	2	3	4	5	6	7	8
1	0.01	0.33	0.00	0.33	0	0	0.33	0
2	0	0.20	0.00	0.20	0	0.20	0.20	0.20
3	0	0.20	0	0.20	0	0.20	0.20	0.20
4	0	0.17	0.01	0.17	0.17	0.17	0.17	0.17
5	0	0.16	0.05	0.16	0.16	0.16	0.16	0.16
6	0	0.33	0	0.33	0	0	0.33	0
7	0	0.20	0	0.20	0.20	0	0.20	0.20
8	0	0.20	0	0.20	0.20	0	0.20	0.20
9	0	0.50	0	0.50	0	0	0	0
10	0	0	0.33	0.33	0	0	0.33	0

If we divide the functionality epochs of Table 5.11 by the functional epoch (the last column in this table), we obtain estimates for the conditional probability distribution of functionalities given each of the operations. The initial probability estimates are shown in Table 5.13. We can see from this table, for example, that $\Pr(f_2 | o_1) = 0.33$.

It was a characteristic of each user that he or she generated his or her own individual operational profiles. That is, each user employed the operations in a slightly different manner. These operational profiles were shown in Table 3.3. By systematically employing Bayes rule, we can derive the functional profiles for each of the users (as shown in Section 5.3). The functional profiles for each of the users is shown in Table 5.14. Also, the last column in this table is the total functional profile across all users of the system.

Each of the functional profiles for each of the users represents a point in a seven-dimensional space. (We lose one degree of freedom to the sum, which must equal 1.0.) Just as we did with the operational profiles, we can measure the distance between any of the functional profiles and the cumulative or total functional profile represented by the last column in Table 5.14. This distance for user i is

$$d^{(i)} = \sum_{j=1}^{8} \left(p\left(f_j^{(i)}\right) - p\left(f_j^{(t)}\right) \right)^2.$$

Table 5.14. Functional Profiles

Functionality	Users						Total
	1	2	3	4	5	6	
1	0.005	0.005	0.007	0.005	0.006	0.006	0.006
2	0.257	0.242	0.272	0.234	0.256	0.274	0.256
3	0.019	0.020	0.007	0.037	0.010	0.003	0.014
4	0.271	0.258	0.276	0.266	0.263	0.274	0.267
5	0.031	0.056	0.011	0.046	0.030	0.009	0.031
6	0.075	0.061	0.073	0.072	0.084	0.087	0.074
7	0.249	0.252	0.271	0.250	0.258	0.252	0.258
8	0.092	0.106	0.084	0.091	0.094	0.096	0.094

It now becomes relevant to assess the overall departure of the six users from the total functional profile. We can then talk about the average distance

$$\bar{d} = \frac{1}{6} \sum_i d_i$$

for this group of six users and the variance of this distance across these users,

$$Var(d) = \frac{1}{5} \sum_i (d_i - \bar{d})^2.$$

The profile distances for each of the six users are shown in Table 5.15, together with the average and variance for these distances. In that these values tend to be very small, it is useful to examine them by their relative magnitude. To this end, the distance values in this table have been scaled by taking the logarithm to the base 10. These values are shown in the last row of the table. It is quite clear that users 2, 3, 4, and 6 contribute the most to the overall variation in the distance values.

Table 5.15. Functional Profile Distances

1	2	3	4	5	6	Average	Variance
0.00013	0.00134	0.00105	0.00134	0.00012	0.00118	0.00086	0.00000
−3.88	−2.87	−2.98	−2.87	−3.91	−2.93	−3.06	−6.48

Table 5.16. Functional Latencies

Operation	Functionality								Latency
	1	2	3	4	5	6	7	8	
1	0.01	0.33	0.00	0.33	0.00	0.00	0.33	0.00	79
2	0.00	0.20	0.00	0.20	0.00	0.20	0.20	0.20	138
3	0.00	0.20	0.00	0.20	0.00	0.20	0.20	0.20	138
4	0.00	0.17	0.01	0.17	0.17	0.17	0.17	0.17	126
5	0.00	0.16	0.05	0.16	0.16	0.16	0.16	0.16	121
6	0.00	0.33	0.00	0.33	0.00	0.00	0.33	0.00	80
7	0.00	0.20	0.00	0.20	0.20	0.00	0.20	0.20	92
8	0.00	0.20	0.00	0.20	0.20	0.00	0.20	0.20	92
9	0.00	0.50	0.00	0.50	0.00	0.00	0.00	0.00	105
10	0.00	0.00	0.33	0.33	0.00	0.00	0.33	0.00	33
Latency	5	150	10	60	70	300	30	150	

5.6.2 Functional Latency

It is an attribute of each functionality that it takes a certain amount of time to execute. We named this the *functional latency*. The symbol γ_j was employed in Chapter 4 to represent the latency of a functionality j. We also established that γ_i is an expected value for the functional latency under a particular operation as

$$\gamma_i = \sum_{j=1}^{m} \gamma_j \Pr\left(f_j \mid o_i\right).$$

For our `calc` example, the hypothetical functional latencies are shown in the last row of Table 5.16. The conditional probability distributions for the functionalities under each operation are shown in the center of this table. In the final column of Table 5.16 are the operational latencies. These operational latencies, again, were derived as expected values for each operation under the functional conditional probability distribution shown in the rows of this table. These operational latencies were the basis for the values presented in Chapter 3 in Table 3.4.

5.6.3 The Linkage of Operations to Functionalities

Now we turn our attention to the problem of maintaining the linkage between the current operations and the current functionalities. Suppose that the operations, at some build j in the future, are represented by the files

Table 5.17. Operation Linkage Information

Operation Name	Operation Filename	Version
o_1	calc/op/o1	3.1
o_2	calc/op/o2	1.4
o_3	calc/op/o3	1.3
o_4	calc/op/o4	1.3
o_5	calc/op/o5	1.5
o_6	calc/op/o6	1.7
o_7	calc/op/o7	1.0
o_8	calc/op/o8	2.2
o_9	calc/op/o9	1.1
o_{10}	calc/op/o10	1.1

and versions of those files shown in Table 5.17. The operation index vector $\iota^{(j)}$ is the last column of this table. The contents of this table bind the operation name to its filename in the operating system environment and also to the particular version of that filename for the current build.

Now suppose that the functionalities at this same point in the build process, build j, are represented by the contents of Table 5.18. The last column of this table is the functionality index vector $\eta^{(j)}$. As was the case for the operations in build j, the contents of this table bind the functionality names to specific filenames and then to versions of each file.

Table 5.18. Functionality Linkage Information

Functionality Name	Functionality Filename	Version
f_1	calc/func/f1	1.4
f_2	calc/func/f2	1.0
f_3	calc/func/f3	2.4
f_4	calc/func/f4	1.3
f_5	calc/func/f5	1.8
f_6	calc/func/f6	2.1
f_7	calc/func/f7	1.10
f_8	calc/func/f8	2.2

The contents of Tables 5.17 and 5.18 are the primary elements of build lists for build j of the operational and functional specifications. They are missing only the filenames and versions of the operational (functional) overview and the operational (functional) model. With this data we can know exactly which operations (by version) were implemented by the source code on build j. Further, we know exactly how these operations were implemented by specific functionalities.

We now turn our attention to the creation of a mechanism that will bind the most recent version of each operation to the most recent version of the functionalities that implement it. In Tables 5.19a through 5.19j are the actual contents of the files for each of the operations. As we can see from Table 5.19a, for example, each operation has a name that uniquely describes it. We then have a textual description of the operation itself. Finally, there is a linkage section that binds each operation to a specific set of functionalities. We can see that operation o_1 is linked to five different functionalities. We can also see which version of each of these function- alities is the current one. Again the pointer to the functionality consists of the filename, version name pair. The pointer to functionality f_1 is the pair <calc/func/f1, 1.4>.

Each of the functionalities for the calc system is described in tabular form, just as was the case for the operations. The functionalities for the calc system at the same point in its evolution as the above set of opera- tions are presented in Tables 5.20a through 5.20h. These tables are some- what different from those of the operations. The functionalities are differ- entiated from the operations by their control and data binding. The control binding is specified in the Control section of each table. We see in Table 5.20c, for example, that functionality f_3 gives control to functionality f_2 and

Table 5.19a. Current Operation Specification

Operation Name	o_1 <enter number>		
Description	The value of the number is pushed on the stack. A number is a string of the digits "0"–"9". It can be preceded by an optional sign ("+" or "–"). If the integer does not follow the form of a decimal number, the system will display the response "error" followed by a carriage return and a new prompt.		
Linkage	f_1	calc/func/f1	1.4
	f_2	calc/func/f2	1.0
	f_3	calc/func/f3	2.4
	f_4	calc/func/f4	1.3
	f_7	calc/func/f7	1.10

Table 5.19b. Current Operation Specification

Operation Name	o_2 '+'		
Description	The top two values on the stack are popped, added, and their sum pushed back on the stack. The contents of the last register are replaced by a zero.		
Linkage	f_1	calc/func/f1	1.4
	f_2	calc/func/f2	1.0
	f_3	calc/func/f3	2.4
	f_4	calc/func/f4	1.3
	f_5	calc/func/f5	1.8
	f_6	calc/func/f6	2.1
	f_7	calc/func/f7	1.10
	f_8	calc/func/f8	2.2

Table 5.19c. Current Operation Specification

Operation Name	o_3 '−'		
Description	The top two values on the stack are popped, the second number is subtracted from the first, and the difference is pushed back on the stack. The contents of the last register are replaced by a zero.		
Linkage	f_1	calc/func/f1	1.4
	f_2	calc/func/f2	1.0
	f_3	calc/func/f3	2.4
	f_4	calc/func/f4	1.3
	f_5	calc/func/f5	1.8
	f_6	calc/func/f6	2.1
	f_7	calc/func/f7	1.10
	f_8	calc/func/f8	2.2

receives control from f_2 as well. The data flow into and out of each of the functionalities is specified in the Data section of each of the functionality specification blocks. Each of the functionalities can also be characterized in terms of the transformations made on the data passed to them. Finally,

Table 5.19d. Current Operation Specification

Operation Name	o_4 '*'		
Description	The top two values on the stack are popped, multiplied and the least significant 10 digits of the product is pushed back on the stack and then the most significant 10 digits of the product are pushed into the stack. Both registers will carry the sign of the result.		
Linkage	f_1	calc/func/f1	1.4
	f_2	calc/func/f2	1.0
	f_3	calc/func/f3	2.4
	f_4	calc/func/f4	1.3
	f_5	calc/func/f5	1.8
	f_6	calc/func/f6	2.1
	f_7	calc/func/f7	1.10
	f_8	calc/func/f8	2.2

each of the functionalities will be described in terms of the nature of the transformations that they effect on each of the data packets that they send or receive.

A significant amount of the effort in maintaining the description of the functionalities will be in maintaining the linkage among the functionalities and the operations. We can see from Table 5.20a, for example, that functionality f_1 might potentially participate in every operation. The truth of the matter is that, in reality, it will participate in exactly one of the operations to the exclusion of all other operations. The most important observation that can be made at this point is that the functionality f_1 can implement all of the operations. This means that changes to this functionality can potentially influence all the operations. The dependency of operations on the functionalities is the crux of the software maintenance problem. Unless the functionalities remain tightly bound to the operations and this binding is kept current, very soon it will no longer be possible to understand just how a particular operation is implemented. Should we wish to modify any of the operations without current binding information to functionalities, it will be very difficult to make these changes — both in terms of human effort and also in terms of reliability. Currently, on the greatest cost centers in the software maintenance enterprise contained in the process of continually trying to discover how an operation is implemented in the current

Table 5.19e. Current Operation Specification

Operation Name	o_5 '%'		
Description	The top two values on the stack are popped; the first number is the dividend and the second number is the divisor. The signed remainder is pushed onto the stack, followed by the signed quotient. If the divisor is zero, the system will display the response "error" followed by a carriage return and a new prompt. The contents of the register set remain unchanged.		
Linkage	f_1	calc/func/f1	1.4
	f_2	calc/func/f2	1.0
	f_3	calc/func/f3	2.4
	f_4	calc/func/f4	1.3
	f_5	calc/func/f5	1.8
	f_6	calc/func/f6	2.1
	f_7	calc/func/f7	1.10
	f_8	calc/func/f8	2.2

Table 5.19f. Current Operation Specification

Operation Name	o_6 'd'		
Description	The top value on the stack is duplicated. That is, it is copied out by the calc engine and pushed back onto the stack.		
Linkage	f_1	calc/func/f1	1.4
	f_2	calc/func/f2	1.0
	f_3	calc/func/f3	2.4
	f_4	calc/func/f4	1.3
	f_7	calc/func/f7	1.10

build. It might seem, at the outset, that the overhead in maintaining the linkage between operations and functionalities is far too great. The fact of the matter is that it is far cheaper to maintain this on a per-change basis than it is to try to reconstruct the binding at random intervals in the build process.

Table 5.19g. Current Operation Specification

Operation Name	o_7 'p'		
Description	The top value on the stack is printed. The top value remains unchanged.		
Linkage	f_1	calc/func/f1	1.4
	f_2	calc/func/f2	1.0
	f_4	calc/func/f4	1.3
	f_5	calc/func/f5	1.8
	f_7	calc/func/f7	1.10
	f_8	calc/func/f8	2.2

Table 5.19h. Current Operation Specification

Operation Name	o_8 'f'		
Description	All values on the stack are printed with a carriage return separating them.		
Linkage	f_1	calc/func/f1	1.4
	f_2	calc/func/f2	1.0
	f_4	calc/func/f4	1.3
	f_5	calc/func/f5	1.8
	f_7	calc/func/f7	1.10
	f_8	calc/func/f8	2.2

Table 5.19i. Current Operation Specification

Operation Name	o_9 'q'		
Description	Exits the program		
Linkage	f_1	calc/func/f1	1.4
	f_2	calc/func/f2	1.0
	f_4	calc/func/f4	1.3

It should now be apparent that there is a substantial amount of effort necessary to maintain the linkage among the operations and functionalities. It will be necessary to create the infrastructure to support this linkage. However, it is still premature to begin to outline the details of this

Table 5.19j. Current Operation Specification

Operation Name	o_{10} 'c'		
Description	The top stack entry is popped. The contents of the last register are replaced by a zero.		
Linkage	f_1	calc/func/f1	1.4
	f_3	calc/func/f3	2.4
	f_4	calc/func/f4	1.3
	f_7	calc/func/f7	1.10

Table 5.20a. Current Specification for Functionality f_1

Functionality	f_1		
Control	Received from functionality: OS, f_2 Transferred to functionality: f_2, OS		
Data	Incoming packets: None Outgoing packets: None		
Functional Transformations	Stack initialization (registers set to zero)		
Linkage	o_1	calc/op/o1	3.1
	o_2	calc/op/o2	1.4
	o_3	calc/op/o3	1.3
	o_4	calc/op/o4	1.3
	o_5	calc/op/o5	1.5
	o_6	calc/op/o6	1.7
	o_7	calc/op/o7	1.0
	o_8	calc/op/o8	2.2
	o_9	calc/op/o9	1.1
	o_{10}	calc/op/o10	1.1

infrastructure until we have completed the discussion of the low-level design. This discussion will add yet another layer of complexity to the complete description of the functionalities.

Table 5.20b. Current Specification for Functionality f_2

Functionality	f_2		
Control	Received from functionality: f_1, f_3, f_4, f_6, f_7 Transferred to functionality: f_3, f_4, f_6, f_7		
Data	Incoming packets: ASCII string Outgoing packets: Signed binary number Command code Error message		
Functional Transformations	Parse character input into: 32-bit binary number, Operation code, or Error condition		
Linkage	o_1	calc/op/o1	3.1
	o_2	calc/op/o2	1.4
	o_3	calc/op/o3	1.3
	o_4	calc/op/o4	1.3
	o_5	calc/op/o5	1.5
	o_6	calc/op/o6	1.7
	o_7	calc/op/o7	1.0
	o_8	calc/op/o8	2.2
	o_9	calc/op/o9	1.1

Table 5.20c. Current Specification for Functionality f_3

Functionality	f_3		

Control	Received from functionality:
	  f_2
	Transferred to functionality:
	  f_2		

Data	Incoming packets:
	  None
	Outgoing packets:
	  Character string "error"		

Functional Transformations	Generate error message for output.		
Linkage	o_1	calc/op/o1	3.1
	o_2	calc/op/o2	1.4
	o_3	calc/op/o3	1.3
	o_4	calc/op/o4	1.3
	o_5	calc/op/o5	1.5
	o_6	calc/op/o6	1.7
	o_{10}	calc/op/o10	1.1

Table 5.20d. Current Specification for Functionality f_4

Functionality	f_4		
Control	Received from functionality: f_2, OS Transferred to functionality: f_2, OS		

Data	Incoming packets:
	  Character string
	Outgoing packets:
	  Signed 32-bit binary number
	  Character code 'd', 'p', 'f', or 'c'		

Functional Transformations	Data buffering: receive string from the OS and buffer the string		
Linkage	o_1	calc/op/o1	3.1
	o_2	calc/op/o2	1.4
	o_3	calc/op/o3	1.3
	o_4	calc/op/o4	1.3
	o_5	calc/op/o5	1.5
	o_6	calc/op/o6	1.7
	o_7	calc/op/o7	1.0
	o_8	calc/op/o8	2.2
	o_9	calc/op/o9	1.1
	o_{10}	calc/op/o10	1.1

Table 5.20e. Current Specification for Functionality f_5

Functionality	f_5		

Control	Received from functionality:
	  f_3, f_7, OS
	Transferred to functionality:
	  f_3, f_7, OS		

Data	Incoming packets:
	  Character strings
	Outgoing packets:
	  Character string		

Functional Transformations	Data buffering: transmit buffered string to OS		
Linkage	o_2	calc/op/o2	1.4
	o_3	calc/op/o3	1.3
	o_4	calc/op/o4	1.3
	o_5	calc/op/o5	1.5
	o_7	calc/op/o7	1.0
	o_8	calc/op/o8	2.2

Table 5.20f. Current Specification for Functionality f_6

Functionality	f_6		

Control	Received from functionality:
	  f_2, f_8
	Transferred to functionality:
	  f_2, f_8		

Data	Incoming packets:
	  2 32-bit binary numbers
	Outgoing packets:
	  1 or 2 32-bit binary numbers		

Functional Transformations	Capture signs of top two stack elements Sign arithmetic results Addition of top two operands on the stack Multiplication of top two operands on the stack Division of top two operands on the stack		
Linkage	o_2	calc/op/o2	1.4
	o_3	calc/op/o3	1.3
	o_4	calc/op/o4	1.3
	o_5	calc/op/o5	1.5

Table 5.20g. Current Specification for Functionality f_7

Functionality	f_7		
Control	Received from functionality: f_2, f_8 Transferred to functionality: f_2, f_8		
Data	Incoming packets: Character code 'd', 'p', 'f', or 'c' Outgoing packets: Signed 32-bit binary numbers		
Functional Transformations	Change stack locations Zero top of stack Data transfer from stack		
Linkage	o_1	calc/op/o1	3.1
	o_2	calc/op/o2	1.4
	o_3	calc/op/o3	1.3
	o_4	calc/op/o4	1.3
	o_5	calc/op/o5	1.5
	o_6	calc/op/o6	1.7
	o_7	calc/op/o7	1.0
	o_8	calc/op/o8	2.2
	o_9	calc/op/o9	1.1

Table 5.20h. Current Specification for Functionality f_8

Functionality	f_8		
Control	Received from functionality: f_6, f_7 Transferred to functionality: f_8, f_7		
Data	Incoming packets: Signed 32-bit binary number Outgoing packets: Character string		
Functional Transformations	Convert signed 32-bit binary number to character string		
Linkage	o_2	calc/op/o2	1.4
	o_3	calc/op/o3	1.3
	o_4	calc/op/o4	1.3
	o_5	calc/op/o5	1.5
	o_7	calc/op/o7	1.0
	o_8	calc/op/o8	2.2

Chapter 6
Module Specification: Low-Level Design

6.1 Introduction

The module requirements specification is the low-level design specification for the system. At this level, we are concerned for the first time about implementing the system in a programming language model. Each programming language creates a different model. There is, for example, a C++ machine. This particular language model is created through a very large library of runtime support services. There is a distinctly different model created by the Java runtime environment. We do not concern ourselves with this low-level implementation detail until we actually begin to map our high-level design model onto a particular language runtime environment. The module specification is simply a low-level partition of the system functionality. The three central issues that emerge from the module description are the structure of the system, the precise specification of data structures, and the data flow from one module to another. There must be, however, a one-to-one mapping between module specifications and code modules. Each module specification will result in exactly one code module. There will be no code modules that do not have design module specifications.

One thing that will become central to our thinking in the module specification is that there must be a well-defined grammar controlling this specification. Our first automatic system measurements will occur at this level. Essentially all the control flow metrics can be obtained from the design module specifications. All the pertinent data attribute information can be obtained here as well. This is our first real discussion of data. After we have a good idea what data we need and how we are going to transform it, then and only then will we worry about data capture from the operational environment.

We do not expect there to be any comment statements in the source code for program we have specified. All program documentation is kept outside the source code module and each source code module has its own design documentation. All pertinent information about the module will be held in the design documentation. If there is a fault in the design, the design must be modified, followed by the associated code modules. The only circumstance that a code module should ever be modified without modification of its design specification is in the case where the code module does not accurately reflect the design module.

6.2 Architectural Overview

At the lowest level of design granularity, there is an abstract machine that is animated by the algorithms described in the individual modules. The architectural overview summarizes the nature of the abstract machine that the low-level design uses to implement the functionalities.

The precise nature of the abstract machine designed by the software design team depends heavily on the nature of the problem to be solved and the language that will be used to implement the low-level design. If, for example, the software system under construction is a largely text processing system, then it would be useful to invent an abstract machine that is facile in string processing. It would also be useful for this machine to support some type of string data structures.

The main purpose, then, of the architectural overview is to define the nature of the problem being solved and outline the general characteristics of an abstract machine that will perform this work.

6.3 Architectural Model

The architecture model describes in complete detail the third abstract machine that is part of the software specification. This abstract machine represents one step closer to the underlying physical hardware system that actually implements the program. This machine will evolve for each design application as the design process progresses. It is an intermediate step to the next machine, the one represented by the final programming language. It is the purpose of the design abstract machine to provide a framework around which the flow of program control and data can be thoroughly understood. It will be very difficult to establish firm guidelines for the nature of these intermediate machines. We are reminded of the little girl who stood before Abe Lincoln and was astonished by his height. She asked the President, "Just how long should a man's legs be anyhow?" History has it that Abe replied, "Long enough to reach the ground." Exactly the same thing will be true of our intermediate architectural model. It must be sufficiently rich to facilitate the design process. It must not be elaborate to the extent that it complicates the design process.

Let us first understand that the vast majority of problems that we are going to use our software to solve are intrinsically decimal problems. That is because we humans think and solve problems in decimal. Therefore, it is reasonable to suggest that our intermediate design machine will have extensive decimal properties. Once we understand the nature of the problem we are trying to solve in terms of the accuracy and precision of the numbers that we will process, then and only then will we worry about mapping this design onto a binary machine. The very last thing we should worry about at this stage is binary floating-point representation of numbers. We might never choose to use a binary machine in the final mapping of design to source code. It could well be that we will choose a final programming language machine like that of BASIC, which is a decimal machine.

Some problems will not require much at all in the way of numerical computation, decimal or binary. Word processors, for example, manipulate characters. If that is the primary need of the design program at hand, then it would be useful to conceive of a computer that has string processing capabilities. If, on the other hand, the application is to interface with an existing database engine for information storage and retrieval, then the architecture of the design abstract machine could well offer features and operations provided by the database management system.

The underlying structure of the data should be an important factor in the specification of the design machine architecture. For certain types of mathematical processing, it is useful to organize data into arrays or matrices. Then we should create an abstract machine that will have these data structures. We will then contrive a means in the algorithmic section of the module specification to use these arrays and matrices. If it is in our interest to create dynamic data structures, then we can invent a machine that will create and reabsorb new memory elements in which we might place data.

One of the more useful data structures that we could conceive for a file processing or a transaction processing system would be the COBOL type of record structure. In this case we would have sets of characters organized into fields that are, in turn, structured into records. We could then augment the capabilities of our design machine by imbuing it with one or more file access methods to match our particular design problem.

From the standpoint of reliability, a very important feature that the design machine should have is some type of contingency management. If an index value is out of range on an array subscript, then it would be nice if we could raise an exception at the abstract machine level. Similarly, if a variable is poised to receive a value that is out of range for the variable declaration, there should be an intrinsic mechanism to trap that condition. If this feature is built into our abstract machine at this stage, it will be easier to integrate this contingency management concept into the source code program.

In the previous analysis, however rich we make the design abstract machine architecture, reality will quickly rear its ugly head when it comes to the choice of programming language. We will be able to choose just about any language that we like, just as long as it is C, C++, or Java. It is painfully difficult to understand the design problem in the context of these languages. That is the purpose of this intermediate machine. It allows us to create a machine that will let us solve our design problem. Once we thoroughly understand the design issues, then and only then can we map this design onto an actual programming language system.

6.4 Module Specifications

In our evolving specification scheme there will be a separate spec for each program module. The structure of this specification can be developed in terms of a little grammar for the pseudo code implementation. In the interest of brevity, we will not begin to attempt to build module descriptions for the hypothetical `calc` system. The most important thing to establish at this point is that there are certain elements of module description that must be specified very precisely at this point. There are other aspects that are less important to the present discussion.

There are three essential components to the module specification. First, there is the Module Header information where we identify the control and data coupling for the module. Second, there is the Data Section where we identify the exact nature of the data the module will consume or produce. Finally, there is the Algorithm Section where we describe how a module actually transforms the data.

There is no provision, in our module specification scheme, for data structures. The only data we identify at this stage is scalar data. If we want additional data structures, then we are going to have to invent a functional model that has this capability. We might wish, for example, to have simple one-dimensional arrays. Then we will have to build a vector capability into our functional model. If, on the other hand, we wish to have strings, then our functional model will have string manipulation as an intrinsic feature. Moses did not come down from the mountain with a set of stone tablets that demanded, "Thou shalt have arrays." If we need arrays, we will invent them. If we need pointers, we will invent them.

In our presentation of the module specification, we use a simple grammar to simplify this discussion. It is merely a starting point. If we are to imbue our functional model with arrays, then we must describe these structures in our module description grammar. If we are going to need records or structures, then we must describe these structures in our module description grammar. The near-term objective is not to get lost in the forest of data structures. We are very interested in defining the scalars that are the fundamental data building blocks of the design. It is important not to obscure that process at this stage.

6.4.1 Module Header

The Module Header Section articulates the data binding between this module and those that call it. The Call Section of our module specification shows the control flow binding between this module and those it will call and will be called by it. We use this section to module bindings. The Algorithm Section is used to derive the module control flow structures. The Data Definition Section shows the scope of each variable. In addition, this section allows us to specify the precise nature of each data variable and the range of data it can contain.

There are two specific things we need to define in a Module Header. First, we need to know how data is obtained and returned to the environment external to each module. Second, we want to know which modules are called by the current module. We also want to know which modules call the current module.

The precise nature of the module header is established in Table 6.1. Parameters have names. Some parameters can also have the property that they will only be interrogated by the current module and not altered by it. These parameters are identified by the IN property. Other parameters are used to send data from the module. These are identified by the OUT property. Still other parameters send data into the module and are also used to send data out of the module. These parameters will have the MODIFY property.

We make absolutely no provision for global data or side effects. There is a vast collection of fault reports in our past that all relate to the inappropriate use of global variables. They are a simple convenience for software developers and an astonishing liability for software maintainers. Thus, we must insist that all data consumed or produced by each module will arrive and depart through a formal parameter list. To do otherwise is to create a maintenance nightmare.

Table 6.1. Module Header Information

```
HEADER <module name>
  PARAMETERS
    <parameter_list> | <empty> IN
    <parameter_list> | <empty> OUT
    <parameter_list> | <empty> MODIFY
  CALLED MODULES
    <module name list>|<empty>
  CALLING MODULES
    <module name list>|<empty>
```

141

Now let us turn our attention to the control linkage of each of the modules. Each module can potentially call one or more other modules. In turn, it can be called by a host of other modules. We would like to capture this data in the module specifications themselves. It is clear how we prepare the list of called modules. We need merely look through the module design algorithm section and identify all such calls. The real problem comes from identifying the calling modules. This is vital information yet it is not encapsulated very neatly in the module specification. It can only be obtained by inspection of the CALLED MODULES section of all other module specifications. As new modules are developed or even as existing modules are modified, it is possible that they will invoke multiple existing modules. We can either retrieve each of those modules one at a time to update their CALLED MODULES section or we can periodically run a simple software update routine that will perform this task for us. We must know, however, which modules might be impacted by any change to any other program module.

6.4.2 Data Section

Data can be obtained from the environment external to the module as arguments at the point of call. The only data that we choose to discuss at this point is scalar data. This data is atomic. We will have character data but no strings. Similarly, we will have decimal numbers but no arrays of these numbers. If we need strings, then our functional model and functionalities must define them and show how they will be manipulated. Then and only then can we talk about them as artifacts in our low-level design. Data can also be passed back to the external environment through arguments.

We declare variables in the module specification that are either parameters for receiving and transmitting data to the external environment or local variables that can be used to hold intermediate values used in computation. These variables are declared as elements of a parameter list or as local variables, as is shown in Table 6.2.

Table 6.2. The Data Section

```
VARIABLES
  PARAMETER_LIST
    <variable dcl> ::= <variable name>; <type> |
    <variable name>; <type> <CR><variable dcl> | <empty>
  LOCAL_VARIABLES
    <variable dcl> ::= <variable name>; <type> |
    <variable name>; <type> <CR><variable dcl> | <empty>
CONSTANTS
  <constant list>
```

Each variable in our design has a name. It is not really important how we choose to define this name. It would be useful, however, if the variable name somehow referred to its contents. If, for example, we have a variable that was to serve as a counter in a loop, it would be nice to call it Loop_Counter, or something equally obvious.

Now we get to the most important aspect of the design process and one that is totally ignored by modern design and programming language environments. The data must be precisely and accurately specified. To do so, we must specify the context from which the data will derive, the accuracy of this data, the range on which the specific variable is defined, and the scale of the variable. These notions are shown in Table 6.3.

A variable has a type attribute. For our purposes, there are two type attributes: numeric and character. Variables that have the character attribute are defined on a range of values corresponding to the values of the ASCII characters. Variables that have the numeric attribute can be either binary or decimal. People do not think in terms of binary number systems; computers do. Thus, if the numbers that we are manipulating in our algorithms are numbers that we obtained from the external people environment, then they are decimal numbers. A user might, for example, wish to compute the velocity of a rocket at various stages of its trajectory. The inputs to this calculation are clearly decimal values and the results are clearly decimal numbers. A bank teller will enter a decimal value for a customer's deposit to his or her account. The account will increase by a decimal value. If, on the other hand, the number represents the contents of a status register of some device in the computer, then the number is clearly a binary one. It has no sense in the decimal world. Memory addresses are yet another example of binary numbers. They are used in their binary context by a binary machine. Thus, those numbers that are intrinsic to the operation of a binary machine have the binary property and those numbers that are intrinsic to a human environment have the decimal property.

Table 6.3. Variable Attributes

```
<type>  ::= <numeric>  |  <character>
<numeric>  ::= Binary <number type>  |
  Decimal <number type>
<character>  ::= ASCII <range>
<number type>  ::= Whole <size>  |  Fractional <accuracy>
<accuracy>  ::= 1|2|...|n Digits Rounded  |  Truncated
<size>  ::= 1|2|...|n Digits
<scale>  ::= Nominal  |  Ordinal  |  Interval  |  Ratio
<range>  ::= [ <value>, <value> ]
```

There are some very disturbing concepts that we have inherited from our background in mathematics. We seem to believe that we are working with integer and real numbers in our programming language implementations. Nothing could be further from the truth. As any beginning math student is aware, the set of integers is infinite. The amount of memory that we have in our biggest computers is, of course, finite. Therefore, we will never be able to use integers on our computers. This creates some real problems. There are some mathematical constructs that have absolutely no direct implementation capabilities in the world of computing. The notion of factorials comes to mind immediately. The mathematical notion of $N!$ simply cannot be implemented in an algorithm for any reasonable value of N, say 1000. Furthermore, we do not have the concept of rational numbers on computers either. A rational number is simply the ratio of two integers. If we do not have integers, then we surely do not have rational numbers either. The set of real numbers is derived from the set of rational numbers through the square root function. If we do not have rational numbers in our computing environment, then it follows that we do not have real numbers either. In short, we cannot really do mathematics on our computers. We can play an approximate mathematical game, but it is only an approximation. It would put us in good stead to keep this notion on the forefront of our thinking when we are doing design.

In our years of experience in wading through untold stacks of fault reports (bug reports, internal anomaly reports, program trouble reports, or whatever), we have observed countless numbers of problems that have arisen from this very problem. Software engineers assume that they are working with real numbers when, in fact, they are working with a very small subset of rational numbers. Repetitive calculations create serious accuracy problems. Most software engineers are simply unaware of this problem. Their programming language leads them to believe that they are working with real numbers.

Thus, we eschew the notion of integer, rational, and real numbers in our design context. We have *whole* numbers and we have *fractional* numbers. Whole numbers are finite subsets of integers. They have no fractional part. Fractional numbers, on the other hand, are finite subsets of rational numbers. They do have fractional parts and possibly even whole parts. A whole number is represented as a signed or unsigned string of decimal or binary digits to wit: 192023 or 1101011001. A fractional number has a decimal or binary point as part of the number, to wit: 123.323, 0.234, 111.01001, or 0.11000111.

Whole numbers do not, of course, have decimal or binary points. They are exact numbers. As such, we must know in advance exactly how large (or small) these numbers might be. If a whole number is of binary type, then we need to know how many binary digits it takes to represent this number. If, on the other hand, the number is a decimal whole number, then we need to know how many decimal digits it takes to represent this decimal number. The number of digits necessary to represent the largest value in magnitude is therefore the *size* of the number.

Fractional numbers are not necessarily exact numbers. They represent approximations. A good example of this is the constant value of *pi* (π). The value 3 is an approximation for the value of *pi*. The value of 3.1 is a better approximation. The value of 3.1416 is an even better approximation. We can continue this process indefinitely. The real value of *pi* can, of course, never be represented precisely on a computer. Any calculations that we do with our approximate value of *pi* will yield approximate values as well. Thus, if we are to use fractional numbers in our calculations, we must constantly worry about the accuracy of our results. Each variable that is of number type fractional must specify the accuracy of the number that is to be kept in that variable. Accuracy will be specific in terms of decimal digits if the number is of type decimal, or binary digits if the number is of type binary.

Numerical accuracy can only decay as a result of computation. If, for example, we have a value in variable A that has been declared to be a fractional number with three digits of accuracy and it is added to a variable B that has been declared to be a fractional number of five digits of accuracy, the result of the sum of these two variables will have three places of accuracy. The accuracy of variable A is a limiting factor in this computation. We will never gain accuracy in any calculation; we can only lose it.

Another problem arises when we take the contents of one variable with, say, nine digits of accuracy and copy this value to another variable with fewer digits of accuracy, say seven. We lose two digits of accuracy in this translation. The real question is what we wish to do with the two digits in question. We can simply truncate them or we can analyze them to see if we should round the result. If the two digits to be thrown away are less than 50 in decimal, then we can discard them. If the two digits are greater than or equal to 50, then we would add one to the least significant digit of the receiving variable. In either case, whether we choose truncation or rounding, we must specify for each fractional number just exactly how values of greater accuracy should be treated when placed into any variable.

No engineer would ever consider using numbers in any calculation without some basic understanding of the accuracy of these numbers. This is just a matter of good engineering training and discipline. Unfortunately, this is not a matter of training for software engineers. In fact, modern computation environments such as C, C++, and Java actually hide these considerations of accuracy from the designer or developer. We must learn to compensate for the inadequacies in specification of these languages by ensuring that we have dealt effectively with them at the design stage.

145

The actual assignment of the numbers and symbols by the rules is determined by a *scale* of measurement. The term "scale" can be taken as the measuring instrument or the standard of measurement. It determines what operations among the numbers (symbols) assigned in a measurement will yield results significant for the particular attribute that is being measured. There are essentially two classes of these scales. There are scales of intensive (qualitative) and extensive (quantitative) measurement. Qualitative scales permit us to determine, at most, a degree of the relationship between two or more instances of an entity. Quantitative scales, on the other hand, permit us to answer questions of how much or how many.

The *nominal scale* is one where numbers (symbols) are assigned only as labels or names. The mappings on this scale are into mutually exclusive qualitative categories. An instance of the entity *automobile* can be perceived to belong to exactly one of the classes of *automobile manufacturer.* An instance of a *human being* has the gender property of *male* or *female*. Eye color and political affiliation are other examples of measures defined on a nominal scale.

Measures defined on nominal scales do not permit the use of arithmetic operators or relational operators. In this new age, one could get into serious trouble by presuming that males were in some sense better than females. Furthermore, the sum of two males is not a female. Sometimes, a number will be used to represent this assignment. For example, we might let a variable $x_1 = 0$ represent the observation that a particular instance of the entity person is a male. Similarly, we might also let $x_2 = 1$ represent the observation that a particular instance of the same entity is a female. It would not be politically correct (nor accurate) for us to present the fact that $x_1 < x_2$.

Sometimes, these nominal scales lurk in the guises of numbers. In particular is the case of social security numbers. This personal attribute is strictly nominal. That someone has a social security number less than mine carries no essential information. Similarly, the numerical difference between two such numbers has no meaning. This fact is lost on many computer analysts and programmers who employ numerical conversions on this nominal data.

The *partially ordered scale* orders some relatively homogeneous subset of objects. The movie rating scale (G, PG-13, PG, R, and X) is an example of such a scale. The assignment of movies to each of these groups largely depends on preference dictated by cultural imperatives. In the United States, it is thought that children should be shielded from aspects of human sexuality. The exposure of gratuitous violence to these same children is not thought to be important. Other, more pacific cultures might well accept human sexuality as quite normal and regard gratuitous violence as something from which to shield their children. These people would rate the very same movies that we have classified as X-rated as suitable for teenagers (PG-13) as long as these movies were free from violence. Similarly, the assignment of a person on the political scale of liberalism is very much a matter of perspective. A conservative politician to me might well be your view of a liberal renegade. It is also most unfortunate that this type of scale dominates the current standard for employee evaluation, the assessment of the worth of computer software, etc.

The *ordinal scale* provides for the numerical ordering of a set of objects, although this may be a weak ordering with the same number being assigned to two or more elements of the set. We generally associate this scale with the concept of ranking. With this scale it is possible to take a set of programs and rank them according to some criterion such as cost, performance, or reliability. The ordinal scale permits us to use the set of relational operators $\{<, \leq, =, \neq, \geq, >\}$ on the rank attributes of objects assigned values on an ordinal scale. Thus, it is possible to say that program A performs better than program B. Further, measures defined on this scale exhibit transitivity. Thus, if A > B, and B > C, then A > C.

What is lacking from the ordinal scale is some sense of the distance between objects of differing ranks. That is, if programmer A is the fifth-ranked programmer in our company, programmer B is the sixth-ranked programmer, and programmer C is the seventh-ranked programmer, the differences between A and B can be inconsequentially small, whereas the differences between B and C can be very large. If we are able to make such assertions that the differences between the sets of programmers are meaningful, then the scale is not just ordinal but constitutes an *ordered metric*. Not only are the objects ordered but also the intervals between them are at least partially ordered.

The *interval scale* is a scale that provides equal intervals from some arbitrary numerical point on the scale. An example of such a scale is the Fahrenheit (or Centigrade) temperature scale. Neither of these scales has an absolute zero point. While there is a $0°$ point on the Fahrenheit scale, a negative temperature does not represent the loss of anything and a positive temperature a gain in anything.

Interval scales do make use of the arithmetic operators of $\{+, -\}$. If the high temperature today is $60°$ and yesterday's high was $50°$, then I can assert with meaning that today it is $10°$ warmer that it was yesterday. As an aside, it is interesting to note that multiplicative relationships can be used on the sums (differences) of these same temperatures. Thus, the difference in temperature between $50°$ and $70°$ is twice as great as the difference between $50°$ and $60°$.

The *ratio scale*, on the other hand, does have an absolute zero point. The multiplying and exponentiation operators $\{\times, \div, \uparrow\}$ can be used with measures on this scale. It is also true that any of the relational operators and adding operators can also be used. A ratio scale, for example, can be used to define the amount of money in my bank account. In this case, there is real meaning to the statement that I have a –$50.00 in my account. I am overdrawn. I owe the bank $50.00. If I have a current balance of $500.00, then the bank owes me $500.00. Further, if someone else has $1000.00 in his account, then he has twice as much as I do. If another individual has $5,000.00 in her account, then she has an order of magnitude more money than I.

From a design perspective, any variable that has the nominal scale attribute can only be an operand to and of the operators of the set $\{=, \neq\}$. We can actually verify this in the algorithm section. Exactly the same case can be made for variables that have the ordinal, interval, and ratio attributes. By asserting that each variable is only an operand of the appropriate operator, we can eliminate an entire class of potential faults in the design.

Characters and character sets do not really exist at the computational level. They are really whole numbers. They become characters at the periphery of the computation environment. It would be destructive to our thinking to believe in characters at the design level. We have spent too many years of our lives trying to teach computer science students the difference between the decimal digit 0 and the ASCII character '0'. We must learn to deal with the ASCII character set only when we need to map from one set of numbers, say the ASCII digits '0' to '9' to the decimal numbers 0 through 9. If we really need ASCII characters, we can invent them in our functional model. It is difficult, however, to think of a computational circumstance when we would really need them. In the last analysis, characters are really *binary whole ordinal* values.

The final consideration in the Data Section of our module specification is the fact that all variables will be defined in a range of possible values. This range is a closed interval containing the smallest and the largest value that the variable might have. If, for example, we have a variable, Age, that contains the possible values for the age of a student at the university, then we might define age as: Age; Decimal, Whole 2 Digits, Interval, [15,80]. If the variable in question is intrinsically fractional, such as a temperature value obtained from a thermocouple that is accurate to four places, the variable would then be defined to be Temperature; Decimal, Fractional 4 Digits, Interval, [–3000E02, +.2000E03].

We have gone a very long way to the precise specification of numerical types. The real benefit this gives us is that we can now take steps to reduce the number of problems that will occur at runtime from the imprecise specification of variable attributes. At the time when each module is designed, we can now understand very precisely what the outcome of all of our data transformations in the algorithm section will be. Perhaps more importantly, we can identify potential overflow and underflow problems. If, for example, we add two four-digit whole numbers together, the result may well be five digits. If we attempt to replace either of the operands with the resulting sum (vis. a = a + b), we confront a possible overflow problem. Similarly, if we multiply these two whole numbers together, we could possibly get an eight-digit result. We would like very much to deal with these considerations at the design stage rather than to find them after deploying the software.

In the specification of each variable, we will define the range of values of the variable may be drawn. This permits us to put in place the necessary provisions in the source code to ensure that no values are placed into any variable that is outside the range for which that variable is defined. This is a vital consideration for ensuring the software reliability of safety- or mission-critical systems.

6.4.3 Algorithm Section

It is the stated purpose of each design module that it will transform or translate input data to output data. The functional process underlying this transformation is identified in the Algorithm Section of the module specification. Some algorithms tend toward being very complex and bushy. To aid in the understanding of the basic functionality of each module, we insist that there is a short description of the algorithm at the beginning of the Algorithm Sections as shown in Table 6.4.

In Table 6.5 there is a short grammar for the algorithm section. This is a very limited grammar. It contains the essentials for what one would need to outline a simple algorithm. It is intended to be a framework only. We would expect that in a more complex world, the rules of this grammar would be overly simple. We would rather err on the side of simplicity. In far too many cases the design grammar has become an end in itself. For our purposes, this grammar provides the essential control structure for an algorithm. It would be very nice if the simplicity of this grammar could be preserved. What beginning students do at this stage is to attempt to

Table 6.4. Algorithm Description

```
DESCRIPTION
    The description text should give a short but
    comprehensive description of the functionality of the
    module, i.e., start state, end state, how the data is
    transformed, etc.
```

Table 6.5. Simple Grammar for Algorithm

```
ALGORITHM
  <basic algorithm> ::= <entry> <statement_list> <return>
  <statement_list> ::= <statement> | <statement>
<statement_list>
  <statement> ::= <selection> | <biselection> | <loop>
|<block> | <call> |
    <sentence>
  <sentence> ::=
    |   Simple Prose .
  <selection> ::=
    |IF ( <sentence> )
    |         <statement list>
    |FI
  <biselection> ::=
    |IF ( <sentence> )
    |         <statement list>
    |ELSE
    |         <statement list>
    |FI

  <loop> ::= <top loop> | <bottom loop> | <perform loop>
  <top loop> ::=
    |LOOP <condition>
    |      <statement list>
    |POOL
  <bottom loop> ::=
    |LOOP
    |      <statement list>
    |POOL <condition >
  <perform loop> ::=
    |PERFORM <expression> TIMES
    |      <statement>
  <block> ::=
    |BEGIN
    |      <statement list>
    |NIGEB
  <call> ::=
    |CALL <module name> WITH { <argument list>}
       {PROTECTED<argument list>}
  <entry> ::=
    |ENTRY
  <return> ::=
    |RETURN
```

write C code, for example, as the design. We are not coding C as this stage. We are simply trying to define how the data will be transformed — that is all.

Statements in our simple grammar are simply sentences that describe unambiguously what we wish to do with the data. Each sentence ends with a period. If, for example, we wish to increment a counter, we will simply say, 'Increment counter A by one.' What could be simpler? We avoid constructs like A = A + 1, if for no other reason than it is really bad mathematics. There is no number A for which A and A + 1 are equal.

Some points are worth mentioning here. First, every algorithm begins with an ENTRY statement. It ends with a RETURN statement. There can be exactly one of each of these. These are the points that will connect to the module flowgraph. Each statement in our algorithm begins with at least one vertical bar, '|'. At every level of nesting we encounter another vertical bar. At first, this might seem like an onerous thing to do. It really serves as a valuable visual aid in understanding the design. One vertical bar in front of a statement means that we are at the initial module nesting level one. Three vertical bars mean that we are two levels in from the initial level. Call statements have associated argument lists. There are two types of arguments. The called module can alter some arguments. These arguments are listed first. Following the term 'PROTECTED' is another argument list. These arguments cannot be altered by the called module; they are read-only.

One of the primary objectives in the Algorithm Section is to capture the essential control structure of the algorithm. From this we can build a flowgraph that allows us to begin our essential measurement of the design complexity. To this end, there are simple IF statements and LOOP statements. In that counting loops are so common, a perform statement has been included. There are no case statements in our design language. In reality, there are no case statements in computers. Case statements are an artifact of the programming language environment. They are most easily misused. We would prefer nested IF statements to case statements. As it turns out, quite a few programming language constructs, such as case statements, contribute to the colossal overhead that is now an accepted standard for modern software development environments.

There is also no provision for any type of input or output mechanism. In reality, these are nothing more than subroutine calls. Again, it is in our interest to avoid system specific types of information in the design. At the design stage, we are manipulating the functional model and not the programming language or operating system model. We concern ourselves with that level of mapping once we understand the nature of the problem we are trying to solve.

Once the module specifications are complete for all modules, we can then perform a necessary and vital level of sanity checking. First, we have defined the formal parameters in each program module with a high level of specificity. We can identify from the Module Header those other design

151

modules that are going to invoke the current one. One by one, we need to visit these calling modules. Each of the arguments for the calling modules must agree exactly with its parameter counterparts in type, scale, and range. Next we need to ensure that all of the PROTECTED arguments from each of the program modules are protected parameters. That is, the protected parameters are those that precede the word "IN" in the formal parameter list.

The next stage of the sanity check is to verify that all variables are correctly matched with operations that are legitimate for the scale of each variable. If, for example, we have declared a variable to have a nominal scale attribute, then it can only be an operand of two operators, = and ≠. Further, a variable with a nominal scale attribute can only receive values from variables that also have the same nominal scale attribute.

The success of this design methodology is in no way contingent on the above algorithm structure or any of the specific structure of the design that has been articulated. It is merely a framework that establishes exactly what a low-level design module should contain. The focus should clearly be on the very precise definition of all variables and parameters that are used in the design, on the precise nature of the coupling among program modules, and the flowgraph structure of the design algorithm. It would be very easy to build a simple measurement tool that would be able to quantify these attributes of every program module. That, then, is the principal reason why the syntax for this design methodology is presented here. It meets the very basic requirement that we can build measurement tools that can quantify the important design attributes.

No provision has been made in the specification of the syntax for design modules for any type of data structure, yet it is difficult to imagine any application that can be easily designed using only scalar values, as is suggested by this design language. If arrays are needed for the application, then they must first appear in the architecture of a machine that will implement the design. Then the necessary syntax to implement the data structure must be integrated in the VARIABLES section of the design. It was not the purpose of the design template presented above to be a universal one. It was intended to be a framework that could be augmented to suit the needs of a particular application.

As new features and capabilities are added to the design syntax, the ultimate criterion is that the new syntax must be easily measured. That is, it should be relatively simple to design an algorithm to identify and measure new attributes that are added for additional data attributes, data structures, or even new control structures in the Algorithm Section. It is imperative that the measurement integrity of the design is preserved in this augmentation process. The very worst thing that could happen to our design language is that it would suffer from the inevitable feature creep

Table 6.6. Module Definition

```
Header Section
  HEADER
    PARAMETERS
    CALLED MODULES
    CALLING MODULES
Data Section
  VARIABLES
    PARAMETER_LIST
    LOCAL_VARIABLES
  CONSTANTS
Algorithm Description Section
  DESCRIPTION
Algorithm Section
  ALGORITHM
```

that has overtaken just about every other enterprise in the software business. The design language should be parsimonious. It should only do exactly what is necessary to define the problem at hand.

6.5 The Elements of a Module Specification

We can now summarize the elements of a module definition. These are shown in Table 6.6. In essence, a module definition consists of four parts. First is the header section that describes the control and data interface to other modules. Next, the attributes of each datum are described in the data section.

The module definition shown in Table 6.6 is not complete. Chapter 7 discusses the binding between each module and the functionalities that use it. Our focus in this chapter is strictly on the module as an entity. These entities will be woven into a fabric of functionalities through their relationships with specific elements of these functionalities.

6.6 Module Call Graph Structure

Once we have built the module specification for each module, we can clearly model the interaction of each module with its immediate neighbors. We know exactly which module calls another module and those modules that call it. The existence of this call graph structure serves to eliminate one of the most trying of software maintenance problems — that is, when the functionality of a module is changed, any module that invokes the change module will be impacted by the change. The module call graph structure is a graphical image of the system showing the call-return binding of the program modules. Each module, represented by a node in the graph, is connected to each called module by an arc in the graph. From this graph, the relationship among calling modules is easily observed.

The overall structure of an evolving design can be seen in its call graph structure. Each module represents one node in this graph and each call represents one edge in this graph. We represent the call graph as a directed graph. A call graph of a program is constructed from a directed graph representation of the program module that can be defined as follows:

- A directed graph, $G = (N, E, s)$, consists of a set of nodes N, a set of edges E, and a distinguished node s, the start node. An edge is an ordered pair of nodes (a, b) representing a call from module a to module b.
- The in-degree $I(a)$ of node a is the number of entering edges to a.
- The out-degree $O(a)$ of node a is the number of exiting edges from a.
- There is a unique start node s such that $I(s) = 0$.

It is clear that some modules are more tightly woven into the fabric of the program control structure than others are. If, for example, the out-degree of a module is zero, then this module is a leaf node in the graph. It is, in essence, a control sink. It simply passes control back to any calling module. If the in-degree of this module is very high, then it can potentially be used by a large number of other modules. If this module is flawed in its logic, then it can potentially contaminate all the modules that invoke it. From a design standpoint, one of the very worst module architectures that can be created is a module whose in-degree and out-degree are both very high. This structure is analogous to a highway network with an intersection of multiple highways at one point. It creates a traffic nightmare. As we learn to measure aspects of design in Chapter 9, we can quantify the effects of this design decision.

Looking ahead into the measurement aspects of the design, we can enumerate all of the nodes and edges of the call graph. Clearly, the call graph structure becomes more labyrinthine as the ratio of edges to nodes rises during the design process. Design modules whose in-degree is very large are probably good candidates for examination. The degree of control complexity reflected by their control binding to a large number of modules makes for serious maintainability problems. Also, modules whose out-degree is very large are also candidates for examination.

A path within the call graph will be a sequence of edges $\langle \overrightarrow{a_1 a_2}, \overrightarrow{a_2 a_3}, \ldots, \overrightarrow{a_{n-1} a_n} \rangle$ where all a_i ($I = 1, \ldots, n$) are elements of N. P is a path from node a_1 to node a_n. If a module a_i is recursive, then there is a path $\langle a_i a_i \rangle$. This path is a loop. If a module a_i is a member of an indirectly recursive set of modules, then there is a path that begins at a_i and ends at a_i to wit: $\langle a_i a_j, a_j a_k, \ldots, a_l a_i \rangle$. This path is a cycle.

Most modern programming language environments make provisions for recursion and indirection recursion in their runtime environments. The overwhelming number of application programs written in these languages do not avail themselves of either of these two features. The result is that every one of the nonrecursive applications pays an enormous runtime penalty because the developers used a programming language environment that had the capability. This is rather analogous to our buying a huge pickup with a large engine to take the kids to school and go back and forth to work. This vehicle is a horrible mismatch for the manner in which it will be used. It is an egregious mistake to use a programming language runtime environment that expects program modules to have the ability to do recursion when, in fact, they never will.

If we accept the fact that a program that we have just designed does not intentionally use either direct or indirect recursion, then it is a simple matter to test the call graph representation of this design for loops and cycles. If a cycle is detected, this is definitely a problem in the design. It is also a problem that occurs relatively frequently in modern software systems, in that there is no formal mechanism to check for this type of anomaly.

It is a characteristic of the basic architecture of the design that a particular user operational profile will assign a frequency of execution to each module. We exploit this fact to measure the module execution profiles. While it is not possible to assign execution times to each module with any degree of reliability, we can certainly measure transitions from one module to the next. Each of the transitions from one module to the next is a module ***epoch***.

In Figure 6.1 we can see a hypothetical program consisting of 11 modules. These are connected with edges reflecting the transfer of control from one module to another. Even in this very small example we can see that the total number of paths in the control structure is very large. If, for example, we examine the set of paths that begins on module 1, there are 25 such paths in this call graph. The actual paths are shown in Table 6.7. It is quite clear that a poorly designed program of 100,000 modules will have an astonishingly large number of paths among the modules.

While there are 25 potential paths beginning at module 1 in the call graph shown in Figure 6.1, it is quite probable that many of these paths simply cannot execute based on the data that might appear on the functionality interfaces. It is possible to identify a subset of modules that represents a ***feasible path set*** from any module in the call graph. This set consists of those paths that might occur based on predicate clauses in the modules. Unfortunately, while this is an interesting concept, it will be very difficult to establish with any degree of precision the elements of the feasible path set. For all practical purposes, the actual operations performed by the user of the system will determine the operational path set. The ***operational path set*** is the set of those paths that we can actually measure as having occurred when the program is executing a particular operational profile.

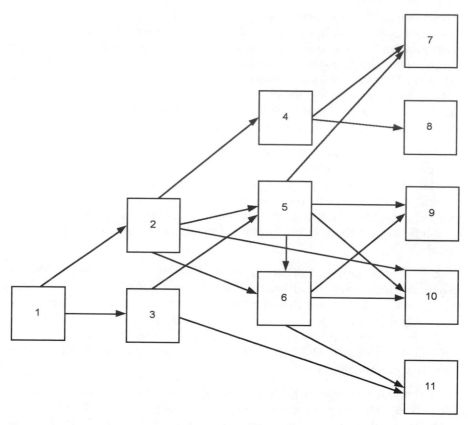

Figure 6.1. Hypothetical program structure.

Table 6.7. Paths in the Flowgraph

1–2	1–2–4	1–2–4–8	1–2–5	1–2–5–7
1–2–5–9	1–2–5–10	1–2–5–6	1–2–5–6–9	1–2–5–6–10
1–2–5–6–11	1–2–6	1–2–6–9	1–2–6–10	1–2–6–11
1–3	1–3–5	1–3–5–7	1–3–5–9	1–3–5–10
1–3–5–6	1–3–5–6–9	1–3–5–6–10	1–3–5–6–11	1–3–11

The notion of a path and the transfer of control up and down this path is somewhat of a mathematical abstraction. The operational structure of these paths is vastly different from the mathematical notion of a path in a flowgraph. Take, for example, the 1–2–4–7 path from Table 6.7. Assume that the call to module 4 from module 2 is located in a loop within module 2. Further assume that module 7 will be called only when some contingency arises in module 7. The actual path from module 1 to module 7

156

might well look something like this: 1–2–4–2–4–2–4–2–4–2-4–2–4-2–4-2–4-2–4–2–4–2–4–2–4–2–4–2–4–2–4–2–4–7. The path from module 1 to module 7 is not a length of 3 arcs; it is really of length 37. This is an example of the functional distance between module 1 and module 7 in one instance of execution and not the minimum distance. In fact, the length of the 1–2–4–7 path may vary substantially. Therefore, we should really think of this path length in statistical terms. Perhaps the best way to characterize each path length, then, is in terms of the mean path length and the variance of that path length.

6.7 Module Profiles

The manner in which a program exercises its many modules as the user chooses to execute the functionalities of the program is determined directly by the design of the program. Indeed, this mapping of functionality onto program modules is the overall objective of the design process. The module profile p is the unconditional probability that a particular module will be executed based on the design of the program. Let X be a random variable defined on the indices of the set of elements of M, the set of program modules. Then, $p_k = \Pr[X = j]$, $j = 1, 2, \ldots, \|M\|$ is the unconditional probability that the user is executing program module k as specified in the functional requirements of the program and $\|M\|$ is the cardinality of the set of functionalities. The problem is that the module profile is not known. We can, however, determine the conditional probability of execution of a module, $u_{jk} = \Pr[X_n = j | Y = k]$. It can be observed by causing each of the functionalities to execute.

The joint probability that a given module is executing and the program is exercising a particular function is given by:

$$\Pr[X_n = j \cap Y = k] = \Pr[Y = k]\Pr[X_n = j | Y = k] = q_k u_{jk}$$

where j is the index of the module and k is the index of the functionality. Thus, the unconditional probability p_i of executing module j under a particular design is:

$$p_i = \Pr[X_n = i]$$

$$= \sum_k \Pr[X_n = i \cap Y = k]$$

$$= \sum_k q_k u_{ik}$$

As was the case for the functional profile and the operational profile, only one event, in this case a module, can be executing at any one time. Hence, the distribution of p is also multinomial for a system consisting of more than two modules.

It is clear that p_i depends on the functional profile. The functional profile, in turn, depends on the operational profile. Remember that

$$q_i = \sum_l o_l w_{il}$$

and that

$$p_i = \sum_k q_k u_{ik}.$$

It follows, then, that

$$p_i = \sum_k u_{ik} \sum_l o_l w_{kl}.$$

It is completely clear now that the behavior of a system directly depends on how the system will be deployed. After all, the operational profile is a direct reflection of how a user distributes his or her activities across the set of operations.

Just as we did with the operational and the functional profile, we can characterize a design *module* profile as a single point in a $k-1$ dimensional space where k is the cardinality of the set of modules. It is, in fact, the centroid in a range of possible departures from the design module profile. That is, each user will use the system in a slightly different manner. Each user will have a slightly different operational profile represented by a different point. Because of the dependency of the module profile on the operational profile, this, in turn, will also mean that there will be some variation in the module profile of a system across a number of users. Let L^p represent the design module profile. Each user will induce a slightly different behavior on the functional machine represented by a module profile, say L^u. Each of the module profiles is, again, a point in a $k-1$ dimensional space. It is possible to compute the distance in this $k-1$ dimensional space between the two points representing a user's actual module and the design module profile as

$$d = \sum_{i=1}^{k} \left(l_i^p - l_i^u \right)^2,$$

where $l_i^p \in L^p$, $l_i^u \in L^u$, and k represents the number of modules. Again, it is also true that $0 \le d \le 2$.

In that no two users will use the system in exactly the same way, it is necessary to understand the distribution of the distances, d. Let d_i represent the distance between a particular module profile for user, i, and the design module profile. We can then talk about the average distance

$$\bar{d} = \frac{1}{m} \sum_i d_i$$

for a group of m users and the variance of this distance across all users

$$Var(d) = \frac{1}{(m-1)} \sum_i (d_i - \bar{d})^2.$$

Just as was the case for the set of user operations and functionalities, we can speak to the issue of the latency of each of the modules. As we get closer to the actual machine that will be running the user operations, we are in a better position to understand and model these latencies. We recall that the latency of each operation is $\lambda_i = l(o_i)$. Each operation is implemented through one or more of the functionalities. Thus, it is clear that there is a functional dependency between the latencies of the functionalities and those of the operations.

Let $v_j = l(m_j)$ represent the latency of a module j. It is clear that v_i is an expected value for the functional latency to wit:

$$v_i = \sum_{j=1}^{k} v_j \Pr\left(m_j \mid f_i\right).$$

Just as was the case for the operational and the functional latency of a system, we can speak to the first two moments about the mean of the module latency. The first statistic we can develop is the expected value for the module latency of the system under a module profile $\boldsymbol{p}$. This is

$$E(v) - \sum_i p_i v_i,$$

where $p_i = \Pr(X = i)$. The variance of the module latency then under the functional profile, $\boldsymbol{p}$, is

$$Var(v) = \sum_i p_i v_i^2 - E(v)^2 = \sum_i p_i v_i^2 - \left(\sum_i p_i v_i\right)^2.$$

From a performance standpoint, if a system is experiencing performance problems, another very good place to look for improvement would be on those functionalities where $p_i v_i$ is very large. In fact, if we were to sort the $p_i v_i$ from largest values to smallest, we would be able to identify potential performance problems in the software system based on its actual usage. As was the case for functionalities, it does not necessarily matter that a particular module is slow. What really matters is that it does not get used frequently.

6.8 The Evolution of the Module Specifications

The module specifications can be expected to evolve in the same manner as the operational and functional specifications. It is difficult to impossible to understand a system completely at the beginning of development. For very large systems, the development process will necessarily be incremental. Each increment adds increasing complexity to the evolving system design. This means that the degree of churn for module specifications at the low-level design stage will be very high. Maintaining an accurate description of the functional machine represented by the high-level design element, the functionalities, the low-level design elements, and the modules will be a very complex task. However, the accurate description of this self-same system is vital to the software development and testing processes.

There is but one type of document that must be managed under some type of configuration control for the modules. As each module evolves, there will be new versions of each of these documents — one for each program module. Again, the design process at the functional level is a particularly dynamic one. It is clear, then, that the documents that describe the functional machine will be very fluid.

We will use the same methodology to reference the set of modules that we developed for the set of operations and functionalities. The same notion of the use of a module index vector μ that will maintain the versioning data on each of the operations will work just as well with the set of modules. The elements μ_i of the functionality index vector represent the version number of the ith modules of the system. The length of the vector μ represents the number of modules that have ever been elements of the system. The length of μ might be much larger than the number of current modules in the system if there has been substantial code churn.

As was the case with the operations and functionalities, there will be a distinct point in the evolution of the modules, called a build, that associates all current modules and their current versions into an entity. There will be multiple builds of the system, sometimes on a daily basis. Typically, a build point is established when the current versions of program source code modules are collected, compiled, and linked into a system. It is conceivable that the low-level design modules will exist well in advance of the source code modules. Therefore, the builds of the low-level design modules will be motivated by a desire to understand the current nature of the functional abstract machine at various points in the evolution of the design of this machine.

The system defined by one build of the set of current module specifications reflects exactly one state of the module index vector μ. This permits the unambiguous interpretation of the functional system that is reflected in the current build of the modules that constitute the low-level design.

The build points of the module specifications are identified with the nomenclature $\mu^{(k)}$ for the kth build of the module specifications. As was the case with the functionality build, the builds of the module specifications occur with the builds of the system source code as the system matures. Thus, $M^{(k)}$ identifies the set of modules at the kth build of the system.

Just as was the case with the operations, each build of the system represents a new build in the module specifications. This fact also has implications in the module profile. As was the case for the functionalities, we should note that the modules profiles of the sets of modules associated with two sequential builds, $M^{(k)}$ and $M^{(k+1)}$, are not necessarily comparable, particularly in the case where the cardinality of $M^{(k)} \cap M^{(k+1)}$ is less than the cardinality of either $M^{(k)}$ or $M^{(k+1)}$.

6.9   An Example

We now extend the `calc` example developed in Chapters 3 and 4 to the low-level design. The first thing we turn our attention to is the nature of the architecture that we will use to describe the problem at this level of design. Then we implement a simple example of a design module that implements the addition of two signed decimal numbers.

6.9.1   Architectural Overview

The machine we need for this application must be capable of nine-digit arithmetic. Communication with the outside environment will be in character form. The machine will have explicit instructions to convert character strings containing decimal numbers to an internal decimal format. It must also be able to input and output character strings that come and go from an Input/Output register. Decimal numbers will be represented internally as signed normalized nine-digit decimal values as integers. The placement of an implied decimal point will be held in a separate register as a scale value. The contents of the I/O register will be interrogated under program control to determine whether a decimal number (operand) or a character representing an operation is present. This is an event-driven machine. That is, it will sit quiescent until either an operator or operand appears in the I/O register. After the contents of this register have been analyzed under program control, a result will be placed back in the I/O register by the program that will then return to its quiescent state.

6.9.2   Architectural Model

For the simple example of the decimal calculator, there is no need for a very complicated machine. It must have minimal provisions for decimal number representation and also for ASCII characters. Decimal numbers will be represented in a normalized scaled form. That is, each decimal number will contain a sign digit, either a 0 for a positive or a 1 for a negative

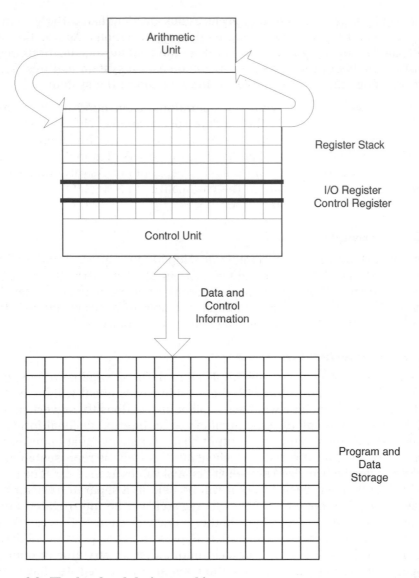

Figure 6.2. The low-level design machine.

number, nine positions for decimal number values from 0 through 9, a single digit for the sign of the exponent or scale factor, and a single position for a decimal digit representing the scale factor for the number. This permits the computer to maintain 10,000,000,000 distinct numbers in each decimal location. In addition to the decimal number representation, there is the ability to represent the set of ASCII values in memory locations that are designated to hold individual characters. This basic architecture of this simple machine is shown in Figure 6.2.

Communication with the outside world will be through a single I/O register. This register holds a total of 12 ASCII digits. When the user enters a command or a number, the result of this action appears in the I/O register. Control is then transferred to the calculator program. If the contents of the I/O represent an operand, the program displaces the contents of the current stack, pushing all values on the stack down and replacing the first stack entry with the contents of the I/O register. Thus, the machine must have a stack push-down capability. If the contents of the I/O register represent an operator, the appropriate module causes the operation to be performed.

There is an Arithmetic Unit that performs the necessary calculator operations. The Arithmetic Unit retrieves the contents of the top two decimal registers from the stack for each binary arithmetic operation. For unary operations, it retrieves only the top register from the stack. The topmost number is the left operand for each operation. The contents of the second stack location constitute the right operand for each operation. The result is placed in the first stack location. The contents of the remaining stack advance one location. Thus, the contents of the third location replace the second location. The contents of the fourth location replace the third. The fourth register position is set to a decimal zero.

The Arithmetic Unit is sent a single character to a single character operation register under program control to initiate its activity. The acceptable operations and their associated character values are addition (+), subtraction (–), multiplication (*), and division (%). After the completion of the arithmetic operation, the Arithmetic Unit displays one of two values in its operation register. If the operation results in a decimal value whose exponent can be represented by a single decimal digit, the register will contain a 0 for a correct operation. In the event that the exponent is outside the range of a single decimal digit, the register will contain a 1, representing either an underflow or overflow during the arithmetic operation. In this circumstance, the Arithmetic Unit returns a decimal zero to the top register of the stack.

At the completion of each user operation, the contents of the first stack register are converted from the decimal format to an ASCII string of ten digits. This ASCII string is then placed into the I/O register.

Program activity is initiated when the user creates data for interpretation of the system. This data is placed in the I/O register and the program is given control. When data is placed back in the I/O register at the completion of an operation, the system returns to its quiescent state. Similarly, when a decimal value is retrieved from the I/O register and placed on the stack, the program then enters its quiescent state.

The individual positions in the decimal number format of the top register stack are individually addressable. This means that the sign can be interrogated as a single entity, as can every one of the decimal digits.

Table 6.8. Decomposition of Modules

Functionality	Description	Decomposition
f_1	System initialization	Program initialization Program termination
f_2	Accept string and convert	Decode the I/O register contents Check and validate the register contents for correct operators and valid decimal numbers
f_3	Send error message	Perform error analysis
f_4	Get string from OS	Initiate read operation
f_5	Put string to OS	Initial write operation
f_6	Do arithmetic	Determine arithmetic option Add operation Subtract operation Multiply operation Divide operation Perform error analysis of result
f_7	Manipulate stack	Duplicate top of stack and push back on the stack Retrieve the top of the stack Retrieve all stack entries
f_8	Convert decimal number to ASCII string	Reformat decimal number for display

6.9.3 The Modules

We can now begin the process of decomposition of the functionalities into a set of program modules. The resulting decomposition of the modules is shown in Table 6.8 with a brief description of the functional decomposition. In a more realistically sized system, each of the modules would be very much larger and richer in behavior. However, the purpose of this exercise is to show the decomposition process.

After sketching the process of functional decomposition, the new functional sub-components can then be structured into program modules, as shown in Table 6.9.

6.9.4 A Sample Module Description

In Table 6.10 there is a sample program module. This module causes the Arithmetic Unit to add two numbers. It then retrieves the result from the

Table 6.9. The Low-Level Design Modules

Module	Description
m_1	Program initialization
m_2	Program termination
m_3	Decode the I/O register contents
m_4	Check and validate the register contents for correct operators and valid decimal numbers
m_5	Error analysis routine
m_6	Read new keyboard input
m_7	Write to display
m_8	Select arithmetic option
m_9	Do addition operation
m_{10}	Do division operation
m_{11}	Do multiplication operation
m_{12}	Do division operation
m_{13}	Duplicate top of stack
m_{14}	Get top of stack
m_{15}	Get all stack entries
m_{16}	Convert decimal number to ASCII string

first decimal stack location and the character value from the operation register. The character result value from the Arithmetic Unit and the contents of the top register are sent to the calling select_operation as output parameters.

While this represents a relatively simple program module, it does serve well to show the basic structure of the module. It is called by a module named select_operation and will return the result of the computation to select_operation. It is worth noting that the range on which the result parameter is defined is in exponential notation. This is so because the decimal point in the result can float from the rightmost position to the leftmost position in the number.

In the Algorithm Section, the use of the vertical bars to indicate the level of nesting of program constructs considerably simplifies the visual representation of the algorithm. It is very easy to know the level of nesting of any sentence in this section.

Table 6.10. Sample Design Module

```
HEADER add_module
  PARAMETERS
    result, error OUT
  CALLED MODULES
  CALLING MODULES
    select_operation

VARIABLES
  PARAMETER_LIST
    result Decimal Fractional 9 Digits
      Rounded Ratio [-.999999999E+9,+.999999999E+9]
    error Decimal Whole 1 Digits
  LOCAL_VARIABLES
```

DESCRIPTION

This program module will accept two signed decimal numbers as parameters. It will first adjust the numbers so that they have the same scale values. It will add the two numbers. Finally, it will check the scale values of the result to ensure that the scale is greater than or equal to zero and less than or equal to 17. If the scale is within this range the sum will be placed in the result register and the ASCII value 'c' will be placed in the error indication.

If the scale of the sum is outside of the range, then a zero will be placed in the result variable and an ASCII 'e' will be placed in the error indication variable. The argument data will be assumed to be accurate and valid decimal numbers in the correct format.

ALGORITHM

```
| ENTRY
|
|     send a '+' operator to the Arithmetic Unit
|     get operation code from the Arithmetic Unit
|   | IF  the operation code is a 'c'
|   |    copy the first stack location to result
|   |    copy a 0 to error
|   | ELSE
|   |     copy a 1 to error
|   | FI
|
| RETURN
```

Chapter 7
Mapping the Operations to Modules

7.1 Introduction

From an engineering perspective, the design process proceeds in a two-step process. First, the user operational environment is mapped onto a functional environment. In this process, each operation of the operational model is mapped onto one or more of the functionalities of the functional model in the functional environment. This constitutes the high-level design process. During this phase there is a very high degree of interaction between the designers of the operational model and the designers of the functional model.

Once the architecture of the functional model is fairly well established, it is then possible to decompose each of the functional elements into its algorithmic constituents. This process is perhaps the most involved of all of the design stages. Each of the functionalities will animate a particular aspect of the functional model. That is clear. What is not so clear, from a program perspective, is just how this is done. A particular functionality, for example, might require a numerical result from an analytical engine. The precise nature of the inputs to this analytical process and the outputs from the process are quite well known. What is not known at this high level are the precise numerical formulae and the mathematical computation that must be performed to obtain the desired result. That level of detail emerges only in the detailed, low-level design process.

7.2 $F \times M$

At the stage of low-level design, each of the functionalities of the high-level design is decomposed into algorithmic units. Thus, the low-level software design process is basically a matter of identifying algorithmic components, or modules, for each functionality f, where $f \in F$. Each of the functionalities is partitioned into a set of design modules. The complete set of design

Table 7.1. Example of the ASSIGNS Relation

$F \times M$	m_1	m_2	m_3	m_4	m_5	m_6	m_7	m_8
f_1	T	T						
f_2	T		T		T			T
f_3	T		T	T	T	T		
f_4	T		T		T	T	T	

modules for all the functionalities is the set M. It is quite likely that many of these design modules will be incorporated in multiple functionalities.

The low-level design process, then, can be thought of as the process of defining a set of relations, ASSIGNS over $F \times M$, such that ASSIGNS(f, m) is true if module m is employed to express functionality f. Table 7.1 shows an example of the ASSIGNS relation for the four functionalities presented in Table 5.1. In this example we can see that the functionality f_1 has been implemented in the design modules m_1 and m_2.

An inspection of Table 7.1 shows that the design modules have some interesting properties with respect to the functionalities. One of these modules, m_1, will be invoked regardless of the functionality. It is common to all functionalities. Other program modules, such as m_2, are distinctly associated with a single functionality. Still other design modules, such as module m_6, can be used in some subset of the functionalities.

Not every design module is employed every time a particular functionality is invoked. They may or may not be needed for the expression of that functionality. Thus, it is a property of a design module that it can be conditionally employed in the expression of a functionality. For each module $m \in M$, there is a relation p over $F \times M$ such that $p(f, m)$ is the proportion of execution events that will involve m when the system is executing function f.

In Table 7.2 there is an example of the relation p. These numbers represent the likelihood that each of the program modules will execute

Table 7.2. Example of the p Relation

$p(f, m)$	m_1	m_2	m_3	m_4	m_5	m_6	m_7	m_8
f_1	1	1	0	0	0	0	0	0
f_2	1	0	1	0	1	0	0	1
f_3	1	0	1	1	0.2	0.3	0	0
f_4	1	0	1	0	1	1	1	0

when a particular functionality is invoked. Table 7.2 represents the proportion of time distributed across each of the six hypothetical program modules. We can see, for example, that $p(f_1, m_1) = 1$. This means that whenever functionality f_1 is invoked, module m_1 will always be executed. On the other hand, we can observe that $p(f_3, m_5) = 0.2$. In this case, there is a relatively low chance that module m_5 will execute given that functionality f_2 has been invoked.

As a system is being designed, it is vital the p relation for that system be developed. Each of the $p(f_i, m_j)$ should be determined as part of the design. These values ultimately constitute the prior probabilities of program code module execution in the final program. They are our best guess as to how the system will be used. After the system has been built and is operating according to specification, we can collect execution data on its actual operating characteristics to validate that the design p relation is accurately reflected in the operation of the system.

There is a relationship between the design functionalities and the modules assigned to those modules. These design modules are assigned to one of three distinct sets of modules that, in turn, are subsets of M. Some modules can be assigned to all of the functionalities of the design; this will be the set of common modules M_c. In a typical program, the main program module is an example of such a module that is common to all operations of the software system. On the other hand, there is a set of modules M_B that is invoked only in response to the execution of one or more functionalities. It is clear, then, that $M_F = M - M_c$.

The set of common modules $M_c \subset M$ is defined as those modules that have the property:

$$M_c = \{m : M \mid \forall f \in F \bullet \text{ASSIGNS(f,m)}\}$$

All these modules will execute, regardless of the specific functionality being executed by the software system.

Another set of software modules may or may not execute when the system is running a particular function. These modules are said to be "potentially involved modules." The set of potentially involved modules for a functionality is:

$$M_p^{(f)} = \{m : M_F \mid \exists f \in F \bullet \text{ASSIGNS}(f,m) \wedge 0 < p(f,m) < 1\}$$

In other program modules, there is extremely tight binding between a particular functionality and a set of program modules. That is, every time a particular function f is executed, a distinct set of software modules will always be invoked. These modules are said to be "indispensably involved" with the functionality f. This set of indispensably involved modules for a particular functionality f is the set of those modules having the property that:

169

$$M_i^{(f)} = \{m : M_F \mid \forall f \in F \bullet \text{ASSIGNS}(f,m) \Rightarrow p(f,m) = 1\}$$

As a direct result of the design of the program, there will be a well-defined set of program modules M_f that might be used to express all aspects of a given functionality f. These are the modules that have the property that:

$$m \in M_f = M_p^{(f)} \cup M_i^{(f)}$$

From the standpoint of software design, the real problems in understanding the dynamic behavior of a system are not necessarily attributable to the set of modules M_i that are tightly bound to a functionality or to the set of common modules M_c that will be invoked for all executing processes. The real problem is the set of potentially invoked modules M_p. The greater the cardinality of this set of modules, the less certain we may be about the behavior of a system performing that function. For any one instance of execution of this functionality, a varying number of the modules in M_p can execute.

For each functionality $f \in F$, there exists a relation c over $F \times M$ such that $c(f, m)$ defines the cardinality of the set of functionalities that can invoke a given module. The c relation can be used to partition the set of program modules into two distinct sets. One set contains the modules associated exclusively with one and only one functionality. This is the set of uniquely related modules M_u, where

$$M_u = \{m : M \mid f \in F, c(f,m) = 1\}$$

The second set contains the modules that might be executed by more than one functionality; that is, the set of shared modules M_s to wit:

$$M_s = \{m : M \mid f \in F \bullet c(f,m) > 1\}$$

There are two distinct ways, then, that we can view program modules associated with functionalities. First, given a functionality, we can characterize each module as indispensably associated with that functionality or potentially associated with it. Second, each program module may or may not be uniquely associated with a given functionality. These two different module classifications are shown in Table 7.3.

A functionality is, by definition, required to have at least two modules and at least one of them is an element of the set of uniquely related modules and not of the set of potentially involved modules. That is, $f_i \in F$ if:

$$\left\| \{ m : M^{f_i} \mid \exists m_j \in M_u \wedge m_j \in M_i \} \right\| > 1$$

Table 7.3. Module Classification

Among Functionalities	Within a Functionality
Unique	Indispensable
Shared	Potential

If each program module is distinctly associated with a single functionality, then the dynamic behavior of a system can be readily understood and modeled. The two sets M_i and M_s are tightly bound to a distinct functionality. The real problem resides in the set of shared modules M_s, and it increases in severity if those modules also belong to M_p. The greater the cardinality of the set of potentially executable modules, the more difficult the task of determining the behavior of a system performing that functionality. In the extreme case, a functionality could express essentially disjoint sets of modules every time it is executed. (Many programs demonstrate this characteristic and they are extremely difficult to test.)

It is clear that each functionality will exercise a certain subset of modules. To return to our example, we can see from Table 7.4 that functionality f_1 does invoke two modules, m_1 and m_2. Both of these modules are indispensable to the execution of functionality f_1. Module m_1 is shared with all other functionalities. Module m_2 is uniquely associated with functionality f_1. In this table we also see that functionality f_3 has some interesting properties. The set $M_p^{(f_3)}$ is non-empty in this case. Whenever we exercise f_3, we can execute from three to five modules. It will be difficult to test this functionality in relation to all other functionalities. Sometimes it will execute module m_5 and sometimes it will not. Sometimes it will execute module m_6 and sometimes it will not. Sometimes it will execute both modules and sometimes it will not.

Sometimes it is desirable to know what functionality is executing at any given moment. We have built a system that will make such a deduction very difficult. For example, if we have just observed the execution of module m_1, we cannot deduce which functionality we are executing. Similarly, there is an equivalent problem with module m_3. There is somewhat

Table 7.4. Modules Associated with Functionalities

	$M_i^{(f)}$	$M_p^{(f)}$	$M_s^{(f)}$	$M_u^{(f)}$
f_1	$\{m_1, m_2\}$	$\{\}$	$\{m_1\}$	$\{m_2\}$
f_2	$\{m_1, m_3, m_5, m_8\}$	$\{\}$	$\{m_1, m_3, m_5\}$	$\{m_8\}$
f_3	$\{m_1, m_3, m_4\}$	$\{m_5, m_6\}$	$\{m_1, m_3, m_5, m_6\}$	$\{m_4\}$
f_4	$\{m_1, m_3, m_5, m_6, m_7\}$	$\{\}$	$\{m_1, m_3, m_5, m_6\}$	$\{m_7\}$

more information in the observation of the execution of module m_6. If we have just observed this module execute, then we know that we are executing either f_3 or f_4. The case for module m_2 is very different. Whenever we see this module executing, we know for a fact that we are now executing functionality f_1.

7.3 $O \times F \times M$

Now let us return to the problem of operations. Users see and perform operations. Functionalities will manipulate the functional machine to implement the set of user operations. From the relationships defined in Chapter 5, we can show the relationship between user operations and specific functionalities that will be exercised in response to a user invoking a particular operation. That is, each operation is implemented by a specific set of functionalities. These functionalities, in turn, invoke a specific set of modules when they are executed. Thus, for each operation o, we can identify a set of program modules that is associated with the expression of that operation at runtime.

Each operation is distinctly expressed by a set of functionalities. If a particular operation o is defined by functionalities a and b, then the set of program modules that are bound to operation o is:

$$M^{(o)} = M^{(f_a)} \cup M^{(f_b)}$$

More generally,

$$M^{(o)} = \bigcup_{i=1}^{n} M^{(f_i)}$$

If one operation is to be distinguished from another, then there must be certain aspects of its implementation in functionalities that will be unique. For an operation to be considered distinct, it will be required to have at least one distinct functionality. That is, $o_i \in O$ if the set of distinct functionalities $F_d^{(o_i)}$ is defined as follows:

$$F_d^{(o_i)} = \{f : F^{(o_i)} \mid \forall j \neq i \bullet \text{IMPLEMENTS}(o_j, f) \Rightarrow p'(o_j, f) = 0\}$$

has cardinality greater than one.

If we insist that each operation has at least one distinct functionality, then it is possible to identify a set of modules for each operation that is uniquely associated with that operation. This set of modules for operation o_i is:

$$M_u^{(o_i)} = \{m : M \mid f \in F^{(o_i)}, c(f, m) = 1\}$$

172

Table 7.5. Modules Associated with Operations

	$M_i^{(o)}$	$M_p^{(o)}$	$M_s^{(o)}$	$M_u^{(o)}$
o_1	$\{m_1, m_3, m_5, m_8\}$	$\{m_2\}$	$\{m_1, m_3, m_5\}$	$\{m_2, m_8\}$
o_2	$\{m_1, m_3, m_5, m_6, m_7\}$	$\{\}$	$\{m_1, m_3, m_5\}$	$\{m_3, m_4, m_6, m_7\}$

When a program is executing a module m where $m \in M_u^{(o_i)}$, it is quite clear that the user is expressing operation o_i. If we wish to determine exactly what the user is doing at any point, we have only to instrument the set of modules $M_u^{(o)}$. As we receive telemetry from each of the modules so instrumented, the sequence of the users operations becomes eminently clear.

We can now map the operations in our example to specific program modules. This mapping is shown in Table 7.5. The specific value of this mapping is twofold. First, if the specification for operation o_1 must be changed, we can identify which modules are associated with this operation. Second, there are certain modules that tag each operation. That is, they uniquely identify the operation. If, for example, we saw either module in the set $\{m_2, m_8\}$, we would then know that operation o_1 was currently being executed by the user.

7.4 Distribution of Activity among the Modules

In Chapter 3 we established the fact that not all operations will get the same amount of usage. The disparity in the distribution of activity was formalized in the notion of an operational profile. Each of the functionalities depends on the activity of the operations. Modules are invoked by functionalities. Thus, it is clear that module activity also depends on the operational profile. The binding between functionalities and modules is detailed in the ASSIGNS relation. It is clear from the p relation that the binding between modules and functionalities is not strictly deterministic. If ASSIGNS(f_a, m_b) is true for functionality f_a and module m_b, this does not imply that functionality f_a will always invoke module m_b.

To capture the essence of these more tenuous relationships between functionalities and operations, we need to characterize the distribution of activity in two different ways. First, we would like to know the strength of the binding between each functionality and the modules that implement it. We can actually measure this relationship by monitoring the proportion of activity each module receives under each functionality. Next, we can establish prior probabilities for the conditional probability distribution $\Pr(f_\bullet | o_a)$.

The conditional probability distribution $\Pr(m | f)$ shows the relationship between each module and the functionalities that might invoke that module.

Table 7.6. Conditional Probability Distribution

Pr(m|f)	m_1	m_2	m_3	m_4	m_5	m_6	m_7	m_8
f_1	0.50	0.50	0.00	0.00	0.00	0.00	0.00	0.00
f_2	0.25	0.00	0.25	0.00	0.25	0.00	0.00	0.25
f_3	0.29	0.00	0.29	0.29	0.06	0.09	0.00	0.00
f_4	0.20	0.00	0.20	0.00	0.20	0.20	0.20	0.00

A hypothetical distribution for these conditional probabilities is shown in Table 7.6. From this table we can see that functionality f_2, for example, will always invoke module m_5. On the other hand, functionality f_3 will only occasionally invoke the same module ($\Pr(m_5 | f_3) = 0.2$).

In Chapter 5 we established that the operational profile for this continuing example was $p(o_1) = 0.3$ and $p(o_2) = 0.7$. We then derived the functional profile to wit:

$$p(f_1) = \sum_{i=1}^{2} p(o_i) p\left(f_1 | o_i\right) = 0.03$$

$$p(f_2) = \sum_{i=1}^{2} p(o_i) p\left(f_2 | o_i\right) = 0.55$$

$$p(f_3) = \sum_{i=1}^{2} p(o_i) p\left(f_3 | o_i\right) = 0.35$$

$$p(f_4) = \sum_{i=1}^{2} p(o_i) p\left(f_4 | o_i\right) = 0.07$$

Observe that the module profile can be derived from the functional profile as:

$$p(m_j) = \sum_{i=1}^{4} p(f_i) p\left(m_j | f_i\right)$$

The values for this conditional probability distribution are shown in Table 7.6. If we multiply the vector of functional profiles by this matrix, we will get a new vector containing the module profiles. The resulting module profile is shown in Table 7.7.

Table 7.7. Module Profile Example

Module							
1	2	3	4	5	6	7	8
0.27	0.02	0.25	0.10	0.17	0.04	0.01	0.14

Table 7.8. New Module Profile Example

Module							
1	2	3	4	5	6	7	8
0.27	0.03	0.24	0.07	0.19	0.03	0.01	0.16

The module profile is the unconditional probability of executing a particular module during an arbitrary module epoch. We can see from this trivial example that the functional profile is directly dependent on the operational profile. If the operational profile were to change, then the functional profile and module profiles would change as well. Let us assume, for example that the operational profile for the two operations has now changed; it is now $p(o_1) = 0.5$ and $p(o_2) = 0.5$. The new module profile for this operational profile is shown in Table 7.8.

Under this new operational profile, the unconditional probability of executing module 3 has diminished. On the other hand, the unconditional probability of executing module 5 has increased. If module 5 were a fault-prone module, we have increased our exposure to the potential problems in this module based on the shift in operational profile. This situation would be even more aggravated if modules 3 and 6 were not fault-prone modules. We have diminished our activity in reliable modules and shifted our activity to a module that has a much greater likelihood of failing.

As long as the user operational profile remains stable, then the manner in which the functional machine actually executes will be stable. This is because the module profile is stable under that operational profile. At the point where there is a major shift in the operational profile by the user, there will be a concomitant shift in the functional profile and the module profile. This will reapportion the activity of the functional machine to a different module profile. It might well be that the shift will cause a fault-prone module that received little exposure under an initial operational profile is increasingly exploited under a new operational profile. This will, of course, result in the diminution of the reliability of the system as a whole. It is apparent, then, that the reliability of a system is directly dependent on how the system is used. One user might well distribute his activity to operations that invoke modules not laden with faults. This user

175

will regard the system as a very reliable system. Another user might distribute his activity to operations that invoke a host of fault-prone modules. This user will think that the software is very unreliable. Software reliability, then, is a function of the operational profile. In this measure, software is very different from hardware. A hardware system can fail or wear out over time. Its reliability, then, will be a function of time. A software system, on the other hand, can fail as a function of usage. Its reliability, then, is a function of the operational profile.

7.5 The Specification Build Process

It is clear that the set of operations and the set of functionalities will change and evolve over the development life of a software system. This means that we can also expect reasonable churn in the set of program modules. This means that the ASSIGNS relation can be expected to change repeatedly as the elements of the set of functionalities F and the set of modules M change.

Again, the defining moment for the set of operations, the set of functionalities, and now the set of modules was established to be the build event. The specific set of operations for a build k was represented by the set $O^{(k)}$ and the set of functionalities by the set $F^{(k)}$. Following this nomenclature, the set of modules on build k is $M^{(k)}$. The set of operations was indexed by the vector $\iota^{(k)}$ and the functionalities by the vector $\eta^{(k)}$, and now the set of modules by the vector $\mu^{(k)}$. A more realistic view of the ASSIGNS$^{(k)}$ relation for the kth build, then, is shown in Table 7.9. The specific functionalities incorporated in build k are those indexed by the vector $\eta^{(k)}$, which in this case has four elements. This means that there have only been four functionalities throughout the evolution of the functional specifications through build k.

At some later point in the evolution of the system at, say, build j, the nature of the ASSIGNS relation will have changed. An example of the system at this new evolutionary point is shown in Table 7.10. At this point in the evolution, we observe that a functionality f_{η_3} is no longer part of the system. A module m_{μ_4} that was distinctly associated with this functionality

Table 7.9. Example of the ASSIGNS$^{(k)}$ Relation

$F \times M$	$m_{\mu_1^{(k)}}$	$m_{\mu_2^{(k)}}$	$m_{\mu_3^{(k)}}$	$m_{\mu_4^{(k)}}$	$m_{\mu_5^{(k)}}$	$m_{\mu_6^{(k)}}$	$m_{\mu_7^{(k)}}$	$m_{\mu_8^{(k)}}$
$f_{\eta_1^{(k)}}$	T	T						
$f_{\eta_2^{(k)}}$	T		T		T			T
$f_{\eta_3^{(k)}}$	T		T	T	T	T		
$f_{\eta_4^{(k)}}$	T		T		T	T	T	

Table 7.10. Example of the ASSIGNS[(i)] Relation

$F \times M$	$m_{\mu_1}^{(k)}$	$m_{\mu_2}^{(k)}$	$m_{\mu_3}^{(k)}$	$m_{\mu_5}^{(k)}$	$m_{\mu_6}^{(k)}$	$m_{\mu_7}^{(k)}$	$m_{\mu_8}^{(k)}$	$m_{\mu_9}^{(k)}$
$f_{\eta_1}^{(k)}$	T	T						
$f_{\eta_2}^{(k)}$	T		T	T			T	
$f_{\eta_4}^{(k)}$	T		T	T	T	T		
$f_{\eta_5}^{(k)}$	T							T

is now gone as well. However, a new functionality $f_{\eta_5^{(j)}}$ and a new module $m_{\mu_9^{(j)}}$ have been added to this system.

It is clear that the ASSIGNS relation serves two distinct binding roles. First, it binds modules to functionalities. Second, it binds versions of these modules to specific versions of functionalities. There are multiple ASSIGNS relations, one for each build.

As was the case for the IMPLEMENTS relation, the defining moment for the ASSIGNS relation is also the document build. Each build will define a new ASSIGNS relation. This relation must also be preserved at each build point in the form of a build list. The build list associates a particular version of an operation to a set of versions of functionalities to a set of versions of modules. Let us assume that at build k the operation index vector is:

$$\iota^{(k)} = \langle 1.2, 1.3 \rangle$$

that the functionality index is:

$$\eta^{(k)} = \langle 1.4, 1.1, 1.3, 1.6 \rangle$$

and that the module index is:

$$\mu^{(k)} = \langle 1.0, 1.2, 1.2, 1.3, 1.1, 1.1, 1.4, 1.3 \rangle$$

The build list for the ASSIGNS[(k)] relation is shown in Table 7.11.

The build lists, then, identify which versions of each of the operations are associated with particular version of functionalities that, in turn, are bound to particular module versions. Each build of the system specifications will represent a different system. We can see that when discussing the software we are developing, we must appreciate that the system is evolving rapidly. Each incremental system is described by its own operational, functional, and module specifications.

Table 7.11. The Build List for Build k

Operation Index	Operation Version	Functionality Index	Functionality Version	Module Index	Module Version
$\iota_1^{(k)}$	1.2	$\eta_1^{(k)}$	1.4	$\mu_1^{(k)}$	1.0
$\iota_1^{(k)}$	1.2	$\eta_1^{(k)}$	1.4	$\mu_2^{(k)}$	1.2
$\iota_1^{(k)}$	1.2	$\eta_2^{(k)}$	1.1	$\mu_1^{(k)}$	1.0
$\iota_1^{(k)}$	1.2	$\eta_2^{(k)}$	1.1	$\mu_3^{(k)}$	1.2
$\iota_1^{(k)}$	1.2	$\eta_2^{(k)}$	1.1	$\mu_5^{(k)}$	1.1
$\iota_1^{(k)}$	1.2	$\eta_2^{(k)}$	1.1	$\mu_8^{(k)}$	1.3
$\iota_2^{(k)}$	1.3	$\eta_2^{(k)}$	1.1	$\mu_1^{(k)}$	1.0
$\iota_2^{(k)}$	1.3	$\eta_2^{(k)}$	1.1	$\mu_3^{(k)}$	1.2
$\iota_2^{(k)}$	1.3	$\eta_2^{(k)}$	1.1	$\mu_5^{(k)}$	1.1
$\iota_2^{(k)}$	1.3	$\eta_2^{(k)}$	1.1	$\mu_8^{(k)}$	1.3
$\iota_2^{(k)}$	1.3	$\eta_3^{(k)}$	1.3	$\mu_1^{(k)}$	1.0
$\iota_2^{(k)}$	1.3	$\eta_3^{(k)}$	1.3	$\mu_3^{(k)}$	1.2
$\iota_2^{(k)}$	1.3	$\eta_3^{(k)}$	1.3	$\mu_4^{(k)}$	1.3
$\iota_2^{(k)}$	1.3	$\eta_3^{(k)}$	1.3	$\mu_5^{(k)}$	1.1
$\iota_2^{(k)}$	1.3	$\eta_3^{(k)}$	1.3	$\mu_6^{(k)}$	1.1
$\iota_2^{(k)}$	1.3	$\eta_4^{(k)}$	1.6	$\mu_1^{(k)}$	1.0
$\iota_2^{(k)}$	1.3	$\eta_4^{(k)}$	1.6	$\mu_3^{(k)}$	1.2
$\iota_2^{(k)}$	1.3	$\eta_4^{(k)}$	1.6	$\mu_5^{(k)}$	1.1
$\iota_2^{(k)}$	1.3	$\eta_4^{(k)}$	1.6	$\mu_6^{(k)}$	1.1
$\iota_2^{(k)}$	1.3	$\eta_4^{(k)}$	1.6	$\mu_7^{(k)}$	1.4

7.6 An Extended Definition of Functionalities and Modules

For each operation it is clear that there are one or more functionalities that will be employed to implement that operation. In turn, each of the functionalities will be implemented by one or more modules in the low-level design. To this point we have linked the operations to the functionalities in their definitions. The functionalities must now be linked to the modules that will implement them. This linkage is shown in Table 7.12 for the revised definition of the functional specification. This specification now includes a linkage section for the modules that are used to implement each functionality. This new functionality specification will permit operations to be mapped to the modules that implement them. It will also allow us to determine which operations are implemented by each operation.

Table 7.12. Specifications for a Functionality

Functionality Name	f_i		
Functionality Index	η_i^k		

Control	Received from functionality:
	   <List of functionalities>
	 Transferred to functionality:
	   <List of functionalities>		

Data	Incoming packets:
	   <Packet list>
	 Outgoing packets:
	   <Packet list>		

Protocol	<Protocol list for data packets>		
Functional Transformations	<List of data transformations>		
Linkage	Operation Name	Operation Filename	Version
	<operation>	<filename>	<version#>
	Module Name	Module Filename	Version
	<module>	<filename>	<version#>

An updated module specification is shown in Table 7.13. This specification now contains the linkage section for the functionalities. There will be an entry in this table for module a for each functionality for which ASSIGNS(m_a, f) is True.

It is clear that the functionalities play a pivotal role in the specification linkage process. Operations can be linked to functionalities that are, in turn, linked to modules. Modules are linked to functionalities that are, in turn, linked to operations. This will permit the reflexive mapping of operations to modules. This linkage for the example build k is shown in Figure 7.1.

7.7 The `calc` System Example

We now turn our attention to the mapping of functionalities to design modules for the `calc` system. The ASSIGNS relation for this mapping is shown in Table 7.14. In that this is a relatively small problem, the mapping between functionalities and modules is very nearly one-to-one. This simple mapping is certainly not characteristic of larger systems. The relationships between the modules and the functionalities will be far more complicated. What is important is that we will have established a methodology for understanding the complexity of these relationships.

179

Table 7.13. Extended Module Definition

Header Section

HEADER
    PARAMETERS
    CALLED MODULES
    CALLING MODULES

Data Section

VARIABLES
    PARAMETER_LIST
    LOCAL_VARIABLES
CONSTANTS

Algorithm Description Section
DESCRIPTION

Algorithm Section
ALGORITHM

Linkage Section		
Functionality Name	Functionality Filename	Version
<functionality>	<filename>	<version #>

7.7.1 Distribution of Activity in Modules

Let us imagine that we have simulated this system at the design stage and have actually obtained some measurement data on the distribution activity of the modules as the system behaved under simulation. The data that we would collect from this exercise might well look like that shown in Table 7.15.

The final column in Table 5.11 tallies all the instances of execution of all the modules while executing each functionality. Another way to say the same thing is that this column represents the total number of module epochs for each user.

If we divide each entry of the functional frequency count from Table 7.15 by the number of functional epochs, we can derive the p relation shown in Table 7.16. Just as was the case with functionalities and operations, the p relation gives us some measure of the strength of the binding between each of the functionalities and modules. We do know, for example, that whenever functionality 1 was invoked in this hypothetical experiment, that modules 1 and 2 always occurred.

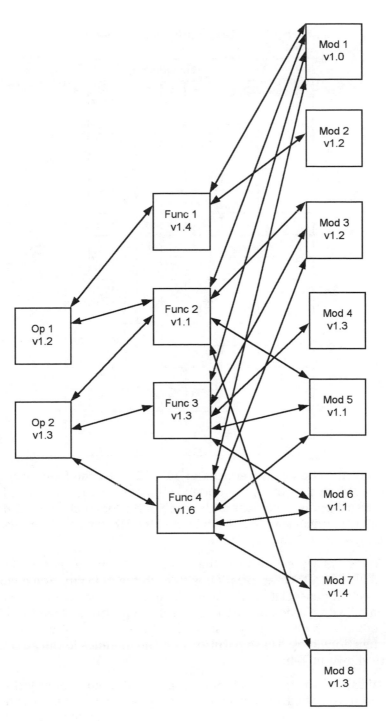

Figure 7.1. Mapping of operations to modules.

Table 7.14. The ASSIGNS Relation for the
calc System

Module	Functionality							
	1	2	3	4	5	6	7	8
1	T							
2	T							
3		T						
4		T						
5			T			T		
6				T				
7					T			
8						T		
9						T		
10						T		
11						T		
12						T		
13							T	
14							T	
15							T	
16								T

If we divide the module epochs of Table 7.15 by the functional epoch (the last row in this table), we obtain estimates for the conditional probability distribution of modules under each of the functionalities. The initial probability estimates are shown in Table 7.17. We can see from this table, for example, that $Pr(m_5 | f_6) = 0.42$.

In Table 7.3 we established that modules might be partitioned into classes based on their association with each functionality. Some modules are potentially associated with a functionality; others are indispensably associated with a functionality. There also is a partition of modules based on whether they are uniquely associated with a functionality or share with other functionalities. These partitions for the modules in the calc example are shown in Table 7.18.

Each user of the calc system will operate it in a different fashion. As such, each user will have a distinct operational profile. These operational profiles were shown in Table 3.3. By systematically employing Bayes rule,

Table 7.15. Simulated Distribution of Activity across Modules

Module	Functionality							
	1	**2**	**3**	**4**	**5**	**6**	**7**	**8**
1	6							
2	6							
3		338						
4		338						
5			16			134		
6				349				
7					58			
8						120		
9						40		
10						13		
11						13		
12						2		
13							212	
14							126	
15							5	
16								168
Total	12	676	16	349	58	322	343	168

we first derived the functional profiles for each of the users, as shown in Section 5.3. By the application of Bayes rule as shown in Section 7.7, it was possible to establish a module profile for each user. Thus, the module profiles for each of the users are shown in Table 7.19. The last column in this table is the distribution of all module activity across all the users of the system.

Each of the modules profiles for each of the users represents a point in a 15-dimensional space. (Again, we lose one degree of freedom to the sum that must equal 1.0.) Just as we did with the functional profiles, we can measure the distance between any of the user-specific module profiles and the cumulative or total module profile represented by the last column of Table 7.15. This distance between the user module profile and the cumulative profile for user i is

Table 7.16. Example of the p Relation for the calc System

Module	Functionality							
	1	2	3	4	5	6	7	8
1	1	0	0	0	0	0	0	0
2	1	0	0	0	0	0	0	0
3	0	1	0	0	0	0	0	0
4	0	1	0	0	0	0	0	0
5	0	0	1	0	0	1	0	0
6	0	0	0	1	0	0	0	0
7	0	0	0	0	1	0	0	0
8	0	0	0	0	0	0.5	0	0
9	0	0	0	0	0	0.3	0	0
10	0	0	0	0	0	0.1	0	0
11	0	0	0	0	0	0.1	0	0
12	0	0	0	0	0	0.001	0	0
13	0	0	0	0	0	0	0.7	0
14	0	0	0	0	0	0	0.2	0
15	0	0	0	0	0	0	0.1	0
16	0	0	0	0	0	0	0	1

$$d^{(i)} = \sum_{j=1}^{16} \left(p\left(f_j^{(i)}\right) - p\left(f_j^{(t)}\right) \right)^2.$$

This will permit us to measure the relative distance between each of the user module profiles and the cumulative system activity over all users. As established in Chapter 5, the average distance was

$$\bar{d} = \frac{1}{6}\sum_i d_i$$

for this group of six users and the variance of this distance across these users was

$$Var(d) = \frac{1}{5}\sum_i (d_i - \bar{d})^2.$$

Table 7.17. Conditional Probability Distribution for the Modules

Module	Functionality							
	1	2	3	4	5	6	7	8
1	0.50	0	0	0	0	0	0	0
2	0.50	0	0	0	0	0	0	0
3	0	0.50	0	0	0	0	0	0
4	0	0.50	0	0	0	0	0	0
5	0	0	1.00	0	0	0.42	0	0
6	0	0	0	1.00	0	0	0	0
7	0	0	0	0	1.00	0	0	0
8	0	0	0	0	0	0.37	0	0
9	0	0	0	0	0	0.12	0	0
10	0	0	0	0	0	0.04	0	0
11	0	0	0	0	0	0.04	0	0
12	0	0	0	0	0	0.01	0	0
13	0	0	0	0	0	0	0.62	0
14	0	0	0	0	0	0	0.37	0
15	0	0	0	0	0	0	0.01	0
16	0	0	0	0	0	0	0	1.00

Table 7.18. Modules Associated with Functionalities

	$M_i^{(f)}$	$M_p^{(f)}$	$M_s^{(f)}$	$M_u^{(f)}$
f_1	$\{m_1, m_2\}$	$\{\}$	$\{\}$	$\{m_1, m_2\}$
f_2	$\{m_3, m_4\}$	$\{\}$	$\{m_5\}$	$\{m_3, m_4\}$
f_3	$\{m_5\}$	$\{\}$	$\{\}$	$\{m_5\}$
f_4	$\{m_6\}$	$\{\}$	$\{\}$	$\{m_6\}$
f_5	$\{m_7\}$	$\{\}$	$\{\}$	$\{m_7\}$
f_6	$\{m_8\}$	$\{m_8, m_9, m_{10}, m_{11}\}$	$\{\}$	$\{m_8\}$
f_7	$\{m_{14}, m_{15}\}$	$\{\}$	$\{m_5\}$	$\{m_{14}, m_{15}\}$
f_8	$\{m_{16}\}$	$\{\}$	$\{\}$	$\{m_{16}\}$

Table 7.19. Module Profiles

Module	Users						Total
	1	2	3	4	5	6	7
1	0.003	0.002	0.003	0.002	0.003	0.003	0.003
2	0.003	0.002	0.003	0.002	0.003	0.003	0.003
3	0.128	0.121	0.136	0.117	0.128	0.137	0.128
4	0.128	0.121	0.136	0.117	0.128	0.137	0.128
5	0.051	0.045	0.037	0.067	0.045	0.039	0.045
6	0.271	0.258	0.276	0.266	0.263	0.274	0.267
7	0.031	0.056	0.011	0.046	0.030	0.009	0.031
8	0.028	0.023	0.027	0.027	0.031	0.032	0.028
9	0.009	0.008	0.009	0.009	0.010	0.011	0.009
10	0.003	0.002	0.003	0.003	0.003	0.004	0.003
11	0.003	0.002	0.003	0.003	0.003	0.004	0.003
12	0.000	0.000	0.000	0.000	0.001	0.001	0.000
13	0.154	0.156	0.167	0.155	0.159	0.156	0.160
14	0.092	0.093	0.099	0.092	0.095	0.093	0.095
15	0.004	0.004	0.004	0.004	0.004	0.004	0.004
16	0.092	0.106	0.084	0.091	0.094	0.096	0.094

The profile distances for each of the six users are shown in Table 7.20, together with the average and variance for these distances. Again, the distance values in this table have been scaled by taking the logarithm to the base 10. These values are shown in the last row of the table. In the case of the module profiles, users 2, 3, 4, and 6 contribute the most to the overall variation in the distance values, a pattern preserved from the functional profiles.

Table 7.20. Module Profile Distances

1	2	3	4	5	6	Average	Variance
0.00010	0.00103	0.00085	0.00100	0.00003	0.00078	0.00063	0.00000
−4.02	−2.99	−3.07	−3.00	−4.49	−3.11	−3.20	−6.70

7.7.2 Module Latency

It is an attribute of each functionality that it will take a certain amount of time to execute. We named this the "functional latency." The symbol v_j was employed in Chapter 6 to represent the latency of a functionality j, where $v_j = l(m_j)$ represents the latency of a module j. It is clear that v_i, the expected value for the module latency was

$$v_i = \sum_{j=1}^{k} \gamma_j \Pr\left(m_j \middle| f_i\right)$$

and the variance

$$Var(v) = \sum_i p_i v_i^2 - E(v)^2 = \sum_i p_i v_i^2 - \left(\sum_i p_i v_i\right)^2.$$

For our `calc` example, the hypothetical module latencies are shown in the last row of Table 7.21. The conditional probability distribution for the modules under each functionality is shown in the center of this table. The last column of Table 7.21 contains the functional latencies. These functional latencies, again, were derived as expected values for each functionality under the module conditional probability distribution shown in the rows of this table. These functional latencies were derived from the values presented in Chapter 5 in Table 5.16.

7.7.3 The Linkage of Functionalities to Modules

Now we turn our attention to the problem of maintaining the linkage between the current functionalities and the current module versions. Recall that the functionalities at this same point in the build process, build j, are represented by the contents of Table 5.18. The last column of this table is the functionality index vector $\eta^{(j)}$. As was the case for the operations in build j, the contents of this table bind the functionality names to specific filenames and then to versions of each file.

The modules will also have undergone some degree of churn by the time build j rolls around. Let us assume that the modules and their versions at this point are represented by the contents of Table 7.23. The last column of this table is the module index vector $\mu^{(j)}$. As was the case for the functionalities in build j, the contents of this table bind the individual module names to specific filenames and then to versions of each file.

The contents of Table 7.22 and Table 7.23 represent the contents of the build lists for build j of the functionalities and the module specifications. With this data and that of Table 5.17 for the operations, we can know exactly which operations (by version) were implemented by the source code on build j. Further, we will also know exactly how these operations were implemented by specific functionalities.

Table 7.21. Functional Latencies

Module	Functionality								Latency
	1	2	3	4	5	6	7	8	
1	0.50	0	0	0	0	0	0	0	3
2	0.50	0	0	0	0	0	0	0	3
3	0	0.50	0	0	0	0	0	0	75
4	0	0.50	0	0	0	0	0	0	75
5	0	0	1.00	0	0	0.42	0	0	135
6	0	0	0	1.00	0	0	0	0	60
7	0	0	0	0	1.00	0	0	0	70
8	0	0	0	0	0	0.37	0	0	112
9	0	0	0	0	0	0.12	0	0	37
10	0	0	0		0	0.04	0	0	12
11	0	0	0	0	0	0.04	0	0	12
12	0	0	0	0	0	0.01	0	0	2
13	0	0	0	0	0	0	0.62	0	19
14	0	0	0	0	0	0	0.37	0	11
15	0	0	0	0	0	0	0.01	0	0
16	0	0	0	0	0	0	0	1.00	150
17	0.50	0	0	0	0	0	0	0	3
18	0.50	0	0	0	0	0	0	0	3
Latency	5	150	10	60	70	300	30	150	

The central role of the functionalities now becomes apparent. We therefore must update the description of the functionalities for this example to also include the linkage to module versions. In this sense, the functionalities play a pivotal role of the mapping from the operations to the modules and back again. The descriptions of the functionalities provide the bridge to the individual operations and thence to the individual modules.

Each of the functionalities for the `calc` system will now be revisited to update its relationship with the modules. The functionalities for the `calc` system at the same point in its evolution as the above set of operations are presented in Tables 7.24a through 7.24h. These tables are somewhat different from those of the operations.

Table 7.22. Functionality Linkage Information

Functionality Name	Functionality Filename	Version
f_1	calc/func/f1	1.4
f_2	calc/func/f2	1.0
f_3	calc/func/f3	2.4
f_4	calc/func/f4	1.3
f_5	calc/func/f5	1.8
f_6	calc/func/f6	2.1
f_7	calc/func/f7	1.10
f_8	calc/func/f8	2.2

Table 7.23. Module Linkage Information

Module Name	Module Filename	Version
m_1	calc/mod/init	4.2
m_2	calc/mod/finish	1.9
m_3	calc/mod/decode	1.2
m_4	calc/mod/error	1.4
m_5	calc/mod/read	1.1
m_6	calc/mod/input	1.8
m_7	calc/mod/write	2.0
m_8	calc/mod/select	3.2
m_9	calc/mod/add	1.5
m_{10}	calc/mod/subt	1.4
m_{11}	calc/mod/mult	2.9
m_{12}	calc/mod/div	3.5
m_{13}	calc/mod/dup	1.2
m_{14}	calc/mod/top	1.1
m_{15}	calc/mod/stack	1.3
m_{16}	calc/mod/convert	1.4

Table 7.24a. Current Specification for Functionality f_1

Functionality	f_1		
Control	Received from functionality: OS, f_2 Transferred to functionality: f_2, OS		
Data	Incoming packets: None Outgoing packets: None		
Functional Transformations	Stack initialization (registers set to zero)		
Operation Linkage	o_1	calc/op/o1	3.1
	o_2	calc/op/o2	1.4
	o_3	calc/op/o3	1.3
	o_4	calc/op/o4	1.3
	o_5	calc/op/o5	1.5
	o_6	calc/op/o6	1.7
	o_7	calc/op/o7	1.0
	o_8	calc/op/o8	2.2
	o_9	calc/op/o9	1.1
	o_{10}	calc/op/o10	1.1
Module Linkage	m_1	calc/mod/init	4.2
	m_2	calc/mod/finish	1.9

There will be a substantial amount of overhead in maintaining the linkage from the operations to the modules. We can readily see that in the linkage section of Table 7.24a, for example, that functionality f_1 might potentially participate in every operation. We can also see from that table the precise relationship between the modules assigned to this functionality and the operations that will be implemented by this functionality.

Tables 7.24b through 7.24h are simply updated versions of the functionality descriptions first introduced in Chapter 5. Now, however, the complete linkage from modules to operations is clearly established in these table contents.

We are now in a position to complete the set of module descriptions for the calc problem. Each of the module descriptions is shown in Tables 7.25a through 7.25o. For simplicity's sake, only the skeleton of each module

Table 7.24b. Current Specification for Functionality f_2

Functionality	f_2		
Control	Received from functionality: f_1, f_3, f_4, f_6, f_7 Transferred to functionality: f_3, f_4, f_6, f_7		

Data	Incoming packets:
	  ASCII string
	Outgoing packets:
	  Signed binary number
	  Command code
	  Error message		

Functional Transformations	Parse character input into:
	  32-bit binary number
	  Operation code or
	  Error condition		

Operation Linkage	o_1	`calc/op/o1`	3.1
	o_2	`calc/op/o2`	1.4
	o_3	`calc/op/o3`	1.3
	o_4	`calc/op/o4`	1.3
	o_5	`calc/op/o5`	1.5
	o_6	`calc/op/o6`	1.7
	o_7	`calc/op/o7`	1.0
	o_8	`calc/op/o8`	2.2
	o_9	`calc/op/o9`	1.1
Module Linkage	m_3	`calc/mod/decode`	1.2
	m_4	`calc/mod/error`	1.4

structure is shown in each of the tables. The sole purpose for these tables at this point is to establish the linkage of each of the modules to one or more of the functionalities.

It should now be apparent that there is a substantial amount of effort necessary to maintain the linkage among the functionalities as well as the modules. This is particularly true for the description of the functionalities, in that they must be linked to both the operations and the modules. It will be necessary to create the infrastructure to support this linkage. We turn our attention to this infrastructure in subsequent chapters. It will clearly not be desirable to maintain the versioning information together with the linkage in the description of each functionality, for example. This would

Table 7.24c. Current Specification for Functionality f_3

Functionality	f_3		
Control	Received from functionality: f_2 Transferred to functionality: f_2		
Data	Incoming packets: None Outgoing packets: Character string "error"		
Functional Transformations	Generate error message for output		
Operation Linkage	o_1	calc/op/o1	3.1
	o_2	calc/op/o2	1.4
	o_3	calc/op/o3	1.3
	o_4	calc/op/o4	1.3
	o_5	calc/op/o5	1.5
	o_6	calc/op/o6	1.7
	o_{10}	calc/op/o10	1.1
Module Linkage	m_5	calc/mod/error	1.1

simply create an update loop problem. This will happen when, say, a module changes. This would mean that the version of the module in the description of the functionality must change. However, changing the description of the functionality to reflect this change will create a new version of the functionality; and the new version of the functionality will create a subsequent change in the module description to reflect this version change in the functionality, etc. We acknowledge the problem at this point but will not attempt to deal with it yet.

Table 7.24d. Current Specification for Functionality f_4

Functionality	f_4		

Control	Received from functionality:
	    f_2, OS
	Transferred to functionality:
	    f_2, OS		

Data	Incoming packets:
	    Character string
	Outgoing packets:
	    Signed 32-bit binary number
	    Character code 'd', 'p', 'f', or 'c'		

Functional Transformations	Data buffering: receive string from the OS and buffer the string		
Operation Linkage	o_1	calc/op/o1	3.1
	o_2	calc/op/o2	1.4
	o_3	calc/op/o3	1.3
	o_4	calc/op/o4	1.3
	o_5	calc/op/o5	1.5
	o_6	calc/op/o6	1.7
	o_7	calc/op/o7	1.0
	o_8	calc/op/o8	2.2
	o_9	calc/op/o9	1.1
	o_{10}	calc/op/o10	1.1
Module Linkage	m_6	calc/mod/input	1.8

Table 7.24e. Current Specification for Functionality f_5

Functionality	f_5		
Control	Received from functionality: f_3, f_7, OS Transferred to functionality: f_3, f_7, OS		
Data	Incoming packets: Character strings Outgoing packets: Character string		
Functional Transformations	Data buffering: Transmit buffered string to OS		
Operation Linkage	o_2	calc/op/o2	1.4
	o_3	calc/op/o3	1.3
	o_4	calc/op/o4	1.3
	o_5	calc/op/o5	1.5
	o_7	calc/op/o7	1.0
	o_8	calc/op/o8	2.2
Module Linkage	m_7	calc/mod/write	2.0

Table 7.24f. Current Specification for Functionality f_6

Functionality	f_6		
Control	Received from functionality: f_2 , f_8 Transferred to functionality: f_2, f_8		
Data	Incoming packets: 2 32-bit binary numbers Outgoing packets: 1 or 2 32-bit binary numbers		
Functional Transformations	Capture signs of top two stack elements Sign arithmetic results Addition of top two operands on the stack Multiplication of top two operands on the stack Division of top two operands on the stack		
Operation Linkage	o_2	calc/op/o2	1.4
	o_3	calc/op/o3	1.3
	o_4	calc/op/o4	1.3
	o_5	calc/op/o5	1.5
Module Linkage	m_5	calc/mod/error	1.1
	m_8	calc/mod/select	3.2
	m_9	calc/mod/add	1.5
	m_{10}	calc/mod/subt	1.4
	m_{11}	calc/mod/mult	2.9
	m_{12}	calc/mod/div	3.5

Table 7.24g. Current Specification for Functionality f_7

Functionality	f_7		
Control	Received from functionality: f_2, f_8 Transferred to functionality: f_2, f_8		
Data	Incoming packets: Character code 'd', 'p', 'f', or 'c' Outgoing packets: Signed 32-bit binary numbers		
Functional Transformations	Change stack locations Zero top of stack Data transfer from stack		
Operation Linkage	o_1	calc/op/o1	3.1
	o_2	calc/op/o2	1.4
	o_3	calc/op/o3	1.3
	o_4	calc/op/o4	1.3
	o_5	calc/op/o5	1.5
	o_6	calc/op/o6	1.7
	o_7	calc/op/o7	1.0
	o_8	calc/op/o8	2.2
	o_9	calc/op/o9	1.1
Module Linkage	m_{13}	calc/mod/dup	1.2
	m_{14}	calc/mod/top	1.1
	m_{15}	calc/mod/stack	1.3

Table 7.24h. Current Specification for Functionality f_8

Functionality	f_8		
Control	Received from functionality: f_6, f_7 Transferred to functionality: f_8, f_7		
Data	Incoming packets: Signed 32-bit binary number Outgoing packets: Character string		
Functional Transformations	Convert signed 32-bit binary number to character string		
Operation Linkage	o_2	calc/op/o2	1.4
	o_3	calc/op/o3	1.3
	o_4	calc/op/o4	1.3
	o_5	calc/op/o5	1.5
	o_7	calc/op/o7	1.0
	o_8	calc/op/o8	2.2
Module Linkage	m_{16}	calc/mod/convert	1.4

Table 7.25a. Current Module Description for Module m_1

Header Section		
Data Section		
Algorithm Description Section		
Algorithm Section		
Linkage Section		
Functionality Name	Functionality Filename	Version
f_1	calc/func/f1	1.4

Table 7.25b. Current Module Description for Module m_2

Header Section		
Data Section		
Algorithm Description Section		
Algorithm Section		
Linkage Section		
Functionality Name	Functionality Filename	Version
f_1	calc/func/f1	1.4

Table 7.25c. Current Module Description for Module m_3

Header Section		
Data Section		
Algorithm Description Section		
Algorithm Section		
Linkage Section		
Functionality Name	Functionality Filename	Version
f_2	calc/func/f2	1.0

Table 7.25d. Current Module Description for Module m_4

Header Section		
Data Section		
Algorithm Description Section		
Algorithm Section		
Linkage Section		
Functionality Name	Functionality Filename	Version
f_2	calc/func/f2	1.0

Table 7.25e. Current Module Description for Module m_5

Header Section		
Data Section		
Algorithm Description Section		
Algorithm Section		
Linkage Section		
Functionality Name	Functionality Filename	Version
f_3	calc/func/f3	2.4
f_6	calc/func/f6	2.1

Table 7.25f. Current Module Description for Module m_6

Header Section		
Data Section		
Algorithm Description Section		
Algorithm Section		
Linkage Section		
Functionality Name	Functionality Filename	Version
f_4	calc/func/f4	1.3

Table 7.25g. Current Module Description for Module m_7

Header Section		
Data Section		
Algorithm Description Section		
Algorithm Section		
Linkage Section		
Functionality Name	Functionality Filename	Version
f_5	calc/func/f5	1.8

Table 7.25h. Current Module Description for Module m_8

Header Section		
Data Section		
Algorithm Description Section		
Algorithm Section		
Linkage Section		
Functionality Name	Functionality Filename	Version
f_6	calc/func/f6	2.1

Table 7.25i. Current Module Description for Module m_9

Header Section		
Data Section		
Algorithm Description Section		
Algorithm Section		
Linkage Section		
Functionality Name	Functionality Filename	Version
f_6	calc/func/f6	2.1

Table 7.25j. Current Module Description for Module m_{10}

Header Section		
Data Section		
Algorithm Description Section		
Algorithm Section		
Linkage Section		
Functionality Name	Functionality Filename	Version
f_6	calc/func/f6	2.1

Table 7.25k. Current Module Description for Module m_{12}

Header Section		
Data Section		
Algorithm Description Section		
Algorithm Section		
Linkage Section		
Functionality Name	Functionality Filename	Version
f_6	calc/func/f6	2.1

Table 7.25l. Current Module Description for Module m_{13}

Header Section		
Data Section		
Algorithm Description Section		
Algorithm Section		
Linkage Section		
Functionality Name	Functionality Filename	Version
f_7	calc/func/f7	1.10

Table 7.25m. Current Module Description for Module m_{14}

Header Section		
Data Section		
Algorithm Description Section		
Algorithm Section		
Linkage Section		
Functionality Name	Functionality Filename	Version
f_7	calc/func/f7	1.10

Table 7.25n. Current Module Description for Module m_{15}

Header Section		
Data Section		
Algorithm Description Section		
Algorithm Section		
Linkage Section		
Functionality Name	Functionality Filename	Version
f_7	calc/func/f7	1.10

Table 7.25o. Current Module Description for Module m_{16}

Header Section		
Data Section		
Algorithm Description Section		
Algorithm Section		
Linkage Section		
Functionality Name	Functionality Filename	Version
f_8	calc/func/f8	2.2

Chapter 8
Choosing the Appropriate Language Metaphor

8.1 Procrustes

There once was an innkeeper in ancient Greece who was concerned about the comfort of his guests. He had a set of beds that were all the same size. Some of Procrustes' guests were tall, too tall for the beds in the inn. For these people, Procrustes simply cut their legs off so that the guests would fit the bed. For those guests who were too short for the beds in Procrustes' inn, he had a rack. He would place the short guests on his rack and make them longer. The bottom line was that everyone fit Procrustes' beds when they went to bed.

Design solutions that start with a specific language metaphor are Procrustean solutions. We see evidence of Procrustean solutions all around us. We bend or chop our designs so they will fit language metaphors that we know and with which we are comfortable.

Procrustes' influence has been very great over the ages. We see evidence of his basic approach throughout many software development organizations. Let us look for a moment at the C programming language environment. The C language was a systems programming language. The first real successful version of UNIX was written in C. The C compiler produces reentrant programs containing recursive function modules. The vast majority of C applications today cannot be in any way construed as systems programs or operating systems. C is literally used for everything. Probably the vast majority of programmers who use the language have absolutely no idea how complex the runtime environments are the programs that they create. It is safe to assume, for example, that an accounting application running on a home personal computer will neither employ recursive algorithms nor will there be multiple instances of this accounting system running simultaneously on this box. Yet, all of the overhead for both recursion and reentrancy will be present in the code that is running.

C is a systems programming language. There are no provisions in the language to deal with real numerical computation. It is very difficult to ascertain the accuracy of numerical results of a C application running across a variety of disparate computer systems, yet there are many computationally complex systems that are written in C. Procrustes has many modern disciples who are coding in C.

A recent derivative of C is C++. This is truly a revolutionary new language. It has, at once, both an ambiguous syntax and an ambiguous set of semantic rules. What a remarkable tool for creating secure and reliable software. It is easy to construct a software system in C++ whose behavior is unknowable. C++ has proven itself as a universal programming language solution. Procrustes would have loved it.

Another very popular language for software development today is Java. This language was developed to support a new SPARC-based, handheld, wireless PDA at Sun Microsystems. A decision was made to create a new virtual machine, the Java Virtual Machine (JVM), that would run byte code that the Java compiler would produce. This would permit small applications to run seamlessly across a large variety of platforms. The key phrase here is *small applications*. Efficiency was not a particular consideration in the Java design and implementation. Small applications could run interpretively under the JVM without particular consideration for the performance hit that this would create. Java is now rapidly supplanting C++ as the language of choice for even very large applications. It is clear that Procrustes has had a profound influence on software development technology.

8.2 Matching Design Architecture to Program Language

To this point we have dealt with three machines that we have designed and developed corresponding to each phase of the specification process. First, there was the operational machine, the machine environment that we created for the end user of the system. This machine will have a hardware component that the user can see, feel, and touch. It will also have an abstract software component that will animate the hardware component. The user will manipulate this operational machine through the functionalities of an underlying abstract software environment represented by the functional machine. This functional machine was yet another abstract machine, permitting us to discuss the implementation of the functional model on an abstract computer model. At the next stage, the functional machine will have to map to an architectural model of a machine that will be used to implement the low-level design specifications. When the low-level design specifications are at last complete, then the low-level design architecture will be mapped onto a virtual machine that will be implemented by the underlying programming language system. There will, for example, be a C machine, an Ada machine, or a Pascal machine. At the very last stage, the programming language will translate the language machine onto an actual computer or real machine. There are, then, a total of five machines that will figure into the complete specification and implementation of a software system.

Each programming language implements a particular virtual machine. This virtual machine is the one that is manipulated by the programmer. There is a C machine, a JVM, a BASIC machine, a FORTRAN machine, etc. Each of these languages was developed to solve a particular class of problems. C, for example, was developed as a systems programming language for the design and implementation of an operating system, UNIX. It was also better than most languages available in the early 1970s for compiler construction. BASIC was a simple decimal machine. It was designed to introduce computer novices to the notion of programming without having to cope with binary numbers at the same time. FORTRAN was created to enable scientists to implement complex numerical algorithms without any in-depth knowledge of the underlying computer hardware. None of the developers of these languages, however, made any claim that the languages were anything other that what they were designed to be.

It is most unfortunate that nearly all these languages were almost immediately used well outside the context for which they were developed. BASIC very rapidly became the *lingua franca* for the rapidly emerging PC market. It was used for nearly all programming applications in that environment. Java was developed for small personal digital assistants that were networked. It is now being used for very large distributed computing applications. C (and C++) is clearly a universal computing solution. It is used everywhere.

Unfortunately, there are no universal tools. Imagine, if you will, employing a carpenter who had at his disposal only a hammer. He would use this hammer for all his carpentry work. If he needed to drive a nail, he would use his trusty hammer. If he needed to cut a board, he would use the claw of the hammer to make the cut. If he needed to measure, he would use the crude marks on the handle of the hammer as an index.

A hammer is not a universal tool. It is used to drive (and pull) nails. That is what hammers are good for; they are not good for cutting wood. They are not good for measuring things, except for those things that need to be exactly as long as the hammer.

When a computing language is used outside the application context for which it was developed, the performance of the application will be suboptimal. In some cases, this mismatch will have serious consequences on both performance and reliability.

8.2.1 A Look at the C Runtime Environment

Although there are many different languages, it is well beyond our ability in this book to examine the runtime representations of each of these languages. It would be useful to visit one of them in detail; thus, we look at the C language for this feature analysis. Let us begin this discussion with an analysis of the computing problem that the C language was designed to solve.

First, every program that was developed in C was assumed to be reentrant. What this means is that the compiler must divide the program into two parts at runtime. The first part is a fixed program part that contains all the instructions and the data constants that a program will use. The second part is the memory space that contains variable data at runtime. For each instance of the operation of this program, a new variable program part is created. Let us call the fixed program part the I part and the variable program part the D part. The first user of this program causes the system to create an I part and D part for the program. The next user uses the existing I part and will have a new program part, D, created for him. The UNIX operating system was designed to support the reentrant program structure created by C. Every program running on a UNIX system is assumed to be reentrant. This may or may not be a good assumption.

Let us now turn our attention to the D program part. The C programming language and its derivatives are strongly influenced by the Algol 60 runtime model. In this model, the data space for each program block and each functional module is created dynamically as these entities are encountered at runtime. This data space is called an activation record. Each activation record is placed on an activation stack as it is created. Thus, whenever a block is executed or a function is called, a new activation record is created. Whenever the block is exited or a return from the function is executed, the activation record is deleted from the activation stack.

During the time that the C runtime system is creating or removing the activation records from the activation stack, the system must cease to perform useful work for the user. The computing cycles taken by the system during the time that these activation records are being created and deleted are lost to the user. This computing activity is pure overhead. It is activity imposed by the C runtime system. It is the price that user has chosen to pay because of the runtime capabilities.

The notion of an activation stack is not vital to the concept of program reentrancy. It would be possible to build a viable runtime environment wherein all of the data storage is created all at once at the beginning of the program execution. The activation stack concept permits a program to have self-reentrant or recursive functions. For programs that have recursive functions in them, the activation stack is a vital part of the runtime environment.

Perhaps one of the greatest liabilities that the C language trap provided to the developer is the closeness of the relationship between C and the UNIX operating system. A very good example of this liability is the UNIX `alloc` command. When a programmer needs (or wants) more storage space, he typically uses one of these `alloc` commands. The operating system then creates the new space and sets a pointer to it for the programmer. This means that the burden of managing the space so obtained falls squarely on the programmer. The language runtime environment does not track these pointers. A C application with an `alloc` in it is practically guaranteed to create memory leaks. A close relationship with an operating system is a very good thing for a systems programming language. This same relationship is probably a very bad thing when the language is used for applications outside that limited context.

The C runtime environment makes no provision for exception handling. When an abnormal condition occurs, such as the use of an invalid pointer or a divide by zero condition arises, the executing C program is simply terminated by the operating system. This is probably acceptable if the application is a computer game. This abnormal termination of the program is certainly not acceptable for a mission-critical piece of software such as an avionics system.

Let us return to the content of Chapter 6. In that chapter we discussed the specification of variables that will be used in the program. Each variable was defined on an exact domain. A variable should never be permitted to receive a value that is outside this domain. The C runtime environment has absolutely no mechanism for the support of the range check for the values that a variable might receive at runtime. If such checking is to be implemented in a program written in C, then the developer will have to do every bit of this checking in C code.

In the module specification process, we very carefully created a mechanism that would permit each parameter that would be used by a program module to be carefully defined and its domain specified. In this manner, the data interface between any two modules was completely specified. The C programming language makes the definition and use of global variables an easy and natural thing to do. This permits the internal action in one module to have an effect well beyond the borders of that module with ill-specified consequences. The use of global variables may be a convenience for developers but it is an anathema to the development of engineered software systems.

The bottom line here is that C is purported as a very easy language with which to create new applications (www.bell-labs.com/history/unix/). It is a very difficult language to use in the engineering of reliable, testable, and maintainable software.

8.2.2   Matching the Low-Level Machine to the Language Machine

So that we can implement the functional machine, we now must investigate our alternatives of programming languages that might best reflect the operation of the functional machine. This task is one of carefully specifying the functional machine and then identifying the programming language environment that creates an abstract machine that is most closely suited for implementation of the functional machine. This is the most vital step of the whole implementation process. It is also the one that is given the least attention. In a Procrustean manner, the programming language environment is generally selected before the functional machine is thoroughly thought out. The application is then shoehorned into the programming language.

There are some obvious mismatches between the language runtime model and the applications that are developed in them. This mismatch is as bad as owning a Ferrari only to use the Ferrari on the congested streets of Manhattan. A Ferrari is an automobile designed to go very fast. It has an astonishing weight-to-horsepower ratio. It is optimized for handling sharp turns at very high speeds. It is very hard on this automobile to sit at idle for extended periods of time. It gets horrible gas mileage in the city. The Ferrari was not designed for city driving. The only reason to drive one in the city is to impress members of the opposite sex. In this context, the Ferrari is a pure pheromone. It is only incidentally a means of transportation.

Now let us look at the vast majority of programs in current operation. Most of these programs have been developed for use on the ubiquitous personal computer. In this environment, they will not be running reentrantly. There is only one user. There is only one version of the program running at any point. It is almost a given that there will be no recursive algorithms used in the development of the program. Yet the C language environment automatically assumes that a program will be reentrant and self-reentrant. It builds the runtime program structure of the application to support this capability at tremendous runtime expense to the user. This is exactly analogous to driving a Ferrari in New York City.

At its core, C is a systems programming language. It was developed as a tool for the construction of operating systems (UNIX in particular) and compilers (the C compiler). The concept of numerical computation was not a driving force for the C language. In fact, it is very difficult to do numerical computation in C. Business applications are difficult to do in C, in that C does not have file systems suitable to support these applications. These are not liabilities of the C language. It was not designed to support either numerical computation or business applications. Its first and most successful application was its use in the implementation of UNIX.

Now let us turn our attention to numerical computation in C. There are some immediate and almost insurmountable problems in attempting to implement problems in this space in the C language. One of the first problems we encounter is the fact that we simply cannot do mathematics on computers as was noted earlier. We have extremely limited mathematical capabilities in the best of the programming languages. Consider the mathematical concept of an integer. Clearly, from a mathematical perspective, the set of integers has an infinite number of elements. On the very best and biggest of computers, we have only a finite subset of these integers. Thus, when we need to do basic mathematics using the notion of integers, we must worry about the cardinality of the subset of integers actually available to us. In C, the cardinality of this subset can vary from one machine and compiler to another. Stated another way, the domain on which integer arithmetic is defined will vary from one compiler to another. This variation is not critical for systems programming work. It is supercritical for numerical computation. An algorithm that might work successfully on one computer might not work at all on another where the subset of integers is smaller.

Another set of numbers is the rational set. A rational number is simply the ratio of two integers. Necessarily, the set of integers is wholly contained in the set of rational numbers. Between any two integers, say n and $n+1$, there are an infinite number of rational numbers. It is clear, then, that computers will give us a very limited milieu in which to do our mathematics. We simply cannot represent rational numbers such as 1/3; we can only represent an approximation for that value. On some machines, this value might be better than others. C does not provide a convenient mechanism for designing around this varying accuracy. Real numbers of the form $\sqrt{c}$, where c is a rational number, simply do not exist on computers. We can only represent this value as a rational number. In the C programming language, we only have the concept of float or double to represent an undefined subset of rational numbers. This is of little consequence if the application we are working on is an operating system. We do not, in general, need a great deal of mathematics in this application domain. This same problem — the lack of definition of the underlying set of rational numbers that has been implemented by the compiler — is a profound liability for mathematical applications.

There is yet another layer of inconvenience in the use of C for numerical computation; C only supports one-dimensional arrays. Further, these arrays are indexed from an initial value of 0. These two decisions that were made during the development of the C language clearly indicate that this language was not designed to do complex mathematical computations. Quite a number of these mathematical computations involve vectors and matrices. These structures are always represented, in their mathematical statement, as being index from 1 to some upper bound n. To implement a vector in C, the array indices must be adjusted to the range of 0 to $n-1$.

This is at once an annoyance and also a splendid opportunity for a developer to make and error that will manifest itself as a fault in the C code.

The implementation of matrices and higher-dimensional arrays in C is really very cumbersome. Again, C does not support n-dimension arrays for $n > 1$. In the case of a matrix, a developer typically defines a matrix as a vector of vectors. He then assumes complete responsibility for indexing into this structure through the use of pointers. This makes the implementation of the mathematical operations almost impossible to read.

C is a systems programming language. It was not designed for business applications. In fact, it is an astonishing liability in the implementation of business applications for many reasons. At the top of this list of reasons are two fundamental considerations. C does not support decimal arithmetic. This really complicates the implementation of applications that involve the manipulation of dollars and cents. Financial applications manipulate decimal numbers, not binary numbers. Basic accounting rules are based on decimal calculations, not binary calculations.

One of the major limitations of C in the implementation of business applications is the simple fact that C can only do simple character Input/Output. It is interesting to note that while C permits structured data types (with struct), it is not capable of writing or reading these structures from its file system. Again, this is not a liability for a systems programming language, but it is a profound liability for applications in the business arena. Yet the number of business applications written in C grows continually.

We now get down to some fundamental voids in the C programming system. These constitute the common-sense issues. The vast majority of these fault reports stem from a basic problem of the C language: it was not designed for engineered software systems. It is a hacker's delight. The very best measure of the liability of the C programming system lies in the fault reports generated by the people using this system. We have spent years pouring over these fault reports at many different commercial and governmental organizations. C has no intrinsic mechanism of either defining domains for numeric values or of ensuring that computation values do not exceed these values. A substantial crop of fault reports relates to overflow or underflow conditions on numerical variables. C invites the use of pointers for nearly everything. They are very frequently used as indices into array structures, for example. There is no provision within the language to ensure that any pointer will have a value within a domain of valid values for that pointer. Thus, invalid pointers constitute a major source of faults in C code.

8.3 Mapping the Modules to Code

In the development of our module specifications, we made provisions for only scalar data values. There was a very good reason for this. The nature of data structures that we might use is really an attribute of the abstract machine defined by the programming language environment. The choice of a language abstract machine that best matches our design needs will be our greatest concern in the mapping of low-level design modules to code.

8.3.1 A Brief Word about the Object-Oriented Language Model

We have made every effort to go wide of a discussion of object-oriented (O-O) software development methodologies. There is a really good reason for this. This methodology is a hacker's delight and an engineer's nightmare. The current computer science literature is replete with anecdotal studies on the O-O metaphor. There are substantive claims made as to the maintainability of O-O systems, yet there is no science to support this conclusion. There are substantive claims made as to the ease of development of systems using this metaphor, yet there is no science to support this conclusion. There are claims that O-O systems are reliable, yet there is plenty of ad hoc evidence to suggest that the contrary is true. There are substantive claims that code reuse is a very strong reason for using the O-O metaphor. That is just the problem. The focus is on the code and not on the functional specification or the operational specification. Very frequently, code reuse leads us to develop systems whose functional and operational characteristics are not well understood. The objective of reuse from a software development standpoint should focus on the design reuse and not the code reuse.

Software systems built in the O-O metaphor resemble the construction work of the ancient Egyptians. The Egyptians built tall buildings by stacking blocks of construction materials on top of each other. Initially, these construction materials were mud bricks. The Egyptians rapidly learned something about the strength of materials from these construction projects. Mud bricks are not very strong. Pyramids built of mud bricks cannot be very tall. On the other hand, stones are much stronger than mud bricks. Pyramids built of stone can be much taller than those built of mud bricks. Whether they used mud bricks or building blocks made of stone, the structures built with these materials were not very usable. The pyramids, in particular, were ponderous in terms of the amount of available interior space versus the height of the structures. They were just plain clumsy, labor-intensive projects. Because of their ponderous nature, they were limited in their height by the structural quality of the building materials. When the structures grew too large, they began to crack and break (reliability problems).

So it is also with O-O code. The systems built with the O-O metaphor are ponderous. The construction of an O-O system, then, is very much like building a pyramid. Objects are stacked on objects until the developers run out of either time or money. We are now beginning to understand that the structures built by these systems collapse as the size of these systems approaches the structural limitations imposed by the mass of code (reliability problems).

Finally, the use of global variables in our design process can lead to horrible problems when these variables are altered by a designer who is not aware of the complete context in which the values of these variables might be used. We have had enough problems with global variables over time to understand that the use of global variables is not good. In fact, it is a practice that must be avoided. If using global variables is a bad thing, then global operations on global variables are certainly worse. This fact is perhaps the greatest problem with the O-O metaphor. Operations on data can be defined to have global scope and visibility. Subsequent changes to these global operations will have a global impact on the system that uses them. The massive amount of interwoven program module data and control dependencies in the O-O metaphor is an anathema to the concept of engineering design. At its best, the O-O software development methodology is a religion.

8.3.2 Data Structures

In Chapter 6 we developed the design for program modules as the lowest level of granularity. Each design module would correspond to exactly one program module. The data passed into the module, used locally by the module, and subsequently passed out of the module was all scalar data. The reason for this is that our sole attention should be devoted, at the design stage, to the precise properties of these data. The structural relationships among these data are properties that we will imbue when we map the low-level design to a particular programming language environment.

The data structures available to use are strictly a function of the language. FORTRAN, for example, is not very rich in data structures. Basically, it gives us dense lists of vectors, matrices, or n-dimensional arrays. It is quite inconvenient to build the notion of a record in FORTRAN. To attempt to do so would lead to some real misuse of developers' time. Therefore, applications that record for processing are not good applications for FORTRAN. On the other hand, those applications that require that the data be organized into matrices are quite naturally implemented in FORTRAN. That is a particular forte of FORTRAN. It would be folly to attempt to implement these same matrix-intensive programs in C. C does not support two-dimensional arrays. What's more, C indexes all of its arrays from 0 instead of 1 as is customary in mathematical computation. The task of remapping these calculations from 1 to n onto the new interval from 0 to $n-1$ provides a real opportunity to make mistakes in the mapping process.

8.3.3 Static versus Dynamic Data Structures

The use of dynamic data structures, such as linked lists, trees, and other structures, is an inherently bad practice. They should be avoided whenever possible. However, that is not to say that their use should be avoided at all costs. There is a time and a place where dynamic data structures are valuable. The key to good design is knowing when that time is nigh.

Dynamic data structures are very attractive for a number of reasons. First, they appear to have great utility in data structures whose elements are rapidly being added, removed, or updated. Second, they can be used with impunity with problems whose scope is really not known. It is possible, for example, to define a linked list to store and organize records. This list can grow indefinitely. We do not need to know how many elements it can contain. One of the obvious candidates for such a structure is a directory system for an operating system. It would be difficult to impossible to estimate the structure and the number of elements in this file system for any context in which the operating system can be deployed.

There are two different reasons that the nature of the problem domain might not be understood in advance. First, it is quite possible that the average number of potential elements in such a structure cannot be estimated with any degree of certainty. It is also probably the case that the variability of the cardinality of the set of elements might also be very great. The second reason that the cardinality of the set of elements in a structure may not be known relates to ignorance or sloth. Many times, for example, simple linked lists are employed as buffers for various user services. In this case, the use of dynamic structures is clearly not warranted. The size of the buffer will depend on exactly two factors: (1) there is a process that places elements into the buffer, (2) there is a process that removes elements from the buffer. The size of the buffer depends entirely on the rates of insertion and of removal. If these rates are not known in advance, this is not a sufficient reason to use a dynamic data structure. This is a reason to do the necessary engineering to understand the rates of insertion and deletion from the buffer. We need to know with some degree of precision both the mean rate of insertion and rate of deletion, and also the variance in these rates. This data will allow us to do two things. First this data permits us to put a reasonable upper bound on the size of the buffer such that we can handle the vast majority of traffic through the buffer. Second, this data defines the operational criterion for reducing the rate of insertion into the buffer. The use of a dynamic data structure for buffer management is a disaster waiting to happen.

The task of management of dynamic memory is clearly something that programmers are not very good at performing. This activity, then, should be part of the runtime support of the programming language environment. Programming languages such as Pascal and Ada provide this level of support. Their runtime environments provide the necessary interface with the operating system to obtain additional dynamic memory allocations from the system, assign pointers to this memory, and potentially manage the pointers to the allocated space. It is clearly possible for the language runtime environment to manage the list of pointers that have been assigned. This, in turn, makes possible the task of defining with precision the domain on which a variable with a pointer attribute can be defined.

8.3.4 Data Domains

During the low-level design process, it is mandatory to specify very precisely the range on which each variable is to be defined. If an integer value, for example, is to contain a value representing the number of seconds on a clock, then the range is clearly from 0 to 59. Any attempt to place a value outside this range should be immediately trapped by the programming language environment. That is a major problem with the use of the C programming language. If there is to be enforcement of this data range, then the programmer is responsible for (1) testing to ensure that incoming values are, in fact, in the appropriate range and (2) handling the contingency that arises when the values are not in the appropriate range. From this simple example, we can begin to see that C is not a language that is conducive for engineered software.

Most of the computation that occurs for most programming applications will be intrinsically decimal. That is, the applications will solve real computational problems for human beings who happen to use decimal arithmetic. Unfortunately, there are very few programming language environments that support decimal arithmetic. COBOL and Ada are notable exceptions. As a result, it becomes a very difficult problem to maintain decimal precision and accuracy in an intrinsically binary programming language. The most common standard now applied to floating point binary arithmetic is the IEEE 754 Floating Point Standard. In single precision, 32 bits, this format provides for numeric values of approximately $\pm 10^{\pm 40}$. The mantissa of a single precision number in this format is effectively 24 bits, that is, approximately seven decimal digits of precision. In double precision, 64 bits, the standard allows arithmetic in the range of approximately $\pm 10^{\pm 310}$. The mantissa of a 64-bit floating point number in this format is effectively 53 binary digits, which is about 16 decimal digits. There are exactly two choices: (1) seven decimal digits of precision or (2) 16 decimal digits.

The unrestricted use of either a single or double precision binary floating point number in the IEEE 754 standard creates for each variable so declared an astonishing range of values. This range of values, in turn, increases the numerical complexity of the underlying computation by a corresponding amount. As the numerical complexity of the problem space increases, so too does the likelihood of a computational fault. In short, the IEEE 754 Floating Point Standard is the computational equivalent of a crescent wrench. A crescent wrench, it can be noted, will adjust to fit a wide range of bolts. It is also very effective at rounding the edges of these bolts because it only touches on two sides of the bolt head.

The translation of decimal values to a binary floating point representation can create severe problems for problems in the financial sector. This conversion process is not exact. Yet all financial problems require exact representation to places to the right of the decimal point. Further, computations that are made on this type of numerical problem will, by law in some cases, be required to be rounded to the second digit after the decimal point. These types of problems are intrinsically decimal. To that end we will look to a programming language such as COBOL to support this type of numerical computation.

There is a similar problem with the use of binary integers to represent decimal integer problems. The choice of binary number representations is somewhat more extensive than that of the floating point representations. A binary number might be 8, 16, 32, or 64 binary digits. In decimal, these formats represent approximately 2.4, 4.8, 9.6, or 19.3 decimal digits. Again, these ranges are arbitrary. There are only four of them. Unfortunately, most of the problems we encounter are not defined on the entirety of any of these ranges. We might, for example, wish to index an array of 100 numbers. To do this we need to define a variable that has a range of integer values from 1 to 100, or 0 to 99, or possibly some other range of integer values such as −5 to 94. To ensure that only a correct value of a variable that will serve as an index on any of these ranges will be used to index the array, the programming language should provide for the necessary runtime checking.

Programming language environments like that of C simply do not provide for the support of the decimal computation that most numerical analysis problems or business applications require. If we are to ensure that a particular design is implemented correctly in C, the programmer must generate the entire necessary domain checking code. This will really increase the complexity of the programming task beyond all reasonable bounds.

8.3.5 The File System

Most of the data that an application program processes will reside on a file. This data is accessible to the application through its interaction with a particular file access method. The greater the richness of this access method, the easier it will be to create and maintain the file.

A file, of course, is an ordered set of records. A record, in turn, is an ordered set of fields. Ultimately, a field is a string of characters of fixed length or a string of characters with some type of field delimiter. Certain programming language environments, most notably COBOL and PL/1, made it very easy to define records, define the relationship of the records one to another, and then bind the sets of records into a logical file. Further, provisions were made to bind the logical file seen by the programmer into a physical file as seen by the operating system.

Major consideration, then, should be given in the selection of an appropriate programming language milieu to the richness of the file definition and processing capabilities of the language.

8.3.6 *Dynamic Memory Allocation*

Dynamic data structures should be avoided at all costs. In the vast majority of cases, their use is simply evidence of very bad design practices. There are occasions that do warrant the use of dynamic data structures, in which case it is vital that the programming language environment offer support for this capability.

Typically, dynamic data structures are composed of elements that are records. Thus, when it is necessary to obtain a new record for incorporation into a data structure, there should be a language command, such as NEW(record-type), that will give a programmer a new element for the data structure. Similarly, there should be a mechanism within the language, such as FREE(pointer), that will release a record back to a memory pool.

When programmers are left to their own devices with such crude operating systems commands as the C `malloc` call, the opportunities for memory leaks are astonishing. It is very difficult to implement the NEW type of command in C. And there is no formal mechanism for releasing a record in a dynamic data structure back to the memory pool in C.

8.3.7 *Simply Bad Programming Practice*

Most modern compilers provide an extensive repertoire of compiler directives. These compiler directives are simply land mines for the undisciplined software developer. They are an anathema to the measurement and the engineering of software systems. We have considered various mechanisms for controlling the use of these compiler directives. Perhaps the most effective mechanism would be to index a programmer's salary so that it is inversely related to the number of compiler directives that the programmer felt it necessary to use.

At the top of the list of offensive compiler directives is the INCLUDE directive. This command is specifically designed to create a nightmare for the build manager. It also makes the measurement of source code systems nearly impossible. The next most egregious compiler directives are the IFDEF directives. They permit multiple programs to be woven together into a single entity. The result is a software maintenance nightmare. If it is necessary to maintain many variants of a program, then these should be managed as branches in a configuration control system.

It would be futile to list all the compiler directives and castigate each one in each distinct programming language environment. Each programming language has its own distinct repertoire of these directives. There are many such commands in any programming language suite. They are there, ostensibly, to facilitate the programmer's task. They do, however, create a maintenance nightmare. They should be avoided at all costs. Suffice it to say that they have no place in an engineering software system. Their presence in a program is clear evidence of engineering immaturity on the part of the software developers.

8.4 $O \times F \times M \times C$

A primary consideration in the selection of a programming language environment will be the ease of mapping the low-level design machine architecture to the underlying architecture provided by the programming language. It is primarily a cost consideration. The more effort required on the part of a programmer to do this mapping on a module to module basis, the more expensive it will be to both create and maintain the program.

There is now a complete linkage between the user operations and the source code that represents the program. The implications of this fact are astonishing. We can identify a particular operation and find the source code modules that implement that operation directly. Similarly, we can identify a program module and have it map directly to a set of operations that it is used to implement. There is just one final element that we must address to ensure that this linkage is maintained. We must link the design modules to the source code modules and the source code modules to the design modules.

To achieve the linkage between the design modules and the source code elements, we will have to revise the contents of Table 7.13 to add the linkage to the code module. This new linkage is shown in Table 8.1. Unlike the functionality linkage, the source code link will only consist of one entry. There must be a one-to-one mapping of the source code elements and the design modules.

8.5 The Bottom Line

Hardware processors have hit a wall. Moore's law is beginning to break down. The next great gains in computer system performance will have to come from software. In fact, the continually increasing overhead imposed as modern programming languages have evolved has mandated that hardware processors become ever more powerful just to keep up with the computational bloat of the software.

Table 8.1. Extended Module Definition

Header Section		

HEADER
  PARAMETERS
  CALLED MODULES
  CALLING MODULES		

Data Section		

VARIABLES
  PARAMETER_LIST
  LOCAL_VARIABLES
CONSTANTS		

Algorithm Description Section		
DESCRIPTION		
Algorithm Section		
ALGORITHM		
Linkage Section		
Source Code Module	Source Code File	Version
	Functionality Filename	Version
<functionality>	<filename>	<version #>

Current overhead rates for today's programming language systems may run as great as 95 percent. It will be relatively easy to make substantial improvements in software performance in the near term. The bloat in these systems is obvious. The future belongs to the new software companies that recognize and exploit this observation. Engineered software systems will have a tremendous market advantage over systems that have been hacked by massive teams of unstructured and undisciplined software developers. A very good place to begin to reverse the current trend is in the selection and use of the right language environment for the right design.

This chapter began with a discussion of Procrustes. Choosing a programming language such as C, C++, or Java and then bending the design to that language is to implement a Procrustean solution. The language should fit the application; the application should not be made to fit the language.

Chapter 9
Measuring Software Design

9.1 Measuring Software Design Alternatives

From a statistical perspective, there are at least three degrees of freedom in the design process. One degree of freedom is attributable to the manner in which the several program modules will be executed. We could, for example, design a program in which all the functionality is implemented in a small number of the total program modules. On the other hand, we might choose to distribute the functionality across a large number of the program modules. The entropy of the design will measure this.

The second degree of freedom in design relates to the complexity of the program modules. We might be able to choose from a series of design alternatives that express the complexity of the set of functionalities in different ways in differing modular structures. This complexity is measured by the modular complexity of the design. We can think of the design process as one of parsing the functional complexity of our design to particular program modules.

The third degree of freedom is related to the choice of functional alternatives for the high-level design. The interesting thing about the design problem is that there are many different ways to implement a set of operational specifications from a functional viewpoint. The important thing, from a user's perspective, is that all the different functional approaches create exactly the same operational model. Some of the functional solutions will result in very complex functional models. These complex models will, in turn, create very complex modular structures. A good functional design is one that minimizes the complexity of the functional model or the design functional complexity as measured by a set of design attributes that we investigate next.

9.2 Understanding Program Modular Structure

As the program functionalities are decomposed into low-level design modules, attention must be given to the complexity of the organization of the modules with regard to two coupling attributes. First, program control can be passed from one module to another. Second, data can be passed to a called module or received from the called module. It is important, in the evaluation of design alternatives, to be able to quantify the precise nature of design alternatives as they emerge. There are several coupling attributes that can be measured to assess this complexity.

9.2.1 Measures of Module Control

The overall structure of an evolving low-level design can be seen in its call graph structure. Each design module represents one node in this graph. Each call/return sequence represents one edge in this graph. A call graph of a program is constructed from a directed graph representation of the program module.

We can define two metrics that are attributes of each module. These are *Indegree* and *Outdegree*. The *Indegree* for a module a is simply $I(a)$ as defind above. Similarly, the *Outdegree* for module a is $O(a)$. A program module with a large value of *Indegree* is closely bound to a large number of other program modules. If there are alterations made to the module, then this will impact more than one functionality as well.

As a measure of the complexity of the program call structure, we can enumerate all the nodes in the metric named *Nodes* and edges of the call graph in a metric named *Edges*. Clearly, the call graph structure becomes more labyrinthine as the ratio of edges to nodes rises during the design process. Design modules whose *Indegree* is very large are probably good candidates for examination. The degree of control complexity reflected by their control binding to a large number of modules makes for serious maintainability problems. Also, modules whose *Outdegree* is very large are also candidates for examination. It very often happens that most of the calls to external modules occur in branches in the flowgraph of the program module. This means that the cardinality of the set of modules $M_p^{(f)}$ is likely to be large for any functionality that is defined by this module.

A subpath within the call graph will be a sequence of edges $\langle \overrightarrow{a_1 a_2}, \overrightarrow{a_2 a_3}, \ldots, \overrightarrow{a_{n-1} a_n} \rangle$, where all a_i ($I = 1, \ldots, n$) are elements of N. P is a subpath from node a_1 to node a_n. If a module a_i is recursive, then there is a path $\langle \overrightarrow{a_i a_i} \rangle$. This subpath is a loop. If a module a_i is a member of an indirectly recursive set of modules, then there is a subpath that begins at a_i and ends at a_i to wit: $\langle \overrightarrow{a_i a_j}, \overrightarrow{a_j a_k}, \ldots, \overrightarrow{a_l a_i} \rangle$. This subpath is a cycle.

A path is a subpath whose initial node is the start node and whose terminal node is a leaf node. The metric value *Path* consists of the total number of paths in a call graph.

If we accept the fact that a program that we have just designed does not intentionally use either direct or indirect recursion, then it is a simple matter to test the call graph representation of this design for loops and cycles. If a cycle is detected, this is definitely a problem in the design. It is also a problem that occurs relatively frequently in modern software systems in that there are no formal mechanisms to check for this type of anomaly.

It is a characteristic of the basic architecture of the design that a particular user operational profile will assign a frequency of execution to each module. We exploit this fact to measure the module execution profiles. While it is not possible to assign execution times to each module with any degree of reliability, we can certainly measure transitions from one module to the next. These transition events we can handily measure in terms of module epochs.

Let us imagine that we can animate our design. Then each of the modules will transfer control to every other module just as it would when the program actually executes. Associated with each edge in the call graph there will be a frequency that a particular path has executed. In Figure 9.1 we can see a hypothetical program consisting of 11 modules. These are

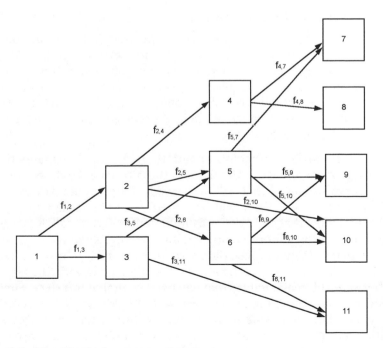

Figure 9.1. Hypothetical program structure.

connected with edges reflecting the transfer of control from one module to another. Let us assume that our hypothetical program has executed for a total of F epochs. The design module profile will apportion these F epochs to each edge in the call graph. The edge, then, between modules a and b will have been traversed $f_{a,b}$ times during the F epochs of simulated execution. The total number of times f_b that module b will have been called in these F epochs will be $f_b = \sum_i f_{i,b}$, where i is an index on the indegree of module b. The proportion of time p_b that module b will execute out of the total F epochs is then $p_b = f_b/F$. We can now describe precisely the activity in the call graph that will be distributed among the set of program modules.

It is now possible to describe the entropy of the design for its execution over the F epochs of observation as $h = -\sum_i p_i \log_{10} p_i$ where p_i is the module profile. The point of maximum entropy for a system of n modules is attained at the point where there is an even distribution of activity across all modules, in which case, $p_i = n/F$. That is, the F epochs are distributed evenly across the set of n modules. Thus, the entropy for this system would be $h = -\sum_i (n/F) \log_{10} (n/F) = -n^2/F \log_{10} (n/F)$. Of course, the point of minimum entropy will occur when modules 1 and 2 or modules 1 and 3 execute to the exclusion of everything else. In this case, $p_1 = F/F = 1$ and $p_2 = 0$. Then the point of minimum entropy will be $h = -\log_{10} 1 = 0$.

9.2.2 *Measures of Data Exchange*

In addition to the transfer of control from one module to another on a call statement, data can also be passed back and forth across the interface. On the calling side there can be one or more arguments drawn from the calling module. On the called side there will be an equivalent list of parameters. Each of the parameters will be defined on a fixed data range. It is imperative that the data range of each of the arguments be defined on a proper subset of that range.

From the standpoint of measurement, there are two attributes that we would like to measure about the data on the interface. First, we count the number of scalar values that will be passed as arguments. For each edge in the call graph, then, there will be a metric *Var* that tallies the number of scalar variables that will appear as arguments on that call. It is possible that an argument is a more complex data structure such as an array or a record or struct. Each of these data structures will contain scalar components. For example, if one of the arguments is an array with 100 elements, then there are 100 scalar values that can appear on that interface. Similarly, a record can have multiple fields. Each of the fields can be a record or a scalar value. Through systematic decomposition, each record or struct will ultimately decompose to a set of scalars. Pointer values are simple scalars. They are defined on a set of ordinal values.

Each of the scalar arguments on this data interface will be defined on a range of values. The greater this range of values, the more complex the calculations in the called module that use this value. A simple Boolean argument is defined as being one of two values: true or false. It is a very simple value. On the other hand, we might have an argument defined as a decimal value on the range from 153.25 to 327.11. There are $32711 - 15325 + 1 = 17387$ possible values for this argument. Thus, each argument a_i will have a range of possible values $r_i = UB_i - LB_i + 1$, where UB_i is the mantissa of the upper bound value of the argument scaled with the decimal point in the rightmost position. Similarly, LB_i is the mantissa of the lower bound value of the argument scaled in a similar manner. The numerical complexity of the arguments on the interface between two modules, say a and b, will be the simple sum of the range values, to wit:

$$Num_{a,b} = \sum_{i=1}^{n} r_i$$

in the case where there are n such arguments.

9.3 Measuring within Module Structure

The computational complexity of a program module depends, to a very large extent, on two factors that can be measured readily at the design state: (1) the complexity of the data that the program module must manipulate, and (2) the associated complexity of the flow of control in the program module.

9.3.1 Module Data Complexity

Just as was the case for the measurement of data attributes for the program module interface, there are two attributes that we would like to measure about the data that will be used as local variables within a program module. First, we count the number of scalar values that the program module has declared in the data section of the module definition. For each design module, then, there is a metric *Var* that will tally the number of scalar variables that are declared in the module.

It is possible that an argument is a more complex data structure such as an array or a record or struct. Each of these data structures will contain scalar components. For example, if one of the arguments is an array with 100 elements, then there are 100 scalar values that can appear on that interface. Similarly, a record can have multiple fields. Each of the fields can be a record or a scalar value. Through systematic decomposition, each record or struct will ultimately decompose to a set of scalars. Pointer values are simple scalars. They are defined on a set of ordinal values.

Each of the scalar arguments declared as local variable within a module will be defined on a range of values in precisely the same manner as was discussed in regard to the module parameters. Each local variable v_i will have a range of possible values $r_i = UB_i - LB_i + 1$, where UB_i is the mantissa of the upper bound value of the local variable scaled with the decimal point in the rightmost position. Similarly, LB_i is the mantissa of the lower bound value of the argument scaled in a similar manner. The numerical complexity of the set of local variables that are declared within a design module a will be the simple sum of the range values, to wit:

$$Num_a = \sum_{i=1}^{n} r_i$$

in the case where there are n local variables.

There will always be a design trade-off that is strongly influenced by the use of data structures. Thus, we must also factor the measurement of data structures complexity into our analysis of design complexity.

There are two broad classes of data structures. There are static data structures that are static and compiled with the source code and those that are created at execution time. Indeed, it is sometimes useful to model the dynamic complexity of programs. It is the purpose of our data structure metric to measure the complexity of static data structures. To a great extent, dynamic data structures are created by algorithms and their complexity will be indirectly measured by the control constructs that surround their creation. The data structures used in a program can influence the type of control structures used and the types of operations that can be used. The programming effort, understandability, and modifiability of a program are greatly influenced by the types of data structures used.

There is a definite difference between the complexity of a data structure as it is mapped to memory and its type complexity, which are the operations that the machine will use to process data from this structure. The type properties of the structure vanish with the compilation, preserved only in the machine operations on the data. In other words, the concept of type is an artifact of the particular programming language metaphor. The data structures persist at runtime. They represent real places in computer memory.

There appear to be many different components contributing to the complexity problem surrounding the notion of data structures. While they represent abstractions in the mind of the programmer, the compiler must make them tangible. In this regard there are two distinctly different components of complexity: (1) the declaration of the object and the subsequent operations that the underlying design architecture will have to perform to manifest the structure; and (2) there are the runtime operations that will manipulate the structure. For the purposes of domain mapping in our complexity domain model, we are interested in the operations surrounding the placement of these objects in the memory map of the design abstract machine.

The attribute complexity $C(D)$ of a data structure D is the cost to implement a data structure on the underlying architecture. This cost is closely associated with the increased complexity of the machine architecture necessary to support the data structure. We would intuitively expect that simple scalar data types are less costly to implement than more complex structures. It would also be reasonable to expect that the attribute complexity of a simple integer would be less than that of a record or struct.

A simple scalar data type like an integer, real, character, or Boolean requires that a compiler manage two distinct attributes: (1) the data type and (2) the address. Actually, the machine will also manage the identifier, or name, that represents the data structure. However, this identifier will be enumerated in the operand count measure. Thus, the attribute complexity $C(scalar)$ could be represented in a table with two entries. This structure table contains all the data attributes that the machine will need to manage for each data structure. We define the structure by the number of entries in this structure table. Thus, the data structure complexity for a scalar will be:

$$C(scalar) = 2$$

To implement an array, the abstract machine requires information as to the fact that it is an array, the memory location in relation to the address of the array, the type attribute of the elements of the array, the dimensionality of the array, the lower bound of each dimension, and the upper bound of each dimension. The structure table for an n-dimensional array is shown in Table 9.1.

In the most general sense, the computation of the attribute complexity of an array would then be governed by the formula:

$$C(Array) = 3 + 2 \times n + C(ArrayElement)$$

where n is number of dimensions the array and $C(ArrayElement)$ is the complexity of the array elements. For some simple machines, the array elements can only be simple scalars. More complex machine architectures can be developed that will support more complex data structures as array elements, in which case the array elements can be chosen from the entire repertoire of possible data structures.

Other kinds of data structures can be seen as variants of the basic theme established above. For example, a string can be considered as an

225

Table 9.1. The Array Structure

Structure: Array
Base Address
Type
Dimensions
Lower Bound #1
Upper Bound #1
Lower Bound #2
Upper Bound #2
•
•
•
Lower Bound #n
Upper Bound #n

array of characters. Therefore, we would compute the attribute complexity of the string as a one-dimensional array.

A record is an ordered set of fields. In the simplest case, these fields are of fixed length, yielding records that are also of fixed length. Each field has the property that it can have its own structure. It can be a scalar, an array, or even a record. The structure table to manage the declaration of a record would have to contain the fact that it is a record type, the number of fields in the record (or, alternatively, the number of bytes in the record), and the attribute complexity of each of the fields of the record. The computation of the attribute complexity of a fixed-length record would be determined from the following formula:

$$C(Record) = 2 + \sum_{i=1}^{n} C(f_i)$$

where n is the number of fields and $C(f_i)$ is the attribute complexity of field i.

Records with variant parts are a slightly different matter. Generally, only one record field of varying length is permitted in a variant record declaration. In this case, the compiler simply treats the variant record as a fixed-length record with a field equal in length to the largest variant field.

The attribute complexities of subranges, sets, and enumerated data types can be similarly specified. They represent special cases of array or

226

record declarations. In each case, the specific activities that the chosen architecture will generate to manage these structures will lead to a measure for that data type. Similarly, a subrange can be represented as a range of integer values, not necessarily positive. The case for sets is somewhat more complicated. A variable with a set attribute is typically represented by a bit array. Each element in the set of declared objects is represented by a bit element in this array. The size of the array is determined by the cardinality of the set.

The notion of a pointer deserves some special attention here. From the perspective of the machine architecture, a pointer is simply a scalar value. A designer might infer that the pointer has the properties of the structure that it references. To the computer, a pointer is simply a location in its memory space. Thus, a pointer is a scalar value on which some special arithmetic is performed. That is all. Hence, a pointer is measured in the same manner as a scalar of integer type. It has a value of two.

The full effect of a pointer and the complexity that this concept will introduce are, in fact, felt at runtime and not at compile time. A relatively complex set of algorithms are necessary to manipulate the values that this scalar object can receive. These values will be derived based on the efforts of the programmer and not the compiler. As a result, in this particular model, the complexity of dynamic data structures, such as linked lists and trees, will be measured in the control structures that are necessary to manipulate these abstract objects.

The data structures complexity of a program module is the sum of the complexities of each of the data structures declared in that module. If, for example, a program has five scalar data items, then the data structures complexity of this module would be 10, or the sum of the five scalar complexity values. If a program module were to contain n instantiations of various data structures, each with a complexity C_i, then the data structures complexity DS of the program module would be:

$$DS = \sum_{i=1}^{n} C_i$$

9.3.2 Module Control Complexity

The internal structure of a program module is a matter of very great interest to us at the design stage. A module that contains a lot of statements but no predicate clauses (such as in if statements) will be very easy to understand and design. It will present little opportunity for the designer to stray from the straight and narrow. Another design module with fewer statements but a really complex control structure will offer the designer plenty of opportunity to introduce faults. To understand and model the internal structure of a design module, we examine its structure through its control flowgraph.

A control flowgraph of a design module is constructed from a directed graph representation of the module that can be defined as follows:

- A directed graph $G = (N, E, s, t)$ consists of a set of nodes N, a set of edges E, a distinguished node s, the start node, and a distinguished node t, the exit node. An edge is an ordered pair of nodes (a, b).
- The indegree $I(a)$ of node a is the number of entering edges to a.
- The outdegree $O(a)$ of node a is the number of exiting edges from a.

This is similar to the definition of the call graph described in the previous section. Design modules are different in that they do contain a single terminal node. Control flow is transferred to the module through the start module s and is passed back to the calling module through the terminal node t.

The flowgraph representation of a program, $F = (E', N', s, t)$, is a directed graph that satisfies the following properties:

- There is a unique start node s such that $I(s) = 0$.
- There is a unique exit node t such that $O(t) = 0$.
- We represent both the start node s and the terminal node t by the symbol

All other nodes are members of exactly one of the following three categories:

- **Processing node**: has one entering edge and one exiting edge. They represent processing node a, $I(a) = 1$ and $O(a) = 1$. In our diagrams we represent a processing node as follows:

- **Predicate node**: represents a decision point in the program as a result of if statements, case statements, or any other statement that will cause an alteration in the control flow. For a predicate node a, $I(a) = 1$ and $O(a) > 1$. We will represent this by the symbol:

- **Receiving node**: represents a point in the program where two or more control flows join, for example, at the end of a while loop. For a receiving node a, $I(a) > 1$ and $O(a) = 1$. This will be represented by the symbol:

If (a, b) is an edge from node a to node b, then node a is an immediate predecessor of node b and node b is an immediate successor of node a. The set of all immediate predecessors for node a is denoted as $IP(a)$. The set of all immediate successors for node b is denoted as $IS(b)$. No node can have itself as a successor. That is, a cannot be a member of $IS(a)$. In addition, no processing node can have a processing node as a successor node. All successor nodes to a processing node must be either predicate nodes or receiving nodes. Similarly, no processing node can have a processing node as its predecessor.

From this control flowgraph representation, two essential control flow primitive metrics emerge:

1. Number of nodes
2. Number of edges

A path P in a flowgraph F is a sequence of edges $\langle \overrightarrow{a_1 a_2}, \overrightarrow{a_2 a_3}, ..., \overrightarrow{a_{n-1} a_n} \rangle$ where all a_i $(I = 1, ..., n)$ are elements of N'. P is a path from node a_1 to node a_n. An execution path in F is any path P from s to t.

The average length of the paths measured in numbers of edges constitutes a second characteristic of a program. A program that has a large number of relatively short control-flow paths differs greatly in terms of testing or maintenance from one having a few relatively long control-flow paths.

Another very important feature of a flowgraph, the representation of control iteration constructs, must be considered. A module can contain cycles of nodes created by IF statements, LOOP statements, or PERFORM statements. These iterative structures are called *cycles*. A loop is simply a cycle of length one (containing one node and one arc). Whether the nodes lie on a cycle relates to the concept of connectedness defined as follows:

- A flowgraph F is weakly connected if any two nodes a and b in the flowgraph are connected by a sequence of edges.
- A flowgraph F is strongly connected if F is weakly connected and each node of F lies on a cycle.

As an aside, all flowgraphs are only weakly connected in that the start node has an indegree of zero and the exit node has an outdegree of zero. However, a flowgraph can be made strongly connected by inserting an edge (t, s) connecting the exit node with the start node.

Any flowgraph might potentially contain weakly connected subsets of nodes that are flowgraphs in their own right. To examine this potential hierarchical structure of the flowgraph representation, the notion of a subflowgraph is essential.

- A *subflowgraph* $F' = (N'', E'', s', t')$ of a flowgraph $F = (N', E', s, t)$ is a flowgraph if the outdegree of every node in F' is the same as the outdegree of the corresponding node in F with the exception of the nodes s' and t'. Further, all nodes in the subflowgraph are weakly connected only to nodes in N''.
- A *subflowgraph* of F is a subflowgraph with the property that the cardinality of $N'' > 2$ and $F' \neq F$. That is, the subflowgraph must contain more nodes than the start and exit nodes and cannot be the same flowgraph.

A flowgraph is an *irreducible flowgraph* if it contains no proper subflowgraph. A flowgraph is a *prime flowgraph* if it contains no proper subflowgraphs for which the property $I(s') = 1$ holds. A prime flowgraph cannot be built by sequencing or nesting other flowgraphs and contains a single entrance and a single exit structure. The primes are the primitive building blocks of a program control flow. In the C language, the prime flowgraphs are the basic control structures shown in Figure 9.2.

The total *path set* of a node a is the set of all paths (s, a) from the start node to the node a itself. The total *path count* of a node a is the cardinality of the path set of the node; hence, each node singles out a distinct number of paths to the node beginning at the start node and ending with the node itself. The path count of a node simply equals the number of such paths.

Now that we have constructed a practical means of discussing the internal structure of a design module, it is now possible to enumerate certain characteristics of the flowgraph to represent the control complexity of the design module. It is our stated objective to learn to measure our design artifacts. Understanding and quantifying attributes of the design artifacts is a very important aspect of the design process.

It is not always very simple to build a flowgraph representation of a module. For the sake of simplicity we temporarily set aside the rule that a processing node cannot have a processing node as its own successor. We use this rule to refine the control flowgraph once we have a working model. The following steps will build the initial flowgraph:

1. The ENTRY statement automatically constitutes the first processing node of the flowgraph. The first node, of course, is the start node, which represents the module name and formal parameter list.
2. Each subsequent statement generates a processing node linked to the previous node.
3. All conditions in IF statements are extracted from the parentheses and constitute one processing node that precedes the predicate node of the selection itself.
4. The IF symbol is replaced with a predicate node linked immediately to the next processing block.

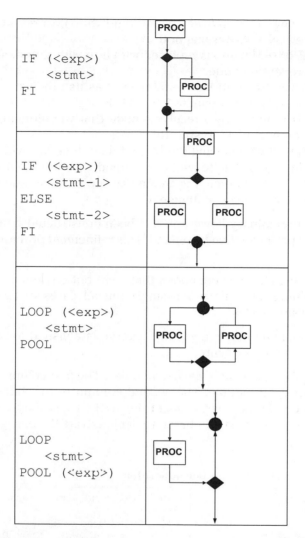

Figure 9.2. Prime flowgraphs.

5. In the case of the iteration statement LOOP, three nodes are generated. First is a receiving node to which control returns after the
   execution of the statement following the while expression. Next, the
   expression is extracted and placed in a processing node. Finally, the
   predicate node is generated and linked to the next processing node
   and to the next statement after the while group. The last processing
   node in the structure is linked to the receiving node at the head the
   structure.

6. In the case of the PERFORM iteration statement, the first expression
   in the expression list is replaced by a processing node, followed by

231

a receiving node and the second (and third) expression(s) is (are) replaced by a processing node.

7. The PERFORM token is replaced with a receiving node linked to the next processing node.
8. The POOL (<conditional>) statement has its predicate node following the statement delimited by LOOP and POOL. First, the LOOP token is replaced by a receiving node that will ultimately be linked to the end of the loop structure.
9. The statement following the LOOP token, together with the expression after the POOL token, are grouped with the LOOP statement.
10. The RETURN statement is treated as the terminal node. There can be but one of these statements.

After the preliminary flowgraph has been constructed by repetition of the above steps, it can then be refined. This refinement process will consist of:

1. Removing all receiving nodes that have but one entering edge
2. Combining into one processing node all cases of two sequential processing nodes

When all remaining nodes meet the criteria established for a flowgraph, its structure can be measured.

Table 9.2 shows a sample design modules. The first column of this table shows the original module. The second column of this table shows the decomposition of this program according to the rules above. In this example, the nodes have been numbered to demonstrate the linkage among the nodes.

Table 9.2. Sample Program Decomposition

```
HEADER average              < 0 START NODE int average(int
PARAMETERS                  number)>
    number IN               < 1 PROCESSING NODE {
    abs_number OUT              int abs_number; LINK 2>
CALLED MODULES              < 2 PROCESSING NODE (number > 0) LINK
CALLING MODULES             3>
    main                    < 3 PREDICATE NODE    if LINK 4, 5>
VARIABLES                   < 4 PROCESSING NODE   abs_number =
  PARAMETER_LIST            number; LINK 7>
    number                  < 5 RECEIVING NODE    else   LINK 6>
ENTRY                       < 6 PROCESSING NODE abs_number = -
  int abs_number;           number;
                                    LINK 7>
  if (number > 0)           < 7 RECEIVING NODE LINK 8>
    abs_number = number;    < 8 PROCESSING NODE abs_number;return
  else                      LINK 9>
    abs_number = -number;   < 9 RECEIVING NODE LINK 10>
                            < 10 EXIT NODE }>
RETURN
```

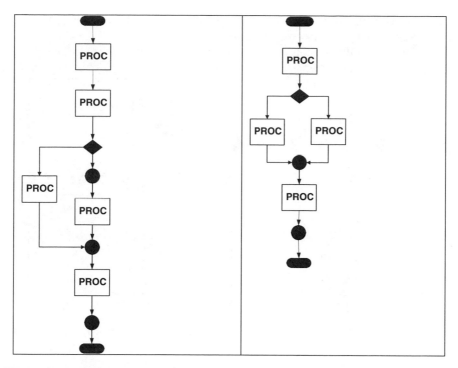

Figure 9.3. Reduction of the flowgraph.

In Figure 9.3, there are two figures. The first figure shows the graphical representation of the initial program decomposition; this is not a flowgraph. We can find, for example, two processing blocks in a row. There is also a receiving node with one entering edge and one exiting edge. When the surplus processing blocks are combined and the unnecessary processing block removed, we get the final flowgraph shown by the second figure in this table.

The *Nodes* metric enumerates the number of nodes in the flowgraph representation of the design module. The minimum number of nodes that a module can have is three: the start node, a single processing node, and the exit node. Although it is possible to create a module with just the starting node and a terminal node, it does not make sense for a real system. Modules with just two nodes can be part of a testing environment as stubs, but they should not be present in a deliverable product (see Figure 9.4).

The *Edges* metric enumerates the edges in the control flow representation of the program module. For a minimal flowgraph of three nodes, there will, of course, be two connecting edges (see Figure 9.5).

A path through a flowgraph is an ordered set of edges (*s*, ..., *t*) that begin on the starting node *s* and end on the terminal node *t*. A path can

(a)

Nodes = 8
Edges = 8
Paths = 2

```
| ENTRY
| IF (number is greater than 0)
| |   Set abs_number to number.
| ELSE
| |   Set abs_number to -number.
| RETURN
```

Nodes = 10
Edges = 11
Paths = 3

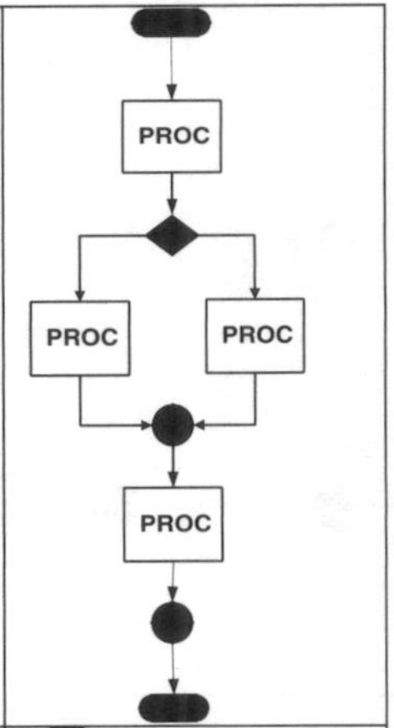

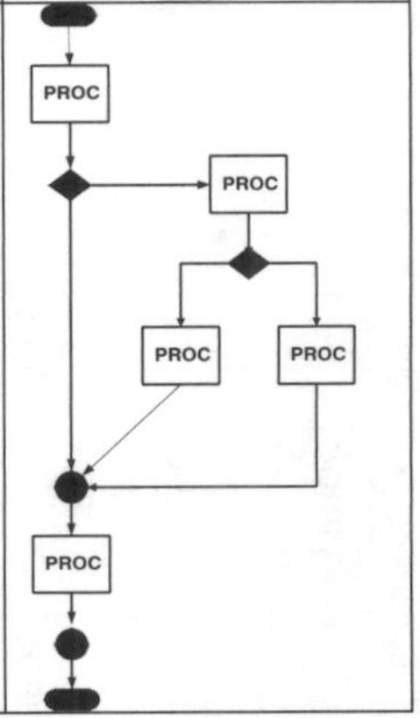

```
| ENTRY
| IF (x is equal to y)
| |   Set max to zero.
| ELSE
| |   IF (x if greater than y)
| | |   Set max to the value of x.
| | ELSE
| | |   Set max to the value of y.
| | FI
| FI
| RETURN
```

(b)

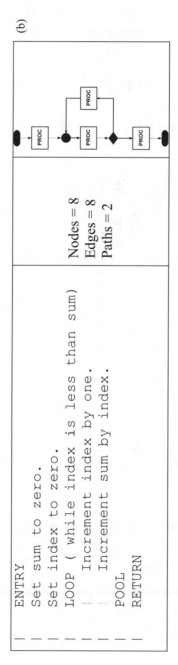

ENTRY	
Set sum to zero.	
Set index to zero.	
LOOP (while index is less than sum)	
Increment index by one.	Nodes = 8
Increment sum by index.	Edges = 8
	Paths = 2
POOL	
RETURN	

Figure 9.4. Enumeration of flowgraph metrics.

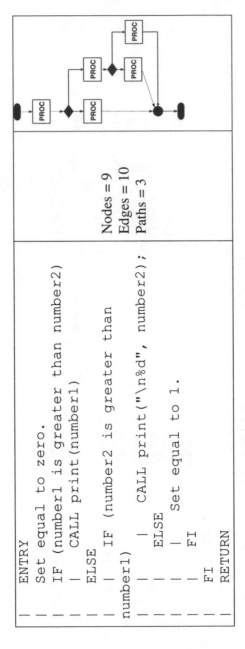

```
| ENTRY
| Set equal to zero.
| IF (number1 is greater than number2)
| | CALL print(number1)
| ELSE
| | IF (number2 is greater than
number1)
| | | CALL print("\n%d", number2);
| | ELSE
| | | Set equal to 1.
| | FI
| FI
| RETURN
```

Nodes = 9
Edges = 10
Paths = 3

Figure 9.5. Enumeration of flowgraph metrics.

236

contain one or more cycles. Each distinct cycle cannot occur more than once in sequence. That is, the subpath (*a, b, c, a*) is a legal subpath but the subpath (*a, b, c, a, b, c, a*) is not, in that the subpath (*a, b, c, a*) occurs twice.

The total path set of a node *a* is the set of all paths (*s, a*) that go from the start node to node *a* itself. The cardinality of the set of paths of node *a* is equal to the total path count of the node *a*. Each node singles out a distinct number of paths to the node that begins at the starting node and ends with the node itself. The path count of a node is the number of such paths.

The *Paths* metric tallies the number of paths that begin at node *s* and end at node *t*. Sample enumeration of the *Nodes*, *Edges*, and *Paths* metrics can be seen in Figures 9.4 and 9.5.

The direct enumeration of paths in a design module might not be functionally possible. Consider the case of a simple IF statement. If a module contains but one IF statement, then the number of paths doubles. In fact, the number of paths doubles for each IF statement in series. We once encountered a module that interrogated each bit in a 64-bit status word one bit at a time. This meant that there were a potential 2^{64} = 18,446,744,073,709,551,616 paths through this module. If our metric tool could count 1000 paths per second in the associated control flowgraph, it would take 584,942,417 years to measure this one module. For large modules, the number of path counts will grow very large. It is very good to know this at the design stage. Program modules with a very large number of paths will be very difficult to test. Common sense should prevail in the design complexity of modules. We think that modules whose path count is in excess of 100 or some other reasonable value N should come under the scrutiny of a design review process.

Cycles are permitted in paths. For each cyclical structure, exactly two paths are counted: one that includes the code in the cycle and one that does not. In this sense, each cycle contributes a minimum of two paths to the total path count. The number of cycles in the module flowgraph will be recorded in the *Cycles* metric. When the path contains control logic, the path count within the module increases (see Figure 9.6).

The *MaxPath* metric represents the number of edges in the longest path. From the set of available paths for a module, all the paths are evaluated by counting the number of edges in each of them. The greatest value is assigned to this metric. This metric gives an estimate of the maximum path flow complexity that might be obtained when running a module. In the example shown in Figure 9.6 for the second row of the table, there will be 2^3 (or 8) paths through the structure. The path length is, of course, the number arcs or edges that comprise the path. Thus, the length of the maximum path is

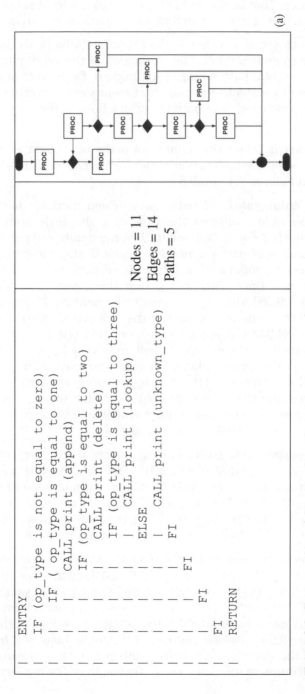

(a)

```
ENTRY
IF (op_type is not equal to zero)
|   IF ( op_type is equal to one)
|   |   CALL print (append)
|   |   IF (op_type is equal to two)
|   |   |   CALL print (delete)
|   |   |   IF (op_type is equal to three)
|   |   |   |   CALL print (lookup)
|   |   |   ELSE
|   |   |   |   CALL print (unknown_type)
|   |   |   FI
|   |   FI
|   FI
FI
RETURN
```

Nodes = 11
Edges = 14
Paths = 5

Figure 9.6. Enumeration of flowgraph path metrics.

238

(b)

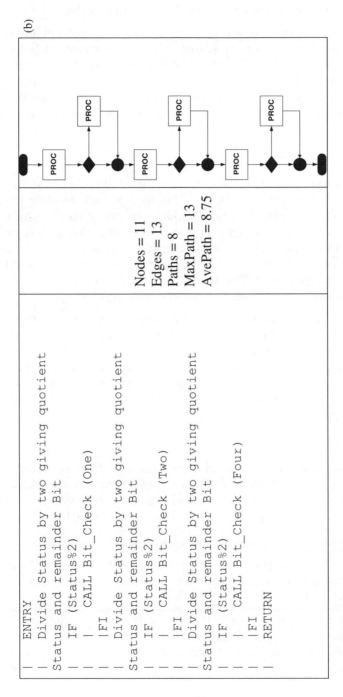

```
|   ENTRY
|   Divide Status by two giving quotient
Status and remainder Bit
|   IF (Status%2)
|   |   CALL Bit_Check (One)
|   |FI
|   Divide Status by two giving quotient
Status and remainder Bit
|   IF (Status%2)
|   |   CALL Bit_Check (Two)
|   |FI
|   Divide Status by two giving quotient
Status and remainder Bit
|   IF (Status%2)
|   |   CALL Bit_Check (Four)
|   |FI
|   RETURN
```

Nodes = 11
Edges = 13
Paths = 8
MaxPath = 13
AvePath = 8.75

Figure 9.6.   (continued)

239

10. There is one path of length 7, one of length 14, one of length 11, and one of length 17. The average path length, *Average-Path,* is then 12.25.

A cycle is a collection of strongly connected nodes. From any node in the cycle to any other, there is a path of length 1 or more, wholly within the cycle. This collection of nodes has a unique entry node. This entry node dominates all nodes in the cycle. A cycle that contains no other cycles is called an inner cycle. The *Cycles* metric contains a count of all the cycles in a flowgraph. A sample function with a cycle in its flowgraph is shown in Table 5.9.

9.4 Design Module Complexity

There are many design trade-offs. We can, for example, choose to write a small number of program modules. This makes each module relatively large and very complex. The total module coupling complexity is very small in this case. At the other extreme, we can decompose our task into lots of very small program modules. In this case, the complexity of each module tends to be very low. The total system coupling complexity, however, is astonishingly large. This type of design alternative is one that very naturally emerges in the object-oriented design model.

Unfortunately, we do not know what the consequences of the various design alternatives are. We do not know, for example, whether low coupling complexity and high module complexity is to be preferred over high coupling complexity and low module complexity. The science simply has not been done. If we are to make sound engineering decisions about our design alternatives, then we must first do the necessary science to evaluate the various alternatives.

9.4.1 Module Cohesion

We would like, now, to understand something about the cohesion of each of the modules that we have designed. In glib terms, a module with the property of cohesion is one whose entire algorithm is devoted to solving a single problem. We could construct, for example, a module to find the square root of a fractional number. It is clear that the vast majority of the procedure blocks associated with this module would be devoted to the steps in the algorithm. The possible exception to this, of course, would be procedural steps to cope with the fact that a negative value was passed to the square root function.

The worst-case scenario from the standpoint of cohesion is a module whose flowgraph looks something similar to that shown in Figure 9.7. In this case, there are three processing blocks, b_1, b_2, and b_3. There are two distinct paths in this module; let us denote the paths by the processing blocks they contain. Thus, $a_1 = \{b_1,b_2\}$ and $a_2 = \{b_1,b_3\}$ are the two paths. There are a total of three processing blocks associated with the module. The

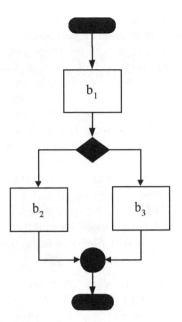

Figure 9.7. Module lacking in cohesion.

intersection set $\{b_1,b_2\} \cap a_1 = \{b_1,b_3\}$ is but one processing block $\{b_1\}$. This design module has essentially two mutually exclusive paths. It will clearly do one of two mutually exclusive things. This is a good example of a module that lacks cohesion.

We are now in a position to quantify the concept of the cohesion. A module demonstrating good cohesion would be one that has a very high proportion of processing blocks that are executed on every execution of the module. In the current example of Figure 9.1, the cardinality of the set of processing blocks in the program module is $t = \|\{b_1,b_2,b_3\}\| = 3$. On the other hand, the cardinality of the set of blocks that is common to all paths is $c = \|\{b_1\}\| = 1$. The ratio of these two terms is, then, a very good index as to module cohesion. We will state this concept thusly, *Cohesion* = c/t. In a more general sense,

$$t = \left\|\bigcup_{i=1}^{n} b_i\right\| \text{ and } c = \left\|\bigcap_{j} p_j\right\|,$$

where p_j is the set of blocks on path j.

9.4.2 Design Trade-Offs

One artifact of the design measurement process is that problem areas in certain design modules become readily apparent. In a typical large program, it is not be uncommon for there to be a number of modules whose path count is well in excess of one million paths, as was the case in the interrogation of the 64-bit status register discussed above. In this case, we saw that there would be 2^{64} or roughly 10^{19} distinct paths in just one program module. While this seems an extreme example, our experience with metric analyzer tools suggests that this is a rather common problem, so much so that our metric analyzers have typically been designed to enumerate the first 50,000 paths and then stop. It is not likely that a correct measurement could be developed by the metric analyzer on such a module in the lifetime remaining of our solar system. Therefore, our first criterion measure in the evaluation of a design will be the total path count for a program. We will seek to reduce the number of paths in the program as the design refinement progresses. This, in turn, will enhance the testability of the ultimate program. It will be far easier to make modifications to the low-level design modules than it will be to modify both the design modules and the code at a later stage in the life cycle.

There are two components to a program path count. First, there is the transition of control flow from program module to program module in the call graph. Each path t_i in the set of all n program paths consists of a set of modules from the main program module to exactly one of the leaf modules in the call graph. Thus, $t_i = \{m_s, m_a, m_b, \ldots, m_x\}$, where m_x is an element of the set of leaf modules and m_s is the main program module. Every path t_i contains the main program module as its initial node. Let $t_i' = \{m_a, m_b, \ldots, m_x\}$ represent the same set of paths as t_i but without the main program module.

Each program module m_a has an associate path count represented by the *PATH* metric. Let s_a represent the path count for module m_a. The total number of execution paths in the program represented by transfers of program control in both call statements and conditional statements is then represented by the total:

$$PROGRAM\_PATHS = s_s + \sum_{i=1}^{n} \sum_{j \in t_i'} s_j$$

We have established a measure of data complexity on the interface between any two program modules a and b as

$$Num_{a,b} = \sum_{i=1}^{n} r_i.$$

A variation on that same theme established the local variable data complexity with each program module as

$$Num_a = \sum_{i=1}^{n} r_i.$$

If A represents the set of all edges in the call graph and B represents the set of all nodes in the call graph, then the total data complexity of a particular design is given by:

$$TOTAL\_DATA = \sum_{a,b \in A} Num_{a,b} + \sum_{a \in B} Num_a$$

In this case, the smaller the value of *TOTAL_DATA* for a given design, the better the design. In a typical modern programming environment, developers use simple declarations of real variables, double-precision real variables, and long integers without regard to the range of values that these variables would then be permitted to assume. This circumstance will create literally astronomical values for *TOTAL_DATA*. This also is a contributing factor to the tremendous amount of testing and maintenance resources that will be consumed by these self-same programs. If an integer variable will be used strictly as a counter for a loop that will have values in the range 1 to 50, then it is preposterous to define this variable as a 32 binary integer that may have values from –4,294,967,295 to +4,294,967,295.

There is a clear trade-off between algorithmic complexity and data structure complexity. As data structure complexity rises, algorithmic complexity will diminish. Similarly, as data structure complexity falls, algorithmic complexity will also rise. Unfortunately, very few software designers or developers are aware of this phenomenon, principally due to the lack of measurement technology employed in the design process. The use of dynamic data structures is a very good example of this trade-off. On the one hand, it is very easy to establish a pointer to a very complex data structure. This pointer is a simple scalar. Its data structure complexity is certainly minimal. The pointer, however, will be manipulated by some very complex algorithms that have very large values of control complexity. It is fair to say that most decisions to use dynamic data structures in the design exercise are misguided. The trade-offs in overall design complexity are certainly not driving factors in this decision-making process as they should be.

9.5 Testability

Testability is a term that has been much used and little defined in the software testing community. We can begin to define and quantify this term in terms of our understanding of the distribution of functionality to program modules. If we were to write a system that always exercised all of its modules, it would be a relatively simple matter to test all the modules in the system. On the other hand, if we were to build a system that seldom or occasionally used some of the constituent program modules, then it would be more difficult to test this system because the circumstances that would cause our shy modules to execute might be obscure or ill defined.

Remember that the cardinality of the set of potentially invoked modules for a functionality f_i was denoted by $\|M_p^{(f_i)}\|$. Then, for a system of k functionalities, we can find the set M_p of all modules that are potentially invoked by at least one functionality by

$$M_p = \bigcup_{i=1}^{k} M_p^{(f_i)}.$$

We can also identify the set those modules M_i that are indispensable to at least one functionality by

$$M_i = \bigcup_{j=1}^{k} M_i^{(f_j)}.$$

Now we want to identify the set of modules M_p' that are also not in the set of indispensable modules for at least one functionality. There is a set of modules M_a in the intersection set $M_a = M_p \cap M_i$. If we remove this intersection set M_a from the set of modules M_p, we are left with the set M_p' to wit: $M_p' = M_p - M_a$. The cardinality of the set M_p' is $l = \|M_p'\|$.

The cardinality l of M_p', in relation to the total number of program modules n, is certainly one attribute dimension of the concept of testability. We could formalize this as $\tau = l/n$. A system where τ is relatively small will have a relatively high testability attribute, testability being inversely related to the cardinality of the set of modules M_p'.

The concept of testability is a multidimensional problem. There are many attributes for testability. One attribute dimension certainly relates to poor design choices that create large sets of modules M_p'. Another testability attribute has to do the with the design entropy. Low entropy designs, a necessary evil of the object-oriented design process, practically guarantee the untestability of the resulting source code. As we progress in our understanding of measurement, other aspects of program testability will become clear. Our objective is to understand the basic principles of what makes a program easy to test and then apply these principles at the design stage.

9.6 The Key Elements of Bad Design

From the standpoint of measurement and engineering, perhaps the worst design practice that can be employed is the use of function pointers to transfer control from one program module to another. There is simply no way to understand the transfer of control in a program that employs this technique. This means that the potential behavior of the program may never be fully understood. There may be latent calls that are seldom or ever expressed. This programming practice is on a par with self-modifying code.

Another very poor design practice involves the use of dynamic data structures. There are a very small number of cases that warrant the use of dynamic data structures. Typically, we will employ linked lists, for example, when there is considerable change activity within the structure. In this case, it is very easy to update list elements, to add list elements, or to delete list elements. This would be an appropriate use of a dynamic data structure. The use of dynamic data structures is most thoroughly abused when the size of the structure is not known to the designer. The simplest solution is to simply use a linked list that can grow indefinitely. The use of a dynamic data structure is not appropriate in such a case. There is considerable overhead both algorithmically and also on the part of the operating system to implement such a structure. The very best thing to do is to spend the resources to determine just what a reasonable upper bound would be on the size of the structure. We might, for example, wish to buffer records arriving from a file system. We could avoid the determination of how many such records there might be at any point through the use of, say, a linked list as a queue. An engineering solution to this same problem would be to conduct an experiment to determine the precise nature of at least the first two moments of the distribution of the number of records that might be expected. The design would then reflect a reasonable size relating to a predetermined maximum number of records that would be allowed, together with a contingency management scheme that would handle the case where this maximum is exceeded.

Bad design elements, then, can be easily recognized. They are techniques that are not founded on fact or observation. Far better it would be to take the time to model and understand the problem at the design stage than it would be to sidestep the problem with the use of design abstractions.

Chapter 10
System Architectural Trade-Offs

10.1 Introduction

To this point, we have discussed only the nature of software systems. All of our representations were for abstract machines: an operational machine, a functional machine, and a language machine. The users of our software systems will reside in a very different tangible physical universe. Users cannot interact with our software directly. They can only do so through some hardware artifact that we will create (or find). What this means is that user manipulation of the operational environment must occur through the manipulation of some physical artifact. This artifact will serve as an interface to the abstract machine.

A hardware machine, then, will always be present in any environment in which our software operates. Just how much functionality there will be on this interface is what the initial stages of the design process determine. In a typical software system running on a personal computer, the interface is well defined and highly stereotyped. As a source of input to such a system, the user has a set of buttons that he or she can push (keyboard or mouse) to generate different signals. As a source of output, there is the ubiquitous display device (LCD or CRT), or possibly a printer. In a modern version of the personal computer, the application software does not even see the keyboard or display. Rather, the software interacts with an operating system that provides the service of interacting with the user.

The software that we create, in this case, is part of a larger, more encompassing system. Some of the functionality of the system can be implemented in hardware; some of the functionality of the system can be implemented in operating system services; and some of the functionality of the system can be derived from other concurrently executing applications. One of the major problems in the design of a modern software system will be to parse the functionalities and assign each to the best environment for implementing that functionality.

10.2 The Actual Operational Model

All software systems are embedded to a greater or lesser extent in hardware and possibly in other software systems. Thus, the actual operational model of a software system consists of a hardware subsystem and a software subsystem. It would be a relatively simple matter to write yet another tic-tac-toe program that a user could play from the keyboard and see the results on the monitor in front of him or her. The system operational model must include a keyboard, a monitor for displaying program output, a computer, and an operating system to drive all of the above. When all is said and done, there are very few degrees of freedom left to the designer of the tic-tac-toe game. The program must be initiated by the operating system. The display of the game on the monitor will be achieved through an interaction with the operating system. The data from the keyboard must be obtained from the operating system. An alternative design approach would be to employ a touch-screen display device. In this approach, the user would touch the screen to place an X (or an O) in one of the nine game positions. The tic-tac-toe engine for this game would be identical to the one played from the keyboard. The rest of the program would be very different. In the first case, the program would simply interpret simple character input from the operating system. In the second case, the program would have to interact with a fairly elaborate windowing system that would be capable of presenting the form of the game on the screen and also intercepting of the coordinates of the user's contact with the screen.

The formulation of the actual operational model for a system must be done with a spectrum of system designers working in concert. In recent history, the operational characteristics of the system were established by hardware designers and then the project was tossed to the software designers to try and make the best of a system in which they had little or no input. The prevalent thinking in that environment was that the software component was simply an add-on. It was "just software." In modern systems, however, the software costs of a system are very rapidly becoming the major cost centers for these projects. It is clear that the software designers must now be part of the overall design effort at the very early stages of any new project development.

The advent of software control in modern hardware systems offers the opportunity for a literally limitless variety in the implementation of the operational characteristics of a system. In the past, the operational characteristics of systems were highly constrained by both the hardware and the characteristics of the user. The actual operating characteristics, for example, of early automobiles were the result of basic human ergonomics. In the early pictures of Henry Ford driving his first vehicle, we see him sitting at the helm of his new automobile. He is controlling the direction of the vehicle with a tiller bar. There is a good reason for this. The tiller bar gives good mechanical advantage to the driver. By grasping the tiller bar closer and farther away from its pivot point, the driver could vary both the amount of steering effort and the sensitivity of the steering mechanism. The downside of the tiller arrangement is that (1) it transmits, almost continuously, the shock of the road to the driver as the front wheels passed over potholes and rock (of which there were plenty in early roads), and (2) a sudden stop of the vehicle as it encountered another vehicle going in the opposite direction or a tree or a brick wall would impale the driver on the tiller. As a result, the tiller was rapidly replaced by a different mechanism, the steering wheel. The steering wheel could be geared to offer sufficient mechanical advantage to the driver. This same gearing mechanism would also isolate the driver from a great deal of the road shock on the front wheels. The steering wheel was also a great deal safer than the tiller bar in the event of an accident.

If both hands were occupied in the act of steering the early automobile, then the feet had to be used to accelerate and decelerate the vehicle. Consequently, a foot pedal was installed for braking. This was very good ergonomically, in that it permitted the driver to use the large muscles of his leg to apply relatively great force to the braking mechanism, which was simply a mechanical friction brake.

The elements of human factors engineering, then, mitigated the design of the user operating interface to the modern automobile. If we examine this interface, we find that we still use a steering wheel for the directional control of the vehicle, although the need for the mechanical advantage of such a mechanism vanished a long time ago. We still use a brake pedal for the vehicle, although the need for the great mechanical advantage offered by such an arrangement also vanished a long time ago. Indeed, this whole user interface is anachronistic in terms of the nature of the task to be performed by the driver.

Let us now revisit this interface and see what can be done to change it based on the new capabilities of the integrated hardware and software capabilities of today's technology. The first thing we find is that there is no need for the user to have any mechanical connection to the vehicle. The entire interface can be controlled electrically and electronically. Therefore, we might consider throwing the whole lot out and starting afresh.

There are relatively few degrees of freedom in the control of an automobile. We can accelerate or decelerate the vehicle. We can cause it go forward or in reverse. We can turn the wheels both left and right. With the exception of climate control and stereo functions, there is little else to do.

Perhaps the first thing we might elect to do in our new automobile design is to limit the control that the driver has over the vehicle. We do know what a reasonable distance should be between our vehicle and the one in front of it at different speeds. The driver should not be permitted to enter this protected sphere except in passing or overtaking situations. Thus, we might elect to install infrared ranging sensors on the vehicle so that our on-board computer could use the data from this sensor to maintain a margin of safety between vehicles. This technology has an added advantage. The reaction time of a human can be measured in seconds. The reaction time of a computer can be measured in nanoseconds. The onboard control computer will be much more effective than the human driver in determining when and how the brakes should be applied. While we are at it, we might want to limit the rate at which the front wheels can be turned. As the automobile begins to increase in speed, the rate of change in the direction of the front tires must be limited to prevent the loss of control of the vehicle. In that sense, we will accept inputs as to directional control from the driver but ensure that the driver will not be able to overact to any situation and subsequently roll over the vehicle. All these measures might seem a bit extreme but they are exactly the ones that are used in modern fly-by-wire systems now employed in commercial aircraft. In that our automobile is now operating under the control of a computer, we are in a position to ensure that it will be operated safely.

Let us now turn attention to the user interface. As we have clearly established, there is very little that a driver can do in controlling the direction and velocity of the vehicle. As a result, we could easily put the necessary controls in a single handle, or joystick, that the driver would manipulate with one hand. The forward velocity of the vehicle could be controlled by the y-axis of this stick. The turning feature would be controlled on the x-axis of the stick. Now the problem becomes very complex. We do not know what it means to push the stick forward or pull it back. This could work in a number of different ways. We could build our control system in such a way that to push the stick forward from the neutral position would cause the vehicle to accelerate in proportion to the distance from neutral that the driver pushed it. Thus, when the stick returned to the neutral position, the vehicle would continue at the new rate of speed. To slow the vehicle, we could slow it in proportion to the amount of travel back from the neutral position. That rate of deceleration would continue when the stick was returned to its neutral position. The vehicle would go into reverse only from a dead stop, in which case the operation of the stick would be just the reverse of its role when the vehicle was moving forward.

An alternative method of interpreting the control inputs from the operator's joystick would be to let the relative position of the stick in a forward position represent the absolute velocity of the vehicle. Thus, if the driver lets go of the stick, assuming that it was spring loaded to return automatically to the neutral position, the vehicle would cease to go forward. The rate of change as the stick moves forward would represent the degree of acceleration required. The faster that the stick moves forward, the greater the acceleration. If the stick is moved backward, then deceleration will occur. The more rapidly that the stick moves backward, the greater the braking function.

Now we need to worry about the braking function. To do this we need to know what it means for the control stick to be in the neutral position. It could be that the control stick in neutral means that the engine has returned to idle; the vehicle is now coasting. This being the case, pulling the stick back from neutral would engage the braking system. The braking system would operate in direct proportion to the amount of displacement from neutral in a backward motion. Reverse direction of the vehicle might be achieved only when the vehicle had reached a complete stop. Then we might simply reverse the sense of interpretation of the stick motion. That is, if the stick is pulled back, the vehicle would accelerate to the reverse. Braking would be achieved by pushing the stick forward from the neutral position.

We could engage in exactly the same discussion with the same two alternatives for the directional control of the vehicle and the movement of the control stick from left to right. There are no clear directives from a higher power as to just how this would work. These operating characteristics are certainly not part of a fundamental law of automobile design. They are merely the product of evolutionary design. These design characteristics should driven by the scientific investigation of how people interact with machines.

The rapid evolution of software capabilities in recent years has completely altered the way we look at the world. In the past, so very much of system design was dictated by the simple fact of availability of materials or, in the case of the automobile example, by the capabilities of the human operator of the system. These constraints have now been removed. There are many more degrees of freedom in the design problem than ever before. Design was previously considered a wicked problem; it is now a heinous problem. Much of what we will need to do to design a system is simply not known. Part of the design process must incorporate the discovery process as well.

It is clear that it is now possible to completely restructure the way a driver will interact with the controls of an automobile. The real question, now, is what is the best way to do this. The answer in most cases will be that the best way is not known. We will have to conduct an experiment to determine which alternative is superior to all others. Science rears its ugly head in the design of these new synergistic systems. In most cases, there are no clear answers as to how to proceed in the formulation of operations for the system. This is new ground. It has not been plowed heretofore. We will have to develop processes to discover the best operations to employ in our system. Fortunately, there is nothing novel in this discovery process. It is called scientific investigation.

To determine the best strategy to employ in the formulation of a set of user operations for the joystick controller for the new automobile, an experiment must be designed to determine the best strategy to use. The first step in the design of this experiment will be to determine suitable, quantifiable criterion measures for the experiment. That is, we must define what the term "best" really means. We could, for example, simply define "best" as the least expensive strategy to implement from a manufacturing perspective. It might well be that this strategy would lead to a host of tragic and fatal accidents on the part of drivers of these new vehicles. The notion of the "best strategy" probably hinges on a multivariate problem space. First of all, to switch from a steering wheel to a joystick will require a substantial leaning curve for both experienced and inexperienced drivers. We would like to minimize the length of time it takes for all types of drivers to acquire the techniques to use the new joystick. Second, we will seek an implementation strategy that will also minimize the reaction time of a typical driver. This reaction time will be measured in the latency between when there is a perceived need to redirect the automobile and the time it takes for the driver to initiate this action. Third, we will be interested in the accuracy of the steering action on the part of the driver. We can measure this in terms of the extent that the driver either oversteers or understeers in response to a direction change. Fourth, we will be interested in the reliability of the steering mechanism. The driver's response to the need to change the direction of the vehicle must result in the appropriate action of the vehicle at all speeds. It would be most inappropriate for a driver to slow the vehicle at high speed, resulting in a rollover of the vehicle. Thus, safety is yet another dimension to the notion of *best strategy*.

Once a determination has been made as to the dimensionality of the criterion measure of "best," then a controlled experiment can be designed to evaluate alternative strategies. In this experiment, for example, we could have two different strategies, as discussed above, for the acceleration and deceleration of the vehicle. In a well-designed experimental environment, we would set up controlling variables for those elements that are outside experimental interest. It may well be, for example, that the gender of the driver might be a significant source of variation in the reaction time or the learning time for the experiment. It might also be that drivers with more driving experience with the current steering wheel technology take much longer to manipulate the new paradigm. These are factors that must be controlled in the experiment.

The most important point in the formulation of the set of operations for the system operational model is the fact that much of what we will need to know to do a good job of this operational partitioning may not be readily available. Thus, conducting a scientific inquiry is a significant part of this design process.

10.3 Parsing Functionalities

From a complete system perspective, functionality can be implemented in a number of different ways. A functionality can be implemented in hardware, firmware, software, or even through the use of library functions. The original radio receivers, for example, were strictly hardware devices. All aspects of the functionality of the radio were resolved into hardware components. Computers simply did not exist in the early days of radio. With today's technology, it is now possible to implement much of the functionality of radio in software. For example, channel modulation waveforms can now be defined and analyzed in software. A radio receiver can extract, down-convert, and demodulate the signal input from a wideband analog-to-digital converter. Indeed, much of what has been regarded as the traditional realm of analog hardware technology can now be handled in software. One of the major problems, then, in the development of a modern system is just how much functionality will be embedded in the software.

The B2 bomber is a very good example of this new type of system. It is the first aircraft development project where the cost of the software system exceeded the hardware development cost. The B2 is a very unstable aircraft. A human being cannot fly it. The level of monitoring of the flight dynamics is simply too great for a human pilot to operate. Therefore, the pilot can only operate the aircraft through an interface to the avionics system. In the good old days, when a pilot moved the control yoke or stick, there was a physical link to the control surface on the outside of the aircraft. This is no longer the case. The control surfaces are manipulated strictly through computer control.

The design process for a complex modern system will involve a considerable number of trade-offs. If we were designing a new automobile, for example, we would have to decide what mechanism we would use to accelerate the vehicle. The traditional method for doing this is to provide the driver with a hinged pedal on the firewall of the engine compartment that the driver would depress in proportion to the speed at which he or she wanted the vehicle to move. The basic accelerate operation would simply be to depress the accelerator pedal. Now we get to the functionality bit. We could attach a rod to the back of the pedal that leads into the engine compartment and thence to the carburetor. In this case, the rod would be affixed to a bellcrank on the carburetor that would, in turn, be connected to a value that would control the volume of air passing through the carburetor. The entire functionality would be strictly mechanical. In a modern automobile, we are less likely to find such a mechanism. Rather, there is a rheostat on the back of the accelerator pedal. A computer in the engine compartment monitors the rheostat for changes in resistance. The change in resistance reflects the extent to which the driver has depressed the pedal. In this case, the functionality of accelerating is implemented strictly in software.

The decision as to whether to implement a given functionality in hardware or in software will be driven by a number of possible criterion variables. Cost might be a factor in this decision. Reliability might also be a factor in the decision process. In the case of the above accelerator example, the decision of how the functionality will be implemented was probably driven by environmental factors. To meet new environmental operating standards for engine emissions, the entire combustion process must be monitored very closely in real-time by an on board computer that will adjust the fuel flow to the cylinders to permit the optimal fuel load for a given operating condition. This being the case, the accelerator functionality must be implemented in such a fashion as to interface directly to the onboard computer.

10.3.1 The System Operational Specification

The system specification process really begins with the hardware system with which the user will interact. The software, after all, is an abstraction. The user can interact with it only through very specific interfaces. Therefore, the hardware environment for the proposed software must be clearly articulated before the software development process begins. An operating system, for example, manages the resources of a hardware system. We could not begin to specify the nature of a new operating system without a hardware context in which it can run.

It does seem reasonable to classify software into three broad taxonomic categories. There are software systems that users will interact with directly. Word-processing systems and spreadsheet systems are classic examples of such software systems. Then there are transaction processing systems. In this case, the software is designed to process data from a stream of transactions from an external source. A Web server and a credit card processing system are examples of transaction processing systems. Finally, there are embedded systems. In these systems, the customer or user of the software is a hardware system. These systems are now ubiquitous in modern automobiles. There are embedded software systems for almost all the basic functionalities of the operation of the automobile.

10.3.2 Hardware versus Software Functionalities

There are some aspects of system functionality that are strictly the domain of hardware. We simply cannot generate, for example, any tangible motive force or energy to drive an automobile. There is no software equivalent for the tires on the automobile. These things are clearly and unambiguously hardware functionalities. Exactly what happens when a driver presses the accelerator pedal of an automobile is no longer strictly a hardware domain. Much of the functionality of the fuel system of a modern automobile is now under the control of a computer and, thus, a software system. It is quite likely, then, that sensing the motion of the accelerator pedal will be a software functionality. It is thus safe to assume that those functionalities that will always be the domain of hardware are those that involve physical interaction with the universe of the user. The control functionality of a jet aircraft can easily be passed to the avionics software. The pilot of the aircraft, however, can only interact with a physical and tangible interface. This will always be the domain of hardware.

Perhaps the best way to look at the partition between hardware and software is that there are two universes for which different principles of physics apply. The universe that we occupy has the properties of time and physical objects. The universe that software systems exist in is an abstract one. Where an application demands attributes such as timing or physical interaction with the user's universe, then the functionality is clearly a hardware one. It is just that simple.

10.3.3 Design Trade-Offs

The physical universe and the abstract universe have a fairly large intersection set. This means that there are a host of design alternatives that can be assigned either to hardware or to software. Thus, in the early stages of the design of a new system, the functionality of the system must be partitioned between hardware and software. Clearly, there are some aspects of functionality that are well beyond the capabilities of software. There are others that can be implemented in either software or hardware. So that the assignment of a functionality into either hardware or software can be made, we must first identify a set of criterion measures that will mitigate in this decision-making process.

One of the primary considerations in the assignment of functionality to either hardware or software will be that of cost. If the implementation and manufacture will be cheaper in hardware than software, then the decision may clearly be to implement a functionality in hardware. It is interesting to note that in the early stages of embedded system design, the decision was frequently made to implement functionality in software wherever possible. As software systems have become much more complex and software overhead costs have escalated, as is particularly the case with object-oriented software development methodologies, the trend in the direction of implementing functionality in software has clearly reversed.

Another controlling factor in the design decision-making process is the time-to-market issue. Decisions to implement a functionality in either software or hardware will be carefully analyzed in terms of the time it takes to develop the product, test it, and deliver it to the marketplace. Again, the complexities and the lack of general engineering discipline in the software development process means that it is increasingly difficult to anticipate product development time in the software application space. This problem strongly biases the decision to implement in hardware wherever possible.

Another factor in the design decision-making process is that of maintainability. It is obvious that if a product is shipped with a fault in the software system, all products will suffer from the design flaw. This creates the circumstance for massive product recalls and a decline in goodwill on the part of the consumers of the product. Another aspect of long-term product maintenance is the enhancement process, wherein new features are added to a product to extend its viability in the marketplace. In this case, it is probably far easier to design new product features into the software rather than the hardware.

Finally, there are two closely linked criteria that play a strong role in the partition of functionality between hardware and software. These are the issues of reliability and security. A design team will certainly evaluate the potential reliability of a software solution and weigh this heavily against the reliability of an equivalent hardware solution. Unfortunately, the current state-of-the-art of software reliability modeling provides for excellent prediction of past software performance but little predictive ability for future software reliability. Precisely the same argument can be made about security. Today's completely unstructured and ad hoc software development methodologies create great potential for security vulnerabilities.

10.4 The Partitioning of Large Systems

Perhaps the best way to think about the partitioning of large systems into their several operational components would be to look at these systems from the standpoint of the operating system environment. In the more simple days of the past, a large system was simply a huge monolithic program. There was one main program module that received control from the operating system. This main program then simply distributed the program activity to a series of sub-tasks within the program entity. Large modern software systems are typically partitioned into a set of independent tasks whose activity will be coordinated by the operating system. These tasks, or processes, will communicate via some type of inter-process communication service, again provided by the operating system. These tasks can be designed to run under the umbrella of a single operating system in a self-contained environment, or they can be designed to run on different machines possibly under different operating systems in a distributed processing environment. The essential characteristic of these systems is that they are sets of independent programs, each with its own distinguished main program module.

Each of the independent programs in this new operating environment can, in turn, be partitioned into a set of very distinct functional subsystems. There might be a Web interface subsystem, a transaction processing system, and a database system in a hypothetical application. A necessary constituent of this functional partition must be that there is an interface between these functional subsystems through which these systems can interact with one another. That is, the interface between any two functional subsystems will include a data interface through which the systems can communicate.

10.4.1 *Partitioning into Independent Systems*

As a software system grows in size, so will the range of functionalities it implements. As the number of functionalities in a system increases, so too will the complexity of the build and maintenance processes. At some point, the complexity of maintaining two separate software systems will be significantly less than that of maintaining a very large monolithic system. When that time arrives, the partition will very naturally occur along functional boundaries in the system. We might be implementing, for example, a network appliance for the processing and maintenance of metric data from the software development process of a number of projects. For this network appliance there are three essential components. There is the Web interface, which presents Web pages to the users of the system and captures data from modifications made to these Web pages by the users of the system. There is a database system underlying the network appliance that is responsible for the storage and retrieval of the metric data from the many builds of the projects being monitored. Finally, there is an analytical engine that transforms the metric data into meaningful information from the consumption of the developers, testers, and project managers who are the users of the system. Logically, the metric network appliance could be divided into three independent programs that will be the subsystems of this appliance.

When a system is partitioned into distinct subsystems as separate programs, the complexity of the interaction among these subsystems will rise correspondingly. Each of the subsystems will be managed as a separate process by the operating system. Communication among the subsystems will now occur through the interprocess communication capabilities of the operating system. As a plus, however, each of the subsystems can be maintained as a separate entity.

From the standpoint of specification and design, each independent program is specified as a separate process. That is, there is a complete set of operational specifications, functional specifications, module specifications, and source code for each of the systems. The inter-process communication among these separate elements appears as the stimuli for the set of operations in each system. In the specific case of our network appliance for software measurement, the set of operations for the Web interface has a user as a client. The analytical engine and the database systems, however, will have the Web interface and each other as users of their operations. The stimuli for these two systems are strictly the inter-process communications that occur between these two systems and the Web interface.

There might also be other reasons for the partitioning of a large system into component subsystems as independent programs. This partitioning will permit each program to run on a separate computing environment as a distributed processing application.

10.4.2 Partitioning Functionality

At the next level of granularity, we now turn our attention to the partitioning of the set of functionalities. Functionalities can be composed of other functionalities. There could, for example, be a set of functionalities that implement basic trigonometric functions. This set of trigonometric functions can be used in a number of different functionalities within the larger system context. As the set of functionalities is designed, a clear hierarchy of these functionalities emerges. At the top of this hierarchical structure is a set of functionalities that are not used in the definition of other functionalities. Some functionalities are used in the definition of other functionalities and, in turn, can include other functionalities in their definition. At the lowest level, there will be a set of functionalities that is not implemented with sub-functionalities.

The set of functionalities, then, can be organized into a functionality tree. The branches of this tree clearly reflect the sequential dependencies among the functionalities. This functionality tree is also the precursor of the program call tree as it will finally be implemented. Each functionality is implemented in one or more low-level design modules. As these modules are defined during the low-level design process, the final structure of the program call graph will emerge.

10.4.3 Threads

Some functionalities are bound to each other sequentially. That is, functionality A must always precede the execution of functionality B. Other functionalities are not bound sequentially to other functionalities. To make effective use of thread during the design process, the sequential binding properties of each functionality must be completely defined. Those functionalities that are not tightly bound sequentially to other functionalities can, in fact, be executed in parallel on two separate CPUs. The careful articulation of sequential dependencies among functionalities will permit the maximum use of the parallel processing capabilities provided by execution threads in the operating system.

10.4.4 APIs

An application program interface (API) is a collection of function calls that provides standard services provided by one program to an adjunct program. From the aspect of the functional specification, we can regard the API as a set of functionalities (services) provided by a software system that is disjoint from an application we are specifying. This adjunct application can be, for example, a database management system that we will use to store and retrieve data for our own application. With the increasing complexity of today's software systems, much of the functionality of a new program will be provided by outside vendors. It is very important from a design and reliability standpoint to understand just how these systems can be integrated into the design process.

From the aspect of high-level design or functional specification, an API presents the system designer with a fixed set of functionalities. It also permits augmentation of the functional model to incorporate the functionality of the services provided by the vendor of the software system who is also the designer of the API. There are, of course, some problems with this approach. Sometimes it is not entirely possible to get a precise definition of the functionality of the system with which we wish to interface. Ambiguities on this interface will certainly affect the reliability of the project under development.

From the standpoint of low-level design, the API will present a series of function calls to specific modules in the supplied application program. At the stage of low-level design, we simply cannot know the internal structure of the modules on the API. We can, however, define very precisely the nature of the data that our program will supply to the API and receive from the API.

The adjunct application can be integrated into the design process in one of two ways. First, we must specify the set of functionalities that we will use from the application. It might well be that the application provides a very broad range of capabilities, of which we will use a very limited subset. In this case, it is necessary to specify the precise set of functionalities that will be incorporated into the current design project. It is neither necessary nor useful to specify the full range of functionality of the application in the current design project, in that it may well introduce functionalities that do not map to specific operations.

In a similar fashion, the low-level design elements that are to be extracted from the API must be included as design elements in the current project. Unfortunately, it is not be possible to implement all aspects of the module design specification. In particular, it certainly is not possible to discuss the algorithm that the external supplier of the API will have used to implement each of the function calls. Further, we only see a simple window into the application. We cannot know how the function module on the interface will interact with other modules in its own environment. We must specify the precise nature of the parameters for each of the function calls. Again, it will not be possible, in most cases, to specify the range on which each of the parameters is defined but it is certainly possible to specify the range for each of the parameters that will match the range of the arguments on the call to the program module.

All the functionalities introduced through the use of an auxiliary application must be included in the $O \times F$ mapping of the complete software system. Similarly, each of the function calls must be included in the mapping on $F \times M$.

The process of binding an external application to the one we are designing and building is fairly well defined. We must excise the functionality from the external application and incorporate that in our functional specification, both in terms of the functional model and the set of functionalities. On the interface to the external application will be a set of function calls for specific modules that will be used on the interface. Low-level design module specifications must be made for the function calls that will be used in the external application. Ultimately, we must have a complete picture of how the external application will be reflected on the set of operations for the application we are developing. This we can understand from the mapping of operations to modules in $O \times F \times M$.

Chapter 11
The Structure of an Executing Program

11.1 Introduction

A program is composed of a set of modules that interact with one another. Control can be passed from one module to another via a call command. Similarly, control can be passed back from a called module to a calling module through a return command. There are two different ways that we can look at these interactions. We can represent the program as a call graph where every program module is represented only once in the structure. Or, we can represent the program as a call tree where a module can be present more than once in the structure. In this case, there will be a node for each module representing the transition of control from a single program module. Thus, if a module A can be called from three different modules, say B, C, and D, then there will be three different occurrences of module A in the call tree.

11.2 A Program Represented as a Call Graph

In the previous chapter we established that a call graph of a program was a 4-tuple $G = (N, E, L, s)$. Further, a path P in a call graph G is a sequence of edges $\langle \overrightarrow{a_1 a_2}, \overrightarrow{a_2 a_3}, ..., \overrightarrow{a_{N-1} a_N} \rangle$ where all a_i $(I = 1, ..., N)$ are elements of N'. P is a path from node a_1 to node a_n. Again, a program can contain cycles of nodes created by direct or indirect recursion. These iterative structures are called *cycles*. A cycle is simply a path from any node a_i to itself. A *loop* is simply a cycle of length 1 (containing one node and one arc).

In Figure 11.1 there is a simple program composed of eight modules. The calling structure of this program is visible from this call graph. The eight program modules constitute the eight nodes of the call graph. The relative complexity of the call graph is reflected in the count of the edges of the graph. In this example, there are ten arcs, each representing a call and return path to and from a module.

The problem with the call graph representation is that when we are executing a given module, say module G, we have no idea of exactly how we got there. There are six different paths from the main program module

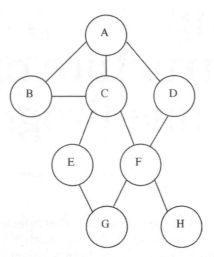

Figure 11.1. Program call graph.

to module G. In the call graph, we simply do not know which of these paths was executed to get to module G.

11.3   A Program as a Call Tree

There is a distinguished entry point in any computer program. This is the point to which the operating system transfers control when the program initiates. It is typically the main program module in set of code modules. The main program can then transfer control to a number of modules through the use of a call instruction. Each of these program modules can, in turn, transfer control, again by a call statement, to a number of other program modules. The control structure represented by these sequences of calls is a program call graph. At its root node is the main program module.

The nodes of the call tree are not unique. If a module is called from a number of program modules, then it appears in the call tree as a number of different nodes. In that this structure is a tree, the indegree of each node will be exactly 1. The outdegree, number of exiting edges, of each module is defined as $0 \leq O(i) \leq n - 1$ for a software system consisting of n program modules.

An alternate means of representing the modular structure of a program is the call tree. It can be derived directly from the call graph. The call tree representation $T = (E', N', L, s)$ is a directed graph that satisfies the following properties:

- There is a unique start node s such that $I(s) = 0$.
- The indegree of $b \in B$ is $I(b) = 1$, where B is a bag of nodes defined on the set of nodes L, the associated call graph.
- There is a bag of nodes B defined on the elements of L such that $O(l) = 0$, $I(l) \geq 1$ for $l \in L$. This is the set of leaf nodes.

In a call graph, the elements of any path P are unique. They may not appear anywhere else in the graph. In a call tree, on the other hand, there may be multiple occurrences of the same path P in the tree.

In a well-specified software system, this call graph can be determined from the low-level design module specifications. All the information necessary to construct the call graph is available within the module specifications. Unfortunately, in the vast majority of modern software systems, it is not possible to construct this call tree with any degree of certainty or accuracy for two reasons. First, there are generally no low-level design specifications for these systems. The call tree must be constructed from the source code alone. It is not always possible to understand exactly what the module binding relationship is among program modules from the source code. Second, they employ a very poor programming practice, that is, the use of function pointers to transfer control from one module to a possible range of other modules. In a software system that uses function pointers, we can never know for certainty that we have been able to specify the call tree with certainty.

The simple program represented as a call graph in Figure 11.1 is shown in Figure 11.2 as a call tree. In this new structure, there are multiple occurrences of some modules. Module G, for example, is present in the tree in three different places. There are 16 nodes in this graph and a total of 15 arcs connecting them.

There is now no ambiguity as to which path was executed to arrive at module G. If, for example, we are executing the module G that is the rightmost node in the tree, then it is obvious that the path of modules A, D, and F was executed to get to this instantiation of module G.

11.3.1 The Structure of Functionalities

It is clear that functionalities consist of program modules. Furthermore, at least one of these program modules must be uniquely associated with each functionality. These modules clearly interact with one another in the fulfillment of their relationship with the functionality. Each functionality, then, is represented by a sub-tree of the program call tree. The contents of these sub-trees is not unique. There may be many instances of a particular functionality sub-tree in the program call tree.

Some functionalities can be used to implement other functionalities, in which case a functionality sub-tree may be composed of one or more

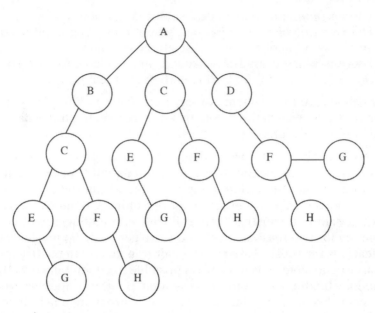

Figure 11.2. Program call tree.

functionality sub-trees. There is an apparent problem with this notion. That is, we will insist that each functionality have at least one module that is uniquely associated with that functionality. This would appear to preclude the possibility that a functionality would be used to implement another functionality. We can solve this dilemma by observing that each functionality sub-tree is an entity in its own right. That is, the modules that implement it are distinctly associated with the root node of the minor functionality sub-tree.

11.3.2 The Structure of Operations

Each operation is implemented by one or more functionalities. Furthermore, the functionalities that implement that operation will interact with one another in the process of expressing the operation. As was the case with the functionalities, the individual operations can be seen as sub-trees of the program call graph.

We have insisted on the principle of mutual exclusion of each of the operations. We will only consider these operations one at a time. It was also an option of each of the operations that it be bound either sequentially or temporally to one or more other operations. Thus, the sub-trees represented by these operations have great implications on the structure of the executing program. Those operations that are not bound sequentially or temporally to other operations may well be executed in parallel with other operations. This has great implications on the functional aspects of the executing program. Among other things, it permits the program to be parsed neatly into threads for parallel execution.

11.3.3 Instrumenting the Call Tree

There are a variety of ways that a program can be instrumented to monitor its operation at runtime. In the previous analysis, all of these instrumentation techniques will be implemented by inserting software probes at selected points in the call tree, depending on the nature of the telemetry required from the operating program.

In the simplest case, a software probe is a call statement within a program module. When the call statement is encountered, control will be transferred to a tally module that records the name (or number) of the calling module. Each module in this scheme has a unique name or number that it will transmit to the tally module as an argument at the point of the call. The tally module is not part of the program functionality; it is part of the control monitoring system. Our software probes will be employed only to monitor the flow of control among the program modules.

The control system is part of a process control infrastructure that we will see later is vital to our monitoring the health of the software system. Early automobile systems ran completely without instrumentation. They ran until they got too hot, they ran out of oil, their electrical systems failed, or some other crisis would befall the mechanical systems. Then the automobile would stop, perhaps irrevocably damaged by the failure condition. This, of course, represents the current state-of-the-art for almost every software system in service today. It soon became evident to automobile manufacturers that they could place sensors in the cooling systems or the oil systems of the engines and warn the driver when an abnormal condition existed in the engine system. This would permit the automobile driver to ameliorate the abnormal condition before the engine was completely destroyed. In like manner, our simple instrumentation of a software system is analogous to the instrumentation that we have come to expect in our automobiles. We want to monitor the operation of a system and detect abnormalities before the software system is irrevocably damaged either by a flaw in the software or some malicious use of the system.

There are two distinct ways that we can instrument the individual program modules. We can put the software probes at the beginning of each program module. In this way we can know when a module is entered. This level of instrumentation will be useful for counting the number of times that each module has been invoked. It will give a good estimate of the distribution of activity across all program modules. We can also instrument at both the module entry point and at its return statement. With this second level of instrumentation, it is possible to trace the path of execution from one program module to another. With this instrumentation strategy, we can know exactly where we are executing in the call tree at any epoch. The downside of instrumenting both the entry point and the return is that the overhead for this level of instrumentation is just about twice that imposed by instrumenting only the module entry points.

Not every module must be instrumented to determine the activity on the system. Instrumenting each module, while it gives tremendous resolution on the system activity, does impose a significant amount of processing overhead. For most purposes, we are only interested in higher-level granularity observations. We know, for example, that each functionality has a module that is uniquely associated with that functionality. By simply instrumenting one module for each functionality that is uniquely associated with that functionality, it will be possible to trace the functionalities that have executed during any particular time interval. At the next higher level of instrumentation, let us observe that each operation is implemented by one or more functionalities. We can identify, then, a distinct module for each operation and place our instrumentation in this module. Thus, we can monitor the execution of sequences of operations on the system as they occur.

11.3.4 Motivation for Extracting High-Level System Observation

The primary motivation for instrumenting and measuring an executing system is to derive estimates for the three profiles — the operational profile, the functional profile, and the module profile. The act of measuring software that is running is a very expensive proposition. The data bandwidth of this process is very large. Unless this data can be filtered in some meaningful way, just the simple task of saving it for future reference can consume a vast number of compute cycles. Data mining on-the-fly will be prohibitively expensive. We must know why we are measuring before we start.

There are a couple of very good reasons to measure systems that are running. First, we can monitor their activity in real-time to ensure that the software is performing in a normal way. If the user is forcing a system into some new execution territory, at best he or she might be inadvertently pushing the system into new and uncertified execution territory and, at worst, be trying to penetrate the security of the system. Second, it is very useful to know what code we have touched during the course of the execution of a specific test. Any observation of code activity, however, must be seen for what it is. The activity that we observe in the code is a reflection of user activity. We are measuring the code to determine how it is being used; we are not measuring the code for code coverage. That is measurement for measurement's sake. We do not care that all code in a program has been touched in some way during its certification. We do care that the code can do what the user will request of it. Our interest in code measurement will be in what we will learn about the functionality of the program.

By keeping track of the state transitions from module to module and operation to operation, we can learn exactly where a system is fragile. This information, coupled with the operational profile, will tell us just how reliable the system will be when we use it as specified. Programs make transitions from module to module as they execute. These transitions can be observed. We can model these transitions as a stochastic process. Ultimately, by developing a mathematical description for the behavior of the software as it transitions from one module to another driven by the operations that it is performing, we can effectively measure what the user is doing with the system.

As a program is exercising any one of its many operations in the normal course of executing the program, the user will apportion his time across a set of operations. The proportion of execution activity that the user spends in each operation is the *operational profile* of the program. The proportion of time that a program spends in each of its functionalities is the *functional profile* of the program. Further, within the functionality, it will apportion its activities across one to many program modules. This distribution of processing activity is represented by the concept of the execution profile. That is, if we have a program structured into n distinct modules, the *execution profile* for a given functionality will be the proportion of program activity for each program module while the functionality is being expressed.

11.3.5 Retrofitting Instrumentation for Functionality Extraction

There are very few, if any, software systems in existence today for which there are complete operational and functional specifications. If we wish to instrument and observe these systems at this level of granularity, we are going to have to extract the functionalities from the module level data. There are two distinct ways we can extract these functionalities from the module data, depending on the nature of the underlying instrumentation. We first explore the possibilities for extracting the functionalities from a simple instrumentation procedure.

One of the first issues we must come to grips with in the measurement of a software system that is running relates to the latency of the observations. We can track the operation of a system at the nanosecond level by observing each module transfer as it occurs. For most purposes, however, we do not need this kind of resolution. For the purposes of reliability and security measurement, latencies on the order of several milliseconds are quite acceptable. Therefore, we only really need to extract information from the operation program only every 1000 epochs or so to monitor is activity with reasonable certainty. This being the case, let us now turn our attention to the problem of extracting the functionalities from the module-level telemetry of the executing program. Keep in mind that there are two levels of instrumentation that we can place in the software: Level 1 instrumentation places probes only at module entry points and Level 2 instrumentation places probes at both the entry and return points from each module. We begin our discussion with Level 1 instrumentation techniques.

In the course of normal program activity, the transitions into each program module at each epoch can be recorded in an execution profile for the program. This execution profile is an n-element vector $\mathbf{X}$ containing one entry for each program module. Each element x_i of this vector $\mathbf{X}$ contains a frequency count for the number of times that the corresponding module m_i has executed during an era of k epochs. Thus, $k = \sum x_i$. We are going to accumulate execution frequencies in this execution profile until the value of k has reached some maximum value of K.

Again, the size of K depends on the nature of the latencies that we can tolerate between observations. There are certain trade-offs that must be made in the determination of K. Smaller values of K mean that the latencies between observations are low. Larger values of K mean that the activity of the program represented by the execution profile is more complete. To be meaningful at all, these data must be captured periodically and transmitted to a control program for analysis. In this context, an execution profile might be recorded whenever the value of k reached a total count of, say, K, at which time the contents of the original execution profile vector would be reset to zero (i.e., $x_i = 0$, $\forall i = 1, 2, ..., n$). The recorded activity of a program during its last $L = jK$ epochs is stored in a sequence of j execution profiles, $X_1, X_2, ..., X_j$. Thus, the value $x_{i,j}$ represents the frequency of execution of the ith program module on the jth execution profile.

The *behavior* of a program is embodied in the manner with which the program modules interact while the program is running. We do know that the modules that implement a functionality are all elements of a common sub-tree. If we observe one module of this sub-tree, then there is a very good likelihood that we will see other elements of the same sub-tree during the same observation interval.

The relative frequency of a particular module, say module m_a, can be established by the two statistics of mean and standard deviation for this module. The mean value for module m_a during a sequence of j execution profiles is

$$\bar{x}_a = \frac{1}{j} \sum_{k=1}^{j} x_{a,k}.$$

The standard deviation in the frequency of execution of module m_a for this same observation interval will be

$$\sigma_a = \sqrt{\frac{1}{j-1}\sum_{k=1}^{j}(x_{a,k}-\bar{x}_a)^2}.$$

The interaction between any two program modules, say, m_a and m_b, during the execution of a program over L epochs or j execution profiles can be expressed in terms of the correlation coefficient

$$r_{ab} = \sum_{i=1}^{j} z_{a,i} z_{b,i},$$

where $z_{a,\bullet} = x_{a,\bullet} - \bar{x}_a/\sigma_a$. We would like to use the correlation information to extract the actual sets of modules that interact with each other over the range of observed behavior of the system. The principal role of the behavioral analysis of program execution will be in the area of application monitoring. In a computer security context, changes in the correlation of the modules over time from some nominal pattern will indicate the presence of new or novel behavior that is potentially threatening. From an availability perspective, these same changes in program behavior may well mean that the program is now executing in a new and uncertified manner.

Our next task is to use a statistical technique to reduce the dimensionality of the problem from a set of n program modules to a set of m functionalities. To achieve this reduction in the dimensionality of the problem space, the statistic techniques of principal components analysis or principal factor analysis can be employed. For either of these two techniques, the $n \times j$, $j > n$ data matrix $D = X_1, X_2, ..., X_j$ will be factored into m virtual orthogonal module components. Each of these new orthogonal sets of modules represents a set of modules that execute in concert with one another. Associated with each of the new m orthogonal components is an eigenvalue λ_i. The number of components extracted in the new orthogonal structure is determined by a stopping rule based on the eigenvalues. Examples of two such stopping rules would be (1) extract all components meeting the condition $\lambda_i \geq t$ where t is some threshold value, or (2) extract those components such that

$$t \geq \frac{1}{n}\sum_{i=1}^{m}\lambda_i,$$

where t represents the relative proportion of variance accounted for by the components represented by the eigenvalues $\lambda_1, \lambda_2, ..., \lambda_m$.

A product of the principal component or factor analysis solution to the factoring of the data matrix, $\mathbf{D}$, is the factor pattern or principal components structure $\mathbf{P}$. The matrix $\mathbf{P}$ is an $n \times m$ structure whose rows $p_{\bullet j}$ contain values showing the degree of relationship of the variation of the ith program module and the jth factor or principal component. Let

$$q_i = \max_{1 \le j \le m} p_{ij}.$$

Let $o_j = \text{index}(q_j)$ represent the column number in which the corresponding value q_j occurs. If, for row j, the largest value of p_{ij} occurs in column 5, then $o_j = 5$. This indicates that the program module, m_j, is most clearly related to the fifth factor or principal component.

The vector $\mathbf{O}$ whose elements are the index values o_j is said to be the *mapping vector* for the execution profile vector. This mapping vector is employed to identify the structure of each of the imputed functionalities. All of the elements, for example, of this vector that contain the same number relate to a common functionality. Stated another way, the elements of the vector $\mathbf{O}$ show the structure of the underlying functionalities.

In essence, the principal components or factor analysis techniques serve to identify m distinct and orthogonal sources of variation in the data vector $\mathbf{D}$ representing the original n program modules. These new m orthogonal domains represent the actual manner in which the software system is executing in terms of the underlying functionalities. Whereas the raw measurements taken on the non-reduced software system reflect n distinct modules, these modules are actually interacting as m distinct functional units $m < n$.

On each of the original raw profiles, the module frequency count was represented in the elements $x_{i,j}$ of the profile vector $\mathbf{X}_i$. After the mapping vector has been established to map each of the raw module interactions into a new functionality domain, the *virtual functionality vector* $\mathbf{Y}_i$ will be employed to contain the frequency counts for any of the interactions among the virtual module set. Thus,

$$y_{k,\bullet} = \sum_{i=1}^{n} f(x_{i,\bullet})$$

where:

$$f(x_{i,\bullet}) = \begin{cases} 0 & \text{if } o_i \ne k \\ x_{i,\bullet} & \text{otherwise} \end{cases}$$

Each of the vectors $\mathbf{X}_i$ represents a point in an n-dimensional space. Each of the vectors $\mathbf{Y}_i$ represents a point in a substantially reduced m-dimensional space. Each point in the *n*-dimensional raw vector represents a behavioral observation of the software system during *K* epochs. The frequency counts of the module executions are, however, highly correlated. Each of the points in a reduced virtual module execution similarly represents a behavioral observation also during the same *K* epochs. In the new scheme, the virtual module interactions have been eliminated.

If the software system is instrumented for Level 2 types of observations, we can observe the operation of the software in a variety of different contexts, presuming that we have observed the full panoply of operations in doing so. As the program transitions from one program module to another, we can use the telemetry from the software probes to construct the actually operational call tree for the executing program. To extract the actual functionalities from this tree structure, let us first observe that the functionalities will be sub-trees of the full call tree. Some of these sub-trees will occur in multiple places in the call tree.

Remember that each of the functionalities can be implemented by one or more other functionalities. Thus, in the process of identifying functionalities, we must visit the ends of the tree branches first. Each of the functionality sub-trees will have a distinct module in it that is unique. These unique modules serve to identify the individual functionalities. In essence, we can systematically identify one such module in each of the functionality sub-trees. All the other nodes in the sub-tree can be replaced by this unique module. It, alone, will serve to identify the functionality. Thus, by starting at the outermost branches of the call tree, we can identify the low-level functionalities and replace each of the nodes in the functionality sub-tree with a single distinct program module. By applying this reduction process from the outermost branches to the root node of the tree, we will then be able to identify the set of distinct functionalities in the tree.

If we are to instrument the functionalities in the program whose functionalities were disclosed by the above algorithm, we need only instrument the set of unique modules that remain in the call tree after the pruning process has been applied.

11.3.7 *Module Flowgraph Structure*

As discussed previously for a problem of fixed computational complexity, there is a trade-off between the modularity of the implementation of the problem and the internal flowgraph complexity of the module. That is, we can build a program with but one very complex module or we can have a program with a lot of very simple modules with regard to their internal structure. A module with a very bushy control flowgraph will be very difficult to maintain. This complexity was represented by the number of *Nodes*, *Edges,* and *Paths* and in the flowgraph representation of the program

271

module. It is clear that these values are, in a sense, complementary to the call graph values. They are inversely related. If a module is divided into two separate modules, the flowgraph complexity of each of the modules will be considerably less than the original single module. However, the call graph complexity of the total system will rise as a result of the addition of at least one new module.

11.4   Measuring for the Profiles

The actual measurement process for the profiles is complicated. Each new version of a module, of a functionality, and of an operation is a new entity. Essentially, we must discard what we knew about the entity from our past observations. It will be necessary to begin anew our observations of this new module. Each build has a distinct set of modules that went to that build. These modules, in turn, are associated with a distinct set of functionalities. The functionalities are also associated with a distinct set of operations. The only historical data that we can use across builds is the data from identical versions of modules, functionalities, and operations.

11.4.1   Estimates for the Profiles

Now we know what are measurement objectives are. We wish to know the operational, functional, and module profiles. Unfortunately, this data is known only to Nature, who is not anxious to share her knowledge of these profiles with us. We can never know the real distribution of these three things. We can, however, develop reasonable estimates for the profiles.

The focus now shifts to this problem of understanding the nature of the distribution of the probabilities for various profiles. We have thus far come to recognize these profiles in terms of their multinomial nature. The multinomial distribution is useful for representing the outcome of an experiment involving a set of mutually exclusive events. Let

$$S = \bigcup_{i=1}^{M} S_i$$

where S_i is one of M *mutually* exclusive sets of events. Each of these events would correspond to a program executing a particular module in the total set of program modules. Further, let $\Pr(S_i) = w_i$ and

$$w_T = 1 - w_1 - w_2 - \cdots - w_M$$

where $T = M + 1$, in which case w_i is the probability that the outcome of a random experiment is an element of the set S_i. If this experiment is conducted over a period of n trials, then the random variable X_i represents the frequency of S_i outcomes. In this case, the value n represents the number of transitions from one program module to the next. Note that:

$$X_T = n - X_1 - X_2 - \cdots - X_M$$

This particular distribution will be useful in the modeling of a program with a set of k modules. During a set of n program steps, each of the modules can be executed. These, of course, are mutually exclusive events. If module i is executing, then module j cannot be executing.

The multinomial distribution function with parameters n and $w = (w_1, w_2, ..., w_T)$ is given by:

$$f(\mathbf{x} \mid n, \mathbf{w}) = \begin{cases} \dfrac{n!}{\prod\limits_{i=1}^{k-1} x_i!} w_1^{x_1} w_2^{x_2} \cdots w_M^{x_M}, & (x_1, x_2, \cdots, x_M) \in S \\ 0 & \text{elsewhere} \end{cases}$$

where x_i represents the frequency of execution of the ith program module.

The expected values for the x_i are given by:

$$E(x_i) = \bar{x}_i = nw_i, i = 1, 2, ..., k$$

the variances by:

$$Var(x_i) = nw_i(1 - w_i)$$

and the covariance by:

$$Cov(w_i, w_j) = -nw_i w_j, i \neq j$$

We would like to come to understand, for example, the multinomial distribution of a program's execution profile while it is executing a particular functionality. The problem here is that every time a program is run, we will observe that there is some variation in the profile from one execution sample to the next. It will be difficult to estimate the parameters $w = (w_1, w_2, ..., w_T)$ for the multinomial distribution of the execution profile. Rather than estimating these parameters statically, it would be far more useful to get estimates of these parameters dynamically as the program is actually in operation. In essence, we would like to watch the system execute, collect data, and stop when we know that we have enough information about the profiles to satisfy our needs.

Unfortunately, for the multinomial distribution, the probabilities are the parameters of the distribution. We cannot know or measure these. We can, however, observe the frequency that each module has executed. Thus, it is in our interest to choose a probability distribution whose parameters are related to the things that we can measure.

273

To aid in the understanding of the nature of the true underlying multinomial distribution, let us observe that the family of Dirichlet distributions is a conjugate family for observations that have a multinomial distribution. The probability density function for a Dirichlet distribution, $D(\alpha, \alpha_T)$, with a parametric vector $\alpha = (\alpha_1, \alpha_2, ..., \alpha_M)$ where $(\alpha_i > 0; i = 1, 2, ..., M)$ is:

$$f(w \mid \alpha) = \frac{\Gamma(\alpha_1 + \alpha_2 + \cdots + \alpha_M)}{\displaystyle\prod_{i=1}^{M} \Gamma(\alpha_i)} w_1^{\alpha_1 - 1} w_2^{\alpha_2 - 1} \cdots w_M^{\alpha_M - 1}$$

where $(w_i > 0; i = 1, 2, ..., M)$ and

$$\sum_{i=1}^{M} w_i = 1.$$

The expected values of the w_i are given by:

$$E(w_i) = \mu_i = \frac{\alpha_i}{\alpha_0} \tag{11.1}$$

where

$$\alpha_0 = \sum_{i=1}^{T} \alpha_i.$$

In this context, α_0 represents the total epochs. The variance of the w_i is given by:

$$Var(w_i) = \frac{\alpha_i(\alpha_0 - \alpha_i)}{\alpha_0^2(\alpha_0 + 1)} \tag{11.2}$$

and the covariance by

$$Cov(w_i, w_j) = \frac{\alpha_i \alpha_j}{\alpha_0^2(\alpha_0 + 1)}$$

Obtaining confidence intervals for our estimates of the parameters for the Dirichlet distribution is not a very tractable problem. To simplify the process of setting these confidence limits, let us observe that if $w = (w_1, w_2, ..., w_M)$ is a random vector having the M-variate Dirichlet distribution, $D(\alpha, \alpha_T)$, then the sum $z = w_1 + \cdots + w_M$ has the beta distribution:

$$f_\beta(z \mid \gamma, \alpha_T) = \frac{\Gamma(\gamma + \alpha_T)}{\Gamma(\gamma)\Gamma(\alpha_T)} z^\gamma (1-z)^{\alpha_T}$$

or, alternately,

$$f_\beta(w_T \mid \gamma, \alpha_T) = \frac{\Gamma(\gamma + \alpha_T)}{\Gamma(\gamma)\Gamma(\alpha_T)}(1 - w_T)^\gamma (w_T)^{\alpha_T}$$

where $\gamma = \alpha_1 + \alpha_2 + \cdots + \alpha_M$.

Thus, we can obtain $100(1-)\%$ confidence limits for:

$$\mu_T - a \le \mu_T \le \mu_T + b$$

from

$$F_\beta(\mu_T - a \mid \gamma, \alpha_T) = \int_0^{\mu_T - a} f_\beta(w_T \mid \gamma, \alpha_T)\, dw = \frac{\alpha}{2} \qquad (11.3)$$

and

$$F_\beta(\mu_T + b \mid \gamma, \alpha_T) = \int_0^{\mu_T + b} f_\beta(w_T \mid \gamma, \alpha_T)\, dw = 1 - \frac{\alpha}{2} \qquad (11.4)$$

Where this computation is inconvenient, let us observe that the cumulative beta function F_β can also be obtained from existing tables of the cumulative binomial distribution F_b by making use of the knowledge that:

$$F_b(\gamma \mid \mu_T - a, \gamma + \alpha_T) = F_\beta(\mu_T - a \mid \gamma, \alpha_T) \qquad (11.5)$$

and

$$F_b(\alpha_T \mid 1 - (\mu_T + b), \gamma + \alpha_T) = F_\beta(\mu_T + b \mid \gamma, \alpha_T)$$

The value of the use of the Dirichlet conjugate family for modeling purposes is twofold. First, it permits us to estimate the probabilities of the module transitions directly from the observed module frequencies. Second, we are able to obtain revised estimates for these probabilities as the observation process progresses.

Let us now suppose that we wish to obtain better estimates of the parameters for our software system whose execution profile has a multinomial distribution with parameters n and $W = (w_1, w_2, \ldots, w_M)$, where n is the total number of observed module transitions and the values of the w_1 are unknown. Let us assume that the prior distribution of W is a Dirichlet distribution with a parametric vector $\acute{a} = (\alpha_1, \alpha_2, \ldots, \alpha_M)$ where $(\alpha_i > 0; i = 1, 2, \ldots, M)$. In this case, α_i is the observed frequency of execution of module i over $\sum_i a_i$ epochs. If we were to let the system run for an additional, say, $K = \sum_i x_i$ epochs, then we would get better estimates for

275

the parameters for the cost of the observation of these new epochs. Then the posterior distribution of W for the with the additional observations $X = (x_1, x_2, \ldots, x_M)$ is a Dirichlet distribution with parametric vector:

$$\acute{\mathbf{a}}^* = (\alpha_1 + x_1, \alpha_2 + x_2, \ldots, \alpha_M + x_M)$$

As an example, suppose that we now wish to measure the activity of a large software system. At each epoch (operational, functional, or module) we will increment the frequency count for the event. As the system makes sequential transitions from one event to another, the posterior distribution of W at each transition will be a Dirichlet distribution. Further, for $i = 1$, $2, \ldots, T$ the ith component of the augmented parametric vector α will be increased by one unit each time a new event is expressed.

11.4.2 Evolution of the Estimates for the Profiles

At the lowest level of measurement of the profiles is the module profile. After the first complete integration build of the system, it is possible to begin to accumulate data on the frequency of execution of each module during the testing phase. To do this, a module frequency vector $F^{(n)}$ will be set up. The superscript of the vector represents the build number. The elements of the vector F are the set of module versions that went to a particular build. Unfortunately, a system is a very dynamic set of program modules, particularly during the early stages of development. The amount of churn in the program modules will be substantial. Some modules will appear on a particular build and then vanish at some later build. Some modules will enter on later builds and remain with the system until it is delivered to the customer. Some modules will be changed during the course of evolution. It will not be easy to track the evolution of the system from the standpoint of its module composition.

Each of the program modules is a potential candidate for modification as the system evolves during development and maintenance. As each program module is changed, the total system must be reconfigured to incorporate the changed module. We refer to this reconfiguration as a "build." To feel the effect of any change, it must physically be incorporated in a build.

To describe the complexity of a system at each build, it is necessary to know the version of each of the modules in the program at that build. Each of the program modules is a separate entity. It evolves at its own rate. Consider a software system composed of n modules as follows: m_1, $m_2, m_3, \cdots, m_n$. Each build of the system will unify a set of these modules. Not all the builds contain precisely the same modules. Clearly, there are different versions of some of the modules in successive system builds.

We can represent the build configuration in a nomenclature that will permit us to describe the measurement process more precisely by recording module version numbers as vector elements in the following manner: $\mathbf{v}^i = \langle v_1^i, v_2^i, v_3^i, \cdots v_m^i \rangle$ for a system consisting of m modules. This build index vector allows us to preserve the precise structure of each for posterity. Thus, v_i^n in the vector $\mathbf{v}^n$ would represent the version number of the ith module that went to n^{th} build of the system. The cardinality of the set of elements in the vector $\mathbf{v}^n$ is determined by the number of program modules that have been created up to and including the nth build. In this case, the cardinality of the complete set of modules is represented by the index value m. This is also the number of modules in the set of all modules that have ever entered any build.

Program modules are similar to stars in a galaxy. Some of these stars (modules) have a relatively short life span. Other stars burn for a very long time. Thus, there is a constant flux of the stars in the galaxy. In a typical software build environment, there is a constant flux of modules going in and out of the build. Therefore, it is not a simple matter to track the frequency of execution of a particular module through a sequence of builds. Each time the module changes, it essentially becomes a new module with its new version number.

It is now possible to discuss the process of measuring the frequency of execution of each program module. What we are tracking is the frequency of execution of each version of the module as it evolves. Thus, for the ith build of a system, the vector $\mathbf{F}^{(i)}$ will record the frequency of execution of the versions of the modules that were in this build. Thus, the jth element of this vector $f_{v_j^i}^i$ will contain the frequency of execution of module j version v_j^i.

The module profile $\mathbf{P}^{(i)}$ for the system on the ith build can then be derived from the relationship, $p_{v_j^i}^i = f_{v_j^i}^i / F^i$ where $F^i = \sum_j f_{v_j^i}^i$.

What this means is that every time a module changes, it receives a new version number. There will be no frequency data for this new version until the system has executed. For some modules, there will be a substantial history of execution. For other modules, the data will be very weak. Only after a system has achieved relative stability in terms of code churn will it be possible to develop a stable module profile for that system. The very act of testing the system, however, is bound to create some distortions in the module profile. This is particularly the case when there is regression testing to test modules that have been substantially modified. There will be deliberate distortions created in the operational profile to exercise the changed modules.

The final act in the certification of a software system is to run the system as it will be deployed and used by the potential customer base. This means that the system must be exercised to produce an operational profile that is reflective of the conditions under which it will be used. In this case, the resulting functional and operational profiles will be much more reflective of the conditions of use of the system.

Chapter 12
Maintaining the Specifications

12.1 Introduction

In an ideal world, the operational, functional, and module specifications are placed under configuration control in the same manner as the source code itself. These documents can be viewed as source code in exactly the same manner as the source code program. They would be stored in a file system or database managed by SCCS or RCS in the same manner as for source code to maintain the various versions of each of the specification elements. These specifications constitute a document in exactly the same manner as the source code itself. As the various specifications evolve, they must be tracked and managed in precisely the same manner as the source code. Some specification elements will come and go. The code representing these eliminated versions will also come and go. As the source code base changes, it is extremely important to know how the version of each requirement element is represented by the code base.

In a new software system, the operational specifications are in a state of flux. They are constantly changing. The functional specifications must also change very rapidly to keep pace with the rapidly evolving operational specifications. Similarly, the design elements for the modules representing the functionalities will change as well. The code base itself is a very dynamic document. Each code module must be linked to the specific design element that it represents. As the code changes, so too must the design element. Each design element, in turn, implements one or more functionalities. As the functionalities change, the design elements must change and the code must change. Every version of every operation must be traceable to the functional specification and the design to a set of code modules.

A change in an operational specification, in terms of a new operation being added, has a cascade effect on the functional specifications, module specifications, and source code, as shown in Figure 12.1. In this figure we can see that the new operation results in the creation of two new functionalities. Each of these functionalities, in turn, is implemented in one existing design module and one new design module. The two resulting design modules also result in two new source code modules.

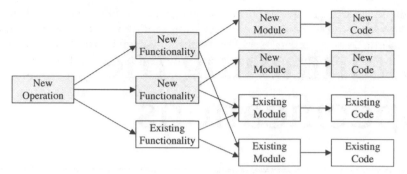

Figure 12.1. Change in operational specification having a cascade effect.

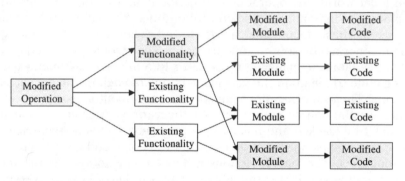

Figure 12.2. Change to an existing operation.

A change or modification to an existing operation has a similar cascade effect. The impact of such a change is shown in Figure 12.2. In this figure it is clear that there is a dependency of three functionalities on the modified operation. One of these functionalities changes as a result of the modifications made to the operation (although it is quite possible that, in some cases, a new functionality will be required based on the modification). The modification to the basic functionality, in turn, requires that two existing module specifications must change as well. This also means that two source code modules must change.

What is most interesting about Figure 12.2 is that when a change is made to one of the modules, the one at the bottom of the figure, we can seen that this module is also used to implement an existing functionality that has not been modified. Herein is the beginning of most maintenance nightmares. If we have complete specification traceability, as is the case in this example, then we are aware of the dependency of an existing unmodified functionality on a module specification that just changed. Now the logical thing for us to do is to follow all the entering edges to the changed module to see if the change to the module design will have a fundamental impact on any other existing modules. If, on the other hand, we do not have complete traceability, it might well be that subtle changes in our design module might have unknown impacts on other functionalities. We will not be able to review the structure of the system to determine these changes, and will discover them only when the software runs amok during the testing phase. Then it will be genuinely difficult to sort out just why the software has failed.

There are exactly two reasons that a source code module would change. First, the source code module might not be a faithful implementation of the module design specification. This means that there is a fault in the source code. In this case, the source code module can be altered to reflect more precisely the design specifications. No other document in the specification traceability hierarchy will change as a consequence of this source code update.

The second reason that a source code module might change is in response to an enhancement. In this case, the enhancement must first be implemented in the module design specification before the change is made to the source code module. It might well be, for example, that a better algorithm has been identified that will result in the performance enhancement of the module at runtime. This change effect will clearly impact only the module design specification and the source code module. The functionality of the module has not changed. Only a nonfunctional performance enhancement has been made to the design of the module. Therefore, none of the functionalities implemented by this module will be impacted by the change. As a result, only two elements in the traceability hierarchy will change.

It should be clear at this point that enhancements in program functionality or operation must occur from the top down. First, the operational model should be modified. Then the appropriate functionalities must be updated. Next, the low-level design elements, the module specifications, will be modified to implement the new functionalities. Only after these low-level design elements have finally been changed can the source code elements change. At the moment the first enhancement is made to a source code element that is not reflected in the corresponding module design element module, the entire specification process will fail. The source code no longer accurately reflects the design. The maintenance nightmare has begun.

It is clear that a rapidly evolving system will have many changes to operations, functionalities, low-level design elements, and source code. Without complete, updated, and accurate specification traceability, the functional and operational characteristics of the code base will no longer be known with any degree of certainty. One major consequence of this ad hoc change activity is that this software system is probably imbued with a substantial amount of dead code. This code implements operations or functionalities that have materially changed or have even been eliminated. Without complete specification traceability at the version level, it is almost impossible to control the problem of dead code. Without complete specification traceability at the version level, it is almost impossible to determine whether the source code actually implements the current operational specifications.

12.2 Configuration Control for the Specifications

There are clearly four sets of documents that represent the specifications for a system. These are the operational specifications, the functional specifications, the module specifications, and the source code files themselves. All of these documents are living documents for a rapidly evolving software system. They are constantly changing. Thus, each of these document systems should be maintained under a document configuration control system.

12.2.1 Configuration Control for the Operational Specifications

Let us reflect, for a moment, on the structure of the operational specification of a software system. There are three distinct document categories in this operational specification. First is the system overview; this is a text document that describes the system from an operational viewpoint. This document evolves in the same manner as any source code module. It has an initial version and then incremental changes can be made to the initial version. The same is true for the second document type of the operational requirements, the operational system model. This model can contain both text documents and figures representing the model. Finally, each operation is a separate entity. Each operation is maintained as a separate text element or module in the configuration control system.

The entire document structure for the operational specifications must be maintained under a configuration control system such as sccs or rcs. Each time one of the constituent elements of the operational specifications changes, a new version of that document element is created in precisely the same manner that source code elements are managed under configuration control.

At various intervals during its evolution, the various elements of the operational specification are brought together into a single document. For the sake of convenience, we call this collection a build. Each build consists of a set of document elements. Each document element has an associated version number. Thus, a build can be characterized in terms of a list of document elements and their version numbers. This will be called the build list. The build list will define the operational specification of a system very precisely for a particular point in time. The complete operational specification is a living document. It will evolve as the system evolves.

Maintaining the operational specification by itself is merely an academic exercise. The operational specification must also be linked to the functional specification. Changes in the operational specification will certainly have an immediate impact on the functional specification. Maintaining the linkage among the operations to their functionalities, however, is not an easy matter. In a rapidly evolving software system, operations may come and go as the software product matures. Operations can also change many times during the course of this evolution. Each time an operation is updated or changed, a new version of the operation is created from the standpoint of a configuration control system.

In that there can be multiple versions of an operation, there should be a mechanism to distinguish one version from another. To this end, we insist that each operation have a unique identifier, <OpID>. In that there can be multiple versions of an operation, it is clear that we must also have a version number, <version>, for each of the operations as well. Thus, each operation can be uniquely identified by the ID-version number pair: <OpID><version>. It is clear that the operational model will evolve with the changing operations. Thus, the operational overview has multiple versions as does the operational model. For purposes of closure, we denote the version of the operational overview as <OpOvVersion> and the version of the operational model as <OpModelVersion>.

With the evolution of the operational specification, new operations are created, existing operations can be modified, and some operations can be deleted. Operations that have been deleted, however, cannot be removed from the configuration control system in that they are a part of an earlier operational system specification. Thus, if an operation is to be deleted, we simply mark the specification as deleted and do not consider it as part of any current system specification. By the same token, an operation that is not deleted is active.

There are significant events in the life of an evolving operational specification. These occur when we bring all the most current versions of the active operations, the operational overview, and the operational model together into a **build** of the operational specification. This build represents the status of the operational specification at a particular instant. We can identify the elements of this build in a **build list** so that the nature of the operational specification at this instant can be preserved for posterity. The build list consists of the version numbers of current operational overview, the operational model, and the ID-version number pairs for all current operations, as shown in Table 12.1.

Table 12.1. Build List No. 1

Overview	<OpOvVersion>
Model	<OpModVersion>
<Op$_1$ID>	<Op$_1$Version>
<Op$_2$ID>	<Op$_2$Version>
$\bullet$ $\bullet$ $\bullet$	$\bullet$ $\bullet$ $\bullet$
<Op$_n$ID>	<Op$_n$Version>

Table 12.2. Build List No. 2

Overview	<FuncOvVersion>
Model	<FuncModVersion>
<Func$_1$ID>	<Func$_1$Version>
<Func$_2$ID>	<Func$_2$Version>
$\bullet$ $\bullet$ $\bullet$	$\bullet$ $\bullet$ $\bullet$
<Func$_m$ID>	<Func$_m$Version>

12.2.2 Configuration Control for the Functional Specifications

The functional specifications are managed under configuration control in precisely the same manner as the operational specification. Each functionality must have a unique identifier <FuncID> and an associated version <version>. A functionality can be uniquely identified by its ID-version number pair: <FuncID><version>. The evolving versions of the functional overview are denoted by <FuncOvVersion>. The evolving version of the functional model is denoted by <FuncModVersion>.

As was the case with the operational specifications, at any instant there is a current set of active specifications for functionalities and a current version for the functional overview and the functional model. This data can be captured in a build list, as shown in Table 12.2.

12.2.3 Maintaining the Mapping between Operations and Functionalities

The mapping of operations to functionalities $O \times F$ will also be stored under version control. Each operation is a separate document or file in the configuration control system. Each operation is implemented by one or more functionalities. However, each operation can have multiple versions. Each of these versions can be implemented by different functionalities or different versions of functionalities. Thus, every version of every operation must be linked to specific versions of one or more functionalities. This is a very complex process and a very vital part of the mechanism for maintaining specification traceability.

In the initial state of a new software system, there are no functional or module specifications. We are in the formative state of describing the basic operations of our new system. In this case, there are no functional specifications and thus the mapping between operations and functionalities are empty. It might well be, however, that we will cycle among many different versions of the operations and the operational model during this initial stage of system specification and development. Each of the versions of the operations, however, can be uniquely identified by its operation ID–version number pair. The same thing is true of the functionalities. Each of the functionalities can also be uniquely identified by its functionality ID–version number pair. These ID–version number pairs then serve as pointers to distinct versions of operations and functionalities.

At the point when the first functionality is created, it must be linked to the operations that it will implement. That is, a pointer must be established from each of the operations so involved to the particular functionality. This operation–functionality relationship is reflexive, meaning that there must be a path from the functionality back to each of the operations that implement it. We can see this relationship for a subset of operations and functionalities for a hypothetical system as shown in Figure 12.3. In this figure we can see that Functionality 5 is used to implement three operations: Operation A, Operation F, and Operation R. Operation A is implemented by Functionalities 5 and 61.

The relationship between the operations and the functionalities is not necessarily static. It might well be that Functionality 46 will be modified at some point in the future. If this is the case, there will be a new version of this functionality and the operations that it implements (Operations F and R) must be updated to reflect the new version of the functionality. Let us suppose, for example, that Operations F and R have version numbers of 2.3 and 3.1, respectively. Also, for the sake of discussion, assume that Functionality 46 has a current version number of 1.2. Then the link from Operation F to Functionality 46 might look like this: (OP-F, 2.3) ↔ (Func-46, 1.2). Similarly, the link from Operation R to Functionality 46 might look like this: (OP-R, 3.1) ↔ (Func-46, 1.2).

At the point where Functionality 46 is changed, it will cycle from version 1.2 to, say, 1.3. The links to this functionality must now be updated to (OP-F, 2.3) ↔ (Func-46, 1.3) and (OP-R, 3.1) ↔ (Func-46, 1.3). These are

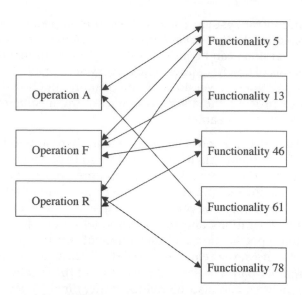

Figure 12.3. Reflexive operation-functionality relationship.

now the current links to Functionality 46. However, from a historical perspective, we must also preserve the past links.

It is now apparent that we must maintain two distinct tables that contain mapping information from the operations to the functionalities. The "Current $O \times F$ Link Table" contains the most recent version numbers of the nondeleted operations and the link to each of the functionalities that implement these individual operations. Second, there must be a "Past $O \times F$ Link Table" that maintains a record of all past associations between all previous operation versions and their associated functionalities.

Remember that periodically we will create a new operational specification for the software system. The specific operations and the versions of these operations in this operational specification are listed in a build list. There can be many different build lists. There might be several of these builds in a single day. The "Current $O \times F$ Link Table" might not reflect the contents of either the most recent builds of the operational or functional specifications. There might have been some changes to the current operational specifications since the last operational specification build. Similarly, there might also have been changes to the functional specifications since the last build of the functional specifications.

For the hypothetical operations and functionalities shown in Figure 12.3, the "Current $O \times F$ Link Table" might look something like the contents of Table 12.3. This table is organized with the operations as the major key and the functionalities as the minor key. It describes the mapping from the set of operations O to the set of functionalities F. In that the mapping is

Table 12.3. Current $O \times F$
Link Table

Current Operation	Current Functionality
OP-A, 1.2	Func-5, 1.4
OP-A, 1.2	Func-61, 1.7
OP-F, 2.3	Func-5, 1.4
OP-F, 2.3	Func-13, 2.1
OP-F, 2.3	Func-46, 1.3
OP-R, 3.1	Func-5, 1.4
OP-R, 3.1	Func-46, 1.3
OP-R, 3.1	Func-78, 1.5

Table 12.4. Reflexive Mapping

Current Functionality	Current Operation
Func-5, 1.4	OP-A, 1.2
Func-5, 1.4	OP-F, 2.3
Func-5, 1.4	OP-R, 3.1
Func-13, 2.1	OP-F, 2.3
Func-46, 1.3	OP-F, 2.3
Func-46, 1.3	OP-R, 3.1
Func-61, 1.7	OP-A, 1.2
Func-78, 1.5	OP-R, 3.1

reflexive, we can easily invert the contents of Table 12.3 to reflect the mapping of the functionalities onto the set of operations as shown in Table 12.4.

12.2.4 Configuration Control for the Module Specifications

Just as was the case for the operational specification and the functional specifications, each design module must have a unique identifier <ModID> and an associated version <version>. A design module can also be uniquely identified by its ID-version number pair: <ModID><version>. The low-level design also includes two new elements, the architectural overview and the architectural model, which relate to the abstract machine that will be used by the programming language to implement the low-level specification. This architecture will certainly evolve as the software system evolves.

Table 12.5. Build List No. 3

Overview	<ArchOvVersion>
Model	<ArchModelVersion>
<Mod$_1$ID>	<Mod$_1$Version>
<Mod$_2$ID>	<Mod$_2$Version>
• • •	• • •
<Mod$_m$ID>	<Mod$_k$Version>

Thus we will also have an evolving architectural overview that will be uniquely identified by the <ArchOvVersion>. The evolving version of the architectural model is denoted by <ArchModelVersion>.

The functional specifications are managed under configuration control in precisely the same manner as the operational specification. Each functionality must have a unique identifier <FuncID> and an associated version <version>. A functionality can be uniquely identified by its ID-version number pair: <FuncID><version>. The evolving versions of the functional overview are denoted by <FuncOvVersion> and the evolving version of the functional model is denoted by <FuncModVersion>.

As was the case with the operational and functional specifications, at any instant there is a current set of active specifications for the design modules and a current version for the architectural overview and the architectural model. This data can be captured in a build list, as shown in Table 12.5. Again, this build list represents the state of the function specifications at a point when it is necessary to archive or to print these specifications.

12.2.5 *Maintaining the Mapping of Functionalities to Modules*

In an argument that is parallel to that of the $O \times F$ mapping, we must also maintain an $F \times M$ mapping from the functionalities to the low-level design modules. For the sample functionalities shown in Figure 12.3, we can imagine a hypothetical mapping of these functionalities to specific design modules. This hypothetical mapping is shown in Figure 12.4. In this figure we can see that one module, Module 43, is used to implement three different functionalities: Functionality 13, 46, and 61. We can also observe that Functionality 46 is implemented by four different modules: Module 43, 54, 57, and 72. In one case, Functionality 78, the functionality is implemented by one and only one module, Module 77.

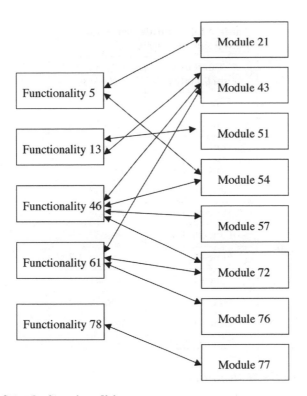

Figure 12.4. Sample functionalities.

Again, there can be multiple versions of each of the functionalities and each of the design modules. The linkage between functionalities and modules can be represented by the 4-tuple of module name, module version, functionality name, and functionality version.

As was the case with the linkage between the operations and the functionalities, we must maintain two distinct tables that contain mapping information from the functionalities to the modules. The "Current $F \times M$ Link Table" contains the most recent version numbers of the nondeleted functionalities and the link to each of the design modules that implement these individual functionalities. Second, there must be a "Past $F \times M$ Link Table" that maintains a record of all past associations between all previous functionality versions and their associated design modules.

Some hypothetical values for these module versions and functionality versions are shown in Table 12.6. Whenever there is an update to a functionality, say Functionality 13, then the contents of Table 12.6 must also be updated. In this particular case, there are exactly two table entries that will be affected by this change.

**Table 12.6. Module Versions and
Functionality Versions No. 1**

Current Functionality	Current Module
Func-5, 1.4	Mod-21, 1.4
Func-5, 1.4	Mod-54, 1.1
Func-13, 2.1	Mod-43, 2.4
Func-13, 2.1	Mod-51, 1.8
Func-46, 1.3	Mod-43, 2.4
Func-46, 1.3	Mod-54, 1.1
Func-46, 1.3	Mod-57, 1.5
Func-46, 1.3	Mod-72, 1.7
Func-61, 1.7	Mod-21, 1.4
Func-61, 1.7	Mod-72, 1.7
Func-61, 1.7	Mod-76, 1.2
Func-78, 1.5	Mod-77, 2.2

12.2.6 The $O \times F \times M$ Mapping

If we were perform an inner join on the contents of Table 12.3 and Table 12.6 on the Current Functionality column, we would produce a table like that shown in Table 12.7. This table is ordered by operation, by functionality, and by module. It shows the simultaneous dependencies of functionalities on operations and also modules on operations. Thus, if we were to make significant changes to the Operation A, then we can see from Table 12.7 that this would have a potential impact on Functionalities 5 and 61. Also, this change would then potentially impact Modules 21, 54, 72, and 76. The bindings between all the operations and all the modules are clear from this table.

If we invert the key structure of Table 12.7 so that the Current Module key is now the major key, followed by Current Functionality followed by Current Operation, we can see the precise dependencies of operations to modules, as shown in Table 12.8. In this case, for example, we can see that Module 21 is used to implement all three operations: A, F, and R. Changes to this module will impact all three operations.

12.2.7 Configuration Control for the Source Code

Not much has been said to this point about the source code of a given system in terms of configuration control. This is because most software development organizations now regard source code configuration control

Table 12.7. Operation, Functionality, and Module Versions No. 1

Current Operation	Current Functionality	Current Module
OP-A, 1.2	Func-5, 1.4	Mod-21, 1.4
OP-A, 1.2	Func-5, 1.4	Mod-54, 1.1
OP-A, 1.2	Func-61, 1.7	Mod-21, 1.4
OP-A, 1.2	Func-61, 1.7	Mod-72, 1.7
OP-A, 1.2	Func-61, 1.7	Mod-76, 1.2
OP-F, 2.3	Func-5, 1.4	Mod-21, 1.4
OP-F, 2.3	Func-5, 1.4	Mod-54, 1.1
OP-F, 2.3	Func-13, 2.1	Mod-43, 2.4
OP-F, 2.3	Func-13, 2.1	Mod-51, 1.8
OP-F, 2.3	Func-46, 1.3	Mod-43, 2.4
OP-F, 2.3	Func-46, 1.3	Mod-54, 1.1
OP-F, 2.3	Func-46, 1.3	Mod-57, 1.5
OP-F, 2.3	Func-46, 1.3	Mod-72, 1.7
OP-R, 3.1	Func-5, 1.4	Mod-21, 1.4
OP-R, 3.1	Func-5, 1.4	Mod-54, 1.1
OP-R, 3.1	Func-46, 1.3	Mod-43, 2.4
OP-R, 3.1	Func-46, 1.3	Mod-54, 1.1
OP-R, 3.1	Func-46, 1.3	Mod-57, 1.5
OP-R, 3.1	Func-46, 1.3	Mod-72, 1.7
OP-R, 3.1	Func-78, 1.5	Mod-77, 2.2

as a given. It will be done. All we really need to do at this point is to integrate the source code configuration control process with the configuration control for the specifications.

As it turns out, there is a one-to-one mapping of source code elements and design elements as shown in Figure 12.5. The design element Module 21 is implemented exactly by Code Module D.

There is, however, not a direct relationship in the version numbers of the design modules and those of the code modules. A code module that does not exactly represent the design module must be modified. This source code module contains one or more source code faults.[1] It requires one or more revisions to remove this fault. Thus, the version numbers of

291

Table 12.8. Operation, Functionality, and Module Versions No. 2

Current Operation	Current Functionality	Current Module
OP-A, 1.2	Func-5, 1.4	Mod-21, 1.4
OP-F, 2.3	Func-5, 1.4	Mod-21, 1.4
OP-R, 3.1	Func-5, 1.4	Mod-21, 1.4
OP-A, 1.2	Func-61, 1.7	Mod-21, 1.4
OP-F, 2.3	Func-13, 2.1	Mod-43, 2.4
OP-F, 2.3	Func-46, 1.3	Mod-43, 2.4
OP-R, 3.1	Func-46, 1.3	Mod-43, 2.4
OP-F, 2.3	Func-13, 2.1	Mod-51, 1.8
OP-A, 1.2	Func-5, 1.4	Mod-54, 1.1
OP-F, 2.3	Func-5, 1.4	Mod-54, 1.1
OP-R, 3.1	Func-5, 1.4	Mod-54, 1.1
OP-F, 2.3	Func-46, 1.3	Mod-54, 1.1
OP-R, 3.1	Func-46, 1.3	Mod-54, 1.1
OP-F, 2.3	Func-46, 1.3	Mod-57, 1.5
OP-R, 3.1	Func-46, 1.3	Mod-57, 1.5
OP-R, 3.1	Func-46, 1.3	Mod-72, 1.7
OP-F, 2.3	Func-46, 1.3	Mod-72, 1.7
OP-A, 1.2	Func-61, 1.7	Mod-72, 1.7
OP-A, 1.2	Func-61, 1.7	Mod-76, 1.2
OP-R, 3.1	Func-78, 1.5	Mod-77, 2.2

the source code modules will cycle more or less independently from those of the program modules. This requires us to introduce two more tables for the mapping of the software specifications to the source code modules. First there is the "Current $M \times C$ Link Table." An example of this table structure can be seen in Table 12.9. Here we can see that the current design Module 21, version 1.4, is now represented by source code Module D, version 2.7.

12.2.8 The $O \times F \times M \times C$ Mapping

There is one final step in the mapping process. The operational specification must be linked to the source code base. In Table 12.10 we have

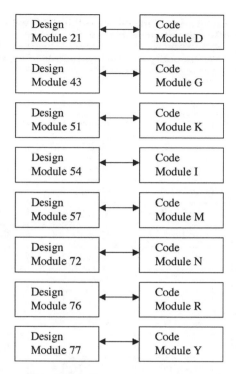

Figure 12.5. One-to-one mapping of source code elements and design elements.

Table 12.9. Module Versions and Functionality Versions No. 2

Current Functionality	Current Module
Mod-21, 1.4	Code-D, 2.7
Mod-43, 2.4	Code-G, 3.1
Mod-51, 1.8	Code-K, 1.2
Mod-54, 1.1	Code-I, 1.1
Mod-57, 1.5	Code-M, 1.6
Mod-72, 1.7	Code-N, 1.7
Mod-76, 1.2	Code-R, 1.2
Mod-77, 2.2	Code-Y, 2.2

integrated the contents of Table 12.9 with those of Table 12.7. Now there is a direct linkage from each of the source elements to a design module specification and thence to one or more functionalities and thence to one or more operations.

Table 12.10. Integrating Contents of Table 12.9 with Table 12.7

Current Operation	Current Functionality	Current Design Module	Current Code Module
OP-A, 1.2	Func-5, 1.4	Mod-21, 1.4	Code-D, 2.7
OP-A, 1.2	Func-5, 1.4	Mod-54, 1.1	Code-I, 1.1
OP-A, 1.2	Func-61, 1.7	Mod-21, 1.4	Code-D, 2.7
OP-A, 1.2	Func-61, 1.7	Mod-72, 1.7	Code-N, 1.7
OP-A, 1.2	Func-61, 1.7	Mod-76, 1.2	Code-R, 1.2
OP-F, 2.3	Func-5, 1.4	Mod-21, 1.4	Code-D, 2.7
OP-F, 2.3	Func-5, 1.4	Mod-54, 1.1	Code-I, 1.1
OP-F, 2.3	Func-13, 2.1	Mod-43, 2.4	Code-G, 3.1
OP-F, 2.3	Func-13, 2.1	Mod-51, 1.8	Code-K, 1.2
OP-F, 2.3	Func-46, 1.3	Mod-43, 2.4	Code-G, 3.1
OP-F, 2.3	Func-46, 1.3	Mod-54, 1.1	Code-I, 1.1
OP-F, 2.3	Func-46, 1.3	Mod-57, 1.5	Code-M, 1.6
OP-F, 2.3	Func-46, 1.3	Mod-72, 1.7	Code-N, 1.7
OP-R, 3.1	Func-5, 1.4	Mod-21, 1.4	Code-D, 2.7
OP-R, 3.1	Func-5, 1.4	Mod-54, 1.1	Code-I, 1.1
OP-R, 3.1	Func-46, 1.3	Mod-43, 2.4	Code-G, 3.1
OP-R, 3.1	Func-46, 1.3	Mod-54, 1.1	Code-I, 1.1
OP-R, 3.1	Func-46, 1.3	Mod-57, 1.5	Code-M, 1.6
OP-R, 3.1	Func-46, 1.3	Mod-72, 1.7	Code-N, 1.7
OP-R, 3.1	Func-78, 1.5	Mod-77, 2.2	Code-Y, 2.2

The complete mapping of the small example we have been developing in this chapter can be seen in Figure 12.6. In this figure it is clear that there may be a one-to-many mapping of operations to functionalities and also from functionalities to design modules. However, this is a one-to-one mapping of design module to source code module.

12.3 Maintaining the Specifications

Just about any large modern software system is a maintenance nightmare. This is because there is absolutely no engineering blueprint for the code. The system will have been carefully crafted by a team (sometimes a horde) of developers. It would be difficult to impossible to find a hardware project of equivalent complexity that had been similarly crafted. The consequences,

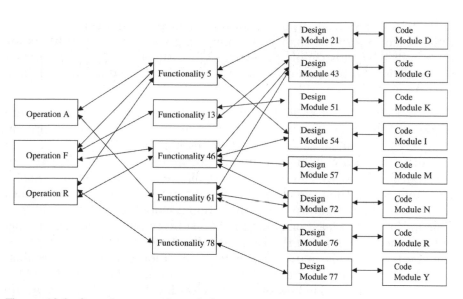

Figure 12.6. Complete mapping of chapter example.

both economic and social, are far too great. There are elaborate design specifications for modern office buildings. There are astonishingly complex design documents on modern integrated circuits. It would be unthinkable to modify one of these two structures without first updating the blueprints or design documents. It should be equally unthinkable to do this same thing with code.

We do not empower carpenters to make design decisions on the buildings we are constructing. They merely implement the design. The same discipline should be enforced on software developers as well. There should be operational and functional specifications for every software system. These documents must reflect the precise state of the system as it now exists. We can no longer afford to pay software maintainers to retrofit a set of design elements every time we want to change the functionality of the code base. This process takes too long and is much too expensive.

If changes are made to the electrical systems of a modern jet aircraft, then the design documents (the blueprints) for the aircraft must also be modified. The precise configuration of the aircraft that is now flying must be known. There is a very good reason for this. Should the electrical system of the aircraft require service in the future, no airline could afford the luxury of paying the maintenance staff to retrace the electrical circuits of the aircraft before beginning their work. We would never attempt to deduce the structure of the aircraft electrical system by inspection. We should, by the same token, not regard this as a good practice for the maintenance of software source code.

We have heard it said by many software development organizations that they cannot afford the luxury of maintaining software specifications for their code base. It is simply too expensive. Nothing could be further from the truth. It is far too expensive, both in terms of elapsed time and staffing cost, to maintain only the source code.

From Figure 12.6 it should be clear that there is a dependency of the entire specification structure on each code module. Under no circumstances can an enhancement be made to the functionality of a source code module without a concomitant update to the entire dependency tree of the specifications. We can identify three different types of enhancements and understand their effect on the specification dependency tree. First, we can change the nature of the operational model to add new features. This means that at least one operation must be changed as a result of this enhancement. This being the case, new functionality must be added for the new feature. This, in turn, means that one or more functionalities must be added or modified. Each of these new or modified functionalities must be implemented in new or modified low-level design modules. At the end of this very long cascading process are the source code modules. These are changed or added to in response to low-level design modules changes.

It is quite possible that we might only want to change the functional model. This means that we are not changing what the user will do the abstract operational model; we are simply modifying the functional model that will change how the system implements the user's operations. In this case, only a functional dependency sub-tree of the specification tree is modified.

Finally, we might only want to change the algorithm that is used to implement one or more functionalities. This algorithm, of course, will be implemented at the module level. This means that only one design module must be changed, together with one source code module.

In this new approach, in is no longer possible to change a source code module. There is only one reason that we would ever change a single source code module and not the entire sub-tree of which it is a leaf node; that is, in the case that the source code module does not accurately reflect the design module. In our new world, no developer will ever again be permitted to hack the source code base. Everyone from the requirements analysts to the designers to the developers must be involved in this change process.

We next turn our attention to the infrastructure necessary to implement this brave new world of software specification, design, and development.

References

1. Munson, J.C., *Software Engineering Measurement,* Auerbach Publications, Boca Raton, FL, 2003.

Chapter 13
The Software Development Infrastructure

13.1 Multiple Projects

In a typical software development organization, there are multiple projects under development at any point. There are typically many elements of functionality that are common to many or all of these software systems. Further, many common operations can be shared across a wide family of products. It is clear, for example, that a large number of services provided to a telephone subscriber by a particular model of telephone switch will be the same across most of the telephone switch product line. The customer will, in fact, never even know what type of switch is handling his or her call. Operationally, all the systems are essentially the same for the entire customer base. In this case, the operational specifications for all of the switches have a very large common core of operations and very similar operational models. It is also quite likely that the functional relationship among the various telephone switches also involves substantial commu nality in the set of functionalities. There are, for example, a rather limited number of ways to poll the set of inactive subscriber lines for new activity.

Most hardware and software projects are evolutionary rather than revolutionary. There are simply just not that many new ideas. Software products evolve from existing bases of operational specifications, functional specifications, and module specifications. This means that there is a great deal of commonality of operations across these evolving systems. There is also a great deal of shared functionality among these systems. This, in turn, means that there are a large number of module specifications that are common to these evolving systems. Because of this overlap in the common elements of specification, much of the development and specification work of the historical systems can be reused.

There has been a great deal of emphasis on the notion of code reuse over the past few years. This effort has been largely wasted. Code is not the focus. It is the operations and the functionality that are reused from one system to the next. That is where the major investment in the development work should be. The source code is almost incidental to the process. As established in Chapter 1, source code is not meant to be read by human beings. It is not a very good place to store design specifications. The same design specification can be implemented in a number of different languages. The translation from the low-level module specification to a source code module should be a largely mechanical one. The most important criterion in this process is that the source code module faithfully implements the design specification.

We now turn our attention to the problem of specification and design reuse across multiple projects. The key to the success of this endeavor is that we are able to build the necessary infrastructure to support this activity.

13.1.1 Common Operations

There are two distinct classes of software systems that share common operational specifications. First there is the case of operating systems such as Linux. The outward face of the Linux OS is the same across multiple platforms. The internals of this system, of course, heavily depend on the underlying hardware architecture. Second there are generations of software systems that share a common set of operations. We can conceive, for example, of a family of telephone switches that offer more features (operations), depending on cost and size of the switch. The big problem with these two classes of systems is one of coordination. If there is a change in the nature of an operation, then this operational change must be propagated across the entire family of common systems lest we unintentionally begin to build entirely different families of software. Thus, it is an attribute of each operation that it is used to animate one or more software projects.

From this new perspective, the attributes of each operation as was developed in Table 3.1 must be augmented by a new Project field, as shown in Table 13.1. Associated with each operation there must also be a list of project identifiers that uniquely describe each project in which the operation participates.

In the particular case where the operational characteristics of the system across all projects are the same, there will be but one set of operational specifications. Further, the Project field for all operations will be the same. This will distinctly be the case when there are multiple versions of a operating system such as Linux that run on different platforms. It is clear that all these systems will and should have the same operational characteristics. A user should be able to switch from one of the systems to any other without any change in the operational model. Thus, if there are four versions of the Linux distribution representing four different machine

Table 13.1. Multi-Project Operation Attributes

Attribute	Description
Operation Name	A unique identifier for this operation
Stimulus	Text describing the precise event that occurs in the external environment that will announce the initiation of the operation
Operation	Text describing the actions that will be taken by the operational model in response to the stimulus
Sequential Dependencies	A list of operations that must occur prior to the initiation of the current operation
Latency	Possible upper and lower bounds on the real-time performance of the operation by the operational model

Project	A list of project identifiers:
	<Project-ID-1>
	<Project-ID-2>
	    •
	    •
	    •

architectures, then there will be four projects that must be maintained as separate entities.

It is most distressing to observe how multiple distribution of a system are handled in most existing cases. The various distributions are all embedded in the same source code distribution. Each distinct system is isolated from all others through the massive use of compiler directives. Not only does this make for a massive amount of source code to maintain as a single distribution, but it also makes for a maintenance nightmare. It is a very difficult task to identify just exactly what the precise components of each system might be.

13.1.2 Common Functionalities

Each software project has its own distinct functional model. That is what distinguishes, at a minimum, one project from another. As such, each project will have two distinct text documents for the functional specifications that are uniquely associated with that project. These are the functional overview and the functional model. The set of functionalities can be shared from one system to another. In the Linux example, the functionality of the task scheduler is probably common to every one of the separate Linux functional systems for the various architectures. Scheduling of tasks is largely independent of the underlying architecture.

A far more interesting case is where a particular functionality is used on multiple projects. We might, for example, envision a functional machine that performs trigonometric transformations. A single-precision sine transformation will function the same across a multiplicity of projects that require such a transformation. Thus, we can define a single trigonometric transformation functionality that can be used in a variety of applications. Each of these applications will use precisely the same functionality.

For the circumstance where functionalities will span multiple projects, then Table 13.2, which lists the attributes of a functionality, must be augmented for this new context. For multiple projects, there must also be a Project attribute, as shown in Table 13.2. Again, if a functionality is to be modified, then it will be necessary to track the potential effect of this change across all the projects that use the functionality.

Now we are coming very close to the concept of object-oriented design. A shared library of functionalities can be used by a variety of different projects. There is a significant advantage to this approach.

Table 13.2. Augmented Specifications for a Functionality

Functionality Name	f_i		
Functionality Index	η_i^k		
Control	Received from functionality: ·<List of functionalities> Transferred to functionality: <List of functionalities>		
Data	Incoming packets: <Packet list> Outgoing packets: <Packet list>		
Protocol	<Protocol list for data packets>		
Functional Transformations	<List of data transformations>		

Project	A list of project identifiers
	  <Project-ID-1>
	  <Project-ID-2>
	    •
	    •
	    •		

Linkage	Operation Name	Operation Filename	Version
	<operation>	<filename>	<version#>
	Module Name	Module Filename	Version
	<module>	<filename>	<version#>

The fundamental problem with the current object-oriented design approach is that there is no infrastructure to assess the impact of a change to a particular functionality. If we are to maintain a particular functionality, we need to know exactly what the effect of this maintenance activity will be on *all* of the projects that invoke it. Very early in the discipline of computer science we learned that the use of global variables across a structure of program modules is a very bad idea. The object model takes this very bad idea and ratchets it one step forward. Operations are made global. Thus, a subtle change to such a global operation can have profound consequences for the multiple contexts in which the operation is used. It is virtually impossible to assess the effect of a change because there is no linkage within a project, much less across multiple projects.

13.1.3 Common Modules

If there are common functionalities across projects, then there will also be common low-level design modules across projects. Functionalities, after all, are implemented in design modules. That said, the specific format of a module definition as shown in Table 7.13 must be augmented to include project information as shown in Table 13.3.

Recall that the low-level design modules animate an underlying machine architecture. For these design modules to participate in multiple projects, the elements of the architecture used specifically by the design objects must also be common to those projects that employ them. We might, for example, have created a virtual machine with vector arithmetic for our architectural model for a given set of low-level design modules. It should be quite clear, then, that any other systems that use these modules should also support an architecture that implements vector arithmetic.

13.1.4 Project Source Code

There should be no particular requirement that all projects sharing functional and design elements must be written in the same programming language. In fact, there are reasons not to impose this requirement. The Space Shuttle Primary Avionics Software System is written in the HAL/S programming language, in that it was a project requirement that the language compiler is flight certified. There is a very good reason for this; it is simply not possible to build a flight-certified software avionics system without a flight-certified compiler. The HAL/S programming language is very difficult to use and there are not that many software developers who are familiar with the language. In fact, a convention of the developers who do know HAL/S could be handily held in a small conference room.

The choice of a particular programming language model should be an independent consideration. It should relate directly to the context in which the final system will operate. These considerations may involve particular

Table 13.3. Augmented Module Definition

Header Section		
| ```
HEADER
  PARAMETERS
  CALLED MODULES
  CALLING MODULES
``` | | |
| Data Section | | |
| ```
VARIABLES
  PARAMETER_LIST
  LOCAL_VARIABLES
CONSTANTS
``` | | |
Algorithm Description Section		
`DESCRIPTION`		
Algorithm Section		
`ALGORITHM`		
Linkage Section		
Project	A list of project identifiers <Project-ID-1> <Project-ID-2> • • •	
Functionality Name	Functionality Filename	Version
<functionality>	<filename>	<version #>

needs for reliability, availability, or security. Economic considerations may also govern the choice of a language. There are quite a few developers who know how to create C or C++ programs. There are not that many developers who know Ada. While it might be desirable to use Ada for reliability considerations, it may be very difficult and expensive to staff the development of such a system.

The real investment in a project should have very little to do with the choice of the underlying program language. The real investment in a software project should be in the specification of the operational and functional systems and in the low-level design.

The bottom line with source code development is that there should be a one-to-one mapping between each low-level design element, or module, and a source code module.

13.1.5 The Notion of a Project

Now we are in a position to describe the concept of a software project in a software development organization that might have many different developments projects occurring at the same time. From an operational specification perspective, each project must have a distinct operational model. It is clear that some elements of the operational model will be shared across multiple projects. However, the operational model, and the operational overview for that matter, will be distinctly different documents. They are atomic. There are no constituent pieces that can be shared from one project to another. Each project will also have a set of operations that animate the operational model.

Each project will also have its own functional model. There will be distinct elements of this functional model that are unique to the project. This means that a project, from a functional aspect, will have two distinct elements: a functional model and a functional overview. These specification documents will not be shared with other projects; each project has its own. The set functionalities, however, can be shared with a host of other projects.

It is quite likely that the architectural model that will be used to implement an abstract functional machine for a particular project will also contain distinct features that are not shared with other projects. Thus, the architectural model will be distinctly associated with each project. The specification of this architectural model will not be shared with other projects. The basic algorithms that constitute the foundation of the program modules can be shared with a variety of other projects.

Finally, it is not a given that all projects that share the same design elements must be written in the same programming language. Thus, the actual language implementation of each project is an attribute of that project. It may well be that a decision is made to use one programming language for all development work. However, this is not a requirement of the specification or design processes.

The elements of a project are summarized in Table 13.4. There are two columns in this table representing the specification elements that are distinctly associated with each project and those specification elements that can be shared across multiple projects.

An example of two systems that share common specification objects is shown in Figure 13.1. In this figure we can see that the operational model, the operational overview, the functional model, the system architecture, and the programming language are distinctly associated with System 1 and System 2 independently. Necessarily, there will be considerable overlap in the architectures of these two systems in that they share a considerable

Table 13.4. The Elements of a Project

Distinctly Associated with a Project	Possibly Shared with Other Projects
Operational Overview Operational Model	Operations: o1 o2 • • •
Functional Overview Functional Model	Functionalities: f1 f2 • • •
Architectural Model	Module Specs: m1 m2 • • •
Programming Language	Source Code Modules: c1 c2 • • •

amount of functionality and low-level design modules. Also, the programming languages are shown to be distinct. That, again, does not necessarily have to be the case; they could both be written in C, for example. It is conceivable, however, that System 1 is compiled under the GCC 3.3.1 compiler and System 2 is compiled under 3.2.1, in which case they would not necessarily share a common runtime library system.

Both of the systems shown in Figure 13.1 have a considerable amount of commonality in terms of shared operations, functionalities, and design modules. In this particular example, the code modules are in the intersection set of source code modules for both systems. This can only be the case if both systems are written in the same programming language.

13.2 Security Considerations

The overwhelming majority of security vulnerabilities in software systems today are simply design problems. The systems are ill specified or may be completely lacking in design specifications. It is not surprising that these systems are easily hacked. The possibilities for unintentional software

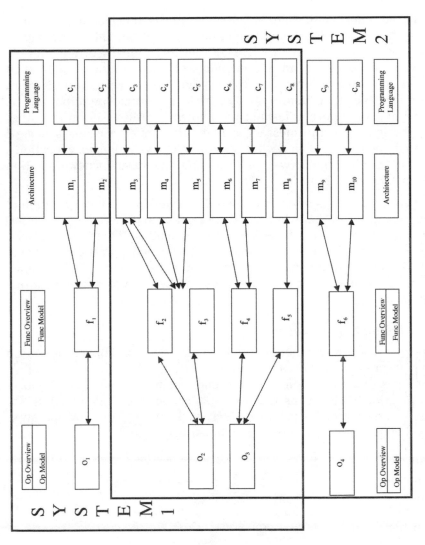

Figure 13.1. Two systems sharing common specification objects.

behavior are very large. We return to the solution for these types of security problems in Chapter 15. What is of interest at this point is the prevention of intentional or unintentional operations in software systems. If the set of operations is not specified precisely and unambiguous, there is room for misinterpretation — either deliberately or accidentally — in the implementation of these operations.

If, on the other hand, there is ambiguity in the specification of a functionality, this may well introduce an implicit operation. This is the crux of a large number of security problems. Either intentionally or unintentionally, systems built in an ad hoc fashion will include hidden or implicit operations. A stimulus for this operation might well be very subtle. It might be, for example, that a normal input to a buffering operation will be handled in a very normal fashion by a given operation. If, on the other hand, the length of the message sent to the buffer exceeds a normal threshold, the residual value will overwrite some valid memory locations. This, in turn, will permit new code, new functionality, and a new operation to be introduced at runtime.

Our concern, at this point, is to identify the deliberate incorporation of hidden functionality that will permit the system to perform implicit operations that are not part of the normal specification. There are basically two ways to do this. First, subtle actions can be incorporated into the set of functionalities. Alternatively, source code constructs can fail to implement design elements faithfully and thus can be used to create nefarious functionality.

13.2.1 Trojan Functionality

The purpose of Trojan functionality is to introduce an implicit operation into a software system. We can see a pictorial example of this in Figure 13.2, where Functionalities 2 and 3, in fact, implement an implicit and unspecified operation. This means that the system has been sabotaged. It will recognize a new stimulus for the implicit operation o_i. This new operation will be implemented in the two Functionalities 2 and 3.

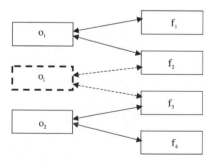

Figure 13.2. Implicit operation.

13.2.2 Trojan Code

Trojan code is a source code structure that has been introduced for nefarious purposes by a untrustworthy developer. The purpose of the Trojan code is to introduce a new implicit functionality that will, in turn, implement an implicit operation. This is an interesting practice. It can only flourish in a system that is completely lacking in the enforcement of good software implementation processes.

It is clear that there must be a design review process in place. Each source code module must implement the complete design module specification. Every aspect of the source code module must be examined to ensure that this mapping is exact and faithful. In essence, there is no room in our well-specified software projects for Trojan code. It would be nearly impossible to introduce behavior in a source module that was not precisely specified in the design.

13.2.3 Security Infrastructure

It is clear that the intention of the introduction of either Trojan functionality or code is to create a new set of implicit operations. These operations, just like any other operation, are triggered by the appropriate stimulus. That was a requirement of an operation — that it has a stimulus that will initiate the operation. This is clear from Table 13.1 where the structure of the stimulus is shown.

The precise nature of all the stimuli for a software system can be gathered from the set of operations. The range and possible values for these stimuli can be ascertained from each of the operations. It might well be that a particular operation will accept a string of text from the user's keyboard. A complete and careful specification of the string stimulus will immediately limit the nature of the string input space. We could, for example, insist that a string is a set of characters that is delimited by a carriage return. Further, this string can be no more that 80 characters long. A string that is 81 characters long, then, is not a valid stimulus for our input operation.

The normal mechanism for dealing with invalid stimuli is to create a contingency management system. This contingency management system consists of one or more operations that will accept all stimuli that are not elements of the set of valid stimuli for our system.

Thus, the final step of specification of the operation model is to create a contingency management system. We partition the set of all possible stimuli to our system into two compartments: one compartment processes normal stimuli and the other compartment processes all other stimuli.

Chapter 14
Specification-Driven Verification and Validation

14.1 Introduction

One of the most important aspects of the software development process is that of the verification and validation processes that occur in parallel with all software specification, design, and development. In this development process, there are two basic concerns: (1) did we build the right software, and (2) did we build the software right? The verification process is used to ensure that we did build the right software. That is, the customer was delivered a software system that was exactly what he or she wanted. The validation process is used to ensure that we did build the software right. That is, the software not only works but also does so reliably.

It turns out that the whole notion of software verification and validation has as its foundation specification traceability. At every stage in the development of the software specification and design, we will have specified very precisely the exact nature of the operational and functional models. In the development of the operational system, the customer is heavily involved with the requirements analysts to ensure that the operational system specified is one that will meet all the customer's requirements. In the development of the specification of the functional system, the high-level architecture of the functional system will be laid out. The role of the verification process at this stage is to ensure that the functional model that is developed will exactly implement the operational model.

14.2 Software Verification

One of the fundamental tenets of this book has been the necessity of the precise articulation of the concept of specification traceability. We defined, with a fair amount of precision, the concept of an operation on an operational model. We then demonstrated how this operation can be implemented in one or more functionalities that will animate a functional model. The mapping between all operations and all functionalities was defined by the

IMPLEMENTS relation defined on $O \times F$. The individual functionalities were further decomposed into functional modules that defined how specific algorithms would be used on a particular low-level architecture to implement each of the functionalities. Again, the mapping between each functionality and a set of low-level design modules was defined by an ASSIGNS relation on $F \times M$.

14.2.1 The Operational Model Development

At the outset of the development of the operational model, we must remember that the operational specification discusses only what the system will do for the user and not how this will be done. Our whole objective in this approach is to disambiguate the operational specification of the system. A user approaches a software developer with a set of needs. We call this set of needs the *requirements*. A requirements analyst works closely with the user to develop a real understanding of the user's wishes. The requirements analyst also works closely with a software system analyst in the development of an operational model of the system that will serve as the first cut of the operational specification. The user is heavily involved in the development of the operational model.

The next step in the development of a viable set of operational specifications is for the requirements analyst and the system analyst to animate the operational model with a set of operations. Remember that each of the operations is initiated by a particular stimulus. Again, wherever possible, the user is involved in the specification of these stimuli. It might well be, also, that there are temporal properties with some operations. That is, these operations must occur in a timely fashion with a specific upper and lower bound on the time from the initiation of the operation until its completion.

The most important consideration, from a security point of view, is that the operations specified are the only those that can be expressed. There are no implicit operations. The system only does what is explicitly specified in the set of explicit operations.

The complete set of operational specifications, including the operational overview, the operational model, and the set of operations, will constitute a legal and binding contract with the user. The verification process, at this stage, is one of building the specifications for an operational system that will meet the user's needs. At the point where this process has been fulfilled, then and only then can the next step in the design process occur — that is, functional model development.

14.2.2 The Functional Model Development

There are three steps in the development of the functional specifications. First, a functional model must be developed that has the capabilities of implementing the operations of the operational specification. Second, a set of functionalities must be developed that will animate this model, just as was the case in the development of the operational specifications. Third, there must be an exact mapping of each of the operations in the operational specifications to one or more of the functionalities in the functional specification.

The formulation of the functional model and the functionalities is the domain of the systems analysis and design group. This group is also responsible for mapping the set of operations onto the functional model.

The verification process at this stage of development depends heavily on review processes at every stage of development. These reviews proceed in incremental fashion with the evolving specification of each of the functionalities. The driving force behind the review process at every step is the systematic implementation of each operation. Protocols are developed for each of the review sessions that focus strictly on the correct implementation of each operation. The bottom line of the verification process is that a good and correct IMPLEMENTS relation be developed on $O{\times}F$, the mapping of the operations to functionality.

14.2.3 The Functional Machine Architecture

Once the basic functional system has been adequately specified, a new team is now ready for their work. These are the system design architects. They are responsible for the implementation of the basic functionalities on an abstract computer capable of performing these functionalities. Their initial responsibility in this process is twofold. First they must design the abstract machine and they must also ensure that this machine can be realistically implemented in a suitable programming language.

After the architecture of the abstract functional machine has been established, each of the functionalities must be decomposed into activities that can be expressed on the functional machine. In essence, the system design architects will implement the low-level design. Their primary task is to create the ASSIGNS relation on $F \times M$. Each functionality is assigned to one or more low-level design modules by this team. For this stage of design, the ASSIGNS relation on $F \times M$ represents the essence of the verification process.

14.2.4 Mapping the Low-Level Design to Code

The final stage of the development process is the implementation of low-level design modules in source code. Of course, the appropriate program language model must first be selected for this implementation. Our primary criterion for this selection is that the programming language can easily and faithfully implement the basic functionality of the abstract machine around which the low-level design has been constructed.

At this last stage, the verification process is very simple. Each program module implements exactly one design module. The task of the programming staff is to ensure that this exercise is completed with precision and exactitude. The review process at this point warrants the faithful translation of the low-level design modules into the corresponding source code modules.

14.3 Some Definitions

In anticipation of the discussion of software validation, it would be appropriate to nail down some terms that we will need in this discussion. One of the most destructive terms ever introduced into the software world was the term "bug." It is typically used as follows: there is a bug in my code. This is a completely vacuous statement. We do not know whether the code failed when it was executed or whether there was a major design problem. In fact, we know little or nothing about what went wrong with the code. Therefore, we need some precisely defined terms to aid us in the discussion of validation.

14.3.1 Errors

An error is an act on the part of a human being. It is a mistake made by that person. There are two distinct types of errors that a person can make. There are errors of omission; the person failed to perform some act and therefore something is missing from a specification. There are also errors of commission; the person did something wrong. The act itself is the error, not the result of the act.

14.3.2 Faults

When a person makes an error, the result of this error is a fault in the document the person is creating. That is, a fault is a physical characteristic of the system of which the type and extent can be measured using the same ideas used to measure the properties of more traditional physical systems. People making errors in their tasks introduce faults into a system. These errors can be errors of commission or errors of omission. There are, of course, differing etiologies for each fault. Some faults are attributable to errors in the operational specification. Some faults are directly attributable to errors committed in the design process. Finally, there are faults that are introduced directly into the source code.

There are two major subdivisions of faults in our fault taxonomy. There are faults of *commission* and faults of *omission*. Faults of commission involve deliberate, albeit unwitting, implementation of a behavior that is not part of the specification or design. Faults of omission involve lapses wherein a behavior specified in the design was not implemented. It is important to make these distinctions, especially so the inspection protocol can be used as a checklist for specific faults that have been found in the past.

T count faults, there must be a well-defined method of identification that is repeatable, consistent, and identifies faults at the same level of granularity as our static source code measurements. In a careful examination of software faults over the years, we have observed that the overwhelming number of faults recorded as code faults are really design faults. Some software faults are really faults in the specification. The design implements the specification and the code implements the design. We must be very careful to distinguish among these fault categories.

There can be faults in the specification. The specification may not meet the customer's needs. If this problem first manifests itself in the code, it still is not a code fault. It is a fault in the program specification or a *specification fault*. The software design might not implement the software requirements specification. Again, these design problems tend to manifest themselves during software testing. Any such design faults must be identified correctly as *design faults*. In a small proportion of faults, the problem is actually a code problem. In these isolated cases, the problem should be reported a *code fault*.

We observed an example of this type of problem recently in a project on a large embedded software system. The program in question was supposed to interrogate a status register on a particular hardware subsystem for a particular bit setting. The code repeatedly misread this bit. This was reported as a source code problem. What really happened was that the hardware engineers had implemented a hardware modification that shifted the position of the status bit in the status register. They had failed to notify the software developers of this material change in the hardware specification. The software system did exactly what it was supposed to do. It is just that this no longer met the hardware requirements. Yet, the problem remains on record to this date as a source code fault.

It is clear, then, that the etiology of the fault must be determined. We should be able to do this mechanically. That is, it should be possible to develop a tool that can count the faults for us. Further, some program changes to fix faults are substantially larger than others. We would like our fault count to reflect that fact. If we have accidentally mistyped a relational operator like '<' instead of '>', this is very different from having messed up an entire predicate clause from an IF statement. The actual changes made to a code module or a specification document are tracked for us in configuration control systems such as rcs or sccs as code deltas. All we must learn to do is to classify the deltas that we make as to the origin of the fix. That is, each change to each text document should reflect a specific code fault fix, a design problem, or a functional or operational specification problem.

We will find faults **within** statements in the source code and in the text of the specifications. The specification documents can be perceived to contain basic lexical units of words and punctuation. Similarly, the source code modules can be perceived to be sets of operators and operands. Through lexical analysis, then, we can view the specification documents as being composed of bags of tokens organized into lines delimited by end-of-line markers. Similarly, source code statements can also be organized bags of tokens delimited in the same fashion. We can then measure faults in these documents in terms of the tokens that comprise them. Specifically, the granularity of measurement for faults will be in terms of tokens that have changed. Thus, if I typed the following statement in C:

$$a = b + c * d;$$

but I had meant to type:

$$a = b + c/d;$$

then there is but one token that I got wrong. In this example, there are eight tokens in each statement. There is one token that has changed. There is one fault. This circumstance is very different when wholesale changes are made to the statement. Consider that the following statement:

$$a = b + c * d;$$

was changed to

$$a = b + (c * x) + \sin(z);$$

We are going to assume for the moment that the second statement is a correct implementation of the design and that the first is not. This is clearly a coding error. (Generally, when changes of this magnitude occur, they are design problems.) In this case, there are eight tokens in the first statement and fifteen tokens in the second statement. This is a fairly substantial change in the code. Our fault recording methodology should reflect the degree of the change. This is not an unreasonable or implausible notion. If we are driving a car and the car ceases to run, we will seek to identify the problem or have a mechanic do so for us. The mechanic will perform the necessary diagnostics to isolate the problem. The fan belt may have failed. That is a single problem and a simple one. The fan belt may have failed because the bearing on the idler pulley failed. We expect that the mechanic will isolate *all* the problems and itemize the failed items on our bill. How much information would we have if the mechanic simply reported that the engine broke? Most of us would feel that we would like to know just exactly what pieces of the engine had failed and were subsequently replaced. We expect this level of granularity in reporting engine problems. We should expect the same level of granularity of reporting on code fixes.

The important consideration with this fault measurement strategy is that there must be some indication as to the number of tokens that have changed in resolving a problem in the document. We have regularly witnessed changes to tens or even hundreds of lines of code recorded as a single "bug" or fault. The only really good index of the degree of the change is the number of tokens that have changed to ameliorate the original problem. To simplify and disambiguate further discussion, consider the following definition:

> **Definition:** *A fault is an invalid token or bag of tokens in a specification document or source code that will cause a failure when the compiled code that implements the specification document token is executed.*

When a software developer changes a line of code in response to the detection of a fault, either through normal inspection, code review processes, or as a result of a failure event in a program module, the tokens on that line will change. New tokens can be added; invalid tokens can be removed; and the sequence of tokens can be changed. Enumeration of faults under this definition is simple and straightforward. Most important of all, this process can be automated. Measurement of faults can be performed very precisely, which will eliminate the errors of observation introduced by existing ad hoc fault reporting schemes.

An example would be useful to show this fault measurement process. Consider the following line in an operational specification:

(1) The lights displayed should be yellow orange or red.

There are ten tokens on this line of operational specification. They are B_1 = {<the>, <light>, <displayed>, <should>, <be>, <yellow>, <orange>, <or> <red>, <.>}, where B_1 is the bag representing this token sequence. This operational specification talks about the existence of two lights, one that is yellow-orange and one that is red. Let us suppose that the intent of the specification was to indicate that there were to be three lights, one yellow, one orange, and one red. The operation specification should have read:

(2) The lights displayed should be yellow, orange or red.

There will again be eleven tokens in the new line of code. This will be the bag B_2 = {<the>, <light>, <displayed>, <should>, <be>, <yellow>,<,>, <orange>, <or> <red>, <.>}. The bag difference is $B_1 - B_2$ = {<,> }. There is one token in the difference. Clearly, one token has changed from one version of the specification to another. There is one fault.

It is possible that a change will span multiple lines of code. All the tokens in all the changed lines so spanned will be included in one bag.

This allows us to determine just how many tokens have changed in the one sequence.

The source code control system should be used as a vehicle for managing and monitoring the changes to code that are attributable to faults and to design modifications and enhancements. Changes to the specification document or source code modules should be discrete. That is, multiple faults should not be fixed by one version of the code module. Each version of the specification or code module should represent exactly one enhancement or one defect.

The fundamental point here is that we now have a very precise way of discussing the nature of changes made to documents to repair problems in them. Not all changes are of the same magnitude. Some changes will be very large and others might simply involve the change of a single token. If we are to model the processes that produce these faults with any degree of accuracy, then we must quantify the size of the faults.

14.3.3 Failures

A failure is an event in the operation of an executing program. It occurs when a fault has been executed. This does not mean that the program will cease executing. It does mean that the program is now expressing behavior that is outside the range of acceptable behavior in terms of the operational specification. It is doing something that the user did not want it to do. It is clear that there might be faults in the operational specification. These faults will cause an incorrect implementation at the functional level that, in turn, will be made manifest in the source code program. The source code may execute perfectly well. It will not break. But, it will be doing something that is outside of the user's requirements. Thus, it will have failed as soon as it executes this code. Similarly, there might also be faults in the functional specification, in the low-level design modules, and also in the source code. The execution of any one of these faults is a failure event.

Unfortunately, the notion of a failure in today's software development milieu is the singular event when the program stops working altogether, usually with a software fault. In reality, if there are no real operational or functional specifications, then this is the only type of failure event that can be recognized. However, these types of failure events are only a very small fraction of the total failure event space.

14.4 Software Validation

At the core of the software validation process is the test activity. There are basically two distinct reasons that motivate us to test software. First, we want to assure ourselves that the software system works reliably for the customer. Second, we need to establish clearly that the software demonstrates the behavior specified by the operational specifications. Any changes to the source code base as the software evolves can potentially cause problems in both domains.

With regard to the reliability problem, no large software system will ever be fault-free. The mantra that suggests that defect-free software is a realizable goal is simply religious dogma. People make mistakes. Big systems will, therefore, be fraught with faults. It is in the natural order of things. The more rapidly a system changes, the greater the likelihood that there will be new faults introduced at a corresponding rate. In the last analysis, it is not particularly relevant how many faults there are in a software system. What is relevant from a reliability standpoint is that the existing faults are not in an execution path that will ever be used by the customer. These faults are quiescent. They will not cause problems as long as the user's operational profile does not vary.

It will simply cost too much for us to remove all the faults from a large system. We should not expect to do so. As we come to understand the improbability of defect-free software, our attention will naturally shift to the real problem at hand. To develop a reliable software system, we must concern ourselves with how the user will use the system. That is, we must have some very good data on just what the user's operational profile will be. When we test the code for reliability, we will be assuring ourselves that this code base will not fail under its basic design constraints. This notion is completely consistent with best engineering practice. It is theoretically possible to build a highway bridge that is free from flaws and would support vehicles of any weight. No rational civil engineer would ever think to design a bridge to meet these criteria or test the final product in a similar manner. We would waste untold monies in this unobtainable and improbable project. Rather, a well-trained engineer would first ask what types of loads the bridge might realistically be expected to carry and design and test accordingly.

Therefore, before the software testing process can really get underway, we must first understand how the customer will use the software. That is, we must invest heavily in the development of an operational profile that is representative of the customer's use of the system. We cannot test all possible user inputs. We can, however, determine with some degree of certainty just how the software will be used and ensure that it will work well within some boundary conditions related to the operational profile.

14.4.1 Unit Testing

In the process of creating the low-level design specifications for the individual program modules, we have determined exactly what the relationship between any one module and all other program modules is. We will know which modules will invoke a given module. We will know which modules will be called by that module. We will know exactly what arguments will be passed to the module. And, we will know what the data range is for each of those arguments. We will know what all of the variables are that will be used locally in the module. We will know exactly what range these variables are defined on. We will have specified the algorithm that will define the substance of the module.

From Chapter 11, we established that a module might be used in the implementation of a number of different functionalities. This would mean the module would be an element in a sub-tree for a number of different functionalities. This means that the context for the module will vary from one of these sub-trees to another. In one context, a module B might be called, say, by module A and will call modules D and E. In yet another context, the same module might be called by module C and will call modules E and F. Clearly, the behavior of this module will be different, depending on the context. Thus, we find that unit testing is not just a question of creating a driver for the module and stubs for the calls it will make. We must first determine the context in which the module can be used and then create a driver for each of these contexts. In this sense, each module will be the root of a sub-tree in the call tree. It will be invoked by exactly one module and will call a limited set of modules. The module can participate in a number of different sub-trees in this manner. In the case where a module is invoked through the use of one or more function pointers, it will be almost impossible to determine these sub-trees before the complete system is up and running. The bottom line is that the use of function pointers will destroy the potential for effective module unit testing.

To return to the case where module B is called by module A, it may well be that one of the parameters in module B will have been defined to be a positive three-digit decimal number on the interval [0,500]. If we were to examine the corresponding argument that is actually passed into module B by module A, we might well find that the argument is defined as a two-digit decimal integer on the interval [1,10]. Thus, in the context of this call, it is really irrelevant to test module B over the whole interval [0,500]. Extreme values for this parameter in this context are 1 and 10 at the low and the high ends, respectively. We could make precisely the same argument for values that are to be received from modules that module B might call. This is vital information in the sense that we will have to create realistic stub calls for these modules.

It may well be that a module might be mapped to an operation that has temporal constraints. We can easily identify such modules from the mapping from operations to source code modules in $O \times F \times M \times C$. If this is the case, the performance of the module in a real-time environment is a subject of the test process. It might well be, for example, that the particular algorithm chosen at the low-level design stage is simply not fast enough when implemented in a particular programming language to meet the temporal constraints laid down in the operational specification. In this case, the module algorithm must be changed to one that provides a reduced time to execute.

We can see that the context in which a module is used will determine the nature of the testing necessary to certify in that context. Unit testing, then, is a two-step process. The first step, and the most critical, in the unit testing process is to identify the contexts in which a module will be used.

14.4.2 Integration Testing

The notion of integration testing is most easily understood in terms of the call tree model. We have seen that basic functionalities are, in fact, sub-trees in the call tree. Some functionalities can be constructed from other functionalities. For our purposes, then, integration testing will be driven from the lowest level of functionality to the highest level of functional granularity. Each functionality has a distinct module that is the root of the sub-tree that constitutes the functionality. This root node is the interface between the functionality and the remainder of the call-tree. Thus, the parameter list for the root node module determines the nature of data that might flow from the functionality. The specific arguments for each of the contexts in which each functionality can be employed will determine the specific nature of the testing that must occur to validate the operation of the functionality in each of the contexts in which it might occur.

Just as was the case for unit testing, as the integration and aggregation process proceeds, we find that some functionalities can be used to implement operations that have temporal constraints imposed on them. We can clearly determine these functionalities from the IMPLEMENTS relation on $O \times F$. As the individual modules are integrated into larger and larger subsets of modules as the system integration proceeds, the performance issues become more critical. Those functionalities that must meet certain timing constraints must be identified and the precise nature of these timings established.

Thus, integration testing will occur through the systematic aggregation of functional sub-trees. Each of the functional sub-trees is compiled into a program unit. This program unit is then tested in precisely the same fashion as was the case in unit testing.

14.4.3 Software System Testing

The final step in the software integration process is the complete build of the final system. At this level of testing, the focus should strictly be on the operational characteristics of the system and not on its functional characteristics. We must understand that we are highly constrained during this last phase of testing. There are probably hundreds of thousands of permutations of possible user actions. At the last stage in the testing process, both the testing time available and the need to deliver the product to market mandate that this testing phase proceed as rapidly as possible. The bottom line is that the test activity during the final system testing phase is restricted to a very limited set of resources based on the complexity of the system. These resources must be distributed in an optimal fashion. If we allocate any of these limited resources to test operations that users simply will not express, then these resources will be wasted.

In the case where test resources are a very limited resource in both time and personnel, it behooves us to use these resources wisely. This situation is analogous to the plight faced by a city with limited resources. Let us suppose that the city can afford to buy a single truckload of cold patch asphalt to patch potholes in the city roads. When they have used all the cold patch, there will be neither time nor money to get more. The city can simply instruct the truck repair team to drive around to fill whatever potholes they might encounter. A wiser director of public works would like to achieve the maximum benefit from the limited amount of patch material. He would observe, correctly, that roads in the city can be divided into, say, three categories. There are busy highways, primary roads that carry somewhat less traffic, and secondary roads that carry limited traffic into residential neighborhoods. For the cold patch to have the greatest repair impact on the greatest number of motorists, the potholes in the highways should be repaired first. If and only if there is remaining cold patch should the potholes in the primary roads be patched. Finally, whatever residual cold patch is left in the truck after the highways and primary roads have been fixed will then be allocated to secondary roads. The most important aspect of this approach is that it allocates the cold patch to those street problems that will have the greatest impact on the greatest number of motorists. We acknowledge at the outset that it will not be possible to fill all the potholes. We do not have enough resources to do that. We will take our limited resources and apply them to where they will do the most good. For us to do that, however, we must first have a very good understanding of how much traffic is carried by each of the roads in our town.

A good director of software testing approaches the software system testing in the same manner as the director of public works used the cold patch for road repair. The first thing the software test manager must determine is how the software is going to be used when it is placed in service. The distribution of user activity across the set of operations is given by the operational profile. Thus, before the system testing process can begin, we must first have a very good idea of the operational profile.

If no such operational profile exists prior to the onset of the testing process, then the first step in the system test activity must be to conduct an experiment with real customers using the system as they would normally do to build a reasonable estimate for the operational profile. The operational profile so obtained will be a single point in the n-dimensional space of operations. Also, each operation is initiated by a stimulus from a stimulus set for that operation. The set of stimuli the users employ to initiate each of the operations will be of interest as well.

Unfortunately, not every user can distribute his or her activity in exactly the same way, in which case there will be different operational profiles for each user. The ith user operational profile will be a point $\mathbf{P}^i = \langle p_1^i, p_1^i, \ldots, p_n^i \rangle$ in the n-dimensional space of operations. For a set of m users, we can find a centroid, $\overline{\mathbf{P}} = \langle \overline{p}_1, \overline{p}_2, \ldots, \overline{p}_n \rangle$ where

$$\overline{p}_{\bullet} = \frac{1}{m} \sum_{i=1}^{m} p_{\bullet}^i,$$

that represents the set of operational profiles for these users. We can also establish a measure of dispersion for the observed m operational profiles. Let d^i represent the distance between the ith user operational profile and the centroid of the operational profile cluster. We can compute d^i as

$$d^i = \sum_{i=1}^{n} (p_j^i - \overline{p}_j)^2.$$

The mean of these distances is:

$$\overline{d} = \frac{1}{m} \sum_{i=1}^{m} d^i$$

and the variance is:

$$Var(d) = \frac{1}{m-1} \sum_{i=1}^{m} (d^i - \overline{d})^2$$

From a statistical perspective, the length of the system testing process will be determined by two factors. First will be the length of time necessary to get good point estimates for each of the user operational profiles. Second, the greater the dispersion in the distances of the individual operational profiles from the centroid, the more testing will have to occur to replicate this variation. In the special case where $Var(d) = 0$, testing can be discontinued when we have arrived at decent point estimates for the individual operational profile.

From a data perspective, we simply will not be able to test a system exhaustively. Let us note that for each operation there is a set of stimuli that will initiate that operation. If, for example, we are entering an adding operation into a decimal calculator, then the range of stimuli that initiates this operation is, possibly, the set of two buttons labeled '+' and '−'. While this is an apparently trivial example, the same case can be made for far more complex problem scenarios. We might well observe that when the calculator is used, the distribution of activity of the two stimuli for the adding operation is not the same. When we actually measure this distribution during a field evaluation of the calculator, we might hypothetically observe that 80 percent of the time one of the adding operations is performed, it is a '+'. If, in this circumstance, we distribute our test activity evenly between the adding operators, we would spend a disproportionate amount of time testing the '−' operator, possibly missing a fault in the functionality that implements the '+' operation.

The bottom line in the system testing process is that we simply cannot do an effective job of testing unless we first know how the software will be used. This means that the first step in the system testing process is to perform a pilot experiment on the system at the operational level. To perform this pilot test, we do not necessarily have to have a fully functional system. An operational pilot test may well be performed on a simple prototype system or even a vaporware system. The objective of this pilot test is to get value insight as to the distribution of the operational profile and some sense about the set of stimuli that will commonly be used to elicit that operational profile.

14.4.4 Software Certification

Times are rapidly changing. In the good old days, it was possible to publish a user license or a caveat for your software that simply said that the enclosed software system was guaranteed to fail and when it trashed your life that you had no legal recourse but to suffer in silence. Those were the good old days. It is quite common now that a disgruntled user will seek redress for damages that occur when software purchased by that user, in good faith, trashes that user's data and application. The current software environment is very similar to the automobile market of the 1960s. Detroit built big, ugly, and terribly unsafe and inefficient automobiles. The position of the automobile manufacturers of that era was that if they built it, folks would buy it. Many hapless automobile buyers died unnecessarily with their faces impaled on the dashboard protrusions that were put there by the manufacturers to *look pretty*. This grand old era of automobile history ended on two notes. First, the automobile manufacturers were determined to be liable for the deaths of people who bought unsafe vehicles. Second, new and more reliable and safe models were introduced into the U.S. marketplace that also provided an alternative for the consumer. We are just now beginning to turn a similar corner in the software industry. The age of accountability is dawning.

The crass and cavalier attitude of today's software industry leaders has led to a generation of big, ugly, and terribly unsafe and inefficient software systems. The position of the leading software manufacturers is that if they build it, folks will buy it. Many hapless software users have lost their livelihood through the excesses of the software industry. However, this cavalier attitude of today's software manufacturers has **created the greatest business opportunity in the history of mankind**. The first software vendor to recognize the need for safe, reliable, and efficient software will rapidly displace the monolithic software giants of today's software industry. We are rapidly approaching the point that hardware processing capability cannot be increased at the rates that were possible in the past. The end of that rate of increase in speed is now clearly in sight. Future gains in the processing capabilities of tomorrow's software systems will have to be made in software and not in hardware.

The key to the success of these new emerging software firms will be software certification. Each software system that they produce will be warranted. The warrantee will guarantee that the user will not be damaged by the software. And, in the unlikely event that the software system should fail and cause damage to the user, that damage will be the responsibility of the software firm.

To certify a software system using current software development methodologies is to guarantee the failure of the software development organization that tries it. A system can only be certified if it is thoroughly understood. It can only be thoroughly understood if (1) it is completely specified and (2) its properties have been completely measured and modeled. The problem is no different than that of manufacturers that want to sell bolts for use in aircraft assemblies. These bolts must be certified as airworthy. They must be manufactured with a precise metal composition. They must meet stringent failure standards, to be determined by measuring the stress that a bolt can take before it fails. The bolts must meet stringent manufacturing tolerances in thread depth and thread pitch. Again, these must be monitored by precise measurement processes. In essence, the key to the certification process is the underlying measurement process. Precisely the same thing is true for computer software. Software attributes that are closely related to faults can easily be measured. Software testing outcomes can be easily measured. Operational profiles for tested software can be clearly established. That is, the path to software certification is precisely the same as that of hardware certification. *Measurement* is the key.

There are two major issues in the measurement of software systems. First there is the measurement and assessment of the software product itself, that is, static measurement. Then there is the measurement and assessment of the software product in execution, that is, dynamic measurement. Static software measurements give a clear indication as to where the potential faults in a system might be. It is one thing to know where the potential faults in code might be but it is quite another thing to see whether the program actually executes in the region where the faults reside. Static software measurement is like one hand clapping. Dynamic software measurement, then, is the other hand clapping. Static measurement is useful in that it shows where the potential problems are in the source code. Dynamic code measurement shows what code was executed and how intensively. Both static and dynamic measurements come together in the measurement of the software testing enterprise. It is vital to be able to measure program behavior at runtime to determine our exposure to the potential faults in the code. If we are to be able to certify a software system, we must know both the probable locations of the faults in the code and the extent to which the software test execution profiles have exposed the potential faults.

It seems entirely reasonable that if we know where the faults in the code likely are, then our test activity should exploit this information. Unfortunately, the code base is a moving target. Most software systems will evolve very rapidly from the first build to the last. This means that there are essentially two different types of faults we must deal with during the certification process. First, we have faults that were introduced in the initial code as it was first built. Second, we have faults that were introduced in subsequent builds. The certification process must carefully track both types of faults and ensure that each type of fault has received maximum exposure during the testing process.

As the software system is exercised during the testing process, we are really learning about the behavior of the system. As the testing process proceeds, we are accumulating more and more information about the reliability of each of the program modules. From a statistical perspective, the quality of our estimates for the tested operation profile becomes increasingly better during this process. If, at the end of the testing process, we have both good statistical estimates for the operational profile and our exposure to faults under this operational profile, we will then be in a position to certify the operation of our software within the range of an established operational profile.

Certification of software must not be confused with warranting the software to be free from defects. We are only guaranteeing the operation of the software within the confines of an established operational profile. An automobile, for example, can be reasonably expected to turn a corner at 40 kilometers per hour (KPH). In fact, we can certify that this automobile will do this safely. We will not certify, however, that this same automobile will turn the same corner safely at 100 KPH. Thus, for every operation that the automobile might reasonably be expected to perform during normal operation, it is possible to guarantee that it will do these operations with complete assurance. If the user operates the vehicle outside these certified boundary conditions, then the safe operation of the automobile cannot be certified or warranted by the manufacturer.

This then brings us to an interesting point. A fragile system will operate only within a very tight framework around the operational profile. As previously established, it is possible to measure the distance between a certified operational profile and a current operational profile. In essence, the certified operational profile is the centroid of the suite of test operational profiles. We can measure the distance between the current use of a system and the certified operational profile as d^i as defined earlier. A *fragile* system is one where the $Var(d)$ is very small. A **robust** system is one where the certified behavior represented by $Var(d)$ is very large. Thus, it is possible to certify a system with a very small $Var(d)$ or one with a very large variance. Clearly, there would be a competitive advantage to a software supplier that is able to certify a software system for a wider range of user operational profiles represented by a relatively large value of $Var(d)$.

14.5 Testing Objectives

It would help clarify our thinking about the testing process if we can establish some reasonable test objectives. Here we can draw from the centuries of test experience from hardware and electronic engineering enterprises. We do not care that our software has faults in it. No matter how careful we are, there will always be faults in our code. As we attempt to remove old faults, we run the risk of adding new faults. It is entirely possible to remove an innocuous fault only to introduce a severe one in the repair process. Removing all the software faults, then, is neither a viable nor practical goal. We would just like to remove those faults that will impair the way that the system is used when it is deployed.

Sometimes there is ambiguity in the goals and objectives of the software testing process. For our purposes, we would like to remove this ambiguity. The objective of the testing process is to certify a software system for a range of behaviors thought to be representative of a typical user's operation profile. In this guise, the software should perform reliably as long as it is operated within the limits of behavior we have certified. Our real objective in this process is to be able to guarantee the reliable operation of our software. The testing process will be used to achieve this objective.

The corporate survivors in the new world of software development will be those that can certify and guarantee the safe and reliable operation of their software. Sound engineering practice is essentially the only way to guarantee reliable software operation. The one thing that we have learned over the years is that it is not possible to use the software testing process to achieve reliability. By the time the system arrives in the tester's hands, the damage has been done. Bad software processes cannot be redeemed during testing. That will not be an objective of the testing process. Rather, the testing process is used to certify that the software will perform reliably within the context of a well-defined operating environment.

Each test activity exercises one or more functionalities. This will, in turn, causes the execution of subsets of code modules. Not all modules are equal. Some are potentially fault prone while others are not so fault prone. The astonishing level of complexity of modern software will guarantee that there will not be the resources to identify all possible faults and fix them. Further, as we have seen, an attempt to fix one fault might well introduce additional faults. We would like, then, to have the ability to marshal our resources so that we can have the greatest impact for the very limited resources available to the test activity. The test activity is perhaps the most resource-poor activity in the entire software development cycle. We need to know how to get the biggest bang for the limited test dollars.

The results of each test activity can be quantified. It is possible to evaluate that test activity in terms of the benefit derived from it. It would be pure folly to devote test resources to an activity that provides little or no exposure to latent faults in the system. The test measurement enterprise allows us to quantify and evaluate each test. This knowledge then guides us in our future test activity.

The software testing process is made far more complex by the simple fact that the object being tested is typically undergoing substantial change activity. A family of software modules might lay quiescent in the system for many build cycles and receive little or no attention from developers. As a result, the reliability of these modules probably increases over time. We must learn to accept the reliability of this family and devote our test resources to other, more active code. All of a sudden, the attention of the developers may well turn to this code backwater. In the face of heavy change activity, our code family that was once reliable might now begin to acquire more and more faults. This code family must now be promoted to be a center of attention for future test activity. In that the code base is not static, there can be no static test plan. A test plan must be a living document that changes as the code base changes.

14.6 Measuring Test Outcomes

Deterministically testing a large software system is virtually impossible. Trivial systems, on the order of 20 or 30 modules, often have far too many possible execution paths for complete deterministic testing. This being the case, we must revisit what we hope to accomplish by testing the system. Our goal might be to remove all the faults within the code. If this is our goal, then we will need to know when we found all these faults. Given unlimited time and resources, identification and removal of all faults might be a noble goal, but real-world constraints make this largely unattainable. The problem is that we must provide an adequate level of reliability in light of the fact that we cannot find and remove all the faults. Through the use of software measurement, we hope to identify which modules contain the most faults and, based on execution profiles of the system, how these potential faults can impact software reliability. The fundamental principle is that a fault that never executes will never cause a failure. A fault that lies along the path of normal execution will cause frequent failures. The majority of the testing effort should be spent finding those faults that are most likely to cause failure.

The first step toward this testing paradigm is the identification of those modules that are likely to contain the most faults. We can know this through our static measurement techniques. In the current state, the objectives of the software test process are not clearly specified and sometimes not clearly understood. An implicit objective of a deterministic approach to testing is to design a systematic and deterministic test procedure that will guarantee sufficient test exposure for the random faults distributed throughout a program. By ensuring, for example, that all possible paths have been executed, then any potential faults on these paths will have had the opportunity to be expressed.

We must, however, come to accept the fact that some faults will always be present in the code. We will not be able to eliminate them all, nor should we try. The objective of the testing process should be to find those faults that will have the greatest impact on the reliability, safety, and survivability of the code. Under this view of the software testing process, the act of testing can be thought of as conducting an experiment on the behavior of the code under typical execution conditions. We will determine, *a priori*, exactly what we want to learn about the code in the test process and conduct the experiment until this stopping condition has been reached.

14.6.1 Simple Measures for the Test Process

At the completion of each test case, we would like to be able to measure the performance of that test activity. There are many different aspects of the test activity, so there will also be a host of different measurements that we can make. The important thing is that the test activity must be measured and evaluated. We must learn to evaluate every aspect of the test activity. Our objective is not just to drive the code until it fails or fails to fail. We want to know exactly what the test did in terms of the distribution of its activity and where potential faults likely are.

The first measure we use in this regard examines how the test activity was distributed across the modules actually exercised by the test. The distribution of the activity is an important assessment of the ultimate testability of the program. If each of the tests distributes all the activity on a small subset of the modules, the majority of program modules will not execute. If, on the hand, the test activity is distributed evenly across each module, then each of the modules will have had equal exposure during the test. A very useful measure of program dynamics is the program entropy measure

$$h = -\sum_{i=1}^{n} p_i \log_2 p_i$$

Each test generates a different test execution profile. Hence, entropy is a good measure of how the test effort was distributed among the various program modules. For the test execution profile $\mathbf{P}^{(i)}$, the test entropy will be:

$$h^{(i)} = -\sum_{i=1}^{n} p_i^{(i)} \log_2 p_i^{(i)}$$

where n is the cardinality of the set of all program modules. A low entropy test is one that spends all its time in a relatively small number of modules. Maximum entropy is, of course, $\log_2 n$ for a test suite of n program modules.

Some tests will have a low entropy value and others will have a high entropy value. A large entropy value indicates that the test tended to distribute its activity fairly evenly across the modules of the system. A small entropy value indicates that only a small number of modules received the majority of the test activity.

The process of measuring the test process for evolving software systems is very complicated. Existing systems are continually being modified as a normal part of the software maintenance activity. Changes will be introduced into this system based on the need for corrections, adaptations to changing requirements, and enhancements to make the system perform faster or better. The precise effects of changes to software modules in terms of the number of latent faults are now reasonably well understood. From a statistical testing perspective, the test effort should focus on those modules that are most likely to contain faults. Each program module that has been modified should be tested in proportion to the number of anticipated faults that might have been introduced into it. Thus, the second measure of test activity relates to the location of potential faults in the system.

in the face of the evolving nature of the software system, the impact of a single test might change from one build to the next. Through an analysis of the distribution of software faults, it is possible to construct a proxy for software faults ρ_i. Whereas it will never be possible to know and to measure just how many faults a particular module might have, it is possible to develop reasonable predictive models to anticipate these faults.[1] We can employ this modeling methodology to build a reasonable fault proxy value that will adequately substitute for the actual fault count. Again, ρ_i is just such a fault proxy or a fault surrogate. The larger the value of ρ_i, the greater the fault potential a module has. If a given module has a large fault potential but limited exposure (small profile value), then the **fault exposure** of that module is also small.[2] One objective of the test phase is to maximize exposure to the faults in the system. Another way to say this is that we want to maximize fault exposure ϕ, given by

$$\phi_i^{(k)} = \sum_{j=1}^{n} p_j^{(k)} \rho_j^i$$

where ρ_j^i is the fault index or fault proxy of the jth module on the ith system build and $\mathbf{p}^{(k)}$ is the test execution profile of the kth test suite.[1] In this case, $\phi_i^{(k)}$, is the expected value for ϕ under the kth test case profile.

We now have two relatively simple measures of test outcomes. The test entropy measure $h^{(k)}$ tells us about how each test case distributes its activity across modules. The fault exposure measure $\phi^{(k)}$ will tell us how well the test activity was distributed in terms of where the potential faults likely are. The main point is that we should learn to measure the test outcomes of individual tests and evaluate them as we perform each test case. Unfortunately, the current measurement in use in most organizations is a binary outcome: the test failed or the test succeeded.

These two measures will serve well to introduce the notion of test measurement. We must remember, however, that the code base is constantly changing. New modules are entering the code base, modules are being modified, and modules are being deleted. A single test case applied over a series of sequential builds may well produce very different values, depending on the nature of the changes that have occurred and the total code churn.

16.6.2 Cumulative Measure of Testing

Each test activity generates a Test Execution Frequency Vector (TEFV). This vector represents the frequency at which each module will have been exercised in a particular test. At the conclusion of each test, we can add each element of that TEFV to a Cumulative Test Execution Frequency Vector (CTEFV). The CTEFV, then, will contain the frequency of execution of each module over the entire lot of test cases that have been executed to date. From this CTEFV we can compute a cumulative test execution profile $\mathbf{p}^{(c)}$, which shows the distribution of test activity across all program modules to date. We can easily compute the cumulative test entropy to date using the CTEFV and our cumulative failure exposure $\phi^{(c)}$.

Let us assume, for the moment, that our test objectives are strictly to find faults. The measure ϕ is clearly a measure of exposure to potential faults in the program. Therefore, a test that maximizes ϕ would be an *optimal test*. It turns out, however, that the maximum value of ϕ is obtained when the one module with the highest ρ_i is executed to the exclusion of all others. This is also a point of minimum entropy.

A *fair test*, on the other hand, is one that will spread its activity across all modules, not just the ones that are most likely to contain faults. A single fault in a module with a very low ρ_i has exactly the same consequences as a fault in a module with a much higher ρ_i when a user executes either of these modules. Each module, then, should receive test activity in proportion to the relative likelihood that it will have faults that can be exposed by testing. The proportion of faults in a module on the jth build of the system is a function of the number of latent faults in the module at the first system build and those faults that have been added in subsequent builds.

The change in ρ_i in a single module between two builds can be measured in one of two distinct ways. First, we can simply compute the difference in the module ρ_i between build i and build j. This value is the **code delta** for the module m_a, or $\delta_a^{i,j} = |\rho_a^{B,j}| - |\rho_a^{B,i}|$. The absolute value of the code delta is a measure of **code churn**. In the case of code churn, what is important is the absolute measure of the nature that code has been modified. From the standpoint of fault introduction, removing a lot of code is probably as catastrophic as adding a lot of code. The new measure of code churn, χ, for module m_a is simply $\chi_a^{i,j} = \left|\delta_a^{i,j}\right| = \left|\rho_a^{B,j} - \rho_a^{B,i}\right|$.

It is now possible to compute the total change activity for the aggregate system across all program modules. The total net fault change (NFC) of the system is the sum of the code deltas for a system between two builds i and j is given by:

$$\Delta^{i,j} = \sum_{m_c \in M^i} \delta_c^{i,j} - \sum_{m_a \in M_a^{i,j}} \rho_a^{B,i} + \sum_{m_b \in M_b^{i,j}} \rho_b^{B,j}$$

A limitation to measuring code deltas is that it does not give a good, clear indication as to how much change the system has undergone. If, between builds, several software modules are removed and replaced with modules of roughly equivalent complexity, the code delta for the system will be close to zero. The overall complexity of the system, based on the metric used to compute deltas will not have changed much. However, the reliability of the system could have been severely affected by the process of replacing old modules with new ones. What we need is a measure to accompany the NFC that indicates how much change has occurred. Net code churn (NCC) is a measurement, calculated in a similar manner to code delta, that provides this information. The net code churn of the same system over the same builds is:

$$\nabla^{i,j} = \sum_{m_c \in M_c} \chi_c^{i,j} + \sum_{m_a \in M_a^{i,j}} \rho_a^{B,i} + \sum_{m_b \in M_b^{i,j}} \rho_b^{B,j}$$

We can now derive an estimate for the proportion of faults in a particular module on the jth build as a function of the initial fault burden of the module at the first build (ρ_i^0) and the accrued fault burden in subsequent builds $(\nabla_i^{0,j})$ as the value $r_i^j = (\rho_i^0 + \nabla_i^{0,j})/(R^0 + \nabla^{0,j})$. A fair test of a system is one in which $p_i^{(c)} = r_i^j$ for all I; that is, each module should be tested in proportion to its potential contribution to the total fault count.

We would like to measure the difference between how we have distributed our test activity in relation to where the potential faults might be. Let $\varphi_i^j = |p_i^{(c)} - r_i^j|$ represent the difference between the test activity on module i and the relative fault burden for that module. A measure of the overall test effectiveness of our test effort to date is then:

$$\Gamma^{(j)} = \sum_{i=1}^{n_j} \varphi_i^j = \sum_{i=1}^{n_j} |p_i^{(c)} - r_i^j|$$

where n_j is the cardinality of the set of modules in build j. The maximum value for $\Gamma^{(j)}$ IS 2.0 and its minimum is 0.0. This minimum is attained in the case where the cumulative test profile exactly matches the projected fault burden of the program modules. The maximum value is attained when there Is a complete mismatch between the cumulative test profile and the projected fault burden. This could happen, for example, if $p_i^{(c)} = 1.0$ and $r_i^j = 0.0$.

One thing that is immediately apparent in the computation of these cumulative measures of testing is that they involve an incredible amount of data that must be accumulated over the evolving history of the system. It would be literally impossible for a single human being to begin to manage all this data. This is one of the primary reasons that the test effort at most software development organizations is run strictly by "gut feeling." Unless there is a suitable infrastructure in place to collect and manage the measurement data, the quantification of test outcomes will be impossible.

One of our principal concerns in the test process is that the system should work when the customer uses it. It is not particularly relevant just how many faults are in the system when it is placed in the user's hands for the first time. The important thing is that the user does not execute the residual faults that are in the code. Remember that each user distributes his or her activity on the set of operations according to an operational profile. Each operational profile, in turn, generates a functional profile, which ultimately creates a distinct module profile for that operational profile. Our total test activity is a success if we have tested and certified the software in a manner consistent with how it will be used. That is, $\mathbf{p}^{(c)} = \mathbf{o}$. In other words, our test activity ultimately reflects the user operational profile. It would be a real good idea for us to know something about the user operational profile before we ship our software.

14.6.3 Delta Testing

As the software evolution process progresses, new faults will likely be added to the system in proportion to the changes that have been made to affected modules. This means that the distribution of faults in the code changes as the software system evolves. Our measurement data shows us this shifting distribution of fault distribution. This means that we can know which modules are most likely to contain faults. The real problem will be to craft test cases that expose these faults. Constructing these test cases can be very difficult if we do not know what the system is supposed to do or how it does what it is supposed to do. That is the reason we must insist on having good specification traceability. This means that we can identify either specific functionalities that exercise certain sets of modules for functional testing or we can identify specific user operations that exercise certain modules for operational level testing.

The initial phase of the effective functional testing of changed code is to identify the functionalities that will exercise the modules that have changed. Each of these functionalities so designated will have an associated test suite designed to exercise that functionality. With this information it is now possible to describe the efficiency of a test from a mathematical or statistical perspective. A delta test is one specifically tailored to exercise the functionalities that cause the changed modules to be executed. A delta test can be effective if it does a good job of exercising changed code. It is worth noting, however, that a delta test that is effective on one build might be ineffective on a subsequent build. The **effectiveness** of a delta test between any two builds i and j, then, is given by:

$$\tau_{i,j}^{(k)} = \sum_{a=1}^{m} p_a^{(k)} \chi_a^{i,j}$$

where m represents the cardinality of the modules in the build as defined earlier. In this case, $\tau_{i,j}^{(k)}$ is simply the expected value for code churn under the profile $\mathbf{p}^{(k)}$ between builds i and j.

This concept of test effectiveness permits the numerical evaluation of a test on the actual changes made to the software system. It is simply the expected value of the fault exposure from one build to another under a particular test. If the value of τ is large for a given test, then the test will have done a good job of exercising the changed modules. If the set of τ values for a given release is low, then it is reasonable to suppose that the changed modules have not been tested well in relation to the number of probable faults introduced during the maintenance changes.

Given the nature of the code churn from one build to another, one simple fact emerges with great clarity: there is no such thing as a standard delta test suite. Delta testing must be tailored to the changes made in each build. The functionalities most impacted by the change process are those that use the modules that have been changed the most.

For practical purposes, we need to know something about the upper bound on test effectiveness. That is, if we were to execute the best possible test, what would be the value of test effectiveness. A **best** delta test is one that spends the majority of its time in the functionalities that contain the modules that have changed the most from one build to the next. Let:

$$X^{i,j} = \sum_{a=1}^{n} \chi_a^{i,j}$$

This is the total code churn between the i and j builds. To exercise each module in proportion to the change that has occurred in the module during its current revision, we can compute this proportion as follows:

$$q_a^{i,j} = \chi_a^{i,j} \Big/ X^{i,j}$$

This computation yields a new hypothetical profile called the **best profile**. That is, if all modules were exercised in proportion to the amount of change they had received, we would then theoretically have maximized our exposure to software faults that may have been introduced.

Finally, we seek to develop a measure that relates well to the difference between the actual profile generated by a test and the best profile. To this end, consider the following term $\left| p_i^{(k)} - q_i \right|$. This is the absolute value between the best profile and the actual profile for test case k. This value has a maximum value of 1 and a minimum value of 0. The minimum value is achieved when the module best and actual test profiles are identical. A measure of the **efficiency** of a test (task or program) is:

$$\theta^{(k)} = \left(1 - 0.5 \sum_a \left| p_a^{(k)} - q_a^{i,j} \right| \right) \times 100\%$$

This coverage value has a maximum value of 10 when the best and the actual profiles are identical and 0 when there is a complete mismatch of profiles.

In a rapidly evolving software system, there can be no standard suite of delta test cases. These test cases must be developed to ensure the operability of each functionality in direct response to modules that implement that functionality.

14.7 Maintenance and the V & V Process

The term "maintainability" has been widely used in the software engineering literature. It is clear from the review of this literature that maintainability is certainly a desirable property for a system to have. The main problem with maintainability is that no one really knows what this means. As a result, it is a difficult term to quantify. In the past, many people thought that the number of comment statements in code were somehow related to maintainability, although there were no scientific studies to support this conclusion. Alternatively, the amount of documentation (presumably measured in kilograms) that a program had was supposed to relate directly to maintainability, although, again, there were no scientific studies to this effect.

The software maintenance activity is nothing more than a microcosm of the initial software development process. The user's requirements might change. This will mean an adaptation of the existing operational model. When the operational model changes, then the functional model underneath it must also change. Ultimately, this change process percolates down to the source code level and the software testing and quality assurance processes.

Unfortunately, the canonical model for the software life cycle begins with the requirements analysis and presumes that the user is really informed and sufficiently intelligent to make a clear statement as to what his or her needs are. This is rarely the case. In a more realistic scenario, the set of user requirements will grow in the evolution of the operational model. The mere existence of the operational model and the capabilities expressed by this model will serve to alter the user's notion of what his or her requirements really are.

There are really three different types of software maintenance processes. There is adaptive maintenance. In this circumstance, the user's requirements change after an agreement has been reached on the precise nature of the operational model. There are perfective changes that can be made to the system. In this case, the functional and operational characteristics of the system are exactly right. Changes might be made to the system to enhance its performance or reliability. Finally, there is corrective maintenance, in which there is a mismatch between the operating characteristics of the system and the user's requirements.

Corrective maintenance is taken in the specific case where there is a fault in the operational specification, the functional specification, a low-level design module, or in the source code. In the simplest case, the fault is in the source code. The source code module does not implement the design module specification. In this case, the change activity involves only a single source code module. In the next case, there may be a fault in the module specification, in which case the module specification must be updated and then the source code module that implements the module specification must also be updated.

A fault in the functional specification is far more egregious than a fault in the low-level design elements. A functionality, for example, may well be implemented in several program modules. Thus, a change in a functionality may well propagate to several low-level design modules, which, in turn, will impact an equal number of source program modules.

The impact of a fault at the operational specification level is by far and away the most severe type of fault that can be introduced. This fault repair can involve multiple functionalities and even more low-level design specifications.

In the current state-of-the-art, sans specification traceability, the maintenance effort involved in correcting a fault at the operational specification level represents an enormous investment of developer resources to determine just exactly which source code module might be impacted by this change. There are two aspects of the associated maintenance costs. First, there will be a tremendous personnel cost associated with correcting the source code. Second, and more importantly, there will be a very large time delay while the developers attempt to do the mapping from the operational side to the source code elements that will be impacted by the operational fault. This time delay translates directly into the time-to-market delay.

It is the case with most software systems that as a system matures so too does the user's understanding of problem. As a result, we can expect that a user's requirements will change almost certainly with the beginning of the construction of the specifications. Thus, adaptive maintenance should be considered a realistic part of the software development process. Again, with complete and unambiguous specification traceability, the cost of performing enhancements in the operational specifications can be minimized.

In the case of perfective maintenance, it is clear that most of this activity occurs at the functional level of specification. In the perfective maintenance scenario, we can assume that the operation of the system meets all of the user's basic needs. The enhancements to the system will involve issues relating to performance, reliability, or security. These will impact, primarily, the functional and module specifications.

The bottom line is that software specification traceability and maintainability are one in the same thing. Software maintenance costs will now account for more than 80 percent of the cost of a software system over its life cycle. It only makes sense to make this job as easy as possible. There are direct payoffs for specification traceability in both personnel time and the time it takes to implement changes in a software system. Developers often say that they cannot afford to implement specification traceability; it simply takes too long. The truth is that this is a front-loaded cost. It is necessary only to make this investment once at the beginning of the project. This investment will pay enormous dividends over the life of the software product.

14.7.1 Quantifying the Notion of Maintainability

We would like to be able to quantify the term "maintainability." It is clear that a system will have good maintainability if we can perform adaptive, corrective, and perfective updates to the system with a minimum of human effort. We can take a cue from modern engineering practice in this regard. A modern office building has a vast complex of blueprints that describe how its various systems are laid out. Good building maintenance discipline suggests that anytime that there is a change in any of the subsystems, the blueprints will be modified to reflect the changes that have been made. The larger the building, the more complex the maintenance task. Regardless of how large and complex the building might be, any future maintenance effort is mitigated by maintaining the precise mapping between the building blueprints and the building as it currently exists.

With the mapping of operations to functionalities to modules, it is clear that we can know which modules are used to implement each functionality and each operation. Should we need to change either an operational requirement or a functional specification, we can know which modules will be impacted with this change. Similarly, if a code module does not function appropriately, we can know which functional or operational specifications are linked to that code module. In this context, each source code module can be linked directly to a single design module specification. Further, each data declaration in the source code module is linked to a data description in the design module. We can also insist that each source code statement be linked to a particular statement or element in the design module algorithm pseudo code.

With the configuration control for the design specification as discussed in Chapter 9.6, it is now possible to identify and quantify the attributes of software maintainability. These are listed in Table 14.1.

Table 14.1. Maintainability Attributes

- Requirements attribution
- Number of software operations
- Number of software functionalities
- Number of software design modules
- Operation to functionality mapping
- Functionality to module mapping
- Number of arcs in the call graph
- Number of arcs in the call tree
- Total number of arcs in module flowgraphs
- Total number of nodes in module flowgraphs

Let us begin with the concept of requirements attribution. Each operation in the operational specification must implement a particular requirement on the part of a stakeholder. That is, we implement no features on the system that were not specifically part of a user's requirements. We can quantify this term as the ratio between the numbers of operations that can be directly attributed to a particular stakeholder request to the total number of operations. This ratio will, of course, be a number from 0 to 1 as the traceability varies from no requirements attribution to complete attribution.

Next, we have distinct entities operational, functional, and module specifications. We can enumerate the number of operations, the number of functionalities, and the number of design modules. Clearly, as these number rise, so too will the complexity of the system being specified. The complexity of the implementation of the functional description of the specifications is embodied in the number of elements in the mapping from the set of operations to the set of functionalities. Similarly, the complexity of the low-level design in relation to the functionalities is embodied in the number of elements in the mapping from the set of functionalities to the set of program modules.

There are two distinct aspects to program control. We can describe the flow of program control between program modules in terms of either a call tree or a call graph. We can describe the flow of program control within a module in terms of the program flowgraph. For all three of these control structures, the number of arcs in the data structures is a good, clear indication of the complexity of the underlying flow of control, both between modules and within modules.

The question of operational granularity always arises. It is clearly possible to define a system with one operation implemented with one functionality implemented by one huge design module, in turn implemented by one huge FORTRAN main program. Life is full of trade-offs. The greater the granularity of the operational definition of the system, the more complex the average module flowgraphs become. Granularity of specification is not really the issue that it might seem. Quite simply, specifications should be parsed until they can be parsed no further. At the lowest level, the module, parsing a module into two components will certainly decrease the flowgraph complexity of the module. It will also increase the coupling complexity of that module.

14.7.2 *Specification Traceability*

The foundation of requirements attribution is that every attribute of a source code module can be mapped to a specific requirement. Further, each operational requirement can be mapped directly to a set of source code modules. In that we have to start somewhere, we first look at the mapping from the source code module to the design.

1. Every variable in a source code module is defined in the low-level design module with a variable declaration.
2. Every statement in the source code module has a pseudo code equivalent in the module specification.
3. Every called module in the source code module is listed in the Call_Section of the module specification.

Some elements of the module design specification are not obvious from the source code.

4. Every module that can call a module is listed in the Call_Section of the module specification.

Next we will turn our attention to the mapping at the functional level.

5. Every design module specification is referenced by at least one system functional specification.
6. That reference contains the most current version of the design module specification.
7. Every system functional specification references at least one operational specification.
8. The reference to each operational specification contains the most current version number.

At the level of the system operational specification, we would like to ensure that the links are in place for the mapping to the system functional specifications.

9. Every system operational specification references at least one functional specification.
10. The reference to each functional specification contains the most current version number.

It will not be possible to measure the completeness of the attribution mapping from operations to modules or modules to operations. Sometimes, missing links are made visible through the evolution process when code modules appear that are not traceable to operational specifications or operational specifications that have no associated code modules.

14.7.3 Operational Specification

A very simple system will have but one operation in it. Most logically, this operation would probably read something like this: STOP. Every other system that we might conceive will be more complex than this one. A simple count of the number of user operations is a good leading indicator of the maintainability of a system. That is, maintainability is inversely related to the number of operations that the system can perform.

14.7.4 Functional Specification

Each operation must have at least one functionality associated with it. In most cases, there will probably be many functionalities associated with each operation. Thus, as the operational complexity rises, so too will the functional complexity of the maintenance task. It is clear, then, that the maintainability of a system is also inversely related to the number of functionalities required to implement the set of operations.

14.7.5 Module Specification

Each functionality must have at least one module specification associated with it. Again, there will probably be many modules associated with each functionality. Thus, as the operational complexity rises, so too does the functional complexity, which also causes an attendant rise in module complexity and, hence, of the maintenance task. It is clear, then, that the maintainability of a system is also inversely related to the number of modules required to implement the set of functionalities.

14.7.6 First-Order Mapping

There are really two levels of first-order mapping between operations and modules: (1) the mappings of operations to functionalities, and (2) the mapping of functionalities to modules. We can represent each operation, functionality, and module as one node in a graph. Each node in the set of operations is connected by an arc to at least one node in the set of functionality; this is a first-order mapping. Each functionality is similarly connected by an arc to at least one module.

In the simplest case, each operation is implemented with exactly one functionality and that functionality is implemented with precisely one module. In this case, for a system of n operations, there will be $2n$ nodes in the first-order mapping from operations to functionalities and n arcs between these nodes. As the system becomes more complex, there will be an increase in the complexity of the connections between the operations and functionalities. This is no longer a simple one-to-one connection, in which case there will be $m > n$ arcs in the graph. When m is substantially greater than n, it is clear that the complexity of the relationship between operations and functionalities has increased. Anytime a functionality is modified, this change will impact more than one operation. Hence, m is a good indicator of this maintainability attribute. Again, the maintainability of the system is inversely related to m.

Exactly the same argument could be made for the first-order mapping of functionalities to modules. If there are n functionalities, then the simplest mapping to modules leads to n modules. If there are more modules, say k, than functionalities, then there must be at least k arcs connecting these two sets. As the relationship between the set of functionalities and modules increases in complexity, the number of arcs will also increase. Let l represent this new value of arcs where $l > k$. This new value l representing the number of arcs is also a measure of the maintainability of the system. Maintainability is also inversely related to l.

14.7.7 Second-Order Mapping

There is also a second-order mapping of operations to modules. We can characterize this relationship with a graph of n_1 operations, n_2 functionalities, and n_3 modules for a total of $N = n_1 + n_2 + n_3$ nodes. Connecting the sets of operations and functionalities, there are m_1 arcs. Connecting the sets of functionalities and modules, there are m_2 arcs for a total of $M = m_1 + m_2$ arcs. Intuitively, the maintainability of the complete system is inversely proportional to both N and M.

14.7.8 Call Graph Structure

As the structure of a program becomes more complex, the modules interact to an increasing extent with one another. This interaction can be represented through a call graph, as discussed in Chapter 11. The simplest call graph of a software system composed of n modules has n nodes and $n-1$ arcs connecting them. There is but one main program module and one leaf node module in this graph. All other nodes have one entering edge and one exiting edge. From the standpoint of intra-module complexity, this is the most simple call graph structure, the most easily understood, and thus, the most maintainable. The complexity of the call graph can only get worse. The number of nodes in this call graph is fixed; the number of arcs is not. If c represents the actual number of arcs in the flowgraph where $c > n - 1$, then the call graph maintainability attribute is inversely proportional to c.

14.7.9 Measuring Maintainability Attributes

There are clearly several distinct maintainability attributes. The above list presented in Table 14.1 is probably not at all exhaustive. What we have done, however, is to define maintainability attributes that can be measured. That is the first step in understanding the nature of the maintainability beast. We should be wise enough at this point to know that we cannot simply add the maintainability attribute values together to compute some arbitrary maintainability index. Each attribute has its own measure. These attribute domains are, in fact, potentially dependent variables in the modeling process that we will engage in to understand how maintainability might be related to other software attributes such as number of faults, total development time, and possibly the number of changes made to the various levels of specification during the development process.

Reference

1. J.C. Munson, *Software Engineering Measurement,* Auerbach Publications, Boca Raton, FL, 2003.

Chapter 15
Direct Benefits of Specification Traceability

15.1 Introduction

The development costs for a system with specification traceability are front loaded. That is, the development organization must commit far more resources in the initial stages of the software development process than it is currently accustomed to doing. There are, however, astonishing benefits that will flow from this disciplined approach to specification and design. Of primary interest is the ability of the concept of specification traceability to solve some major problems in the arena of software availability.

The term "availability" in a hardware context has a well-defined meaning. It is fundamentally related to the proportion of time that a piece of hardware is in operable condition. When a piece of hardware is placed in service, it will typically run for a period of time and then it will fail. After it has failed, it is then fixed and placed back in service. Each hardware system is unique. It shares only its form and shape with other hardware systems built just like it. Take, for example, a cell phone. All cell phones produced on the same assembly line look the same. They are supposed to function identically but each of these cell phones is completely different from its neighbor on the assembly line. If nothing else, there are different atoms that make up each of the cell phones. This means that each cell phone is fundamentally different from its compatriots on the assembly line. They may look the same but they are really very different.

The intrinsic differences in the physical composition of the cell phones means that there are variances in their individual components. Not all the capacitors will have precisely the same capacitance. Not all the resistors in each unit will have precisely the same resistance. If the cell phones are made under conditions of tight quality control, these variances will tend to be very small. If, on the other hand, there is no attempt to control the quality of the cell phone components, then the differences among the cell phones will be large.

The important point here is that each cell phone is physically different from any other cell phone of a different type. Therefore, each cell phone can be expected to last for a different amount of time before it fails. We could easily measure the length of time that each cell phone worked before it failed. From this data, we could then compute the average or mean time between failure events, or mean time between failure (MTBF).

When a cell phone breaks or fails, it remains out of service until it is repaired. Again, we can measure the amount of time it takes to get each of the failed cell phones operable again. This time will, of course, depend on a number of factors. First, the cell phone must be sent to a service facility. Then the service facility must diagnose the problem. Next, the appropriate parts must be found. Finally, the part that is defective must be replaced by a trained technician. All these steps take time. There may be, for example, only one service facility. Then the length of time it takes to get the cell phone to the service facility will vary, depending on the distance between the customer and the service facility. The service facility may have a limited staff. Therefore, the amount of time it takes to diagnose the problem will depend on the number of units waiting to be serviced. The service depot may have a limited inventory of parts. Therefore, depending on the nature of the part that failed, the cell phone being repaired may have to wait for a part to be shipped to the service depot. All these factors contribute to the variation in the length of time that is required to service each of the defective cell phones.

Over time, we can collect data on the length of time required to service each cell phone. From this data we can then compute the average time it takes from the time that the cell phone fails until it is placed back into service. Over the range of all cell phones of a given product line, we can develop the statistic of mean time to repair (MTTR).

Over the life of cell phones of a given type, each cell phone will work for a while, fail, and then be repaired. The total service time for each can be established as:

$$\text{Total Time} = \text{MTBF} + \text{MTTR}$$

A cell phone is available for use when it is not sitting in the repair depot waiting for service. Thus, the proportion of time that a given product line is available for use by the cell phone customer is:

$$\text{Availability} = \text{MTBF}/(\text{MTBF} + \text{MTTR})$$

Unfortunately, the concept of availability in the hardware context simply does not apply to software for a very simple reason. There is no variability in the manufacture of the software systems. Each of the cell phones in the above example will have exactly the same software loaded in it. If the software system placed in the cell phones is fault-free, then all the cell phones will be perfect. They will all be identical from a software standpoint. There is no variation in the software load across all cell phones. If, on the other hand, there is a manufacturing defect (fault) in one of the modules of the software load, then all the cell phones will fail when they execute this same fault.

This, then, is a key point in the analysis of software availability. The exposure to a fault in a particular module has everything to do with how the software is used and not with the length of time it has been used. As we learned earlier, the distribution of activity across modules, the module profile, is directly dependent on the operational profile. This means that our exposure to a fault depends only on what we do and how we distribute our activity across program modules. All the users who exploit a feature or operation of the cell phone that will cause a module containing a fault will experience the same failure. If they never exploit that feature, then they will never experience the failure.

In very simple terms, if we are to discuss software availability, then we are going to have to learn what this term means in the software context. Let us begin with the user's exposure to a software fault. This fault has a definite location. It is located in a single code module. The operations that can be impacted by this fault are those that are implemented by functionalities that, in turn, use the program module. A user might accidentally expose this fault during his or her normal use of the software. In this case, the software will be unreliable for that user. On the other hand, a user might have knowledge of the software fault. He or she might exploit this knowledge to force the software to fail. This type of failure, then, is a security problem. This means that software systems can fail for a variety of reasons. These systems can execute faults embedded in the code modules. They can also be deliberately made to fail by assaults on them from hackers who exploit certain vulnerabilities that have been built into the code. The main point here is that software systems will fail as a result of their use and not as a function of time. It is clear that software will not wear out over time. It is also clear that there is no variability in the manufacture of the software. The only source of variability in the execution of software systems is that induced by the patterns of use of the user.

The operation of a software system simply cannot be deduced from outside the system. The only way we can know what a system is doing is to instrument the software so that we can monitor its activity as it runs. This concept of actively monitoring software systems as a normal course of their execution is a very novel thing. There are very few, if any, examples of such software systems in existence today. The same is not true for hardware systems. It would be difficult to imagine a nuclear power plant operating without a myriad of sensors embedded throughout the entire reactor assembly. All of these sensors would be monitored for safe operation in real-time by a real-time process controller. A modern operating system is far more complex than a nuclear power plant. Many of these operating systems are functioning in safety-critical systems yet none of these systems are subject to any type of process control. We **hope** that they are doing their job well but we do not have any way of knowing anything about the health of these operating systems until they melt down and do something really wrong.

This, then, is the nut of the software availability assessment problem. Our large computer software systems are running unmonitored and operating totally out of control. We must institute processes in the specification and design stage to incorporate measurement and control systems in these complex software systems. All large, complex software systems should be designed with real-time control systems built into them. We now take a look at what it is that we need to know about these systems to do this.

The vast majority of software security vulnerabilities in software are there for a very simple reason: the software has not been engineered. It has been crafted. It would be difficult to conceive of a nuclear power plant operating without any process monitoring hardware in place. It would be equally difficult to imagine an oil refinery that could safely operate without extensive process monitoring probes in place. In both of these hardware systems, vital information is monitored in real-time for all aspects of plant operation. This information is obtained in a sufficiently timely manner to react to operating conditions that exceed normal parameters. In essence, both of these systems are operating under real-time feedback control systems.

Modern operating systems are far more complex than most oil refineries or nuclear power plants. Modern command and control software is far more complex than the hardware systems controlled by these C^4I systems. Yet, no modern software systems have any form of process control built into them. They are essentially running out of control. It is not surprising, therefore, that even a novice hacker can gain control of these complex systems. No one is watching. No mechanism has been provided to exercise the necessary restraints to prevent unwanted incursions into these systems.

The solution to the current crisis in software security and reliability lies in the application of basic engineering principles that have dominated mechanical, electrical, and civil engineering for some time. Software systems simply need to be measured as they are designed and tested. They must have the basic real-time controls built into them that we have come to enjoy in our microwave ovens and our automobiles. It would be very difficult to sabotage a military installation because of the real-time monitoring that is built in to protect it. It is relatively easy to render this same installation inoperable in that the software that forms the nucleus of the entire system in not subject to the same level of engineering discipline.

In essence, we do not have a security problem. We have a control problem. Interested parties can hijack our software because we are not watching its operation. Similarly, we do not have a software reliability problem. We have a monitoring problem. Software is allowed to perform uncertified functions that will certainly increase the risk of its failure. Our current problems with software security can easily be eliminated when we understand the need for building real-time controls into these systems.

15.2 Reliability

Now let us turn our attention to the problem of software reliability. It should be relatively clear that a reliable software system is one that does not fail. What is not quite clear is just what a failure event is. It is clear that a catastrophic failure event where the software simply stops executing is clear evidence that a failure has occurred. The real problem here is that the actual failure event might have occurred millions of epochs before the system actually crashed and burned. Many of us do not need to wait for the spectacular collapse of the operating systems on our personal computers. We feel that things are not quite right. Maybe certain commands are taking longer than they normally do. Maybe a command is not executed in exactly the manner that we have learned to expect. In any event, there is a sense that things are not right on our machine. Either we reboot the system or we are going to be trashed in short order. We will never ask what went wrong. What is worse, we probably could never find out just where the failure event really occurred. Common sense simply says that things are not right and it is time to save everything and get a fresh start with the operating system.

A typical statement about a software system that has faults in it is that it is buggy. This term "bug" is very destructive to our thinking about software reliability. It is a vacuous term. It is literally without meaning. Before we can begin to solve the mysteries of software reliability, we are going to have to learn to be very much more precise in our thinking.

15.2.1 Understanding Software Reliability

A software system is quite unlike a hardware system from a reliability standpoint. A hardware system is typically the sum of its components. A software system, on the other hand, is only its components. Only one software module executes on any given CPU at any time. If that module fails, then the system fails. The reliability of a software system, then, can be characterized in terms of the individual software modules that comprise the system. From the standpoint of the logical description of the system, these functional components of the larger system are, in fact, operating in series. If any one of these components fails, the entire system fails. The likelihood that a component will fail is directly related to the complexity of that module. If it is very complex, the fault probability is also large. The system is as reliable as its weakest component.

If a module is flawed, it may or may not be a problem to a particular user. The fault is exposed only if the user chooses an operation that causes that module to execute. Thus we can see that the perceived reliability of a software system by a user depends on how the software is exercised by that user. If the user's operational profile results in a module profile that provides for a very low probability of execution of a flawed module, then the perceived reliability of the system will be high for that user.

To capture the essence of the concept of software failure, let us suppose that our software system is well designed and that any fault will be trapped by an exception handler to which control is automatically passed at the instant that the program departs from its specified behavior. We can easily accomplish this action with assertions built into the design. In essence, we cannot perceive a failure event if we are not watching. Some program activities, such as a divide by zero, are trapped by the system automatically. The hardware and operating system, however, cannot know our intentions for the successful execution of a module on a more global scale. We must instrument the code to know whether it is operating correctly. Programming assertions into the code is a very good way of measuring for failure events.

There are really three levels of granularity of program reliability. At the lowest level of granularity, there is ***module reliability***. The module design process has specified each program module very carefully. We know what it should be doing. We can easily define the parameters for its successful operation. That is, we can know whether the program module is operating within its design specifications. The moment it begins to operate outside its design framework, we imagine that the module transfers control to the exception handler. The fact of this transfer represents the transition of the program to a failure state. Thus, if we have a system of n program modules, we imagine that this system is augmented by a module, say m_{n+1}, that traps all contingencies that arise when any program module has failed.

Each program module, then, might or might not fail when it is executed. We can know this and we can remember these failure events. A program module can be considered reliable if we have used it frequently and it has failed infrequently. A program module is considered unreliable if we have used it frequently and it has failed frequently. A program module that is used infrequently is neither reliable nor unreliable.

Any program module can transfer control to the exception handler. This transfer, of course, can only happen if the current module has departed from the program specifications. With our dynamic instrumentation and measurement technique, we can clearly count the number of times that control has been transferred to each module. This data can accumulate in a module execution frequency vector (MEFV). We can also count the number of times that control has transferred from any module to the exception handler. This data can accumulate in a failure frequency vector (FFV) for each module. A module is considered reliable if there is a small chance that it will transfer control to the exception handler.

Let t_i represent the ith element of the MEFV. It contains the number of times that module i has received control during the last $\sum_{i=1}^{m} t_i$ epochs for a system with m modules. Similarly, let s_i represent the number of times that module i has transferred control to the exception handler during the same number of epochs. It is clear that $s_i \leq t_i$; that is, a module could have failed every time it was executed or it could have executed successfully at least once. Our current estimate for the failure probability of module i on the kth epoch is $z_i^{(k)} = s_i^{(k)}/t_i^{(k)}$. This means that of the total $t_i^{(k)}$ epochs that module i has received control, it has worked successfully on $e_i^{(k)} = t_i^{(k)} - s_i^{(k)}$ epochs. The reliability of this module is simply one minus its failure probability to wit: $r_i^{(k)} = 1 - z_i^{(k)}$. From these observations we can then construct a vector $\mathbf{z}^{(k)} = \langle z_1^{(k)}, z_2^{(k)}, ..., z_n^{(k)} \rangle$ of failure probabilities for each module on the kth epoch.

It is clear that if module i has executed successfully for a large number of epochs (e.g., 100,000) and failed but once over these epochs, then the module will be fairly reliable. In contrast, consider another module j that has executed only ten times and has not failed at all. At face value, the reliability of module j is 1.0, whereas the reliability of module i is 0.99999. However, we really lack enough information on module j to make a truly accurate assessment of the likelihood of failure of that module. In other words, our confidence in our reliability estimate is low.

What we are really interested in is the current point estimate for the failure probability of a module and a lower confidence bound for that estimate. It is clear that we can derive our estimate for the failure probability $z_i^{(k)}$ from the relationship $z_i^{(k)} = s_i^{(k)}/t_i^{(k)}$. It is also clear that executing module i will have exactly two outcomes: it executes successfully or it fails. The distribution of the outcome of each trial is binomial. Let us observe that, for relatively large n, we can use the binomial approximation to a normal distribution with a mean of np and a standard deviation of $\sqrt{np(1-p)}$.

An estimate a, for the $(1 - \alpha)$ upper bound on this failure probability can be derived from the binomial approximation to the normal distribution where

$$\frac{1}{\sqrt{2\pi}} \int_{-\infty}^{a} e^{-\frac{1}{2}(x-np)/np(1-p)}\, dx = \alpha.$$

349

If, for example, we wished to find the 95 percent confidence interval $u_i^{(m)}$ for $z_i^{(m)}$, we could compute this from:

$$
u_i^{(k)} = \left(s_i^{(k)} + 1.65\sqrt{t_i^{(k)} z_i^{(k)}(1 - z_i^{(k)})} \right) \Big/ t_i^{(k)}
$$

$$
= \left(s_i^{(k)} + 1.65\sqrt{t_i^{(k)} \frac{s_i^{(k)}}{t_i^{(k)}}\left(1 - \frac{s_i^{(k)}}{t_i^{(k)}}\right)} \right) \Big/ t_i^{(k)}
$$

$$
= \left(s_i^{(k)} + 1.65\sqrt{s_i^{(k)}\left(1 - \frac{s_i^{(k)}}{t_i^{(k)}}\right)} \right) \Big/ t_i^{(k)}
$$

where 1.65 is the x ordinate value from the standard normal $(N(0,1))$ distribution for $\alpha = 0.95$. This estimate, $u_i^{(k)}$, is an unbiased estimate for the upper bound of $z_i^{(k)}$. The problem is that if we have executed a particular module only a very few times and it has not failed, then the number of failures $s_i^{(k)}$ for this module will be zero and the estimate for the upper bound $u_i^{(k)}$ will also be zero. This would seem to imply that an untested module is also highly reliable and we are very confident about that estimate. Nothing could be further from the truth.

A more realistic assumption for the reliability of each module is to assume that it is unreliable until it is proven reliable. To this end, we assume that each module has, at the beginning, been executed exactly once and it has failed. Thus, the number of measured epochs for each module increases by one and the number of failures experienced by that module also increases by one. Let $s_i'^{(k)} = s_i^{(k)} + 1$ and $t_i'^{(k)} = t_i^{(k)} + 1$. Thus, a more suitable estimate for the initial failure probability for a module is $z_i^{(k)} = s_i'^{(k)}/t_i'^{(k)}$ with an upper bound on this estimate of:

$$
u_i^{(k)} = \left(s_i'^{(k)} + 1.65\sqrt{s_i'^{(k)}\left(1 - \frac{s_i'^{(k)}}{t_i'^{(k)}}\right)} \right) \Big/ t_i'^{(k)}
$$

We can construct a vector $\mathbf{u}^{(k)}$ whose elements are the $(1 - \alpha)$ upper bounds on the estimates for the failure probabilities. Thus, with the vector of failure probabilities $\mathbf{z}^{(k)}$ and the vector of upper bounds on these estimates $\mathbf{u}^{(k)}$, we can characterize the failure potential and our confidence in this estimate of set of modules that comprise the complete software system.

As each functionality f_i is exercised, it induces on the set of n program modules a module execution profile $\mathbf{p}^{(f_i)}$. That is, each functionality exercises the set of program modules differently. Therefore, each functionality has a different failure potential, depending on the failure probability of the module. It executes. We can compute an expected value for the functionality failure probability of each functionality on the kth execution epoch as follows:

$$q^{(f_i)} = \sum_{i=1}^{n} p_i^{(f_i)} z_i^{(k)}$$

In matrix form we can represent the vector of functional failure probabilities as $\mathbf{q} = \mathbf{p}\mathbf{z}^{(k)}$, where $\mathbf{p}$ is an $m \times n$ matrix of module execution profiles for each functionality. We can also compute an upper bound on the expected value of the functional failure probabilities as $\mathbf{q}' = \mathbf{p}\mathbf{u}^{(m)}$.

As the user exercises each operation ω_i in the set of l operations, it will induce on the set of k functionalities a functional profile $\mathbf{p}^{(\omega_i)}$. That is, for every operation, there is a vector of conditional probabilities for the execution of each functionality given that operation. Let $\mathbf{p}'$ represent the $l \times h$ matrix of the conditional probabilities of the h functionalities for the l operations.

It is clear that each operation will exercise the set of program functionalities differently. Therefore, each operation has a different failure potential, depending on the failure probability of the functionalities it executes. We can compute an expected value for the operational failure probability of each operation on the kth execution epoch as follows:

$$x^{(\omega_i)} = \sum_{i=1}^{k} p_i^{(\omega_i)} q^{(f_i)}$$

In matrix form we can represent the vector of operational failure probabilities as $\mathbf{x} = \mathbf{p}'\mathbf{q}$, where $\mathbf{p}'$ is an $l \times h$ matrix of functional profiles. Substituting for $\mathbf{q}$, we can define $\mathbf{x}$ directly in terms of the measurable module failure probabilities to wit: $\mathbf{x} = \mathbf{p}'\mathbf{p}\mathbf{z}^{(m)}$. We can also establish an upper bound on the operational failure probabilities as $\mathbf{x}' = \mathbf{p}'\mathbf{p}\mathbf{u}^{(m)}$.

The elements of the vector $\mathbf{x}$ represent the failure probabilities for each of the l operations. The reliability of operation ω_i can be derived from its failure probability as follows: $r_i = 1 - x_i$. Thus, we can construct a vector of operational reliability estimates $\mathbf{r} = \mathbf{I} - \mathbf{x}$, where $\mathbf{I}$ is a vector of ones. We can also construct a vector of lower bounds on these reliability estimates $\mathbf{r}' = \mathbf{I} - \mathbf{x}'$.

The reliability of a software system is, therefore, not a static attribute of the system. It is an artifact of how the system will be used. There is a different reliability estimate for each operation, depending on how that operation exercises different modules. Furthermore, there is a lower bound on that reliability estimate, depending on how much we know about the modules that comprise that operation. A user's perception of the reliability a system depends on how he or she uses that system. The operational profile **o** represents the distribution of user activity across the system. Therefore, the user's reliability perception of the system ρ is simply $\rho = $ **or** and the lower bound for this estimate is $\rho' = $ **or**$'$.

15.2.2 Data Collection for Reliability Estimation

It seems pointless to engage in the academic exercise of software reliability modeling without making at least the slightest attempt to discuss the process of measuring failure events. A failure occurs immediately at the point that the program departs from its specification, not when we first perceive this departure. The latencies between when a system fails and when this failure event is perceived by the user can be substantial. We could, for example, have a small memory leak in our Web browser. We will have to run this program for some time before it self-destructs, but die it will with this memory leak. The actual failure occurs at the point that the browser software failed to release some memory it had used. The instant that this first happened is when the failure occurred. If we are not watching, we will fail to see this happen. We will see it only when some functionality is first impaired. The user may not see the problem until the Web browser crashes or slows his or her machine to a crawl.

The basic premise of our approach to reliability modeling is that we really cannot measure temporal aspects of program failure. There are, however, certain aspects of program behavior that we can measure and also measure with accuracy. We can measure transitions to program modules, for example. We can measure the frequency of executions of functions if the program is suitably instrumented. We can also measure the frequency of executions of program operations, again supposing that the program has been instrumented to do this.

Let us now turn to the measurement scenario for the modeling process described above. Consider a system whose requirements specify a set O of user operations. These operations, again specified by a set of functional requirements, are mapped into a set F of elementary program functions. The functions, in turn, are mapped by the design process into the set of M program modules.

The software is designed to function optimally under a known and predetermined operational profile. We need a mechanism for tracking the actual behavior of the user of the system. To this end, we require a vector O in which the program will count the frequency of each operation. That is, an element o_i of this vector is incremented every time the program initiates the ith user operation. This is, of course, assumes that the system performs only operations within the set O. A system that has failed will depart from the specified set of operations. It will do something else. We really do not care what it does specifically. The point is that the system has performed an operation outside of the set O. We know that it failed as a result. This implies the existence of an additional operational state of the system, a failure state. That is, the system is performing an operation o_{n+1} completely outside the repertoire of the normal set of n specified user operations. This fact has strong implications in the area of computer security. It is clear that if a program is executing within a predefined set of operational specifications, it is operating normally. Once it has departed from this scenario, it is operating abnormally. This likely means that the program is now operating in a potentially unsafe manner.

When we first start using a program, we will have little or no information about how its components will interact. The initial test activity is, in essence, the start of a learning process wherein we will come to understand how program components actually work together.

The very nature of the milieu in which programs operate dictates that they will modify the behavior of the individuals who are using them. The result of this is that the user's initial use of the system as characterized by the operational profile will not necessarily reflect his or her future use of the software. There might be a dramatic shift in the operational profile of the software user based directly on the impact of the software or due to the fact the users' needs have changed over time. A design that has been established as robust under one operational profile can become less than satisfactory under new profiles. We must come to understand that some systems may become less reliable as they mature due to circumstances external to the program environment.

The continuing evaluation of the execution, function, and module profiles over the life of a system can provide substantial information as to the changing nature of the program's execution environment. It is clear that as we execute a particular piece of software, we will continue to collect data on the execution of the system. In all likelihood, the system will run quite well for many thousands of epochs. Thus, our perceptions of the reliability of our system will tend to be enhanced the more we work with the system. Also, our confidence in these estimates will grow over time.

15.3 Software Security

Problems in computer security can be classified into one of three distinct bins. First, there are problems in the design of a system. Exploits are created by hackers to leverage these design flaws to attack a system. Second, there are access control problems. In this case, a hacker can attain privileges to perform actions that are not normally permitted. Third, there are behavioral problems. In this case, a user is performing actions that are outside of his or her normal use of a system.

15.3.1 Security by Design

It is an astonishing fact that the overwhelming majority of computer security problems relate directly to design inadequacies. Take, for example, the buffer overflow exploits. In this case, a developer will have allocated, say, 4K bytes to receive data from some type of IP traffic. In the code that actually transfers data to the buffer, there are no provisions made to ensure that the 4K bytes are not exceeded during the transfer. This is clearly a problem that occurs in the specification of the low-level design module. No data transfers over the size of the buffer should ever occur. If data transfers that exceed the size of the buffer are attempted, the action must be referred to an appropriate exception handler.

The most implausible fact of the current security problem is that there is exactly no learning in the system. At the first occurrence of a buffer overflow, it would seem reasonable to examine all other buffer transfers in the operating system to see if the same condition could arise at any other point. Further, as new code is added to a system, an automatic check should be performed for data transfers of this kind before the code is added to the system. However, such is not the case. Security vulnerabilities are simply patched as they are discovered by hackers. Perhaps this is largely true in that there are no real design documents for the majority of the operating systems in use today. The most egregious example of such a system is the Linux operating system. There are no design documents for this system or any sense of a set of operational specifications. The source code constitutes the entire documentation for the system. It is a prime example of a software system that has grown to the point that it is literally no longer maintainable. The opportunities for new security problems in such a system are rife, primarily due to the absence of engineering design specifications for the system.

15.3.2 Security by Access Control

As previously noted, a second means of providing security for a software system is to limit access to system resources through the use of passwords and privileges. This is analogous to the act of putting locks on every system resource. This means that each user can be given a limited set of keys and have access to those facilities for which he or she has the keys. The obvious extreme in this system is to place locks on everything to provide for complete security. This is a strategy that is, in fact, employed at some of the better houses in Latin America. Literally every closet door, room door, cabinet drawer, and pantry is secured by locks. Each domestic employee has access only to (i.e., has a limited set of keys) for those facilities that he or she will actually need to service. Only the cooks, for example, would have access to the refrigerator, the pantry, and the dish cabinet.

There are several problems with access control security mechanisms. First, they are very cumbersome. Imagine, if you will, what it would be like to live in a house secured in that manner. To move through such a house and have access to your personal belongings would mean carrying a keychain containing several hundred keys. The second problem with such a strategy is that it presumes something about the integrity of each person having a subset of these keys. A cook has access to the pantry. This does not make the cook an honest person. The integrity of the contents of the pantry depends, ultimately, on the integrity of the cook. It is a sad fact that the criterion most frequently used to evaluate a good cook is that the cook does not steal too much. As long as people have keyed access to limited resources, there will always be a social engineering security problem.

15.3.3 Security by Control

The third way that security can be imposed on a software system is to monitor the activity of the system as it is running. Again, this is a common-sense strategy. It is ubiquitous in every aspect of our daily life except in our software systems. Hence, the exposure is great. These problems now make every personal computer a source of great liability for its user, not to mention the tremendous losses incurred on a daily basis by the world's financial community. The solution to these problems is rather quite simple. We just need to learn how to monitor the execution of our software systems to analyze the behavior of activity on those systems. It turns out that normal, legitimate activity on a software systems can be easily modeled and understood. Departures from this normal activity are quite easy to detect. It might well be, for example, that a nuclear scientist has access to a secure database for the design of nuclear weapons. This person might also have access to removable disk storage media to provide backup for the work he or she is performing on his or her own workstation. The use of the disk subsystem by this individual is quite normal. They do so on a daily basis. The use of the database is quite normal for this individual. It is not, however, normal for this individual to use the database and the disk backup at the same time. That is the problem. In all likelihood, the secrets of the database are migrating on removable disk storage for transportation outside the secure area.

When we monitor systems that are executing, their patterns of execution of program modules readily become apparent. This is not surprising. We saw in Chapter 7 that there is a direct mapping from what a user does to a specific set of program modules. That is, when a user exercises an operation, this operation is implemented by one or more system functionalities. These functionalities will, in turn, be implemented by one or more program modules. The pattern of activity of the modules under each user operation becomes the **behavior** of the system. Each user ultimately generates an operational profile that describes how he or she has used the system. At the module level, there is a rather small set of module profiles that characterize this operation profile. These profiles constitute the normal system behavior.

Most computer security methods now in place attempt to characterize the abnormal conditions that occur during each security violation. Signatures of this abnormal activity can be developed for the behavior of the system such that whenever we recognize a certain pattern of behavior, we will know that we are under attack by the Manama virus or the Blorch Buffer Overflow exploit. The basic problem with this approach is that the state space for abnormal behavior is unknowably large. This creates a real advantage for the attacker who would exploit our system. The state space for normal behavior in a typical operating system or any other large software system is really quite small. We can know and understand this normal behavior quite well. If we know what a system's normal activity is, we can quite easily determine when the system is no longer operating within the bounds of normal activity.

As we have clearly established, a software system is constructed to perform a distinct set of operations O for the customer. These are a set of mutually exclusive operations. An example of such an operation might be the activity of adding a new user to a computer system. At the software level, these operations must be reduced to a well-defined set of functions F. These functions represent the decomposition of operations into subproblems that can be implemented on computer systems. The operation of adding a new user to the system might involve the functional activities of changing from the current directory to a password file, updating the password file, establishing user authorizations, and creating a new file for the new user.

From the standpoint of computer security, not all operations are equal. Some user operations might have little or no impact on computer security considerations. Other operations, such as system maintenance activities, have a much greater impact on security. System maintenance activities performed by systems administrators would be considered nominal system behavior. System maintenance activities performed by dial-up users, on the other hand, would **not** be considered nominal system behavior. To formalize this decomposition process, a formal description of these relationships must be established.

It can be seen that there is a distinct relationship between any given operation o and a given set of program modules. That is, if the user performs a particular operation, then this operation manifests itself in certain modules receiving control. It is also possible to detect, inversely, which program operations are being executed by observing the pattern of modules executing (i.e., the module profile. In a sense, then, the mapping of operations to modules and the mapping of modules to operations are reflexive.

It is a most unfortunate accident of most software design efforts that there are really two distinct sets of operations. This is particularly true of systems that lack a set of operational specifications and a mapping of each of these operations to specific functionalities. On the one hand, there is a set of explicit operations O_E. These are the intended operations that appear in the operational specification. On the other hand, there is also a set of implicit operations O_I that represent unadvertised features of the software that have been implemented through designer carelessness or ignorance. These are neither documented nor well known except by a group of knowledgeable or patient system specialists, called hackers.

The set of implicit operations O_I is not well known for most systems. Most system administrators are obliged to find out the hard way what they are. Hackers and other interested citizens will find them and exploit them. What is known is the set of operations O_E and the mappings of the operations onto the set of modules M. For each of the explicit operations, there is an associated module profile. That is, if an explicit operation is executed, then a well-defined set of modules will execute in a very predictable fashion. This fact can be exploited to develop a reasonable profile of the system when it is executing a set of operations from the set of explicit operations. This nominal system behavior will serve as a stable platform against which intrusive activity can be measured. That is, when an observation is made of module profiles that is not representative of the operations in O_E, then the assumption can be made that the new observation is one or more operations from the set O_I; there is an intruder present.

15.3.4 Measuring for Dynamic Security Monitoring

A software security violation is really just the aberrant behavior of a software system caused by the malicious use of the system. In every case, the behavior of the system changes as result of this violation. From a software measurement standpoint, the behavior of the program is embodied in the distribution of the activity of the program modules in response to specific user operations. In essence, a security violation, then, is really a change in user behavior. When the user's behavior departs from normal user behavior, this change is represented in the operational profile of that user. The operational profile of the user will change. This change in the nominal operational profile will be visible in the functional profile. The change in the functional profile will be visible as a substantial change in the module profile.

The real solution to the computer security problem lies in the dynamic measurement of software system activity. In that the module profile depends on the user operational profile, it is only necessary to monitor the module profile to determine whether the user has departed from a nominal operational profile.

There are two significant problems that must be solved to make this level of software measurement a viable prospect for real-time security monitoring. First, the data bandwidth of the measurement activity at the module level is extremely large. Just the simple act of processing the data representing the transition from one module to another will induce a substantial amount of overhead on any type of application due to the over-head of the measurement process. We are really not interested in the module activity, however. We are interested in the user activity. This user activity is reflected in the functional profile. Remember that each function-ality must have a unique module associated with that functionality. It is merely necessary to instrument the software modules that are uniquely associated with each functionality. This permits a realistic functional pro-file to be maintained in real-time with a minimum of overhead.

The second problem that arises in the dynamic monitoring of the oper-ation of a software system for the detection of aberrant behavior is that of the representation of normal behavior. There are many different ways to do this. A neural net can be conditioned to accept the transition from one functionality to another. A Kalman filter can be used to screen the data for abnormal activity. A genetic algorithm can be employed to learn and recognize the normal distribution of activity in the functionality data.

Perhaps the simplest means of representing normal program activity is to use a simple clustering algorithm. To implement this solution, we can build a functionality observation vector, say, $\mathbf{F}$. In this vector we accumu-late the frequency of execution of each functionality. Thus, the element f_i represents the frequency of execution of the ith functionality during the particular observation interval. Remember that we can measure the tran-sition from one functionality to another in terms of functionality epochs. When a program is executing normally, the contents of the vector $\mathbf{F}$ reflect the distribution of activity across functionalities induced by normal user operations. As the number of observations of functionality epochs becomes large, the variation the contents of the vector $\mathbf{F}$ tend to become very small for normal program activity. Dramatic changes in the variation of the contents of $\mathbf{F}$ serve to identify abnormal program activity.

Alternatively, we can choose to monitor the functionality of the system for a constant number of epochs, say n such epochs. At the end of each observation interval of n epochs, the contents of the vector $\mathbf{F}$ can be saved and the vector reset to zeros everywhere. Each one of these saved vectors represents a point in an $m-1$ dimensional space, where m is the number of functionalities that have been instrumented. As time progresses, the set of points representing normal program behavior will form clusters in this $m-1$ dimensional space. Each of the clusters can be represented by its centroid. We can determine this centroid by defining a value ε and grouping all points within a distance ε from this point. There are a variety of clustering algorithms that serve to form a set of centroids. Each centroid represents a cluster of functional behaviors of the system. In the nominal operation of a typical system, there are very few of such centroids necessary to represent the entire behavioral repertoire of the system.

Of course, the first step in the determination of normal behavior is the calibration step. The system must be observed in its normal operating mode. During this calibration phase, each type of nominal program activity must be observed. After a while, the number of points that will form new clusters will begin to diminish until a point is reached when no new clusters are formed by continuing observation.

Once the nominal behavior of the system has been determined, it is relatively simple to identify abnormal behavior. It will be represented by a new point that is more than ε from all of the centroids that represent normal behavior. Again, abnormal system activity results in a shift in the normal distribution of the functional profile. This abnormal system activity is readily identified as a new point in the $m-1$ dimensional space representing normal functionality that is at some distance from other points in this space.

This is not intended to be an exhaustive discussion of specific analysis techniques for computer security. Rather, the point is that it is possible to measure the activity of a system, determine what is normal activity for that system, and then monitor the activity of that system in real-time for departures from this nominal activity.

As many software development organizations have discovered to their chagrin, security is simply not an attribute that can be added on to a system after it is built. Security must be built into a system from its inception. Securing computer software must be handled in precisely the same way as securing a physical location. The activity of the software must be monitored in real-time as the system is operating. The monitoring system must be an integral part of the system.

As an aside, it also worth noting that most folks in the computer security industry are simply barking up the wrong tree. They are looking for signs of abnormal data activity surrounding the execution of a program. It turns out that the state space of abnormal data activity is huge. On the other hand, the state space of normal program behavior is very small. It is relatively simple to understand normal program activity through dynamic measurement and identify program activity that is a clear departure from the activity. Moreover, this monitoring activity can be performed in real-time.

Abnormal activity can be arrested at its inception and not after an intruder has adversely affected the system.

15.4 Maintainability

When a large operating system fails during the normal course of operation, the normal course of action is to reboot the system and hope for the best. There is very little that the typical user of such a system can do to ameliorate the problem. The very best the user can do is hope that the problem does not reoccur. Alternatively, if such a failure event occurs in a large transaction processing system, a typical response would be to roll back to the last checkpoint, restart the system at that checkpoint, and then update the system from a transaction audit trail before bringing the system online. In either event, the very last thing a typical user would do is attempt to fix the software. The fault that caused the failure event will remain intact. This means that there is a lingering potential for the system to fail again. The actual maintenance activity, if any, that will ensue as a result of this failure will be on the part of the software supplier if and only if the customer takes the time to provide a detailed account of the nature of the failure event.

The important point here is that when a system fails, it has failed in a particular user operation. It is operating outside its specified behavior. The failure event occurs in the user operational space. The user was performing an operation when the system departed from its specified operating characteristics.

The first step in fixing a problem is determining the precise nature of the problem. When the set of user operations is completely and unambiguously articulated, it is possible to identify the precise nature of the operation that failed. With specification traceability, we can then determine the specific functionalities that implement that operation. Each of these functionalities, in turn, is implemented in a set of design modules. Each design module maps directly to one code module. Thus, the process of diagnosing the problem is relatively straightforward. We can focus immediately on a very small subset of program functionalities and modules. The time necessary to identify the problem is thereby reduced enormously.

15.5 Survivability

In very large software systems, the functionalities can be distributed across a number of very large programs. These programs can, in turn, operate on many different computers in a distributed processing system. Maintaining the integrity of these systems is of paramount importance. Reliability problems in individual system components or security assaults on elements of the system should not bring about the complete loss of the system as a whole.

We can now clearly see that the set of operations that a system performs for a user are distinctly associated with a set of functionalities that is, in turn, associated with a set of program modules. A failure event, when it occurs, will occur in a particular program module. The functionality implemented by that module will fail, which in turn results in the failure of a particular operation.

It is not necessary that the whole system fails just because a particular operation fails. The set of operations can be segregated into two distinct sets. There are some operations that are vital to the functioning of a system, and others that are nice but not necessary. The word processor being used to prepare this text has a tab set operation. The system will continue to function quite well for most purposes should a failure event occur in one of the program modules associated with the tab function. The word processor should not fail completely because the tabbing functionality is lost. On the other hand, there is the file save operation. If this operation is lost, then it is pointless to continue interacting with the word processor, in that none of the subsequent work can be saved.

It is reasonable to expect that a software system should continue operating in the face of a failure of one or more nonvital operations. Just because there has been a failure in a module that implements, say, a tab functionality, the user should not lose all of his or her work in the current word-processing system. The user should be notified of the failure event and that a specific operation has now been cordoned off.

There should be, as part of the design of a system, a functionality that can handle failure events that occur within the set of nonvital operations. This functionality should notify the user of the failure of an operation, log the nature of the failure and the events that led to the failure, and return the system to a more or less normal operating mode.

Designing a system for graceful degradation is a difficult task. If a particular program module is used to implement a number of functionalities, then a failure event in that module can potentially affect all the functionalities of which it is a member module. The exposure to a failure of a particular module, then, is a direct function of the number of different functionalities that will use that module. With a clear mapping from operations to functionalities to modules to code, it is possible to assess this impact for any module in the system.

A much more egregious problem arises in the use of modules that may or may not be invoked in the expression of a functionality. Let us assume that a program module is potentially associated with one or more functionalities. If the program module is a member of the set $M_p^{(f)}$, the set of potentially invoked modules for any functionality, then that functionality might, or might not, invoke the module — in which case it might or might not fail. This is not a particular problem for those operations (functionalities) that can be partitioned into the set of nonvital operations. It is a terrible problem for those operations that are vital. They may or may not fail. If the cardinality of the set of potentially invoked program modules $M_o^{(f)}$ for a vital operation is large, then it will be very difficult to test and certify that operation.

15.6 The Software Blackbox Recorder

Embedded software systems are now ubiquitous. They are found in essentially every type of hardware we might buy. Some of these embedded systems play a safety-critical role. In particular, modern avionic software systems control almost every aspect of a flight profile for modern commercial aircraft. It is considered to be a state-of-the-art procedure to instrument and measure every aspect of the mechanical operation of these aircraft and record the results in a software blackbox recorder. In the event of a crash of the aircraft, the data on the blackbox recorder will give some indication as to what the pilot was doing and how the mechanical systems were functioning at the point of the crash. This data, while summary in nature, serves to identify what went wrong with the mechanical systems in a post-mortem crash investigation. Unfortunately, essentially all of these mechanical systems are driven by the avionics software system. There is no mechanism for determining just what the state of this system was in the event of a crash. The crash may, in fact, have been due to the fact that there was a catastrophic failure in the avionics software. Without a software blackbox recorder, it will be very difficult to impossible to deduce just exactly what happened in the avionics system to precipitate a disaster.

When software fails, it is often very difficult to determine the precise cause of the failure. This is largely because insufficient information has been retained external to the program to permit the reconstruction of the circumstances that led to the failure. Often, the systems whose failures we must diagnose are in remote locations, which makes the interaction with the software system difficult to impossible. There is also a demand for being able to reconstruct the causes of the extreme failure of software avionics systems. Of particular interest are those systems that have led to the crash of a vehicle. The objective is to formulate a functional history of a software system in a fashion equivalent to the traditional flight data recorder or blackbox. It is now possible to specify the characteristics of a system that will preserve the essential information on the operation of a program to permit the diagnosis of the circumstances that led to its failure.

The formulation of the software blackbox failure isolation system is based on the construction of the best model for representing the failure event. It is not the software system that fails; it is the software system executing a particular functionality that fails. From this perspective, it is important to capture the sequential execution of program functionalities. In particular, the program functionalities are physically expressed within a program as sub-trees of modules in a program call tree hierarchy. The transitions between the program modules in a pair wise fashion are the arcs in a program call graph.

It is clear that the likelihood of a software failure is simply not time dependent. A system can operate without failure for years and then suddenly become very unreliable based on the changing functions that the system must execute. A new model for software systems would focus on the functionality that the code is executing and not the software as a monolithic system. In computer software systems, a single functionality is being expressed when the system ceases to execute. It is possible, then, to reconstruct the activities of a system from historical data on its execution of various functionalities.

The main problem in the construction of a software blackbox is getting the granularity of the observation right. Software systems are designed to implement each of their functionalities in one or more code modules. In some cases, there is a direct correspondence between a particular program module and a particular functionality. That is, if the program is expressing that functionality, it will execute exclusively in the module in question. In most cases, however, there will not be this distinct traceability of functionality to modules. The functionality will be expressed in many different code modules. It is the individual code module that fails. A code module will, of course, be executing a particular functionality when it fails. We must come to understand that it is the functionality that fails. From these observations, it will become fairly obvious just what data will be needed to describe accurately the functionality of the system. In essence, the system will be able to apprise us of its own activity. This can be accomplished dynamically while the program is executing.

Let us now turn to the measurement scenario for the modeling process described above. Consider a system whose requirements specify a set of a user operations. These operations, again specified by a set of functional requirements, are mapped into a set of b elementary program functions. The functions, in turn, are mapped by the design process into a set of m program modules.

The software is designed to function optimally under an *a priori* operational profile. We need a mechanism for tracking the actual behavior of the user of the system. To this end we will require a vector O in which the program counts the frequency of each of the operations. That is, an element o_i of this vector is incremented every time the program initiates the ith user operation. Each of the operations is distinct and they are mutually exclusive. Thus, we can use the Bayesian estimation process to compute estimates for the actual posterior operational profile for the software.

The next, static, matrix Q that must be maintained is the matrix that describes the mapping $O \times F$ of the operations to the program functions. Each element of this matrix will have the property that:

$$q_{ij} = \begin{cases} 1 & \text{if IMPLEMENTS } (o_i, f_j) \text{ is TRUE} \\ 0 & \text{if IMPLEMENTS } (o_i, f_j) \text{ is FALSE} \end{cases}$$

The next static matrix S that must be maintained is the matrix that describes the mapping $F \times M$ of the function to the program modules as a result of the program design process. Each element of this matrix will have the property that:

$$s_{jk} = \begin{cases} 1 & \text{if ASSIGNS } (f_j, m_k) \text{ is TRUE} \\ 0 & \text{if ASSIGNS } (f_j, m_k) \text{ is FALSE} \end{cases}$$

A current assessment of the frequency with which functions are executed can be maintained in a matrix S. As was the case with the operational profile, an element o_j of this vector will be incremented every time the program initiates the jth function.

Finally, we need to record the behavior of the total system as it transitions from one program module to another. If there are a total of m modules, then we need an $n \times n$ $(n = m + 1)$ matrix T to record these transitions. Whenever the program transfers control from module m_i to module m_j, the element t_{ij} of T will increase by one. The rows of the transition matrix P can be obtained dynamically from the estimation methods presented above.

The index pair (i, j) constitutes the transition event from module m_i to module m_j. If we preserve the sequence of (i, j) from the 0th epoch to the present, we are able to reconstruct the functional (operational) sequences of program behavior. However, in that the number of epochs will be extremely large for reliable program operation, an alternate mechanism might be to preserve simply the last n (i, j) pairs. This can be done by pushing each of the (i, j) pairs onto a stack C of length n that will preserve only the (i, j) pairs of the last n epochs.

Thus, the software blackbox will consist of the components C, O, Q, S, and T. From these data elements we can construct the functional behavior of any system through its final n epochs. If a program is augmented to include these fundamental matrices and mechanism, either within the operating system or even the program itself, to record the necessary entries in these matrices, it would be possible to reconstruct the functionality that a program was executing when it met its untimely demise. The sequence of prior activities, together with the final functionality, can be reconstructed from this abstract model of the software blackbox recorder. This would constitute the minimum configuration for the software analog of the hardware blackbox recorder now implemented on commercial and military aircraft.

The important thing about this approach to the blackbox software recorder is that the focus is on what the user was doing. If we are to try and analyze the last moments in the life of a software system, it is not particularly relevant what that software was doing. However, it is very relevant that we know what the user was doing. It would be almost impossible to reproduce the sequence of states at the code level that led to the failure of a system. On the other hand, it would be very easy to reproduce the sequence of user operations that led to the failure event. That is the essence of the blackbox recorder concept.

15.7 Summary

The major thrust of this book has been to provide a foundation for the engineering of software systems. The key to the engineering of a system is the precise specification and design of the system. This means that we must be able to measure every aspect of the system as it evolves. It would be difficult to conceive of a set of blueprints for the construction of a new building that is completely free of any measurements or scaled drawings, but that is exactly the current state of the art of software development.

There have been many efforts to deal with the problem of software specification. Some of these efforts at specification languages have attempted to impose mathematical rigor on the process. We should not confuse mathematical rigor with engineering discipline. They are not the same thing. The software specification and implementation process should have at its core the need to measure the product outcomes at every step.

The most important aspect of the specification and implementation processes is that the operational specification and design process remains linked throughout the life of the software system. This linkage is absolutely vital for the software maintenance activity. Now that most of the actual programming of software systems is being outsourced overseas, it is even more imperative that the specification and design processes become the primary focus of the software development effort. If we have done the design correctly, there will be absolutely no freedom accorded to the developer in the creation of a system. Their task will simply be one of implementation.

Finally, specification traceability is absolutely vital to the software quality process. It is imperative that faults be traced to their point of origin. Faults can be attributable to problems at the source code level, at the low-level design level, at the high-level design level, and also at the operational specification level. We simply cannot begin to improve the quality of the software development process if we do not know precisely where in the various stages of the software life cycle the problems are being introduced.

Engineering, in general, is a front-loaded process. No one would think to start building a new commercial jet aircraft without extensive operational and functional specifications for the new jet. The aircraft engineering community has come to understand that this is a very front-loaded process as far as development costs are concerned. So too must the software development community come to understand exactly the same principle. The first software development company that truly embraces the principles of engineering will rapidly come to dominate the software industry. The road to today's computing milieu is littered with the carcasses of some very big hardware and software companies. That a company is dominant in the industry today gives little hope that this same company will be around in another ten years. The future of the software industry will belong to the company that first learns to engineer software.

Index